# WHO CAN AFFORD TO IMPROVISE?

# WHO CAN AFFORD TO IMPROVISE?

## JAMES BALDWIN AND BLACK MUSIC, THE LYRIC AND THE LISTENERS

### ED PAVLIĆ

Fordham University Press

New York  2016

*For Stacey Cecile in the Echo Café*

# Contents

Go back to Miles, Max, Dizzy, Yardbird, Billie, Coltrane: who were not, as the striking—not to say quaint—European phrase would have it, "improvising": who can afford to improvise, at those prices?

—James Baldwin, "Of the Sorrow Songs: The Cross of Redemption" (1979)

# Introduction
## "To the listeners, for those that have an ear for this"

I began to think, that is to say to listen harder.

—*Samuel Beckett,* Molloy

In the fall of 1969, James Baldwin was living in Istanbul. He had rented a flat in the Üçler Apartments at the intersection of Gümüşsuyu Cad-desi and Çiftevav Sokak, a steeply inclined street between the German and Japanese embassies.[1] The neighborhood was about two blocks toward the Bosporus from Taksim Square; the famed literary meeting place, the Park Hotel, was located around the corner. Baldwin had lived in Istanbul off and on since first arriving in the city to visit late in 1961. In early July, with his every move noted by the FBI, and feeling nearly as stalked by his own highly politicized public persona, he had exited Hollywood and abandoned his attempts to convert *The Autobiography of Malcolm X* into a film starring Billy Dee Williams for Columbia Studios. He was leaving more than a film project, however. Following the publication of *The Fire Next Time* (1963), which catapulted him into literary and cultural stardom, Baldwin had been immersed in near-constant struggle with the cultural politics of the era. Many of the activists with whom he had joined forces had been murdered and imprisoned. The freedom movement had splintered; the political mainstream was veering to the right. Baldwin sensed that the road through what would be remembered as "the sixties" was ending. He was searching for a new beginning; for him, that meant he was *listening*, intensely.

Baldwin took the failure of the film project as a cue to renegotiate his hypervisible, visceral relationship to American culture. Assassinations and mass violence in the preceding years had taken their tolls. Emotionally in tatters, politically exhausted, and personally, at least partially, defeated,

1

Front entrance of the apartment building in the Ayazpasa neighborhood, Istanbul, where Baldwin lived in the fall of 1969. (Photo by author, 2013.)

he meant to change his approach. As it stood, he was in a very, very bad way. In *No Name in the Street* (1972), he would go back and tell the story of his experience since *The Fire Next Time*. He had gone to Istanbul to regain a sense of his private life en route to finding a point of view, a voice, capable of telling a version of the past that would be relevant to the future. In Sedat Pakay's *James Baldwin: From Another Place*, shot in Istanbul during the summer of 1970, Baldwin assessed the task and scanned the near future of the book he had yet to write: "I think that all poets, and I'm a kind of poet . . . have a very difficult role to play. . . . My own effort is to try to bear witness to something which will have to be there when the storm is over. To help us get through the next storm; storms are always coming."[2]

From his vantage point, on July 13, as he boarded the Pan Am flight in Paris for the second leg of his trip to Istanbul, the road he'd traveled resembled a disaster if not a slaughter. He was in search of another way to engage what had happened, desperately in need of signs of life that hadn't been imprisoned and murdered by recent history. In *No Name in the Street*, he underscored the need for a kind of precision: "I want to avoid generalities as far as possible."[3] When it came to people, those in his work and in his life, he decided: "One tries to treat them as the miracles they are, while trying to protect oneself from the disasters they've become" (*CE*, 357). But, where, at the time, could he find a guide for the precision and discernment he needed?

The first place was in the daily rhythms of his relationship to people he loved. He had spent five days in Paris before completing the second leg of his journey. Once back in Istanbul, Baldwin would live with his oldest artistic mentor and friend, the painter Beauford Delaney, and his lover, Alain, a younger Frenchman whose family was from Martinique. The three men got along beautifully. Beauford was feeling good, spent a lot of time in the late-summer sunshine, and tutored Alain in painting. Every day, Baldwin measured and remeasured where he stood and what he'd become in the eyes of those around him, often watching Alain watch visitors for signs of who he appeared to be in their eyes. Getting along beautifully doesn't mean all was peaceful. Baldwin's personal life could be molten in its intensity. He knew it wasn't easy—if it was possible at all—for Alain to handle. Even in Istanbul, his political notoriety hadn't been left behind; in initial surveys of his neighborhood, he marked the Japanese embassy as likely the best place to go should he need emergency political asylum. Amid those kinds of triangulations, later that fall, Beauford went back to France and Jimmy and Alain went about their lives together. The period between July 1969 and March 1970, when he sent Alain to France, would be the longest, continuous stretch of domestic life shared with a lover Baldwin had ever experienced, about nine months.[4] He would put off writing *No Name in the Street* until he was able to find a way around seeing only the disasters, the generalities, until he could teach himself, again, to touch the miracle of possibility which, he knew, was still alive around and within him.

In addition to clarifying and deepening his first-person experience, most importantly his experience of other people, music provided a touchstone crucial in what he had to do and what he needed to write. On September 10, he wrote to ask his brother David to send him his favorite record at the time, "Oh Happy Day," by the Edwin Hawkins Singers.[5] Worried about mailing the vinyl, he suggested that David might put the record on a reel-to-reel tape. He told David he missed hearing the song, which, in the United States, was on its way to a 1970 Grammy Award for Best Soul Gospel Performance.

By the title, the song might appear to be a strange choice. Baldwin's sense of what lay behind and immediately before him certainly didn't provide cause for celebration. The choice looks even stranger in that, in "The Uses of the Blues" (1964), amid the initial wave of fame and violence that eventually delivered him to Istanbul in such bad shape, he'd written that "happiness . . . is not a real state and does not really exist."[6] Given his embattled and embittered state, the obviously misaligned terminology rewards closer attention. In that essay, Baldwin argued that "the acceptance of this anguish one finds in the blues, and the expression of it, creates, however odd this may sound, a kind of joy."[7] Heard in this way, the music provides traces of a counterintuitive method of surviving disasters, a method for creating a transformative energy in the person, in people, and in the world. Of that energy, he wrote: "Now joy is a true state, it is a reality; it has nothing to do with what most people have in mind when they talk of happiness."[8]

People performing this kind of creative work generated real power. It was exactly that sense of engaged and joyful precision that Baldwin needed. He'd been immersed in the creation of that reality as a child; he'd known it all of his life. Near the close of his first novel, *Go Tell It on the Mountain* (1953), John Grimes emerges into the street from his all-night immersion in the music of the church and realizes: "Where joy was, there strength followed; where strength was, sorrow came—forever? Forever and forever, said the arm of Elisha, heavy on his shoulder."[9] Music and the intimate presence of people was almost always nearby as one encountered that sense of embodied possibility. In *Go Tell It on the Mountain*, the message comes to John directly from the arm that the boy, Elijah, has put around him. It's not accidental that Elisha is the church piano player. In *The Fire Next Time*, the paradoxical energy capable of wringing miracles (or living precision from deadening generality) from disasters emanates directly from the church, both music and the presence of the people singing it: "There is no music like that music, no drama like the drama of the saints rejoicing, the sinners moaning, the tambourines racing, and all those voices coming together and crying holy . . . speaking from the depths of a visible, tangible, continuing despair of the goodness of the Lord."[10]

So, instead of a happy song, Baldwin was asking his brother to send him a kind of paradoxical particular, documentary evidence of joy, a reality he trusted, a point of view he would use to renegotiate his relationship to his life, to the world, and to his work. Baldwin heard *something* in Dorothy Combs Morrison's lead vocal, echoed by the chorus, singing "Oh Happy Day." That something most certainly involved the textures and rhythms of the music supporting the description of rebirth when "Jesus, he washed my sins away." But, it's also clear that Baldwin didn't take being "happy" very seriously nor did he believe that Jesus could (or should) wash the world out of the self as the lyrics claim. It's something else. In Baldwin's mind, that song, and black music writ large, testified to an experience without an exact name in American life and history. Even more, the *sound* offered a complex and powerful link between words and what they meant in experience, in black American experience first, and, after that, in encounters with human experience radiating around the world. In Baldwin's listening ear at the time, as in his work throughout his career, so much depended upon something unnamed added by the tone and rhythm of the speaker, even more by the *singer*, to the word. So much, as it were, depended upon the texture of a voice. As if translating William Carlos Williams's thing-based, American modernist poetic rule into black culture, Baldwin's approach said: Sing it, no ideas but in song.

Apparently David sent the recording or someone found a copy in Turkey. In *James Baldwin's Turkish Decade*, Magdalena Zaborowska notes that the record was played to greet Baldwin, whenever he entered the "famous Club 12" near his apartment, off Taksim Square in Istanbul between the fall of 1969 and his return to France in the summer of 1970.[11] One can only guess at the nuanced transit between pain and joy, between disaster and miracle, made possible by Baldwin's repeated listening to "Oh Happy Day," either in private, on his Grundig De La Versatile III tape player, or in public, often deep into the morning at Club 12. These listenings patterned that pivotal year when, while reconfiguring his private and public lives, he would collaborate with Engin Cezzar and, most notably, jazz avant-gardist Don Cherry, by directing John Herbert's *Fortune and Men's Eyes* (translated into Turkish as *Düsenin Dostu*). The play was a controversy and a sensation. Early in its run, Baldwin marveled that the police had come to shut down the packed house but, instead, stood at the back and watched the performance. The production was voted the Play of the Year in Istanbul. As always, music played a leading role in Baldwin's encounters in his life and explorations in his work. Via a shifting series of approaches, *Who Can Afford to Improvise?* searches for the crux of what music meant to Baldwin and his work and what that can mean to us.

On November 4, 1971, the poet Nikki Giovanni met Baldwin in London. As part of the shift in point of view he heard in the music, he'd taken increasingly to calling himself a poet. The two were there to record a conversation to be aired as episodes of Ellis Haizlip's television show, *Soul!* During the second episode, discussing the way American history had politicized the relationship between artist and audience, and between writers and critics, Nikki Giovanni said, "personally, I hate critics," to which Baldwin replied: "Actually, I love critics, but they're very rare. A real critic is very rare."[12] Baldwin continued, "I will be able to accept critical judgments when I understand that they understand Ray Charles."[13] Giovanni, twenty-eight years old at the time, cast the possibility aside, "It'll never happen." Playing the elder, Baldwin left the door ajar, "When that day comes . . . we'll play it as we see it."[14] Speaking in shorthand, and signifying a mix of openness and skepticism, Baldwin highlights the crucial importance of music, musicians, and of listening itself to his or anyone else's sense of his work's place in the world. Within months of the publication of *A Dialogue*—the book version of Baldwin's conversation with Giovanni in London—Baldwin placed his finger on the critical scales by performing *with* Ray Charles at Carnegie Hall on July 1, 1973 (see Chapter 6). It was a performance critics at the time responded to in ways that certainly didn't contradict Giovanni's skeptical sense of the timing involved and that no one since has responded to at all.

Throughout his life and career, in essays, plays, novels, interviews and conversations, Baldwin repeatedly signaled the importance of listening, of hearing, and of music. That importance wasn't contained in a song; it didn't begin or end there. In *The Amen Corner*, from the mid-1950s, Luke explains: "When you really swinging—then you joined to everything, to everybody, to skies and stars and every living thing . . . the music don't come out of the air, baby. It comes out of the man who's blowing it."[15] Listening led back to living, to the world. To cite a telling instance, in the fall of 1963, just weeks after six black children were murdered in one day in Birmingham, Alabama, Baldwin went to live in Lee Strasberg's summer home on Fire Island. He went there to work on his play *Blues for Mister Charlie*, which is loosely based on the Emmett Till murder. Baldwin's mother came along. Her description of the time they spent together catches the place of music in his life and work perfectly. Mrs. Baldwin told

Fern Eckman: "He seemed to subsist on music rather than calories:'The minute he'd get out of bed, he'd put records on and keep them going all day. He played spirituals constantly. I had no idea he played them so much."[16] Concluding, she noted: "I like spirituals. Fortunately. Because Jimmy plays them very high." Baldwin's trust in black music spanned the genres from spirituals and gospel to soul, R&B, and jazz; it spanned generations from Bessie Smith to Billie Holiday, Dinah Washington and Nina Simone, from Miles Davis and Ray Charles to Aretha Franklin and beyond.[17] It's a constant presence in his work, not just in pieces that explicitly feature musical subject matter.

*Who Can Afford to Improvise?* records my own musically informed, open-ended encounters with Baldwin's work and life, with a few of the musicians that meant the most to him, and, finally, with contemporary encounters that illuminate our cultural, social, and political worlds. In these chapters, explorations really, I position music, and lyrics, and the *lyric*, at the hub of a series of encounters with Baldwin's career, the textures and rhythms of its development over the decades between the mid-1940s and the late 1980s. My lyrical approach to Baldwin takes place in three stages, or books. Each book focuses on a specific kind, or modality, of listening. In this way, *Who Can Afford to Improvise?* builds upon and invests in a burgeoning and diverse conversation taking place around Baldwin's life and work.[18] Rarely in these pages do I engage the critical discourse directly. Rather, I provide a narrative of Baldwin's work in sync with its moorings in the textures and structures of black music and emphasizing its complex, at times radical, sense of artistic social and political engagement.

*Who Can Afford to Improvise?* depends upon a notion of the *lyric* as a generally disruptive propensity of language, a metaphorically or literally *musical* interruption of the report-function usually assigned to what is called prose. The lyrical mode bridges the distinction between discourse and experience by becoming an experience itself. A song is discourse *as* experience, interrupting the boomerang from word to referent, holding our attention to physical and emotional textures woven in the rhythms of the utterance itself. Poets and translators have long pursued strategies for liberating language from its utilitarian job as pack mule in human communication and commerce (including the *cognitive commerce* between signifier and signified). But, as Baldwin knew, singers generally operate in lyrical mode better and the greatest singers do things with language possible nowhere else. Considering language in general, and Baldwin's work in particular, in this musical-lyrical way emphasizes how phrases and statements carry multiple possibilities, distinct tonalities that communicate at several simultaneous levels. That complexity, that color and timbre in lyrical utterance, 'is one of the reasons why all lyrics beg and bear repeated attention. People don't listen to their favorite song *once*. A lyrical entity isn't an object in linear time; experiencing the lyrical dimension of language stirs the impulse to listen again. And, again. And, also, requires the artist to state and restate, always in slightly different ways, with different inflections and emphases. All of these facets of language are common to poetry, even more so in musical performances, and intensely so in the black musical world. Baldwin's exploration of these kinds of repetitive, lyrical, textural (as opposed to textual) dimensions of black music intensified steadily throughout his career.

What would it be, then, to approach Baldwin's work in this way? What do we hear if we pay lyrical—and experiential—attention to work that was conceived and performed (on pages and on stages) precisely, and increasingly, in these terms? One way to go at this task would be to focus on pieces of Baldwin's work where he's writing explicitly about music, quoting songs, naming musicians, and so on. There are many of these. But, there aren't as many such instances as the foundational role of music in his life and work might forecast. And this is one key lyrical point. To focus on Baldwin's writing *about* music is still a prose—not to say a prosaic—exercise, one that misses the instances, on almost every page, where he's *writing* a kind of music no matter the subject matter.

Another more valuable approach to Baldwin's lyrical power is to listen to the way his clarity and musical disruption deepen our sense of collective, as well as individual, elements of experience. There are difficulties inherent in this approach. In *Audiotopia*, Josh Kun closely attends Baldwin's listening but concludes that "Baldwin listened to Bessie Smith, and he heard himself."[19] Kun notes the lyrical opening in which musicality in language *connects* people across barriers (individual, gendered, sexual, geographical, generational). It's true that, to some degree, we hear our own voices in any lyrical utterance. That is an absolutely crucial feature of the kind of listening *Who Can Afford to Improvise?* charts and enacts. But, in the end, Bessie Smith's sound, and the sounds in black music more generally, ushered Baldwin into contact with much more than himself; it figured floods, families, and communities, illuminated epic journeys in his imagination: The world in a jug. An important feature in Baldwin's listening echoes what Langston Hughes meant when he described the "disc-tortions of the music of a *community* in transition."[20] This collective, lyrical element is key. Signals of that importance are everywhere in Baldwin's work. In *Just Above My Head*, his final novel, Baldwin concluded:

"Our history is each other. That is our only guide. Perhaps that is what the gospel singer is singing."[21] This statement itself serves as a kind of refrain throughout this book.

To listen is very often to encounter links between (as well as within) human interiors. Part of the action of what we mean when we say "lyrical" lives in those links. In *Go Tell It on the Mountain*, Florence hears the saints in the Temple of the Fire Baptized sing "*Standing in the need of prayer*" and "gained again from the song the meaning it had held for her mother, and gained a new meaning for herself" (*ENS*, 61). Such lyrical links turn upon repetition. When Baldwin's autobiographical protagonist, John Grimes, falls on the floor of the church, he falls into the sound of the music surrounding him. At a threshold in his musical descent, Baldwin writes: "But now he knew, for irony had left him, that he was searching for something hidden in the darkness" (193). Strictly speaking the sound is as much experiential as musical, the singing and the music provide John lyrical access to otherwise unspeakable facets of his world, facets well beyond himself:

> This sound had filled John's life, so it now seemed, from the moment he had first drawn breath. He had heard it everywhere, in prayer and in daily speech, and wherever the saints were gathered, and in the unbelieving streets. It was in his father's anger, and in his mother's calm insistence, and in the vehement mockery of his aunt; it had rung, so oddly, in Roy's voice this afternoon, and when Elisha played the piano it was there; it was in the beat and jangle of Sister McCandless's tambourine, it was in the very cadence of her testimony, and invested that testimony with a matchless, unimpeachable authority. Yes, he had heard it all his life, but it was only now that his ears were opened to this sound that came from darkness, that could only come from darkness, that yet bore such sure witness to the glory of the light. (194)

Close and repeated listening links personal interiors to each other and opens renewed engagements with the worlds within and around them.

Baldwin's valences of listening emphasize a subtle and very powerful distinction in the deep structure of black language, culture, and black music most of all. Throughout this book, I revisit the way this "musicality" signals complexly collective dynamics in Baldwin's work and in the culture at large. Echoing Zora Neale Hurston's meditations on "Angularity" and "Asymmetry" in "The Characteristics of Negro Expression" (1934), Robin D. G. Kelley places collective lyricism at the center of *The-*

*lonious Monk: The Life and Times of an American Original.* Grappling with
the difficulty of describing Monk's "originality" in ways that conserve his
deep connections to his family and San Juan Hill community, past and
present, Kelley notes Monk's nonironic handling of dissonance in the recordings of "Memories of You" and "You Are Too Beautiful" from the
spring of 1956. Meditating on the songs as homage to Monk's recently
deceased mother and to his piano teacher, Kelley writes:

> His unaccompanied rendering of Andy Razaf and Eubie Blake's
> "Memories of You" should be heard as his tribute to Alberta Sim-
> mons, the neighborhood piano player who took Thelonious under
> her wing, helped him with his stride technique, and taught him
> songs by the old black composers. She had befriended Blake, met
> Razaf, and played "Memories of You" so often it was as if it were
> her own composition. Thelonious thought of Miss Simmons often,
> and his memories of her grew in prominence as he grappled with
> his mother's absence.... Monk didn't soften his dissonant sonori-
> ties, yet [the recording] contained not a hint of irony and never lost
> its romantic lyricism.[22]

This kind of confrontation with irresolvable complexities which refuses to
withdraw (via irony) from the effort to mean (or at least to mean to mean)
what one feels, says, or plays is a distinct feature in African American
experiences, utterances, and performances at the border between the
American modern and postmodern. Throughout black modernity, along
with a necessary intensity of self-regard, the artist's descent bears unmis-
takably and communicably empathic energies.[23]

Baldwin's dynamic angularities (often criticized as contradictions) and
dissonances often carry a similarly distinct tonality. The genealogy of this
tone is largely musical. It sounds in the way Billie Holiday loaded up one
melismatic autobiographical "I" stretched over six adagio beats in "Billie's Blues"; it resembles what Miles Davis twisted into "My Funny Valentine" or Charles Mingus into "Orange Was the Color of Her Dress"
or "Fables of Faubus"; it sounds like John Coltrane's dissonant devotion
to Nat Cole in "Nature Boy" or his resuscitation of Bronislau Kaper's
"While My Lady Sleeps." This list provides but a few instances of this
distinct form of musical disruption. Disc-tortion. Monk's music is a ver-
itable universe of nonironic angularity; he's at his most elusively obvious,
harmonically devastating and miraculously precise in his version of "Just a
Gigolo" recorded for Prestige on September 22, 1954. Consider the immediate background. He'd begun that summer in Paris, making his Euro-

pean debut which one British reviewer described as "a man committing artistic suicide."[24] He'd picked up the pieces later that evening in a jam session with Gerry Mulligan and salvaged his Paris sojourn by touring the city with Mary Lou Williams and his new acquaintance, Baroness Pannonica de Koenigswarter who would become a lifelong companion. Back in Manhattan, he was out of work during the summer. Monk's beloved wife, Nellie, supported the family while he took care of their two toddler-aged children changing diapers and touring the neighborhood with them in tow. A few weeks before his thirty-seventh birthday, on the first day of fall 1954, in Rudy Van Gelder's studio, Monk ran short of music he needed for his next ten-inch LP, and so he laid down his singular portrait of the gigolo as loving husband, out-of-work musical genius, and devoted stay-at-home dad. In general, this kind of African American use of polyphony and dissonance conserves the will to mean it (as in Robert Hayden's incomparable "Mean mean mean to be free"[25] in "Runagate Runagate," a poem Baldwin quotes in No Name in the Street) and informs what and how these performances communicate to people in a challenging, political, possibly tragic, but collective and resilient human design.

At bottom, this musical angularity conveys complexity to a community in ways that move beyond late modernist and postmodernist enumerations of splintered facets in an isolated—and thereby often ever-increasingly so—solitary consciousness. It supports the need to convey multiple meanings between people who refuse—or who can't afford—to be irrelevant to each other. Michael Ondaatje's meditation on Fats Waller, "In a Yellow Room" (1984), pinpoints these dynamics. Ondaatje writes: "I have always loved him but I love him most in the company of friends. Because his body was a crowd and we desire to imitate such community."[26] He then marks the crux of what musical angularity is all about, "the fact that Fats Waller was talking to someone over your shoulder as well as to you."[27] Although the terms overlap, it's this collective or plural method of meaning, the need to simultaneously convey distinct messages to different people, Baldwin had in mind in The Fire Next Time when he observed "the freedom one hears in some gospel songs, for example, and in jazz. In all jazz, and especially in the blues, there is something tart and ironic, something authoritative and double-edged" (CE, 311). And, for much of the popular tradition, as Baldwin's Arthur Montana notes in Just Above My Head, black musicians and singers played to listeners, and to listeners over the shoulders of listeners, "and [kept] both of them going, too, baby, and all the time grinning in Mr. Charlie's face" (375).

Musicians more than most, African American artists of all types have noted this kind of distinct relationship to their audience and communities. In a letter to the editor of *Down Beat* magazine in June 1962, John Coltrane noted that, unlike American composers such as Aaron Copland, the "'Jazz' musician ... does not have to worry about ... finding himself an integral part of the musical community."[28] Coltrane observed, "You can believe all of us would have perished long ago if this were not so." In shifting terms, and often in explicit connection to music, to musicians, and to his role as a "poet," Baldwin sought means to a musically angular address throughout his career.[29] He became aware of this need in stages, by degrees. As I discuss in Chapter 3, in one crucial moment in March 1968, while listening to Aretha Franklin's album *Aretha Arrives* in California, Baldwin heard in her voice a way to address the *people* as well as the *person*. Ultimately, Aretha's guidance, refocused by "Oh Happy Day" and, doubtless, many other voices, would lead him to the voice he needed to complete *No Name in the Street* (1972). This newly expansive and versatile lyricism would further both the personal and political depth and scope of his work in the 1970s and 1980s. In Chapters 8 and 9, I describe this interpersonal, collective angularity as a feature of the contemporary "diasporic lyric," key in the effort to chart shifts in communities in transition across geographies, through history, even between life and death.

That kind of lyrical, angular transformation of language and the assumptions that guide it was an ever-present feature of Baldwin's methods. With obvious caution, he called *that* improvising. In a speech delivered at UC Berkeley in April 1979, he said:

> I'm going to improvise, like a writer, on some assumptions. And, though I feel a little uneasy in doing this, in saying this, nevertheless, what a writer is obliged to realize is that he is involved with a language which he has to change ... for a black writer, especially in this country, to be born into the English language is to realize that the assumptions of the language, the assumptions on which the language operates, are his enemy.[30]

Writing about Baldwin shortly after his death in December 1987, Toni Morrison characterized the sum of his lyrical, if uneasy, improvisations, his recreation of the language in which we think, write, and speak, even the language in which we sing: "You went into that forbidden territory and decolonized it, 'robbed it of the jewel of its naiveté,' and un-gated it for black people so that in your wake we could enter it, occupy it, restructure it in order to accommodate our complicated passion—not our vanities but our intricate, difficult, demanding beauty, our tragic, insistent knowledge, our lived reality ... while refusing 'to be defined by a language that has never been able to recognize [us]'."[31] Black music's textures, its logics and structures—what Baldwin would famously call "the beat"—are the most important sources among the many that informed the transformative work he accomplished via lyrical improvisations, the implications of which we're just beginning to explore. This was undoubtedly a space for black people attuned to the necessities, trials, and ambiguous (not to say treacherous) blessings of American life. It was also a message for anyone reading, or listening, as it were, over black people's shoulder.

A "listening" to writing attunes itself to what's encoded and entailed (as well as what's stated) in the work. In his essay "Listening," Roland Barthes—echoing Luke in *The Amen Corner* quoted earlier—traced a multidimensional capacity to musical dimensions of "the singing voice, that very specific space in which a tongue encounters a voice and permits those who know how to listen to it to hear what we can call its 'grain'—the singing voice is not the breath but indeed that materiality of the body emerging from the throat ... 'What such listening offers is precisely what the speaking subject does not say ... an active texture which reactualizes ... the totality of his history.'"[32] In this sense, I often found myself traveling with the "grain" of Baldwin's voice, listening for where his sense of lyric, of music, and of their interaction converged. These convergences in craft, like the substance of any meeting between people, as Baldwin would come to realize, were *political*. Signaling the importance of these mutual—if angular—resonances and inflections, he told *The Black Scholar* in 1973: "History was someone you touched, you know, on Sunday mornings or in the barbershop. It's all around you. It's in the music, it's in the way you talk, it's in the way you cry, it's in the way you make love. Because you are denied your official history you are forced to excavate your real history even though you can never say that's what you are doing. That is what you are doing."[33] As was the case with what John Grimes heard in the musically encoded "darkness" within and around him and the "light" that came from it, the historical "song" of the world is everywhere if one is able to listen. In these songs, with the body of the singer "emerging from the throat," music writes "real history" in the air.

History, here, is not simply a matter of archives and the rigor of established facts. It's a living, embodied energy that permeates and inflects our actual lives, whether or not we attend. These are lyric energies in that they're not under the control of—nor do they transcend—the institutional and intellectual structures of our world. Baldwin's voice carries a very rare musical grain that accesses those living, lyric energies in an extremely wide—as close as is possible to a universal—audience. In his 1992 essay "A Prophet Is Not Without Honor," Ekwueme Michael Thelwell described a fundraising mailer devised by the Student Non-Violent Coordinating Committee in New York City to support the effort, in the summer of 1964, to "drag Mississippi into the twentieth century."[34] The mailer bore the image of a letter addressed to each recipient that appeared to have been personally written by James Baldwin. Thelwell reported the astonishment of the workers in the office, including himself, when confronted by the tens of thousands of deeply personal responses sent in "from every state, both sexes, every social stratum, every age group."[35] Thelwell spent a day leafing through the stacks of letters, gripped by the obvious reality that "the authors felt themselves in intimate and direct communication with James Baldwin." He pondered "what exactly was it about that voice and persona that could, in those times, so compel the attention" of readers who responded so profoundly to Baldwin's address?[36] There's obviously no one answer. But, the responses testify to a vital, lyrical traffic within, and especially *between*, persons touched by Baldwin's voice.

Baldwin himself considered it a matter of confession. He came upon the idea that all "art is a kind of confession, more or less oblique" while interviewing Swedish director Ingmar Bergman outside Stockholm in October 1959 (*CE*, 246). In 1961, talking with Studs Terkel, he clarified his meaning setting it apart from popular apprehension at the time: "I don't mean a true confession in the sense of that dreary magazine."[37] Confession, for Baldwin, combined energies from different, often disparate, levels of experience into forms that expressed the complexity of life with as little evasion as possible. Among many reciprocal formulations, confessions infused the passion of a lover into a public forum or the deep insight from solitary concentration into a friendly dinner, the pain of historical conflict in a brother's touch. Framed by a dispute with social structures that "rationalized" such levels of experience and divided them into their separate containers, Baldwin transformed the tensions into the driving engine of his creative force. In ways that resonated racially, sexually, personally, and politically, he forced each level of his experience to connect with the others.

The result was a chronic (if instructive) state of turbulence and disruption, a sense of always impending, if not always encroaching, danger. As an artist, he said many times that he thought of himself as "a disturber of the peace." In his approach to experience, love was in no way restricted to what Americans would call private life. It was neither a fuzzy sentimentality nor an emotional or sexual indulgence. It was certainly not a safe space. Within the mode of confession, love was a serious, joyous, and dangerous, at times even disastrous, vein of connection across persons' dissociations from themselves and separations from each other. In *The Fire Next Time*, he'd written that "one can give nothing whatever without giving oneself—that is to say, risking oneself" (*CE*, 336). A few months later, of the small crowd assembled at a late-night party in his Manhattan apartment at 81 Horatio Street in 1963, he told Jane Howard of *Life* magazine "they don't know that to get you have to give, and giving, baby, isn't a day at the bargain counter but a total risk of who you are and what you want to be."[38] That sense of risk was by no means restricted to personal life; it was a social and political pact as well. In his essay "The Creative Process" (1962), he wrote that the "war of an artist with his society is a lover's war" (*CE*, 672). In ways that directly conflicted with at least some social philosophies of the era, the soaring vision at the end of *The Fire Next Time* virtually hinged upon the role of personal passion in interracial, social terms.[39] The shifting—now augmented, now diminished—chords of Baldwin's approach to confession spanned his career and were, sometimes, drastic and distant and, at other times, close up and subtle. Subtle instances lace conversations such as his 1984 interview with Richard Goldstein for the *Village Voice*. Noting that Baldwin had elevated homosexuality "*into the realm of literature*," Goldstein emphasized the public and historical importance of Baldwin's novel *Giovanni's Room* (1956). Shifting registers drastically to an intimate effect, Baldwin responded, "I had to do it to clarify something for myself."[40] Summing up the crossed paradigms of confession, he allowed, "I made a public statement that we're private, if you see what I mean."

Baldwin's most basic goals involved much more than the skilled application of literary craft. Despite public comments in the 1950s and early 1960s,[41] by the early 1970s he had made it clear that his ambitions went far beyond simply being a good writer; the world, he observed with a sardonic tinge, was full of those. The work he envisioned required his interrogation of his personal experience in ways that radiated beyond his individual life and beyond the page. So he called himself a poet, and his best paragraphs were often closer to being songs than they were to being prose. In his mind, confession involved his life as citizen as well as brother, friend, writer, and lover. At once a calculated aesthetic and a spiritual discipline, confession was a need organic to Baldwin's personality. This need included an impulse to push beyond his personality; it operated in his life in ways he felt beyond his intentional control. Confessions often engaged forces in the world that operate in brutally impersonal terms. Confession, then, was Baldwin's term for not allowing one's sense of self, of reality, even of time, to be dictated by the structures imposed by history and articulated (or not) in the prevailing cultural languages. By joining levels of experience held separate or simply denied in mainstream American life, confessions created their own sense of time and filled names with a subversive sense of the person, the act if never really the actor. A lyrical sense of musicality was the most important guide he had in figuring, in improvising, new, fluid structures that could articulate themselves and sense their way to each other despite the social and intellectual worlds that held them captive in isolation.

Musical at its core, Baldwin's was an intensely analytical and passionate imagination. Sexual and sensual energies were never far away. The disciplined disorder of his work in this regard has challenged all manner of attempts at academic and intellectual rigor. The real tension between Baldwin and his critics was (and still is) his increasingly direct attacks on the intellectual modes and commercial-cultural institutions that gird (and imprison) American self-understanding, accord status, and support popular and academic institutions. Ray Charles, indeed. Near the close of his 1979 speech at UC Berkeley, Baldwin paused his remarks to add, ruefully, smiling momentarily if only to himself, "All this will be, well . . . contested."[42] In fact, evidenced in the release of *The Cross of Redemption: Uncollected Writings* (2010), despite the rich and varied scholarly discourse noted above, reception of Baldwin's work in the most highly visible cultural reviews still bears marks of this tension.[43] Critics still resist the depth and radical structure of Baldwin's vision. At the very least, it's deflected.[44] *Who Can Afford to Improvise?* traces a musically informed, politically engaged, and historically and biographically grounded sense of Baldwin's most intensely lyrical thought. Part of this work entails a precise, period-by-period reading of Baldwin's development. But, it is not a strictly historical timeline. This is because any real lyrical moment is, almost by definition, a moment made of other moments, echoes. Riffs. There are bridges between Baldwin's statements across decades; they're twisted by the demands of history and the echoes bear a musical logic. Even more complexly, and lyrically, the bridge that connects lyrical meanings across eras depends upon the experience—the necessities and desires—of the listener.

In the summer of 1955, explaining the chaotic intensity of his life to his brother, and resisting his friends in New York who urged him to settle down,[45] Baldwin scripted an asymmetry that would inform all of his life and work. He told his brother David that the world, including his friends, wanted him to change, which he refused to do; instead, he was determined to develop. According to the tension between these terms, Baldwin's life and work would echo and riff in a complex, historically engaged tandem, and in ways impossible to reduce into a rise-and-fall narrative, over the full course of his career.

The most important aspect of *Who Can Afford to Improvise?* is the attempt—mine first which I intend as a call to readers—to first listen *to*, then *with*, and, finally, to lyrically *respond* to the long song of Baldwin's work, intricately related to the rhythms of his life. In writing this book I had a resource to which the public doesn't have access. I had read and reread, transcribed, and studied the letters James Baldwin wrote, between 1953 and 1986, to his brother David, the closest person to him in the world. That experience listening to Baldwin's incomparable first-person voice addressing his closest confidant over decades was an experience unlike any I'd had. It conveyed a version of experience, and of love and work and struggle, that carried the subtle timbres of a human speaking— or singing—voice, that at times, indeed, bore the sensations of human touch. The letters brought my ear very, very close to aspects of the published work and public speeches that wouldn't have sounded like they did to me had I not listened so closely to what Baldwin had told his brother about it all in his letters. So while the narrative in those letters rarely surfaces explicitly in *Who Can Afford to Improvise?*, its rich rhythms and complex, love-drenched textures have their undeniable role.

In listening, so much depends upon one's position and what one is positioned to do with what one hears. In *Coltrane: The Story of a Sound*, Ben Ratliff notes Coltrane's own obsession with how microphone placements could affect the fullness of his tone. Dissatisfied with his studio sound, Coltrane said: "They get too close to the horn with the mikes and don't give the sound time to travel as they should. Consequently, they don't get enough of the real timbre and they miss the whole body of the sound. They get the inside of it but not the outside as well."[46] Beyond the general importance of position, Trane's vocabulary is precisely suggestive. *Who Can Afford to Improvise?* pursues a fuller encounter with the body of Baldwin's sound than we've had in a book before, often by altering the position, the angle, from which we listen. Frequently, according to the notion of confession, we'll move between the personal (inside) and the political (outside) dimensions of his sound watching for where they infiltrate each other, illuminating a political interior or injecting personal passion into public issues.

Attuned as it is to what Coltrane termed "the real timbre" and "whole body" of Baldwin's voice in this way, the structure in *Who Can Afford to Improvise?* tracks the process of listening from at least three positions, each with a distinct purpose. Book I listens *to* Baldwin. We pick him up in the initial months of his most intense American visibility in May 1963. As a whole, Book I establishes a new, lyrical narrative of Baldwin's career. It traces his statements as they play over musically inflected analytical structures *he* developed era by era during his life. Chapter 1 accounts for his profile on-screen in the documentary film, *Take This Hammer*, shot in San Francisco in May 1963. Chapter 2 introduces the key terms of Baldwin's lyrical aesthetic: his celebration of "constants," apprehension of "changes," and identification of "chimeras." He outlined and employed this approach in *The Fire Next Time*, the book that initiated his period of peak visibility. Divided into eight chronological periods, Chapter 3 identifies the developing series of structures, key signatures, crucial in guiding a principled, deep listening to the volatile, always shifting contours of Baldwin's career. It begins with his early work as a reviewer for left-leaning journals in the 1940s and extends to his last published and unpublished works from the mid-1980s.

Book II listens *with* Baldwin. It contains essays on the work of three singers closely related to his developing point of view. Chapter 4 listens very closely to key moments in Billie Holiday's career as vocal instrumentalist, singer, and as one of the greatest writer/performers of lyrics, and of the *lyric*, in twentieth-century American culture. Chapter 5 situates Dinah Washington's tonal acuity in blues recordings alongside Baldwin's most densely musical-political essay "The Uses of the Blues," published in *Playboy* in January 1964, within a month of Washington's tragic death. Chapter 6 presents the first detailed account of "The Hallelujah Chorus," a performance from July 1, 1973, in which Baldwin shared the stage in Carnegie Hall with Ray Charles. More than any other single source, "The Hallelujah Chorus" conveys Baldwin's musical approach to his life and his work, a message he attempted to communicate amid one of the most racially and politically volatile and violent moments in American history, and in one of the most turbulent years of his life.

Responding to and extending the listenings in Books I and II, Book III resituates our musically inflected reconsideration of Baldwin's voice into our contemporary culture. Specific passages from Baldwin's work frame each essay and connect them to resonant moments in twenty-first-century music, film, dance, social discourse, and politics. Framed by Baldwin's discussion of "inheritance" and "birthright" from the introduction to the 1984 reissue of *Notes of a Native Son*, Chapter 7 examines the lyrical brilliance and the situation of Amy Winehouse, one celebrated (and vilified) descendant of Holiday, Washington, and Charles. Chapter 8 "inter-views" two films—Richard O. Moore's documentary *Take This Hammer* (1963) and Barry Jenkins's romantic drama *Medicine for Melancholy* (2009)—connected by their directors' deep regard for Baldwin as well as their subtle attention to the lives of black people in a gentrifying San Francisco. Chapter 9 focuses Baldwin's thoughts on the importance and origins of black style, dance in particular, to review a short film, *Turf Feinz* (2009) that depicts street dancers' creation of a diasporic, lyricized space in Oakland. Framed by Baldwin's formulation of the contest between whiteness understood as a "state of mind" and blackness understood as "a condition"—each only partially dependent on skin color—Chapter 10 interrogates the politics of so-called privilege in contemporary American life and culture. And, finally, in the conclusion, I return to the constant, change, and chimera paradigm from *The Fire Next Time* by training a lyrical lens on the contemporary militarization of American life. I focus on President Obama's introduction of the Predator drone program to the American public during the Correspondent's Dinner in May 2010. More a reading of American power than of President Obama himself, the chapter examines how Baldwin's analytical device repositions and refocuses our understanding of the staging of American political and military power in the global theater of the twenty-first century.

This work seeks to describe and enact an angular, musical address. Within and between Books I, II, and III, each section operates in its own way using distinct methods and tones of presentation and, at times, of argument. It is written to the listeners and to the possibility of someone listening over the shoulder of a listener. It's a record of my years traveling across Baldwin's career, and in my own life, guided by my study of the version of his life he told his brother David and by my own needs and experiences as well. Because of the legalities of the James Baldwin Estate, my travel with those letters was intensely private, even secret. *Who Can Afford to Improvise?*, however, is a public offering, not always gentle but usually trying, not *always* angry but often on the verge. At bottom, it's designed to clearly and directly depict—but not always to fully explain, see Billie Holiday—the lyrical and musical dimensions of Baldwin's work and life, the music of a few of the musicians who were most important to him along the way, and selected moments of our contemporary culture.

It's my hope that this musical, structural attention can present the energy Baldwin's work offers an engaged reader in new ways. I've tried to enable an experience of "traveling" with the instructive clarity and the open-ended mystery his work invoked into the world; but I've also attempted to avoid the safe box of celebration. In the film *I Heard It Through the Grapevine* (1980), over footage of him sitting in front of the Martin Luther King Jr. monument in Atlanta, Baldwin discussed how strictly celebratory, commemorative gestures represent "one of the ways the Western world has learned, or thinks it's learned, to outwit history, to outwit time, to make a life and a death irrelevant, to make that passion irrelevant, to make it unusable for you and for our children. There's nothing you can do with that monument . . . and we're confronting that."[47] Part of the tone, texture, and structure of this work owes to my own attempts to address that trap. I'm not sure I've succeeded. I've written in hopes that this book can contribute to the professional, academic conversation; but, much more crucially, I've written it in a way that I hope can be engaged by anyone with a passion to encounter how the complex musicality of Baldwin's work clarifies and intensifies our notion of what human experience is all about.

In 1963, Baldwin told *Life* magazine, "I want to be stretched, shook up, to overreach myself, and to make you feel that way too."[48] In a close echo from 2006, my friend, the poet Adrienne Rich—herself an avid reader and re-reader of Baldwin beginning in her teenage years—wrote that "the medium" of lyric imagination is "language intensified, intensifying our sense of possible reality."[49] These statements came to mind many times, framing part of what I was after while I worked out these chapters. It's only a start. But I think it *is* a start. It's taken a while but, sooner than never, a book has taken form that explores how James Baldwin understood "Ray Charles," what music meant to his work, and what that can mean to us. Evinced in tweets and posts, public events, performances, publications, and conferences, recent years have seen a renewed and enlivened conversation about, arguably, the most important, almost undoubtedly the most undervalued, major twentieth-century American writer. My aim is to move the conversation further along because, as Baldwin wrote at the end of *Just Above My Head*, drawing on something his friend Harry Belafonte told him over dinner in St. Paul de Vence, "ain't nothing up the road but us."[50]

# BOOK I

## The Uses of the Blues
### James Baldwin's Lyrical Quest

You have the right to be immature for quite some time. But, if you're immature let us say beyond the age of twenty-seven, you're not any longer immature you are frozen. You know? And the only way you could then grow up would demand then a cataclysm, you know. You'd have to be broken up into pieces and then put back together again which most people can't survive. In order to, you know, in order to become a man or a woman. But if you're frozen in this peculiar way then you can only be lonely because you haven't got any basis on which to operate, on which to be bound to others. You have no dance floor.

—*James Baldwin to Studs Terkel (1962)*


Everyone on the one hand is fundamentally capable of paying his dues. But no one pays their dues willingly.... As long as you think there's some way to get through life without paying your dues, you're going to be bankrupt.... And the very question now is precisely what we've got in the bank.

—*James Baldwin,* Take This Hammer *(1963)*

# 1

## "Not the country we're sitting in now"
### Amputation/Gangrene Past and Present

By May 1963, James Baldwin had become the most visible "spokesman"—a term he hated—for the civil rights movement, a phrase he didn't like much either. May was an intense month. In an inauspicious beginning, *Harper's* magazine published a set of his letters to his agent Bob Mills.[1] Early in the month, going from San Francisco "to Sacramento, then to San Diego and Los Angeles and back to San Francisco," Baldwin traveled with his personal representative, Eddie Fales, and *Time* magazine correspondent Roger Stone on a tour of California sponsored by the Congress of Racial Equality.[2] Stone described the schedule as "bone jarring" and, signaling attitudes (in this case, relatively mild ones) that would inflect Baldwin's life in uncountable ways, Baldwin as "an eloquent pixy with a sharp tongue."[3] Climbing on and off planes, in and out of cars, moving between venues while snatching papers from newsstands to stay abreast of events in Birmingham, and averaging more than two speeches per day, Baldwin sent a telegram to US Attorney General Robert Kennedy on May 12. The message blamed the violence flaring in Birmingham on the apathy of the federal government. Baldwin didn't go to Alabama during the tumult of that week, but he told Stone: "If I'm called, I will go. I don't want to get castrated any more than anyone else. But I will go."[4] On May 17, one week after the centennial anniversary of Lincoln's Emancipation Proclamation, his portrait appeared on the cover of *Time* magazine. During that week, he filmed the documentary *Take This Hammer* in San Francisco.[5] On May 22, he traveled to Wesleyan University as a guest of novelist Kay Boyle, an engagement that lasted until

2:30 AM. On Thursday May 23, after catching (barely) the 7 AM flight from New York's LaGuardia airport, he had breakfast with Kennedy at the Kennedy home in McLean, Virginia. He returned to New York and spent the rest of the day attending to several business matters, contacting participants for the agreed upon meeting with Kennedy the following day, and then hosting an all-night dance party and planning session for the meeting.

A story titled "At a Crucial Time a Negro Talks Tough" appeared in *Life* magazine on Friday, May 24.[6] It described a recent, "hectic, two-day speaking tour to New Orleans for the Congress of Racial Equality" on which Baldwin "gave five planned and three spontaneous talks." The same day, Baldwin led a group of friends and family (including Lena Horne, Lorraine Hansberry, Harry Belafonte, Rip Torn, his brother David, and freedom rider Jerome Smith) to a meeting with Robert Kennedy in their family's apartment at 24 Central Park South in New York City. Directly after that (by all accounts) disastrous attempt to communicate with the attorney general, he went directly with Kenneth B. Clark to tape an interview with WGBH-TV in New York. On May 27, agents from the New York office of the FBI attempted to gain and were refused entry to the apartment where Baldwin was staying on East Third Street in the Village, initiating intense surveillance that would continue until 1974 and amass a file nearing two thousand pages.[7] A friction at the center of the month's events offers a lens through which to clarify core angularities in Baldwin's life and work. Such a point of view, even decades after Baldwin's death, can also offer valuable perspective on our own lives and the cultural and political worlds around us. In short, Baldwin's work offers a unique gauge for measuring who has how much, and of what, in the bank. At the end of the dispatch for *Time*, Stone concluded, "Baldwin has a face that could soon be forgotten, not so his lengthening shadow, as it steals across the nation."[8] What Stone described as a shadow I approach throughout the book as a disruptive clarity and a constantly refocusing analytical lens.

The meeting with Kennedy in New York became famous as a flash point for the tension between mainstream liberal politics and the street-level realities of race and black consciousness in the early 1960s. In his 1979 essay "Lorraine Hansberry at the Summit," Baldwin recalls Kennedy's invocation of his own immigrant roots and his attempt to calm the group by saying that "a Negro could be president in 40 years."[9] He adds: "He really didn't know why black people were so offended by this attempt at reassurance."[10] Of the gap between perspectives, he wrote, "the meeting took place in that panic-stricken vacuum in which black and white, for the most part, meet in this country."[11] Although the complexity of his response was lost on the vast majority of his original readers, the "panic-stricken vacuum" Baldwin notes both does and *doesn't* refer to meetings between people of different skin color. Baldwin's prose is exact. The abstract situation, "when black and white, for the most part, meet in this country," refers to individual people as well as racialized cultural codes that operate *between* and *within* people in American life. As he had begun to do with his earlier essays and as he would continue to do for the rest of his life, Baldwin portrayed meetings of "black and white" as meetings between persons as well as intersections of impersonal, racialized codes that play out on every level of our psychic and civic lives.

Baldwin had already charted the tension produced by these clashing codes of speech, thought, and what, in *The Souls of Black Folk*, W. E. B. Du Bois referred to as "the peculiar sensation" of interracial coexistence. The tensions were political, social, and personal. Once more, he understood that all those terms were tangled up with each other. In "Notes of a Native Son" (1955), Baldwin attributes the 1943 Harlem riots to "the Negro's real relation to the white American" (*CE*, 82). As happened innumerable times before and since, the peculiar sensation, boiling in a certain way in every resident of Harlem (at least), had simply become "intolerable." Finally, "Harlem had needed something to smash." As a result, and as usual, interracial tension surfaced in intraracial (and intrapersonal) violence—"To smash something is the ghetto's chronic need. Most of the time it is the members of the ghetto who smash each other and themselves." Black Americans, Baldwin held, could not simply embrace white cultural codes, "the white world is too powerful, too complacent, too ready with gratuitous humiliation, and, above all, too ignorant and too innocent for that" (83). And, even privately, rejecting out-of-hand the interracial tangle entailed inordinate costs as well: "one has to blot so much out of the mind—and the heart—that this hatred itself becomes an exhausting and self-destructive pose" (83).

He concludes his sketch of this social and psychological collision, "when black and white meet in this country," and the impossible postures it imposes, with the metaphoric risks of gangrene and amputation. *Gangrene* results as a black American subject negotiates with the "panic-stricken vacuum" thereby absorbing the power, complacency, ignorance, and innocence that characterize the white cultural codes' regard for the black ones. This is poisonous chemistry. *Amputation* is the term Baldwin uses to describe the attempt to cease the negotiation and compartmentalize to rid one's (black) self of the contemptuous assumptions of its white image (and one's "white" self of the contempt of the black one) in the mirror. Baldwin then sets his terms in motion in his most effective and terrifying mid-twentieth-century portrait of what Du Bois had termed double-consciousness in 1903:

> One is absolutely forced to make perpetual qualifications and one's own reactions are always cancelling each other out. It is this, really, which has driven so many people mad, both white and black. One is always in the position of having to decide between amputation and gangrene. Amputation is swift but time may prove that the amputation was not necessary—or one may delay the amputation too long. Gangrene is slow, but it is impossible to be sure that one is reading one's symptoms right. The idea of going through life as a cripple is more than one can bear, and equally unbearable is the risk of swelling up slowly, in agony, with poison. (*CE*, 83)

In Baldwin's mind, there are power dynamics to take into account, but no American escapes these impossible negotiations between amputation and gangrene imposed upon them when the "white" components of the sociopsychological terrain of American life regard the "black" ones and vice versa. No matter the level of consciousness or the relative pressure at which that panic-ridden drama plays out, Baldwin knew that *every* American faced the dilemma that "the trouble, finally, is that the risks are real even if the choices don't exist" (83).

Appearances, however, at the surface of behavior and in American self-regard (then and now) seemed to belie Baldwin's insight. For the most part, at the time of the meeting between Kennedy and Baldwin's group, most mainstream white Americans claimed not to know much about this at all. Whiteness understood (and still understands) itself as a kind of privilege that allowed people to avoid paying dues in the gangrene/amputation dilemmas of the American inheritance. Baldwin knew better. The results (no matter the income bracket) of not engaging were bankruptcy. His understanding of black style, speech and, more than anything else, music, was founded upon this impossible tangle that was far more difficult for black people to ignore than whites. The key difference is, Baldwin thought, that some of the risks of ignoring the transracial tangle interior to the American subject were more obvious—the alternatives more immediately lethal—to black people than they were to white people.

That white innocence had its costs, of course. In the opening moments of *The Fire Next Time*, he noted the paradox: "It is the innocence which constitutes the crime" (*CE*, 292). On the other hand, together with the scars, contending with the amputation/gangrene dynamic produced an undeniable form of strength. In *No Name in the Street* (1972), Baldwin noted both. Of the former, he observed: "White Children, in the main, and whether they are rich or poor, grow up with a grasp of reality so feeble that they can very accurately be described as deluded—about themselves and the world they live in" (431). Of the black contending, he argued that "it is a very different matter, and results in a very different intelligence, to grow up under the necessity of questioning everything—everything from the question of one's identity to the literal, brutal question of how to save one's life in order to live it" (431).

In his biography of Baldwin, about the meeting in New York City, David Leeming writes that it was Kennedy's quip about the presidency that brought Baldwin out of his silence to say, in anger, that "the point was, a Kennedy could already be president while the black man was . . . 'still required to supplicate and beg you for justice.'"[12] It's not clear where Baldwin first heard Kennedy's prediction about a black president, but his offense is on the record as early as June of 1961.[13] That Kennedy's abstractly white liberal patronizing and political pragmatism touched an abstractly black nerve is obvious. But, on that Saturday afternoon on May 24, 1963, Kennedy also touched a much less obvious nerve in James Baldwin, the person, as well. Baldwin absolutely understood and fully embraced the need to make racial, political sense of African American history. In this, by 1963, he knew that *he* was a visible, impersonal part of that racial, political, historical sense and *he* refused to be made part of a liberal myth founded upon the gradual attainment of the so-called American dream. On the other hand, he understood that the cultural politics could not explain the full complexity of his (or anyone else's) personal life. And, he understood that the complexity of personal life was a political reality as well. Baldwin's anger at Kennedy signified a distance between them. It stemmed from the danger and the immediate need for relief, on the centennial of the Emancipation Proclamation. And it sounded an acceptance that it would entail a lifelong—possibly a generations-long—struggle, the outcomes of which would be unrecognizable from where they all sat on that Saturday in New York.

Despite, or because of, that distance, James Baldwin had been in rhetorical territory surprisingly similar to Kennedy's the previous week. Just before leaving California to return east, Baldwin had participated in a documentary film titled *Take This Hammer* in which he talked with dif-

Still image from the opening of *Take This Hammer*, San Francisco, May 1963.

ferent groups of black people about their experiences in San Francisco. In one meeting, a young black man in his late teens or early twenties says, "There'll never be a Negro president in this country."[14] When Baldwin, responding to the man's attempts at amputation, asks why he believes that, the man responds, "We can't get jobs how we gonna be a president?" By which he meant, in a sense, why carry the poison of impossible and abstract ambition around in one's body? To which Baldwin answers: "You *got* me. But, I want you to think about this. There will be a Negro president of this country. But it will not be the country we're sitting in now. . . . It's not important really, you know, whether or not there's a Negro president. I mean, in that way." Baldwin's struggles to suggest a tolerance for the risks of gangrene fall on palpably skeptical ears. While he makes his attempt, one of the two men he's facing, with a deftly stylized theatricality, carefully puts on his sunglasses. "What's important," Baldwin concluded, "is that you should realize that you can, that you can become the president. There's nothing anybody can do that you can't do."

If the man with the shades seems to have seen it coming, the other young men look likewise unconvinced in the moment. In 1951, Langston Hughes had collected this, call it *am*-putative, black perspective in his poem "Children's Rhymes": *By what sends / the white kids / I ain't sent: / I know I can't / be President.*[15] By the early 1960s, only hopelessly criminal innocents (like Kennedy, at least for another few months until his brother was murdered) or adults who mistakenly imagine they're visiting the world of kids (like Baldwin's film persona in San Francisco) would suggest that Hughes's streetwise kids were wrong. Baldwin knew all this well enough. At that moment, he was also living the fact that sociology and probability (what poet Robert Hayden called "riot squads of statistics") don't *fully* map human capacity. So, acting, against even higher stakes in the knowledge that one can, indeed, die from gangrene even in a phantom limb, Baldwin said it anyway. The disease remains real even if the amputated limb has been left far behind.

In one way the separation between Baldwin and Kennedy's rhetoric and the perspective of the young men is actually quite similar. In another way, the gap between Baldwin at that moment and those men was a gap between himself and his own past, as well as evidence of a complex deal he'd made (by exactly risking choices that didn't exist) with his own life in the present. Due to his keen understanding of this fractured territory and the war between amputation and gangrene it entailed, the vacuum between Baldwin and the young men isn't panic-stricken in the least. The gap, however, is vast and the bridge of conversation and style, while important, is hardly adequate. Livable choices, in fact, didn't exist. Neither did communicable connections. That's *why* the vacuum. That's why the panic. Evidence suggests that Baldwin was, in fact, *acting* in the film to dramatize exactly this.

Noting his spokesman status, Leeming described Baldwin's role in *Take This Hammer*: "He walked through the city commenting in a guru-like manner on its possibilities and its inequities."[16] Indeed, Baldwin's monologues in the film take on a kind of oracular if not "guru-like" effect. But, Leeming's account of the documentary misconstrues the complexity of

Skeptical young man with sunglasses, *Take This Hammer.*

Baldwin's position (which is neither as stable nor as self-assured as Leeming implies) in the conversations it chronicles. Often, Baldwin positions himself on an untrustworthy bridge between the anger of young black people in San Francisco and the liberal audience of KQED public television in the Bay Area.

At one point in the film, he is positioned in front of a construction project that has displaced black residents and will result in high-rise apartments at prices no black former resident of the neighborhood could afford. Addressing the role of such gentrification in the American narrative of "progress," Baldwin translates the rage that results in (if it doesn't require) amputations in the minds and lives of the black community. Editors spliced the scene to immediately follow a working class black man addressing the racially coded role of nepotism in San Francisco: "You got to know somebody in San Francisco to get somewhere, and by knowing somebody it got to be somebody with authority and nobody in San Francisco, no colored man got no authority." Cut to Baldwin in front of the construction site where he says:

> Even the least damaged of those kids would have to, to put it as mildly as it can be put at the moment, would have to be a little sardonic, a little sardonic about the, um, the things he sees on television and what the president says and all those movies about being a good American and all that *jazz* and he'll look at this, look over there and look up here and he will despise the people, you know, who are able to have such a tremendous gap between their performance and their profession. But the more damaged kids will simply feel like blowing it up, simply feel like blowing it up. Speaking for myself I feel a little sardonic and I'm civilized, I think, but there was a time in my life when I would have felt like blowing it up . . . how do you get through to the least damaged kids. . . . I don't know what I would say that would make any sense to them, because in fact this doesn't make any sense. [The people who will live in a building like this] will walk down the street and wonder why the first Negro boy they see looks at them like he wants to kill them and if he gets a chance tries . . . he has no ground to stand on here the cat said yesterday "I've got no country I've got no flag" and it isn't because he was born paranoiac that he said that, it's because the performance of the country for his eighteen years on Earth has proven that to him. . . . I'll tell you something about that building. It has absolutely no foundation. It really does not have any foundation. It's going to come down, one way or another. Either we will correct what's wrong or it will be corrected for us.

While *Take This Hammer* documents a real distance between the famous writer and the black people he meets in San Francisco, the footage clearly conveys Baldwin's intense care for and delight in hearing the young voices he's surrounded by in San Francisco's black neighborhoods. The film also documents a brilliant variety of voices, personalities, and energies surrounding Baldwin in the meetings. It's clear that Baldwin fears for their futures and the future of the brilliant, critical vitality, what he would describe in *No Name in the Street* as "a very different intelligence," they invoke into the world (*CE*, 431). The tact of his presence with the groups takes shape despite (and also because he's keenly aware of) the chasms that fracture the discussions. There's an unmistakable humility visible in this footage of Baldwin's conversations. It's a humility rooted in his respect for black people's everyday skill in the face of the acute demands of racially intensified experiences and his familiarity with how words evaporate (although, he knew, not for everyone and not completely) the minute the camera turns away, he gets on a plane, and the young people go back to doing what they do.

But, that's not to wax romantic, either. The risks of amputation and gangrene twisted into the spiritual and material paradigms of American life spare no one. Some, to whatever extent, work them into real masquerades of functional lives. Others can talk a good game, at least. One fast-talking young man in the film says, "I don't have to work for *nobody*, and I can make it." Others agree as Baldwin checks, a little nervously, over each shoulder. Orville Luster asks the man, "How do you make it?" Addressing Luster and referring to Baldwin, he answers: "What you mean how I make it? This is something I'm going to tell him how I make it? Look here I'm indicting myself if I talk to him and you go down and tell the police what I done did!" Ten minutes later the film cuts back to the meeting Baldwin recalls above. Outside a grocery store, he sits surrounded by young men and shielding his eyes from the late afternoon sun. We overhear a man, off-camera: "I got no flag." Another voice: "We have no country, no country." And another: "Get off your knees and take what you want." Then a twenty-three-year-old man recounts his first arrest at the age of eight while someone off camera says, "Never let the white man catch you on your knees, brother." In a way it's a familiar scene, the loudest and quickest voices in the group profiling for the camera to impress their peers. It's part jiving, certainly, and laced with stylized radicalisms, catchphrases likely learned in part from Nation of Islam lectures or flyers. Yet, it's serious business too. The camera returns to the twenty-three-year-old who argues, in a calm and assured voice, that nonviolence and sit-in demonstrations are hopeless. An exchange ensues:

JB: How are we going to do it?
THE MAN: By violence. Violence. An uprising, having a revolution.
JB: But there are twenty million of us.
THE MAN: Twenty million. That's enough.
JB: [*Stammers for his phrasing*] Not, not, not in, not not these days and not in those terms.
THE MAN: Oh, it's enough.

JB: They're scattered, forty-eight states.

THE MAN: Forty-eight states? Get 'em together.

JB: How?

THE MAN: How? Through Islam—

JB: What?

THE MAN: the true religion, you know. Get all the people together get them all to believe in one thing then they can't help but stick together. You know we can't stick together now half of us Christians the other half Baptists, you know, some Jews and all that. Now what good is that going to do us?

JB: Um hm. So you think the only thing that we can do . . .

THE MAN: . . . is get together . . .

JB: . . . is have an armed uprising?

THE MAN: . . . really. Just put blood, you know, let everybody bleed a little bit.

By the end, this young man's tone isn't full of fast-pitch boasts like the others. Counseling moderation and organized protests, or at least playing that role in the film, Baldwin suggests, "Birmingham isn't over yet." As the man counters his voice softens, "They done sent in the state troopers, the federal." By the end, he almost whispers. In a line intoned with the half-sublimated intimate and violent ambiguities of a soul song, he concludes: "It's all over now."

Within a few years, the violence intoned above and forecasted in *The Fire Next Time* and elsewhere was in full view across the nation. In September 1966, the National Guard was mobilized in Hunter's Point. One man in *Take This Hammer*, James Lockett, was nineteen in 1966. Almost fifty years later, he recalled: "They lined up in formation, the first row was on their knees with shotguns and the second row was standing up behind them." Lockett continued to sketch the ominous scene, smiling, "I guess they thought they were intimidating us, so, we had guns, too."[17] A shootout followed involving "hundreds and hundreds of bullets." Of the violence in 1966, Tyrone Primus, who was thirteen when he appeared in *Take This Hammer*, said: "I've never been in a war, you know what I mean? But I felt like I've experienced it." Violence intensified into the 1970s. As I note in Chapter 6, between October 1973 and April 1974, members of a splinter group from the Nation of Islam in San Francisco would kill over a dozen white people in a series of racially motivated murders and attacks known as the "zebra killings" that terrified people in and around the city.

Baldwin and Kennedy's positions in these exchanges are in no way identical. His position with the young men (and at least one young woman who, as I discuss in Chapter 8, speaks bravely and brilliantly about her impending homelessness) and his comments, however, do echo into a vacuum similar to the one over which Robert Kennedy, days later, offered his naïve reassurance to Baldwin and his group. All the parties in both meetings are connected, and none of them can communicate. That language didn't exist. It still doesn't. Baldwin's obsession with revising the basic terms of American conversations targets these vacuums. He knew that the American vocabulary was designed to thwart such conversations. Without question, an echo of the insufficiency of his own assurance to the men in *Take This Hammer* about the future of a black presidency was part of what made Baldwin so angry with Kennedy. Baldwin was a connoisseur of such irresolutions, the always-angular relationships between conceptual (at times, political) identity and any lived reality, or actual lives, as well as the necessary, if partial, disjunction between private and public life. A musicality in the language allowed Baldwin's angularity to communicate with lives lived out privately and publicly in a world people share. These demonstrated, though deeply coded, facets of his work confirm that he was certainly aware of the vacuum he shared with Kennedy in that moment in New York City on Friday, May 24, 1963. The friction in that vacuum fired his syncopated rhetorical precision ("supplicate *and* beg") and his rage.

We don't know what happened to most of the young people with whom Baldwin spoke in San Francisco. But, we do know that Baldwin and Kennedy were both right. November 2008 proved it. Or did it? Kennedy's easy assumption about the future was off by five years, a few months longer than he, at the time age thirty-eight, had to live when he met with Baldwin and his delegation in New York. But, what of Baldwin's idea that the country that elects a black president "won't be the country" in which he sat with those young men in San Francisco? Certainly massive shifts have occurred in what *black* and *white* mean by themselves and to each other, as well as in the contours of the vacuum (panic-stricken or not) between them. Just as certainly, aspects of these shifting, racialized codes between and *within* people continue to inform innocence and delusion on one hand and "a different kind of intelligence" on the other. And, one would guess, that our understanding of which hand is which and what all that means isn't as sure as Baldwin's understanding seemed to be when he wrote *No Name in the Street*. In the final decades of the twentieth and in the opening ones of the twenty-first century, evidence that this American innocence and delusion could be found among people of all colors has, whether cynically or not, been characterized as progress. Even if measured in signs of social delusion, it seems that any narrowing of the gap between people of color and the accouterments of whiteness still often operate as badges of progress.

Much of Baldwin's work sought to produce a coherent map of these changes and a clearer idea of their relationship to things that don't change. A central insight and musically inflected structure of Baldwin's work ca. 1963 involves the interaction between change and constant. For the rest of his life, he would explore and draw attention to the dangerous illusions (what he termed "chimeras") produced by confusion of things that change with things that don't and vice versa. Chimeras remain. The questions that connect Baldwin's meetings with Kennedy to his conversations with black people on the streets of San Francisco are still unasked. The American idiom to ask and answer them in still eludes us. Or we elude it. Today, huge numbers of people assume they can avoid—or are clueless as to how connect to—such questions. Others, trapped inside the questions, can't afford to suspect they don't know the answers. The result is widespread dues unpaid as much American experience occurs in denied territory, uncharted terrains within and noncommunicated spaces between people. Terms shift and slip, but panic-stricken vacuums abound. What changes, what constants, and what illusions made the United States the place that elects a black president? What does *black* president actually mean? And, for whom does what change, exactly? And, what then? No one engaged these questions and sought terms that would force still deeper ones more intensely than James Baldwin. If we're serious about what Baldwin's work can mean in the contemporary world—and evidence exists indicating that we aren't[18]—the place to begin is with a brief look at the structure of the constant changes and changing constants in the musically scored dimensions of Baldwin's thought at the dawn of his period of most intense public visibility.

# 2
# Blues Constants, Jazz Changes
## Toward a Writing Immune to Bullshit

In *The Fire Next Time*, James Baldwin abstracted the quest for cultural and personal awareness: "It is the responsibility of free men to trust and to celebrate what is constant—birth, struggle, and death are constant, and so is love, though we may not think so—and to apprehend the nature of change" (*CE*, 339). Issued at the dawn of his role as a prophetic celebrity, this is the core of his vision ca. 1963. Black musical assumptions inflect the meaning of the key terms, constant and change. In short, blues distills the constants into lyrical truths. With its foundations in blues, in constants—in what Baldwin would simply call "the facts of life" *densified* by blues lyricism—jazz searches options and charts viable changes.[1] Crucially, a gospel-influenced sense of collective purpose permeated all of Baldwin's work, gathering the blues and jazz angularities into a story of complexly shared implications. These inflections were in no way restricted to musical performance and recordings, "The title, 'The Uses of the Blues,' does not refer to music; I don't know anything about music. It does refer to the experience of life, or the state of being, out of which the blues come."[2] Strictly speaking, it wasn't a matter of just listening to music; Baldwin experienced the world and made sense of it via an unceasing dialogue with what he heard in black music. Music worked as a kind of witness to reality and possibility, constants and changes; at its deepest, music was a report from (often) denied territory, from levels of experience held outside—or captive inside—the American myth of what life was supposed to be all about.

Baldwin drew on black music to shade and inflect terms in an idiosyncratic language that engaged the evasions embedded in American writing and speech. He meant his engagement to resonate in the worlds of literary and popular culture, politics, and the media, as well as in daily life. Using "American" words the way Billie Holiday used a Broadway show tune, and often enough with Holiday's voice as an explicit point of reference, he shifted the meanings of words and phrases to engage a sense of experience he had forged from black life, drawn from world art, and honed in his work and experience at home and abroad. Through these shifts, his work pursued what LeRoi Jones termed, "the changing same" (change engaged with, not in flight from, the facts of life) in the human condition.[3] In this way, Baldwin engaged psychological, social, and political complexities via a prose, at times a deceptively *lyrical* prose, crafted in an idiom progressively close to his own speaking voice. He *loved* conversation; he loved to talk "to all kinds of people," and thought, as he wrote in 1959, that "almost everyone, as I hope we still know, loves a man who loves to listen" (*CE*, 140).

Clarifying the notion of change in the previous passage, Baldwin noted the danger of mistaking American ephemera for the facts of life. Ephemera masquerading as constants become dangerous illusions—chimeras—that threaten one's sense of reality. Baldwin's insistence on the blues suggests that one's sense of self and life is threatening in and of itself. That's what makes the blues the *blues*. Threats to this threatening sense of self, then, often appear cloaked as protective devices capable of mitigating the threats inherent in the facts of life. In Baldwin's mind, people can't afford such devices; traffic with them is the road to bankruptcy: "I speak of change not on the surface but in the depths—change in the sense of renewal. But renewal becomes impossible if one supposes things to be constant that are not—safety, for example, or money, or power. One clings then to chimeras, by which one can only be betrayed, and the entire hope—the entire possibility—of freedom disappears" (*CE*, 339). Calculated or compulsive clinging to chimeras, he thought, was the source of a pervasive American evasion of experience. Enter, "whiteness."

Baldwin's most explicit, single engagement with the way black musical inflections expose American chimeras occurs in his 1964 essay "The Uses of the Blues." Published exactly one year after *The Fire Next Time*, this essay associates whiteness directly with the—to his mind dangerously chimerical—American dream and pursuit of happiness. These terms, for Baldwin, indexed people's tendency to seek ephemera in the place of "change in the sense of renewal" precisely as a way of evading constants, the basic intensities—"birth, struggle, death, love"—of experience. Signaling a possibility conveyed in black music and otherwise largely absent from the American sense of life, he points to a crucial surprise produced by successful, lyrical distillations of real constants, joy. He then marks a stark distinction in his musically inflected dynamic: "And I want to suggest that the acceptance of this anguish one finds in the blues, and the expression of it, creates also, however odd this may sound, a kind of joy. Now joy is a real state, it is a reality; it has nothing to do with what most people have in mind when they talk of happiness, which is not a real state and does not really exist."[4] Joy becomes possible through a lyrical relationship with basic intensities of life. In "Color" (1962), he had touched upon the difficulty of accounting for this reality in an American vocabulary in which: "To suggest that joy can be present, in any way, on any level, of Negro life offends, of course, immediately all of our social and sentimental assumptions. Joy is the fruit of Yankee thrift and virtue and makes its sweet appearance only after a lifetime of cruel self-denial and inveterate moneymaking" (CE, 674). "The Uses of the Blues" allows Baldwin to differentiate between the hard-won reality he's naming and the mythology that surrounds and threatens it. When pursued by attempting to elude the facts of life—whether via self-denial, inveterate moneymaking, or whatever else—happiness accrues in a register of experience that, for Baldwin, simply isn't real. It won't sing. Exit, "whiteness."

But not so fast. In a 1979 speech at UC Berkeley, Baldwin made the provocative statement, "Insofar as you think you're white, you're irrelevant."[5] While the audience laughed as if he'd just dismissed the "white" people around them, Baldwin was in fact addressing the constant/change/chimera dynamic in terms that drew directly upon the blues and jazz resonances—or the lack thereof—in the term *white*. Signaling a narrative of constants and changes beneath the terms, to what effect is impossible to know, Baldwin intoned, "We can no longer afford that particular, *romance*." As he noted at the beginning of the speech, the effort to engage terminology such as *black* and *white* was central to his understanding of a writer's job: "What a writer is obliged at some point to realize is that he's involved with a language that he has to change. For example, for a black writer, especially in this country, to be born into the English language, is to realize that the assumptions of the language, the assumptions on which the language operates, are his enemy." Throughout his career, often through direct use of resonances routed in black music,[6] Baldwin shifted enemy assumptions into lyrical lenses on irrelevant chimeras, distillations of the blues constants, and necessary renewals in the changing same of living experience. The tensions in this pursuit informed every stage of his constant development as he refused chimerical changes in the culture around him.

For forty years, Baldwin sought to expose how the great bulk of mainstream American culture and the assumptions upon which it operates prevented the celebration of constants and apprehension of change resulting in alienation from the painful and joyous, living and dying rhythms of actual experience. In this effort he had, as he knew, widespread and distinguished musical company. For instance, in "An Open Letter to Miles Davis" published in *Down Beat* Magazine in November 1955, Charles Mingus sketched the experiential implications of this aesthetic directly: "If someone has been escaping reality, I don't expect him to dig my music."[7] For persons lacking a lyrical, densified account of experience, Baldwin thought, freedom could assume no substantive meaning at all. In "The Uses of the Blues," he wrote:

> The failure on our part to accept the reality of pain, of anguish, of ambiguity, of death, has turned us into a peculiar and sometimes monstrous people. It means, for one thing, and it's very serious, that people who have no experience have no compassion. . . . You can't know anything about life and suppose you can get through it clean. The most monstrous people are those who think they are going to.[8]

Baldwin's guides in the search were many, none more important than the black blues impulse to lyrically *engage* rather than evade the most vexing facets of experience and the jazz impulse to endless improvisation within and around those themes. In his classic essay, "The Changing Same," LeRoi Jones suggested that the blues in black music could best be understood as the "expression of the culture . . . immune to bullshit."[9] In "Mississippi John Hurt," Yusef Komunyakaa credited Hurt's music for its clarity of vision, a "knife-edge of seeing."[10] Baldwin considered such nonreductive, lyrical engagement—and the pain entailed therein—key to the nature of freedom itself. In a 1961 interview with Studs Terkel, he said:

> I think the country has got to find out what it means by freedom. Freedom is a very dangerous thing. Anything else is disastrous, but freedom is dangerous. You've got to make choices you've got to make very dangerous choices. You've got to be taught that your life is in your hands . . . [then, likening Ingmar Bergman to blues artists, Baldwin said that Bergman] had recognized what people in this country have a great deal of trouble recognizing, that life

is very difficult, very difficult for *any*body, anybody born. Now, I
don't think people *can* be free until they recognize this, in the same
way that Bessie Smith was much freer, odd and terrible as this may
sound, much freer than the people who murdered her or let her
die. You know. And, Big Bill Broonzy, a much freer man than these
success-ridden people running around on Madison Avenue today.[11]

Throughout his career, Baldwin summoned American public and private
facts of life focused by his version of the "knife-edge of seeing." He
redirected the American vocabulary in ways that lyricized both the filmy
irrelevance of chimeras and the painful joy of constants. Jones described
this effort in the blues: "The elements that turn our singing into direction
[*sic*] reflections of our selves are heavy and palpable as weather."[12] Baldwin
created many such "elements" by lyrically invoking black musical (which,
to him, meant black experiential) textures that contend with the enemy
assumptions of the language we speak.

Signaling the scale and depth of his dissent from the public languages
and private silences of American life, Baldwin framed the racial implications of the constant/change/chimera paradigm in a letter from Switzerland printed in *Harper's* in 1963. Power, Baldwin understood, can make
chimeras real, dangerous, even deadly. If a chimera takes a liking to you,
it might make you happy, for a while, but Baldwin argued that *no* power
can make a chimera joyous. Ever. He wrote, "I have said for years that
color does not matter. I am now beginning to feel that it does not matter
*at all*, that it masks something else which *does* matter: but this suspicion
changes, for me, the entire nature of reality."[13] People, as Baldwin observed often, are fond of masks. He continued his letter, "There is a very
grim secret hidden in the fact that so many of the people one hoped to
rescue could not be rescued because the prison of color had become their
hiding place."[14] Obviously, Baldwin knew that race matters to American
experience. He also knew that social reality masks other, private, pleasures
and dilemmas in a life. Neither social nor private life could be considered
real (and so derive or sustain joy) in isolation from each other. As he told
Terkel, Baldwin thought that constant truths (be they social or private
ones) originate in people's fallible state and against a pervading sense of
risk, a sense of the tragic. For him, art's first function was to thwart social
customs designed to cover this up. Art put people eye to eye with this
essential state of risk and made an engaged joy possible:

Life is mainly, you know most of us no matter what we say are
walking in the dark ... nobody knows what's going to happen to
him from one moment to the next or how he will bear it. This

is irreducible and it's true for everybody. Now it is true that the nature of society has to be, you know, to create among its citizens an illusion of safety. But it is also absolutely true that this safety is necessarily an illusion and artists are here to disturb the peace. [*Terkel breaks in*: "Artists are here to disturb the peace."] Yes, they have to disturb the peace, otherwise, chaos.[15]

Baldwin closes the conversation with Terkel at exactly where understanding his work begins, a collision between a chimerical torpor (mainstream American peace and happiness masking panic) disturbed by art into contact with the living texture of experience and the chaos that resulted when such efforts failed.

As a long listen to his writing and speeches reveals, no other American writer pursued, let's call it, *a musical immunity to bullshit* with Baldwin's lyrical intensity of vision. On the public stage, in the role of the literary jazzman with one foot in the blues, functioning as what he called "a disturber of the peace," he sought to illuminate the durable, troubling constants deeply embedded in, and forging links between, the public and private life.[16] Indeed, as revealed by listenings in the following chapter, an actual freedom required a radical reorientation of what public and private meant. As he told Terkel, "If you can examine and face your life, you can discover the terms in which you're connected to other lives . . . and this is a great liberation." This is not Jazz at Lincoln Center. This is a jazz for living, a joy which risks its *musical immunity* again and again by betting that, as Jones warns in *Black Music*, it doesn't "become a music of special, not necessarily emotional, occasion."[17]

Even an initial charting of the deep resource offered by these shifting dimensions of Baldwin's work requires a few steps. In Chapter 3, I trace the arc of his career as he constantly developed his encounter with the world and his work. Music arguably is *the* key touchstone at several, simultaneous levels. It provides a nearly continual frame of reference in Baldwin's increasingly lyrical, analytical repertoire of responses to and interventions in post–World War II American life and culture.

# 3

## "Making words *do* something"
### Retracing James Baldwin's Career

In letters to friends and family over decades, Baldwin stressed the importance of writing to his presence in interior, personal, and political worlds. As he would learn, those worlds complexly overlapped. Writing was more than a neatly formal exercise on the page. It was an essential element in a turbulent quest for development within an expanding sense of political, cultural, and historical vitality and veracity. As he explained to his brother in a letter in the summer of 1955, writing should "*do* something"; it should produce a pressure that makes something happen in the person, in people, in the world. In the spring of 1963, he told Jane Howard of *Life*, "I want to be stretched, shook up, to overreach myself, and to make you feel that way too."[1] As if making words *do* that was the key, he continued: "I want to be a great artist, not just a very good one." Wherever he was, the music was close at hand. Describing the routine when Baldwin was in New York, a friend of his told Howard, "You always go back to Jimmy's after an evening . . . never anybody else's. He's got to hear that music."[2] Howard informed, "That music consists largely of Ray Charles, Mahalia Jackson, and the Abyssinian Baptist Choir." The page included a photo of Baldwin dancing "the hitchhike" in New Orleans after a lecture. Another photo from that evening's dancing provides the cover image of this book.

In his 1960 essay "Mass Culture and the Creative Artist," Baldwin considered the relationship between American popular culture and the creative arts. The prevailing nature of the relationship between art and culture, he observed, was conflict. Pointing out the elephant-sized chimera in the room, he wrote: "What passes for the appreciation of serious effort in this country is very often nothing more than the inability to take anything very seriously."[3] Extrapolating from there, he continued: "Perhaps life is not the black, unutterably beautiful, mysterious, and lonely thing the creative artist tends to think of it as being; but it is certainly not the sunlit playpen in which so many Americans lose first their identities and then their minds."[4] Blurring the distinction between art and culture, and linking writing directly to transformative social energy, he signaled a tolerance for shuffling between the conflicting poles:

> I feel very strongly, though, that this amorphous people [Americans] are in desperate search for something which will help them to re-establish their connection with themselves, and with one another. This can only begin to happen as the truth [through art] begins to be told. We are in the middle of an immense metamorphosis here, a metamorphosis which will, it is devoutly to be hoped, rob us of our myths and give us our history, which will destroy our attitudes and give us back our personalities. The mass culture, in the meantime, can only reflect our chaos: and perhaps we had better remember that this chaos contains life—and a great transforming energy.[5]

Time and time again, throughout stages of his constantly shifting point of view, Baldwin wrote with a precise intensity that penetrated and disabled the chimeras of American delusion and proposed alternative terms capable of a more trenchant, if almost always more risky, gauge of experience. The mainstream narrative of Baldwin's career continues to be one of early promise that peaked in 1963 and declined owing to activist and cultural engagements to the detriment of literary virtue. Certainly, Baldwin's willingness to equivocate with views of literary virtue as a disengaged, aesthetic technique diminished after 1963; but his concept of a socially, culturally, politically resonant aesthetic is visible throughout his early writing. The arc of his development, in fact, is an unbroken series of musically informed innovations designed to map a rapidly shifting set of political, cultural, and artistic energies among which he lived. The chart of his transit through four decades is complex. At each stage, his approach is dynamic; the course is nonlinear but betrays unmistakable marks of a deep, soulful logic. The following sections trace the long, shifting song, one route in the epic score of what Baldwin attempted to make words, his words, do. Here we go.

## "The shock of identification": Beginnings and Early Reviews (1947–1950)

In book reviews written in his twenties, Baldwin began his career as a professional writer unmaking established American and international writers in a prose balanced precariously between an ironic wit and an unsparing, critical fury. These pieces, written amid his attempts and failures to realize his own first novel, betray early concerns as well as impulses that would inform his work throughout his career: a scathing attitude toward the fantasies and indulgences of mainstream popular culture, including fiction; a distrust of art in sync with dominant ideologies in favor of the anarchic vitality of human interior and private life; a radical suspicion of and intolerance for psychoanalytic schemes as guides to human complexity; and a skeptical attitude toward quietist philosophers and scientific historians whose thought didn't interact with the immediate and messy urgencies of daily existence nor the vast spaces between historically verifiable facts.

Holding literary art up to demanding standards was serious business for Baldwin and he played his share of dozens along the way. Whether caused by commercial pandering or ignorance, he had little patience for novelists whose characters, plots, and approaches reinforced middlebrow American chimeras. In "Modern Rover Boys," his 1948 review in the *New Leader* of the *Moth* by James M. Cain, Baldwin concluded that the writer's characters were blinded by American myths and were therefore confounded by the most banal facts of life: "the only thing wrong with [Cain's characters] was the fact that they were still reeling from the discovery that they were in possession of visible and functioning sexual organs. It was the impact of this discovery that so hopelessly and murderously disoriented them."[6] This shallow and naïve misperception of the most basic facts of human existence made writing like Cain's an easy target for Baldwin's scorn in his mid-twenties. He admitted the urge to just keep silent, but an assignment was an assignment: "It seemed much kinder, really, to take no notice of him, to adopt with him that same fiercely casual, friendly air, assumed, let us say, when visiting two otherwise harmless people who are, however, shamefully addicted to early-morning drunkenness."[7]

Perhaps a lesser annoyance than middlebrow mawkishness was the great postwar danger of literary writing that scripted human life according to systematic social models and ideologies. In "Maxim Gorki as Artist," his 1947 review in the *Nation* of Gorky's *Best Short Stories*, Baldwin admitted his sympathy with Gorky's care for human misery and the oppressive political and economic power that caused it. However, art, he thought, lived elsewhere. Due to the weight of progressive social duty, the book of stories amounted to "a disquieting and honest report. Its only limitation, and it is a profound one, is that it remains a report. Gorky does not seem capable of the definitive insight, the shock of identification ... his people inspire pity and sometimes rage but never love or terror. Finally we are divorced from them; we see them in relation to oppression but not in relation to ourselves."[8] Baldwin links the failure to get beyond or beneath the level of social report to Gorky's point of view. In a moment that precisely anticipates Baldwin's more famous, 1959 critique of Langston Hughes's *Selected Poems*, he argued that even Gorky's "rare sympathy for people ... did not lead him to that peculiar position of being at once identified with and detached from the humans that he studied. He is never criminal, judge, and hangman simultaneously" (*Cross*, 240). Concluding his review in ways that he would echo in "Everybody's Protest Novel" (1949), his critique of Richard Wright's *Native Son*, he wrote: "[In] Gorky's failure can be found the key to the even more dismal failure of the present-day realistic novelists.... If literature is not to drop completely to the intellectual and moral level of the daily papers, we must recognize the need for further and honest exploration of those provinces, the human heart and mind, which have operated, historically and now, as the no-man's land between us and our salvation" (241).

When it came to the invisible interior provinces of the human heart and mind, as well as to the macro-historical narratives, Baldwin was likewise suspicious of psychological schema and scientific fact. In "Without Grisly Gaiety"—his 1947 review in the *New Leader* of Stuart Engstrand's *The Sling and the Arrow*, a novel involving a host of Freudian-inspired neuroses and a portrait of schizophrenia—Baldwin observed that the novel failed by asking readers to consider "an abnormal psychology" instead of a "personality," "not a study of human helplessness but a carefully embroidered case history" (*Cross*, 252). Without the inside/outside "shock of identification," Baldwin found "no illumination, no pity, no terror," a reader closes the novel "knowing that this happens seldom and can never happen to us." At the close of "Too Late, Too Late," his review of seven volumes of sociology and history for *Commentary* magazine in 1949, Baldwin paused upon Gunnar Myrdal's historic study, *An American Dilemma*. As a symptom of how social duty masks real human encounters in readers as well as writers, in the world as well as in books, Baldwin admits that Myrdal's book was "impressed most forcibly on my mind long before I read it by a landlord, who, having refused to rent me an apartment, but wishing to assure me of his good intentions, told me he was reading it" (272). Taking the books as a whole, he concluded that "they record the facts, but they cannot probe the immense, ambiguous, uncontrollable effect."

With an ax to grind that becomes visible in angular flashes, Baldwin's early reviews frame his early artistic intentions and needs quite precisely. All in all, the reviews are more illuminating and surprising than were their subjects. He saves one counterintuitive surprise, ca. 1949, for the close of his review in *Commentary*: "What is happening to Negroes in this country has been happening for a long time, and it is something quite logical, inevitable, and deadly: they are becoming more American every day" (*Cross*, 272). This point of view would twist along the contradictory path of Baldwin's career as a writer, the first stage of which would depend upon energies largely unrecognized in historical and psychological charts of the reigning intellectual world. When it did happen, recognition often amounted to racist caricature or report terminology that avoided the "shock of identification." For Baldwin, those living, saving energies resided in Harlem and operated deep in the human interiors of his characters.

## "Where only the truth can live": The Poetics of the Heart (1951–1955)

Amid the poverty and suffering, Baldwin sensed he'd grown up amidst the performance rhythms in a cultural tradition that kept people from becoming dominated by their circumstances by enabling a nuanced and vital traffic between interior and social worlds. That tradition enacted a level of experience at the border of the secret and the unconscious. For him, it took its most profound and complex form in black music. In his essay "Many Thousands Gone" (written in 1951 for *Partisan Review* and collected in *Notes of a Native Son* [1955]), Baldwin wrote: "It is only in music, which Americans are able to admire because a protective sentimentality limits their understanding of it, that the Negro in America has been able to tell his story" (*CE,* 19). An organizing drive of Baldwin's career as a writer was to translate the story unheard in the music into what he called "the disastrously explicit medium of [printed] language" (8). He mobilized its malleable message into a series of confrontations with what he called the American "state of mind." In a 1953 interview for the *New York Herald Tribune*, Baldwin, riffing on himself, admitted that he had "always wondered why there has never, or almost never, appeared in American fiction any of the joy of Louis Armstrong or the really bottomless, ironic and mocking sadness of Billie Holiday."[9]

In each era, Baldwin's musical mission would coexist with an irresolvable, dynamic structure at the core of his approach. In Chapter 2, I examined the constant/change paradigm ca. 1963. In fact, it was the descendant of a previous structure. The most resonant instance of the first dynamic paradigm in his early career appears at the close of his essay "Me and My House" (1955), published in *Harper's* and reprinted as the title essay in *Notes of a Native Son* that same year. Abstracting his notion of amputation and gangrene discussed in Chapter 1, he wrote:

> It began to seem that one would have to hold in the mind forever two ideas which seemed to be in opposition. The first idea was acceptance, the acceptance of life as it is, and men as they are: in light of this idea, it goes without saying that injustice is commonplace. But this did not mean that one could be complacent, for the second idea was of equal power: that one must never, in one's own life, accept these injustices as commonplace but must fight them with all one's strength.[10]

The problem, here, was that common American ideas of "life as it is, and men as they are" were drenched in layers of naturalized injustice. Over decades, Baldwin searched for the basic facts of life to accept and then focused on the next layer of injustice to "fight with all one's strength." In 1955, he wasn't buying any available version of what, exactly, must be accepted and by whom. Instead, he sought useful extremities (geographic, social, psychological) from which he could gain critical vantage and begin to figure out what to accept and what to struggle against first. The first extremity was a faculty of discernment, what he came to call "pride," located deep within the person.[11]

In *Go Tell It on the Mountain* (1953), Baldwin's first novel, Elizabeth, who had borne a son without being married, struggled to defend her sense of self against a world which considered her a fallen woman, her son a bastard, her life a scandal. Resisting the false names offered by history and culture and refusing to repent, she thought about the father of her child: "Not even tonight, in the heart's nearly impenetrable secret place, where the truth is hidden and where only the truth can live, could she wish that she had not known him ... that, being forced to choose between Richard and God, she could only, even with weeping, have turned away from God" (*ENS*, 152). In contrast to the existence of her feelings—and the life of her "illegitimate" son—in the world as it was and what it all meant in the eyes of *men* as they were, she felt what was in "the heart's nearly impenetrable secret place, where only the truth could live" (152). While subtle, a lot depends upon Baldwin's use, here, of the indefinite article, *the*, instead of the personal pronoun, *her*. In "Me and My House," he recurred to that resource as the starting place for questioning the relationship between injustice and the world as it was: "This fight begins, however, in the heart, and now it had been laid to my charge to keep my own heart free of hatred and despair."[12] The narrative of the eldest son taking charge upon the death of the father was itself an insidious part of the injustice of the world because of "life as it is" (and has been) as well as "men as they are" (and have been). Baldwin's first resource in his development related directly to a woman's (Elizabeth Grimes and, by extension, his own mother's) weapon in this reckoning. His note to the readers of *Harper's* about keeping his heart "free of hatred and despair" was one, rather comforting, way to put it. But Baldwin was also keeping track of his pride's fierce quest to disturb the world as it was en route to changing things he'd been told—often without being told directly—to accept. He could feel a conflict on the way in which much of the world as it was would be overthrown.

Meditating on her journey and the suicide of John's biological father, Richard, Elizabeth imagines the inescapable trials her son will face. The saints in the church sing "*Somebody needs you, Lord / Come by here*" (*ENS*, 168), but the page seems to sing—possibly with Mahalia Jackson—"My soul looks back and wonders, how I made it over." Elizabeth finds that even the secret reaches of the heart float in another, wider and deeper substance with impersonal capabilities and capacities far beyond those of the subject. Under the pressure of history, the song of the surviving self must find access to both dimensions of being, the "nearly impenetrable" reaches of the heart and the, finally, unfathomable depths of the soul. The music is the best, at times seemingly the only, guide:

> Men spoke of how the heart broke up, but never spoke of how the soul hung speechless in the pause, the void, the terror between the living and the dead; how, all garments rent and cast aside, the naked soul passed over the very mouth of Hell. Once there, there was no turning back; once there, the soul remembered, though the heart sometimes forgot. For the world called to the heart, which stammered to reply; life, and love, and revelry, and, most falsely, hope, called the forgetful, the human heart. Only the soul, obsessed with the journey it had made, and had still to make, pursued its

mysterious and dreadful end; and carried, heavy with weeping and bitterness, the heart along. (169)

Baldwin thought that a deeply subversive force accrued to those who could connect to the "nearly impenetrable, secret" poetics of the heart riding inside the mysterious totality of the soul. In the closing scene of the novel, on the dusty floor at the feet of the enraptured saints of his church, John found: "Of tears there was, yes, a very fountain—springing from a depth never sounded before, from depths John had not known were in him" (*ENS,* 198). It was a revelation of a private—but no ways neatly individual—resource, a source of potential, but as yet inarticulate, power: "The night had given him no language, no second sight, no power to see into the heart of any other" (200). He knew, however, where it came from: "He knew only—and now looking at his mother . . . that the heart was a fearful place" (200). John encountered a distant, unfocused, and personal resource of his mother's in him. And it was frightening. But, he sensed that it was also the root of an insightful and disruptive—possibly subversive—force. He'd felt its power—if he didn't yet understand the profound costs—as his mother and his aunt Florence stood between him and his father's judgment. As he emerged from the church back into the street, his vision now connected to the point of view where only the truth could live, John carried the fearful power to loose the world as it was from its illusions of stability: "That heart, that breath, without which *was not anything made which was made.*" He then saw the world from the nearly impenetrable point of view: "Tears came to his eyes again, making the avenue shiver, causing the houses to shake" (211). John's creator had promised the readers of *Harper's* that he would keep his "heart free of hatred and despair."[13] He meant it. But, he also knew that he carried in his heart the spark, and in his mind a radical, lyrical capacity, determined to cast visions capable of destabilizing the world as it said it was and disturbing men as they thought they were. In order to live, even as yet with "no language, no second sight, no power," he sensed this is what he would have to do.

Baldwin's sense of this tradition of engaged pride lodged deep in the heart linked him directly with his family, especially his mother, and with a tradition of double-edged articulation in black music. He wrote perceptively if often obliquely about Billie Holiday many times in novels, in essays such as "On Catfish Row" (1959) and "The Uses of the Blues" (1964) as well as in *The Devil Finds Work* (1976). In one of her best self-authored songs, "Billie's Blues," most of all in the version she recorded at

Carnegie Hall in January 1944, Holiday sang: "I ain't good looking and my hair ain't curled." After drummer Sid Catlett audibly disagreed and Holiday repeated the line, she concluded the verse, "But, my Mama she give me something that'll carry me through this world." As did Catlett on stage in 1944, agreeing with the latter statement, saying, "it's true, it's true," Baldwin, as well as his mirror-image protagonist in *Go Tell It on the Mountain*, John Grimes, would have had to nod their heads.

In *Go Tell It on the Mountain*, Baldwin only hinted at the way such prideful subjects, in the very shadow of their vaunted autonomy, *needed* each other nonetheless. When Elizabeth sought out Florence, the scene figured what "she then so incoherently felt: how much she needed another human being, somewhere, who knew the truth about her" (*ENS*, 172). Baldwin's earliest work betrays that need as well. Pride needed to be heard, and could only be heard if it avoided its own tendencies toward vanity, toward disguise. No one did that alone. Autonomy could not, Baldwin knew, exist in isolation. A privacy that stayed private, or secret, was doomed to romance.

## Of and Beyond the Heart: Toward an Embodied, Politically Engaged Poetics (1956–1958)

During the fall of 1956 and the spring of 1957, Baldwin was living in Paris, then in Corsica, and enduring a key transitional year of crises that led directly to his first experiences in the American South. During this period, he began to develop terms that linked the poetics of the heart directly to the emerging liberation movements in the United States and elsewhere. The tumult registered in his work, often in his inability to do it. In 1963, remembering that time immediately after finishing *Giovanni's Room*, Baldwin told *Time* magazine correspondent Roger Stone: "'Another Country' didn't work at all . . . because I'd been away from home too much . . . there was something in my background I was trying to avoid."[14] Work on *Another Country* wouldn't budge and, despite news of *Giovanni's Room*'s rapid sales, Baldwin felt gripped in a mounting creative and personal impasse. Once more, the new manuscript seemed perfectly aware of the problem even if its author wasn't. In part one, Cass listens to Vivaldo's description of where he came from while the description echoed Baldwin's own struggles precisely. Watching her friend avoid "change in the depths" (*CE*, 339), she thinks: "he was going back over it, looking at it, trying to put it all together, to understand it, to express it. But he had not expressed it. He had left something of himself back there on the streets of Brooklyn which he was afraid to look at again. . . . Vivaldo's recollections in no sense freed him from the things recalled . . . he regarded it with a fascinated, even romantic horror, and he was looking for a way to deny it" (*ENS*, 464–465).

In Baldwin's case, it was the nameless political texture of his own interior he'd been avoiding. In order to engage those depths, he would find, he would need to *return* to a place he had never been before. Paraphrasing Baldwin's description of this period, Stone wrote: "In European exile, despairing of his own country, James Baldwin ran through a sharp crisis in his life at the age of thirty-two. . . . He was frightened of coming back to America but knew that there was really no place for him anywhere else. . . . In 1957, he left Corsica for Paris, then—flat broke—moved straight to the U.S. and, that summer, straight to the South, (his first time there)."[15] The impossible necessity to return to a place he'd never been isn't romance. The dilemma captures a tension between overlapping interior and social lives as they were scripted by the times. *Who* Baldwin was had never been to the South. True. But, *what* he was came from there and was involved in whoever he'd become. This was a dynamic he would work at intensely during the 1960s, but it dawned on (really in and around) him in the mid-1950s.

Baldwin's first artistic successes proved to him that personal and professional recognition wouldn't deliver him from his condition nor, for that matter, would success in and of itself aid him in the discharge of his artistic talent. As personal success pulled him out of the poverty and minute-by-minute cooperation with friends he'd known during his early years in Paris, he experienced his first taste of where that story led: a world where one's personal world offered the possibility of a privacy ostensibly separate from one's social and public experience. In a letter to his mother from that period, he told her that his first successes had led to the possibility of a private life and conventional happiness; yet, in fact, he'd been more unhappy in those circumstances than ever. Famous for its account of his rivalry with Norman Mailer, "The Black Boy Looks at the White Boy" (originally published in *Esquire*, May 1961) is actually more interesting for its description of Baldwin's desperate struggles with, and wild efforts to avoid facing, what this realization implied. Painting Norman Mailer as a conventional, safe, and married man, he wrote:

When, late in the evening or early in the morning, Norman and Adele returned to their hotel on the Quai Voltaire, I wandered through Paris, the underside of Paris, drinking, screwing, fighting—it's a wonder I wasn't killed. And then it was morning, I would somehow be home—usually, anyway—and the typewriter would be there, staring at me; and the manuscript of the new novel, which it seemed I would never be able to achieve, and from which clearly I was never going to be released, was scattered all over the floor. (*CE,* 274)

The impasse boiled up out of his work and into his life. The structure of his potential, focused and distorted by his initial period of success, proved difficult to bear and impossible to deny. Terms to describe the political dimensions of his heart, so to speak, weren't available; his struggles, he mistakenly felt, were strictly a matter of his personal life. In the introduction to *Nobody Knows My Name* (1961), he exposed the invisible short in the circuit of the times: "It turned out that the question of who I was was not solved because I had removed myself from the social forces which menaced me—anyway, these forces had become interior, and I had dragged them across the ocean with me. The question of who I was had at last become a personal question, and the answer was to be found in me" (*CE,* 135). Here we find Baldwin missing the key in his own observation. He missed it because what he was describing was an oxymoron for the times, a *political interior.* In the 1960s, he would confirm that the connection between who (private) and what (public) one was was inextricable. At the time, the connection was still invisible. As his "poetics of the heart" matured beyond John's adolescence, Baldwin sensed it, now, in his body. In *Another Country*, the transition appears in Eric's account: "One lies about the body but the body does not lie about itself; it cannot lie about the force which drives it" (*ENS,* 555).

In *Giovanni's Room*, Jacques warned David about the costs of not engaging one's experience with every dimension of one's self and vice versa: "'You play it safe long enough,' he said, in a different tone, 'and you'll end up trapped in your own dirty body'" (*ENS,* 267). Despite perilous personal and sexual escapades in Paris, somewhere he sensed he was still playing it safe. In 1961, recalling his position and stymied by this vision of himself, Baldwin wrote:

[I] might really become a great writer. But in order to do this I would have to sit down at the typewriter again, alone—I would have to accept my despair: and I could not do it. It really does not help to be a strong-willed person or, anyway, I think it is a great error to misunderstand the nature of the will. In the most important areas of anybody's life, the will usually operates as a traitor. My own will was busily pointing out to me the most fantastically unreal alternatives to my pain, all of which I tried, all of which—luckily—failed. (*CE*, 274)

Rather than liberate him, success reinforced his sense of self-enclosure in a way that echoed David's predicament in *Giovanni's Room* directly. Baldwin couldn't find a way beyond it: "*How*, indeed, would I be able to keep on working if I could never be released from the prison of my egocentricity? By what act could I escape this horror? For horror it was, let us make no mistake about that" (273). In Baldwin's case, the key missing dimensions weren't narrowly sexual, or even really personal, they were political and they had begun to appear in the news from the United States, from the South. Maddeningly, Baldwin found that social and political "forces which menaced" him "had become interior," indeed, but they had also somehow remained political. In the summer of 1957, seeking a way out of what he called his "egocentricity," he would find himself dragging the tangled, who/what questions back across the ocean, and then *back* to the South where what he was had come from, where who he was had never been before.

Baldwin's foreboding sense of fame's costs and the emptiness of individual success on its own terms predated the dawn of his extra-literary celebrity and the political notoriety—and danger—that came with the use to which he would put the historical spotlight in the coming years. At the time, although he felt it more than he *knew* it, he was gripped by the need to join the artistic and personal parts of his life to a political dimension, a connection that mirrored an interior political terrain the language for which didn't exist at the time. In *Giovanni's Room*, David and Hella's idea of how to escape their sense of self-enclosure links them to the heterosexual, bourgeois vision of starting a family, but it maps directly onto Baldwin's emerging identification with political action. Of her own amorphous desires, Hella tells David: "Oh. Of course I liked Spain, why not? It's very beautiful. I just didn't know what I was doing there. And I'm beginning to be tired of being in places for no particular reason" (*ENS*, 320). In "Princes and Powers" (first published in *Encounter*, January 1957, and reprinted in *Nobody Knows My Name*), Baldwin's experiences at the First International Congress of Black Writers and Artists brought a cloud of political issues to the surface but nothing into focus; he would clarify key moments of the conference for himself in the structures of "Sonny's Blues" (1957) and "Letter from a Region in My Mind" (1962) which would become *The Fire Next Time* (1963).[16] Recalling the transition in his thinking at the time (1956–1957) in *No Name in the Street* (1972), he would write: "I could, simply, no longer sit around in Paris discussing the Algerian and the black American problem. Everybody else was paying their dues, and it was time I went home and paid mine. . . . It was only [in the United States], after all, that I would be able to find out what my journey had meant to me, or what it had made of me" (*CE*, 383).

Baldwin's first trip to the South in the fall of 1957 faced him with profound connections and conundrums that he would revisit many times during his life. From the first reports, he began naming unnamed entities that corresponded to what he was finding in his own politicized interior. In "Nobody Knows My Name: A Letter from the South," published in *Partisan Review* in 1959, he wrote: "What this evasion of the Negro's humanity has done to the nation is not so well known. The really striking thing, for me, in the South was this dreadful paradox, that the black men were stronger than the white. I do not know how they did it, but it certainly has something to do with that as yet unwritten history of the Negro woman" (*CE*, 208). Linking this invisible, paradoxical strength to the earliest dimensions of his own point of view in *Go Tell It on the Mountain*, the energy deep in a black woman's heart, he casts his unseen version of freedom: "Human freedom is a complex, difficult—and private—thing. If we can liken life, for a moment, to a furnace, then freedom is the fire which burns away illusion" (208).

Published in the summer of 1957 in *Partisan Review*, "Sonny's Blues" depicts Baldwin's first successes at imagining a lyrical expression that traverses the threshold between the personal and the political. It was an explicitly musical, lyrical mode that wrung what Baldwin would call "change in the depths" from the constant/change paradigm (*CE*, 339). In the eyes and ears of his brother,

> [Sonny and his band] began to tell us what the blues were all about. They were not about anything very new. He and his boys up there were keeping it new, at the risk of ruin, destruction, madness, and death, in order to find new ways to make us listen. For, while the tale of how we suffer, and how we are delighted, and how we may triumph is never new, it always must be heard. (*ENS*, 862)

And, as if anticipating the reciprocal substance of freedom—"the fire which burns away illusion"—Baldwin would find in his first visit to the South, it was a lyric that exposed a privacy that meant *particular* more than it meant *secret*, even less was it isolated.

It was a lyrical notion of the private and personal, and a release from the prison of the egocentric *individual*. The release required action in at least two connected dimensions: (1) the song builds upon itself in lyrical repetitions and variations; (2) the performance encodes the dynamic, interdependence of personal and collective awareness and freedom. Beginning his piano solo,

> Sonny's fingers filled the air with life, his life. But that life contained so many others. And Sonny went all the way back, he really began with the spare, flat statement of the opening phrase of the song. Then he began to make it his. . . . I seemed to hear with what burning he had made it his, with what burning we had yet to make it ours. . . . Freedom lurked around us and I understood, at last, that he could help us to be free if we would listen, that he would never be free until we did. (*ENS*, 863)

And, finally, a few months before Baldwin went South for the first time, Sonny's private lyric, in naming a space that didn't quite exist yet, or maybe in spacing a thing that as yet had no name, *returns* to a place he'd never been: "He had made it his: that long line, of which we knew only Mama and Daddy. . . . I saw my mother's face again, and felt, for the first time, how the stones of the road she had walked on must have bruised her feet. I saw the moonlit road where my father's brother died" (863). In ways that echo John Grimes emerging into the Harlem street, Sonny's brother's tears testify to disruptions to come: "I felt my own tears begin to rise. And I was yet aware that this was only a moment, that the world waited outside, as hungry as a tiger, and that trouble stretched above us, longer than the sky" (863).

## Toward a Political Interior and a Privacy Beyond Secrets (1959–1963)

Baldwin's politicized interior and the intense, intuitive urge to reach beyond himself didn't mean he'd rejected his former insistence on the power of private energies. He was looking for a way to connect energies in disjointed realms of experience, for ways to use disparate resources of being. In ways before he was fully conscious of the effect, he was resisting discourses that held these realms and resources separate from each other. In his essay "The Northern Protestant" (1959), he'd termed such connective gestures and utterances, especially those that spanned fissures in psychic and social structures, *confessions*. Following the lead of the musicians much more clearly and with deeper vigor than his literary contemporaries and accenting the literary importance of intimate experience, Baldwin wrote:

> Finally for me the difficulty is to remain in touch with the private life. The private life, his own and that of others, is the writer's subject. . . . What the times demand, and in an unprecedented fashion, is that one be—not seem—outrageous, independent, anarchical. That one be thoroughly disciplined—as a means of being spontaneous. That one resist at whatever cost the fearful pressures placed on one to lie about one's own experience.[17]

As mentioned earlier in the introduction,[18] Baldwin's sense of privacy, however, often led *toward* not away from other people. Thinking toward this connection in his 1961 interview with Studs Terkel, Baldwin said:

> I really think, seriously, there's a division of labor in the world and some people are here, to, um . . . well, let me put it this way. There are so many things I'm not good at. I can't drive a truck. I couldn't run a bank. Well alright, so that's you know, other people will have to do that. In a way they're responsible to me and I'm responsible to them. And my responsibility to them is to try to tell the truth as I see it, not so much about my private life as about their private lives. So there's a standard for all of us, you know, that'll get you through your trouble. Because your trouble's always coming, and Cadillacs don't get you through it.[19]

He explored the shared, political importance and implications of privacy. Baldwin thought that reaching past the ideologies and engaging immediate textures and private truths was key to a personal life worth living, a politics worth promoting, and crucial to any viable social world. By the time he'd finished his third novel, *Another Country* (1962), he'd reached back to the "nearly impenetrable secret place" of Elizabeth's pride in *Go Tell It on the Mountain* and upped the ante. In a reprise of Sonny's solo, Baldwin wrote: "The secrets of everyone, were only expressed when the person laboriously dragged them into the light of the world, imposed them on the world, and made them part of the world's experience. Without this effort, the secret place was a dungeon in which the person perished; without this effort, indeed, the entire world would be an uninhabitable darkness" (*ENS*, 465). If the secrets stayed secret, they would become a prison and the social world, absent those energies, a wasteland, and a show window for vanities. In Baldwin's thought, there were no viable public, social or private spaces in the absence of real distinctions *and* fluent connections between them. This dynamic was necessary, irresolvable, and irreducible. The connections were awkward, disruptive, and even dangerous; but the alternative was bankruptcy.

There's much explicit political power in Baldwin's private-public formulations of the writer's tasks during these years, but it's still latent. Liberal readers of, say, *Harper's* in 1960 would be free to misread statements by Baldwin about the private life in accord with the widely held new critical dogma that politics, social realities, and inequities had nothing directly to do with true literature or, more importantly, with *their* own private lives. The editors of the November 1955 issue of *Harper's* where "Notes of a Native Son" was first published (under the title: "Me and My House") provided the following gloss: "In this searching portrait of his father and himself—the author of *Go Tell It on the Mountain* and of the forthcoming *Notes of a Native Son*, explores some depths of the human condition."[20] The racial and historical dimensions of Baldwin's work were reduced to a variation on a universal theme requiring no disruptive examination of one's historically situated, socially constituted self. As for its bearing on the private life, near the end of the essay, Baldwin confessed his intensity on the morning of his father's burial, which also happened to be the morning after the 1943 Harlem race riot, like this: "That was his legacy: nothing is ever escaped. That bleakly memorable morning I hated the unbelievable streets and the Negroes and whites who had, equally, made them that way."[21] While pointing in directions that would emerge as the times, Baldwin, and the literary culture changed, the sentence was also perfectly modulated to reassure white liberals that their private lives weren't being invaded, implicated, and blamed. Framed by the gloss of the editors, "Me in My House" painted a picture of a riven and chaotic social world in which all had an equal hand and signaled to "depths of the human condition" to which all had, at least potentially, equal access.

Just don't look too closely. When reviewers, biographers, and critics discuss Baldwin's perfect pitch from this era, they're very often talking about the nearly impossible rhetorical balance which allowed him to at least apparently serve radically different—and very soon to be violently opposing—masters. Sustaining that balance would prove impossible as the interior (cultural, national, and international as well as individual and psychic) power of the black world began to articulate itself to itself and to the world in increasingly direct terms and as the cozy universalisms (such as "depths of the human condition") began to fracture. As his private life had been insisting for years—and as emerging political movements across the decolonizing globe would proclaim—*that* center would not hold.

In order to describe the political dimensions of his crisis, he would need a new point of view. This became clear to him while visiting Elijah Muhammad in Chicago in July 1961. Baldwin's nerves were on edge as he walked into Muhammad's mansion in Hyde Park. He knew he couldn't drink or smoke while inside, but also suspected something about the inadequacies of his point of view in the face of what Muhammad represented to the historical moment. In *The Fire Next Time*, Baldwin wrote:

> I was frightened, because I had, in effect been summoned into a royal presence. I was frightened for another reason, too. I knew the tension in me between love and power, between pain and rage, and the curious, the grinding way I remained extended between those poles—perpetually attempting to choose the better rather than the worse. But this choice was a choice in terms of a personal, a private better (I was, after all, a writer); what was its relevance in terms of a social worse? (*CE,* 321)

The "social worse" didn't refer simply to an Algerian enclave in Paris, nor even Baldwin's familiar Harlem. There were more black people living on the South Side of Chicago than there were in Harlem, Detroit, and Philadelphia combined. Southern and displaced like his parents, they lived in circumstances neither as foreign as Paris nor as familiar as Harlem. And, he'd been to the South twice by then. The South Side was a flat, Midwestern, unbroken social expanse full of black southerners who, for the most part, had grown too angry to survive—to dance that dance, which he'd now witnessed—where they'd been born. He wrote: "Here was the South Side—a million in captivity—stretching as far as the eye could see. And they didn't even read" (*CE,* 321). How, indeed, was his writer's choice of "a personal, a private better" relevant to *that*? How could he become politically relevant and remain a writer? These questions loomed large in Baldwin's mind as he sat at Elijah Muhammad's dining table that evening in July.

Still, Baldwin knew that no social scientist (nor any royal theologian such as Muhammad) was capable of speaking fully to that reality, either. No less than in his reviews from the 1940s, he still believed those social/ scientific idioms could do little more than quarantine and manipulate human reality. In his 1963 speech "The Artist's Struggle for Integrity," he said: "The poets (by which I mean all artists) are finally the only people who know the truth about us. Soldiers don't. Statesmen don't. Priests don't. Union leaders don't. Only poets" (*Cross*, 42). An artist's integrity depended upon how he engaged that truth, a truth, as he'd learned about his *own* interior life, which had its undeniable social and political dimensions. But, how? Describing the conversation, and the vast expanses of things unsaid, at Muhammad's dinner table, he thought it was still really about a kind of privacy. But this privacy wasn't any individual's secret, it was a communal particularity: "For the horrors of the American Negro's life there has been almost no language. The privacy of his experience, which is only beginning to be recognized in language, and which is denied or ignored in official and popular speech—hence the Negro idiom—lends credibility to any system that pretends to clarify it" (*CE*, 326). Baldwin considered this linguistic chameleon-ism, this tactical silence, to be of a different order than the "thoroughly infantile delusion" of mainstream American silences (*Cross*, 8). Neither approach was, finally, adequate to *his* shifting purposes as a writer reorienting his notion of integrity in response to the demands of the radically shifting world.

Seated at Muhammad's dinner table, Baldwin grappled with the importance, the inevitability and the inadequacies, of the Nation of Islam's political theology. The key moment came when Muhammad asked Baldwin where *he* stood? Recognizing the question as a test of his point of view, with his integrity on the table, he responded: "'I left the church twenty years ago and I haven't joined anything since.' It was my way of saying that I did not intend to join their movement, either" (*CE*, 327). Baldwin knew he wasn't off the hook. In 1962, by the time he was actually writing the scene for what would become *The Fire Next Time*, he was in effect asking *himself* the questions. In the essay, Baldwin describes Muhammad smelling blood in the water and moving in: "And what are you now?" Muhammad's question echoes almost too closely one posed by Studs Terkel from his conversation with Baldwin in Chicago during that same July 1961: "James Baldwin: who are you, now?"[22] Baldwin answered Terkel in beautiful, searching tones, that he just had "to play it by ear, and . . . pray for rain." On the surface, it was an approach far better suited to the "wide, tree-shaded boulevards" (*CE*, 383) of Paris than it was relevant to the lives of "a million in captivity" (321) on the South Side of Chicago. By reassigning Terkel's question to Muhammad and foreclosing the literary romance by changing the terms of the question from "who" to "what," Baldwin was putting himself and his literary point of view on the social, political, and racial spot.

With his voice literally failing under the pressure of the social view Muhammad had put upon the private point, Baldwin considered the possible responses. He found he had none: "I was in something of a bind, for I really could not say—could not allow myself to be stampeded into saying—that I was a Christian. 'I? Now? Nothing.' This was not enough. 'I'm a writer. I like doing things alone.' I heard myself saying this. Elijah smiled at me. 'I don't, anyway,' I said, finally, 'think about it a great deal'" (*CE*, 327). Using Elijah Muhammad to checkmate himself, Baldwin wrote: "Elijah said, to his right, 'I think he ought to think about it *all* the deal'" (327). Thus, in the essay, Baldwin's voice had been pushed— by the necessity of its development—to the edge of this chessboard of a conversation. With the heels of his integrity at the precipice of a silence he couldn't abide, he attempted to hold his ground by talking to himself: "(I said to myself, but not to Elijah), 'I love a few people and they love me and some of them are white, and isn't love more important than color?'" (327). Of course, most readers of *Harper's* ca. 1955 or *The New Yorker* ca. 1962, where the essay made its widely celebrated first appearance, would have said: *yes, of course, love is more important than color. And, isn't the world just a sad and beautiful place?*

But, Baldwin knew better than to make *that* appeal, out loud, on the South Side, in the face of "a million in captivity." And, even more, as Baldwin would find out, what those liberal readers meant—and they didn't know it, but they would find out too, and he would help—was that for them, somehow, love was more important than *their* color, but not more important than *his*. Love was certainly more important on the pages of a magazine; in life, however, and in ways people deny even today, color dominated choices people made about where and how to live their lives, especially their so-called private lives. Insofar as they remained corralled by the power of color as a "social," as opposed to "a private, a personal," force, Baldwin would soon argue, people would remain exiles from themselves in social and political terms. In such social exile, and in the bunkered attempt at privacy it mandated, he would write, they would be incapable of living actual American lives. Those people would eventually fall into some version of Jacques's trap in *Giovanni's Room*. One couldn't "play it safe" (*ENS*, 267) and "play it by ear"[23] at the same time. To avoid the American trap, love had to be more important than color in public as well as private; it had to involve *what* other people saw in public as well as *who* appeared when one looked in the private mirror. The literary language (let alone the social will and courage) for that hardly existed at the time. So such confessions were rare. As a consequence, in *No Name in the Street* (1972), he would write, "i.e., there *are* no American people yet" (*CE*, 358). But, I'm getting ahead of myself.

In *The Fire Next Time*, Baldwin handed the victory to Elijah Muhammad, a victory he would attempt to steal back—in the name of a liberal coalition he knew didn't really exist—in the concluding section of the book. In an aria of high eloquence that made him a literary star, Baldwin *did* steal back the victory on the page. In theory, Americans were capable of risking lives that spanned fissures confining them in pods—whether bodies, apartments, or neighborhoods—situated within existing hierarchies. Concluding the book with maybe his most quoted passage, Baldwin demanded the impossible, noting that it "was the least that one can demand": "If we—and now I mean the relatively conscious whites and the relatively conscious blacks, who must, like lovers, insist on, or create, the consciousness of the others—do not falter in our duty now, we may be able, handful that we are, to end the racial nightmare, and achieve our country, and change the history of the world. If we do not now dare everything, the fulfillment of that prophecy, recreated from the Bible in song by a slave, is upon us: *God gave Noah the rainbow sign, No more water, the fire next time!*" (*CE,* 346–347). According to the terms of American success, a success that he wanted very very badly, the victory was certainly *his.* He got paid. Writing me from Portugal in 2013, Baldwin's longtime friend, jazz pianist, and composer Alonzo Levister, remembered: "when *FIRE* came out in *The New Yorker* I was at Horatio St. He was an overnight star and I took him to an upscale store, British America House, for him to buy what I think were the first nice clothes he ever had 'til that time. That's how I remember it."[24] But, left where it was, success at that level would reinforce with a vengeance the "prison of my egocentricity" dilemma he'd barely survived in the mid-1950s. If he was to avoid changing and to continue developing, matters couldn't stay where they were. In fact, matters were already elsewhere and, by the early 1960s, he knew it.

If he didn't fully believe it himself—the violent complexities between the relatively sophisticated New Yorkers in *Another Country* show plainly enough he had good reason to doubt—Baldwin lived with the mistaken scorecard during most of 1963 as he was giving speeches such as "The Artist's Search for Integrity" and "We Can Change This Country." Call it a truce. Or success. For the eight months between the publication of *The Fire Next Time* (January 1963) and the March on Washington (August 1963), one might even have called it hope. The bomb that killed the girls in the Sunday school of the 16th Street Baptist Church, and the accompanying violence that killed two young black men, in Birmingham on September 15, 1963, ended the truce and accelerated developments in point of view that Baldwin's debate with Elijah Muhammad, as reported in *The Fire Next Time*, already required. Maybe, with morning coffee and a stroll in Central Park, his liberal readers could swallow his strange truce with Elijah Muhammad in the face of "a million in captivity." But, Baldwin couldn't; his sense of integrity demanded more. His craft as a writer already inflicted upon him an impersonal trajectory of development aligned with rapidly accelerating shifts in the cultural and political worlds. Make no mistake; Baldwin's complex reckoning with the political subtleties of personal presence at Elijah Muhammad's dining table most certainly didn't (as some thought it might) signal a tolerance for the Nation of Islam's racial theology. He made that clear enough in *Life* magazine in May 1963: "The Black Muslims serve one extremely useful function: they scare white people. Otherwise they are just another racist organization and the only place they can go is to disaster."[25]

If the personal was undeniably political, Baldwin had long known that the personal was also impersonal. His 1947 critique of Gorky's "social reports" turned upon exactly this realization. In *Go Tell It on the Mountain*, John Grimes's inheritance from his mother worked that way, as did Giovanni's challenge to David's life in *Giovanni's Room*. In "Sonny's Blues," the brothers work from opposing directions to arrive at the place where each is at once inside and outside his personal point of view. In his review of Langston Hughes's *Selected Poems* from 1959, Baldwin wrote, "the poetic trick, so to speak, is to be within the experience and outside it at the same time" (*CE*, 614). He knew that arriving at the *human reality* of the personal required impersonal routes; one's personal identity not only depended upon *who* one saw in the mirror but also *what* the world saw. The conversation with Elijah Muhammad forced Baldwin to realize that the private (who) and political (what) must wash together in such a way that they couldn't be separated, not even when examined in someone else's terms on someone else's turf. From *that* realization, as the world seemed to veer toward revolution, Baldwin reshaped his life, from 1964 to 1969, as part of a quest for *that* point of view and for an experience that could vouch for it.

Already leaning this way, Baldwin addressed the interdependence of private and social dynamics in "The Artist's Struggle for Integrity." The "crime of which you discover slowly you are guilty," he wrote, "is not so much that you are aware, which is bad enough, but that other people see that you are and cannot bear to watch it, because it testifies to the fact that they are not."[26] In his turn away from political equivocations, phrasings that left room for literary romance and visions of personal transcendence, he knew his lyrical flashlight into the political dimensions of the human interior wouldn't make the mainstream critics nor his liberal readership happy. He would be very right about that. He also knew that there were other audiences out there to be addressed; audiences, he suspected, positioned to react to his call in more dynamic ways because, he thought, the structure of their lives didn't compel an immobilizing worship of the mainstream American chimeras. There were people out there already "playing it by ear," mostly because they didn't have (the illusion of) the option of "playing it safe." Evidence at the time, however, suggested that *that* road would be rough as well.

As background for the cover story about Baldwin in *Time* magazine (May 17, 1963), Washington correspondent Loye Miller reported back to the bureau from Harlem on May 10. He'd been sent to gauge Baldwin's notoriety at home, uptown. Miller's dispatch begins by twisting Baldwin's sense of political anonymity into a gauge of his popularity: "It is as you suspected, in Harlem, Malcolm X is a man of fame, but James Baldwin was right when he wrote that nobody knows his name."[27] Miller interviewed John Burnell, "chief organizer for a prominently-Negro labor union (Hospital Workers Local 144)," Jeff Greenup, a black attorney in Harlem, and Connie C. Stamps, "pastor of the big (2,000 members) Metropolitan Baptist Church on Seventh Avenue and president of the Baptist ministers conference of Greater New York (250 churches with membership totaling conservatively a half million)." Miller reported that Burnell had "never heard of James Baldwin. So far as he knows, few if any of the 14,000 members of his union ever have either." Greenup had heard of him but said, "I really can't talk to you about Baldwin intelligently. . . . I've saved some newspaper clippings about him but I haven't gotten around to reading them." Echoing Baldwin's feeling at Elijah Muhammad's in Chicago—that literary goals and methods ca. 1963 were bound to insignificance in social and political terms, were, in fact, designed to stay out of those arenas—Miller's conclusion was that Baldwin's national literary fame meant little in the eyes of average black people in the United States. In Harlem, people knew him from the neighborhood. Quoting an anonymous person on the street, Miller wrote: "He grew up and went to school just a couple of blocks away over here, and he's writin' books now."[28]

Miller was able to find at least one person in Harlem with a considered opinion of Baldwin and his work in 1963. A prominent lawyer, Gang of Four member, and future Manhattan borough president, his statement warrants quotation in full as a gauge for contending pressures into which Baldwin's career took him. Miller wrote:

Says a top Harlem Negro leader (Percy Sutton, no attribution). "Baldwin is interesting reading, and we quote him when he serves our purposes. But he really has no influence. For one thing, he's difficult reading, so only the Negro intellectual reads Baldwin, and that severely limits his communication. Remember that Negroes are not really influenced by a writer, any writer, because we are not in the main intellectuals. Not enough of us read. The Negroes are influenced by the lecturers, the compelling speakers, the men like Martin Luther King and Malcolm X. And Baldwin can't be effective as a lecturer. When you see him as a lecturer, you see an effeminate, and that ruins him even with those who have read him. He's a faggot, a fairy. And we as Negroes have much greater animosity toward lesbians and homosexuals than does the white man, because this is weakness, and there is already too much weakness among Negroes without that. So Baldwin doesn't impress most Negroes, even among the few that really know about him, and if he doesn't impress, he can't influence."[29]

No matter the cloud of resistances, in the open and behind the scenes, to his developing sense of his work and the world, Baldwin determined to follow the cues (in his heart, body, family, and personal life) he'd learned to read. The private, political poetics, the change in the depths, he would continue to develop for the rest of his career would be the basis for his most socially important—and most intellectually misunderstood—work. Some people, he knew, would respond in the moment, others would come later, and some never would come at all; there it was. In "The Black Boy Looks at the White Boy," measuring his quest against his friend and rival Norman Mailer's bid to be mayor of New York City, and thinking back to where he'd been, he knew he was working across dimensions: "My revenge, I decided very early, would be to achieve a power which outlasts kingdoms" (CE, 279).

## Riffin' on Black Power: The Poetics of Political Confrontation (1964–1971)

Baldwin wrote and performed his most direct and relentlessly political work in the era immediately following his description of the musically inflected change/constant paradigm that could identify American "chimeras" and connect citizens to churnings of renewal within and between them in their lives. The mid-1950s dynamics of acceptance and struggle had morphed into a politically explicit charge to embrace life's constants, set chimeras aside, and engage the nature of change. He did exactly that. On camera and behind the scenes, back stage and in the street, it was the period of his most consistent and direct engagement with the political culture. No small percentage of his time was spent either onstage or in the air en route from one intervention to the next. His essays were short, to the point. Many of them were either interviews or speeches. During its tumultuous run from April through August 1964, his play *Blues for Mister Charlie* pushed Broadway toward direct confrontation with the costs of racial violence in the South and in the heart. He lived for most of 1966 in Istanbul, exhausted and working on his next novel. It was a novel he needed to write to remind himself he was, in fact, a writer, not just an impassioned activist. In July 1966 he wrote to his brother David that if he didn't finish the novel, it would mean he wasn't really a writer and *that* would mean his brother wouldn't have a brother anymore.

Not surprisingly, *Tell Me How Long the Train's Been Gone* (1968) is a novel about the demands of performance, an anguished exploration of Baldwin's many-leveled sense of his own experience as performer on overlapping stages. It begins with his protagonist, Leo Proudhammer, suffering a heart attack while onstage. Where else? Signaling the degree to which performance permeated the period, Baldwin depicts even death (or what a figure thinks is death) as a performative act. The scene sings the passionate detachment in the blues point of view. On his back in the throes of a heart attack, Proudhammer thinks: "*My God, this is no way to play a death scene, the audience would never be able to see me.* Then I decided that it was a death scene being played not onstage but on camera and pretended that the camera was placed in the ceiling, just above my head—a huge, long close-up, with lights, and, eventually, music, to heighten my ineffable, dying speech."[30] Until 1969, as assassinations littered the news with the names of his friends and colleagues in the movement, the bright lights of his ambition and his fame and the very real risks of his political visibility accompanied him even at the typewriter, the place he was least, or most, himself and most, or least, alone. He ended the period of head-on engagement—even though it took over a year to adjust—leaving Hollywood in July 1969 after refusing to translate his version of Alex Haley's *The Autobiography of Malcolm X* into a screenplay Columbia Studios could sell to mainstream American viewers.

"The Uses of the Blues," published in *Playboy* in January 1964, announced the new, more direct point of view loud and very clear. Baldwin traced in black music an unmistakable link between private and political life. He had realized that the connection actively sought between "who" and "what" black people were in the eyes of the nation, but more immediately in the eyes of each other and themselves, enabled a coherence, an authority, that popular American culture lacked:

> Right now you find the most unexpected people building bomb shelters. If we had, as human beings, on a personal and private level, our personal authority, we would know better; but because we are so uncertain of all these things, some of us, apparently, are willing to spend the rest of our lives underground in concrete. . . . People who don't know who they are privately, accept as we have accepted for nearly 15 years, the fantastic disaster which we call American foreign policy, and in the incoherence of the one is an exact reflection of the incoherence of the other.[31]

Like the connected private and public world, Baldwin's work from the period stressed the link between domestic and international realities. In a 1967 letter to *Readers Forum*, he amplified his attempts to connect the dire situation of captives within and so-called enemies of Western nations to the inability of the West to face itself person by person, mirror by mirror:

> The American ideal of freedom and, still more, the way this freedom is imposed, have made America the most terrifying nation in the world. We have inherited Spain's title: the nation with the bloody footprint. . . . The terrible probability is that the Western populations, struggling to hold on to what they have stolen from their captives, and unable to look into their mirror will precipitate a chaos throughout the world . . . for which generations yet unborn will curse our names.[32]

Early in the era, he attempted to intercede in the formation of Black Power as a new American political idiom. In *The Fire Next Time*, three years before the term *Black Power* was coined and entered the mainstream, Baldwin had developed and extended his thought about color's place in the structure of power and power's place in the structure of color:

> This urgency on the part of American Negroes *is not to be forgotten!* As they watch black men elsewhere rise, the promise held out, at last, that they may walk the earth with the authority with which white men walk, protected by the power that white men shall have no longer, is enough, and more than enough, to empty the prisons and pull God down from Heaven. It has happened before, many

times, before color was invented, and the hope of Heaven has always been a metaphor for the achievement of this particular state of grace. The song says, "I know my robe's going to fit me well. I tried it on at the gates of Hell." (*CE*, 331)

On the next page, he abstracted the challenge: "How can one, however, dream of power in any other terms than in the symbols of power?" (*CE*, 332). In the third section of "Down at the Cross" in *The Fire Next Time*, he attempted to dream a kind of power *not* based upon the way color had been mobilized in twentieth-century political dominance. Failure to reimagine the symbols and structure of power would lead, according to Baldwin, to war: "*God gave Noah the rainbow sign. No more water the fire next time!*" (144). Tellingly, whether by accident or not, upon the essay's celebrated first appearance, *The New Yorker* ad department promptly followed Baldwin's visionary warning with a full-page add for Piper Champagne, "*pop goes the Piper . . . no wonder the French don't drink water*" (145).

The page in *The New Yorker* magazine facing the final page of James Baldwin's essay "Letter from a Region in My Mind" (1962).

Consider the collision between Baldwin's soaring aria of cross-racial (im)possibility that culminates in an apocalyptic warning of interracial violence and the party-time advert on the facing page of its initial appearance. Is there a mocking corrigendum (at *least*) implied in the placement of this exclamation? In the peripheral—even subconscious—focus of one's attention, does the jack-in-the-box cork at the center of the ad invoke a street corner, pornographic answer to Baldwin's most visible attempt at transformational, interracially resonant high eloquence? To my knowledge, Baldwin never commented upon the coincidence at the time. But, precise lyrical evidence indicates he remarked the juxtaposition of his most high-profile Jeremiad with the ad for Thanksgiving bubbly the *New Yorker* staff placed on the facing page. The image marked the volatile crosscurrents in his role as a prophetic celebrity. In an instance of lyrical acuity that's likely beyond the capability of conscious intention (a subconscious location that is the real target of advertising in any case), the image of juxtaposition resurfaced almost a decade later in *No Name in the Street* when Baldwin, sensing "a million people staring at us both," enters the apartment of his long-lost friend, Arthur Moore. He wrote, "my life came with me into their small, dark, unspeakably respectable, incredibly hard-won rooms like the roar of champagne and the odor of brimstone" (*CE,* 361).

The intended or unintended (complacent or compulsive) mocking of the mainstream, Baldwin knew, was trivia. Transformative cultural and political dynamics were already in motion. In predicting the flames as well as the coming radicalisms, Baldwin had been viewed as ahead of his time. In the late 1960s, he was often characterized as behind the beat, out of touch. Despite—or because of—his misgivings about the emerging discourse, Baldwin eschewed the media and attempted to address the radical ideologues of Black Power directly throughout the era. For much of 1966, immediately following Stokely Carmichael's emergence as the symbol and spokesperson for the Black Power movement, Baldwin watched from Istanbul. He knew he couldn't trust the press for information about Black Power, the changes in the Student Nonviolent Coordinating Committee (SNCC), and the emergence of the Black Panthers. He'd read enough unbelievable "facts" about himself in the press to know better. At first, for information he could trust, he relied directly on letters from his brother David. His letters back to David during the spring and summer of 1966 trace his position on and critique of the Black Power movement in detail and in ways beyond what he ever publicly declared. He didn't dismiss the political voices in the younger generation. He didn't hide his critique either. He resigned from the *Liberator* magazine editorial board upon becoming aware of anti-Semitism in its pages. He distilled his warning against the kind of self-affirmation that dances in the mirror of existing power. In his 1967 essay, "Anti-Semitism and Black Power," he wrote, "I would rather die than see the black American become as hideously empty as the majority of white men have become" (*Cross*, 204).

In a letter to his brother David he dismissed the racial chauvinism of the black cultural nationalists in favor of concrete acts in pursuit of political and economic goals. Later in "Anti-Semitism and Black Power," almost quoting what he'd written to David, he wrote: "Why, when we should be storming capitols, do they suggest to the people they hope to serve that we take refuge in the most ancient and barbaric of the European myths? Do they want us to become better? Or do they want us, after all, carefully manipulating the color black, merely to become white?" (*Cross*, 205). In a 1968 essay based on his speech to the World Council of Churches in Sweden, "White Racism or World Community," he credited Stokely Carmichael for translating a core Western value into "the black idiom" (*CE,* 752). Baldwin wrote, "black power translated means the self-determination of people. It means that, nothing more and nothing less" (752–753). Baldwin took the "nothing less" part of the equation seriously in a way that confronted the premises of Black Power; he knew black people couldn't be "self-determined" if they (1) modeled their power, their determination, on the myths (inverted) white people had designed to hold the black image captive and (2) if they divorced themselves from the complex reality of the "selves," themselves, that were to be "determined" to whatever extent and in whatever way. Amid whirlwinds of violence and change, he held on to constants. He knew a person couldn't be liberated from "the facts of life" (*Cross*, 57), which one must learn "to trust and to celebrate" (*CE,* 339).

In Baldwin's conception, a more deeply resonant black power must elude the blindnesses, pitfalls, and paucities of white power—principal among them, the concept of color itself—and recreate itself in relation to a different mirror. For him, predictably, a crucial key to reflecting black lay in sound not sight. If heard for what they were almost saying, the voices in the music could liberate the face of black power from its white mask in the mirror:

There is a sense in which it can be said that my black flesh is the flesh that St. Paul wanted to have mortified. There is a sense in which it can be said that very long ago, for a complex of reasons, but among them power, the Christian personality split itself in two, split itself into dark and light, in fact, and it is now bewildered, at war with itself, is literally unable to comprehend the force of such a woman as Mahalia Jackson, who does not sound like anyone in Canterbury Cathedral, unable to accept the depth of sorrow, out of which a Ray Charles comes, unable to get itself in touch with itself, with its selfless totality. (CE, 754)

Based upon a tonal narrative—a kind of code, he heard deeply embedded in the sound, structure, and origins of black music—Baldwin advocated a black power freed from the schisms at the core of the Western myth, immune to the blindness staring back from the bottom of the whiteness of the Western well, and refashioned as the determination of a self back in touch (or black and in touch) "with its selfless totality." In his mind, the models of Western power provided but perilous structures, structures *not* to be emulated, certainly not to be repeated:

From my point of view, it seems to me that the flesh and the spirit are one; it seems to me that when you mortify the one, you have mortified the other. It would seem to me that the morality by which the Christian Church claims to live, I mean the public morality, that morality governing our sexual relations and the structure of the family, is terribly inadequate for what the world, and people in the world, must deal with now. (CE, 754)

He understood it was a long shot; a black power movement premised upon "concrete acts" and refashioned as the determination of a black self in touch "with its selfless totality" was going to be a hard sell. Nonetheless, his work from the era evinces *his* self-determined will to sketch its design as clearly as necessary, often just a little clearer than was possible in the present moment. But, Baldwin knew he was addressing the present as well as the future. In Sedat Pakay's *James Baldwin: From Another Place*, filmed in 1970 just before he left Istanbul to live again in France, Baldwin said:

I think all poets, and I'm a kind of poet, are caught in a situation, which is a kind of pre-revolutionary situation, have a very difficult role to play. Insofar as they're real poets they're committed to the welfare of the people, of all the people. But, they don't always read this welfare as simply as politicians might. My own effort is to try to bear witness to something that will have to be there when the storm is over, to help us get through the next storm. Storms are always coming.

In *Just Above My Head*, he would clarify the stakes in unmistakable terms: "What breaks the heart, though, is that self-interest is indispensible to any human endeavor, is the universal human motor, and is noble or ignoble, depending on one's concept of the self."[33] In the 1970s, Baldwin would attempt to intervene into this concept, the self, as new structures, possibilities, and threats emerged.

Baldwin had spent two decades pursuing the kind of success he had attained by 1963. He'd battled his personal demons and worked through his fears about his family's shame. In *Notes of a Native Son*, *Giovanni's Room*, *Nobody Knows My Name*, *Another Country*, and *The Fire Next Time*, he had confronted the core American private and public chimeras and converted the confrontation into a lyrical prose of a uniquely public and private power. And, he'd done most of it high on the best-seller's list. The terms of his engagement shifted with the politics of the time, usually ahead of the beat, always deeper than the foam at the stormy surface. Medgar Evers and Malcolm X, the kids in Birmingham, and many others were already martyrs. Martin Luther King Jr., Robert Kennedy, and many younger activists would soon follow. He couldn't back away. And, he didn't. He couldn't simply stand his ground, either. The ground itself was shifting. Even time didn't seem to be itself anymore. In *No Name in the Street*, he remembered the vortex-like period:

> In this place, and more particularly, in this time, generations appear to flower, flourish, and wither with the speed of light. I don't think that this is merely the inevitable reflection of middle age: I suspect that there really has been some radical alteration in the structure, the nature, of time. One may say that there are no clear images; everything seems superimposed on, at war with something else. There are no clear vistas: the road that seems to pull one forward into the future is also pulling one backward into the past. I felt, anyway, kaleidoscopic, fragmented, walking through the streets of San Francisco, trying to decipher whatever it was that my own consciousness made of all the elements in which I was entangled, and which were all tangled up in me. (*CE*, 463–464)

In an era in which chimerical change seemed the only constant, and where all articulations of "pride" seemed already partially cloaked and vain, his paradigm from 1963 was twisting out of shape. The times demanded a new approach. Amid the kaleidoscope, he would have to keep his own time, matching the rhythm of the changes to his need to develop.

By the end of the 1960s, Baldwin found himself listening to a younger generation. On various accounts, they didn't see eye to eye. Much like his friend Miles Davis with his second quintet and beyond, Baldwin showed that he could hear and respond to a wide range of perspectives younger than his own. He listened. In 1968, in an open letter published in several newspapers—including the *Manchester Guardian* and the *St. Petersburg Times*—he wrote about the generation of black power:

> Now, I might not always agree with Stokely's views, or the ways in which he expresses them. My agreement or disagreement is absolutely irrelevant. I get his message. Stokely Carmichael, a black man under thirty, is saying to me, a black man over forty, that he will not live the life I've lived, or be corralled into some of the awful choices I have been forced to make. And he is perfectly right. . . . I do care—about Stokely's life, my country's life . . . one hopes, always, that something will happen in the human heart which will change our common history.[34]

In ways compatible with—but not identical to—Martin Luther King's vision, Baldwin could, at least in public, hope harder for the moral education of citizens in the United States than could the younger freedom fighters. But, unlike many who had been committed to the Southern-based freedom struggle, he could also recur to his own biography in the Harlem ghetto—really the ghetto, "the bottom," *of* the Harlem ghetto—as a passage to common ground routed in the basic, increasingly urban, blues of the black diaspora. Baldwin labored on behalf of America's moral health, but he understood his labor in relation to firsthand experience with sabotage by the federal government and widespread, deep, and open—overwhelmingly but not totally white—hostility to the goals of the freedom struggle. He also understood his work and life as part of a long history: "if [the change of heart] doesn't happen . . . we, the blacks . . . are simply forced, with both pride and despair, to remember that we come from a long line of runaway slaves who managed to survive without passports" (*CE,* 116). His insistence upon pride *and* despair sounds an important note in his message to the black power messengers not to simplify the complexity of history into what was, to him, a dangerously American epic of pride slipping by the minute into vanity. Disguise. While revolutionary theorists like Mulana Karenga rejected the blues in favor of a masculine, pseudo-African "heroism," Baldwin offered a blues-tinged dialectics of joy and pain, pride and despair, intensified changes and counterintuitive constants, as an alternate texture of heroic struggle. He knew that when pride becomes a mask, a disguise, the result is a vanity incapable of a coherent authority such as sounded deep in the music or such as he recognized in the texture of black people's everyday lives.

The pride/despair dynamic clearly informed Baldwin's most substantive engagements with the Black Power–era and its major figures. His "Dear Sister" (1970), an open letter to Angela Davis in prison, along with "We Are All Viet-Cong" (1970) and many other pieces from the 1970s testify to Baldwin's interest in, sympathy for, and connection to the next generation of activists. Time has revealed that the "awful choices [Baldwin had] been forced to make," the despair with which he'd been forced to coexist, and the pride of his ever-developing point of view informed an analysis several orders of magnitude beyond the younger generation of activists. Some of them, wearing newly fashioned masks, counseling thoroughly chimerical vanities, openly refused the nature of Baldwin's moral-musical vision. Eldridge Cleaver and Amiri Baraka, to name only two, publicly denounced Baldwin while making private appeals (Cleaver for cash while in exile, Baraka while in jail to speak in support of his Defense Fund) for his support. For his part, in letters to his brother, Baldwin wondered how he could respond honorably to calls that were, at least partially, dishonorable. That itself was damned near the paradigm for the period. Meantime he planned at least one lecture tour the proceeds from which he would secretly donate to the Black Panthers. In the end, saying he would arrange himself "around the necessary," it can be said that he did the best he could, maybe a little better than was actually possible.

In "Dear Sister," Baldwin, with a brilliant tact, tried to bridge the divide between the generations:

> I am something like twenty years older than you, of that generation, therefore, of which George Jackson ventures that "there are no healthy brothers—*none at all.*" I am in no way equipped to dispute this speculation . . . for I know too well what he means. My own state of health is certainly precarious enough. In considering you, and Huey, and George, and (especially) Jonathan Jackson, I began to apprehend what you had in mind . . . a whole new generation of people has assessed and absorbed their history, and, in that tremendous action, have freed themselves of it and will never be victims again.[35]

Listening to what the younger generation said, he tried to imagine what they *meant* to say and attempted to honor that meaning and respond, searching for constants to celebrate, the nature of change to apprehend, and chimeras to identify. In describing his own generation and interrogating the changing same, Baldwin writes to Davis: "I'm trying to suggest that you—for example—do not appear to be your father's daughter in the same way that I am my father's son. At bottom, my father's expectations of his generation and mine were the same. . . . For, in fact, to use the brutal parlance of that hour, the interior language of that despair, he was just a nigger—a nigger laborer preacher and so was I."[36] Attempting to discern and gauge relative assumptions, on one level, Baldwin agreed with George Jackson and the revolutionary diagnoses of the relative health of the generations. Then he added two crucial, missing levels to the calculation of "health": first, a private, silent dimension of life that never exactly obeys the ideological current of the day; second, a private, undefined dimension of his generation's experience. Meditating on the constant, if indirect strength of the (in the eyes of revolutionaries, "unhealthy") generations poisoned by despair, he wrote: "There is always, of course, more to any picture than can speedily be perceived and in all of this—groaning and moaning, watching, calculating, clowning, surviving, and outwitting, some tremendous strength was being forged, which is part of our legacy today. But that particular aspect of our journey now begins to be behind us."[37] He also knew that one's relationship to time, and to history, was neither clear nor linear. In *No Name in the Street*, he wrote:

> Time passes and passes. It passes backward and it passes forward and it carries you along, and no one in the whole wide world knows more about time than this: it is carrying you through an element you do not understand into an element you will not remember. Yet, something remembers—it can even be said that something avenges: the trap of our century, and the subject now before us. (*CE*, 365)

What appeared to many (including Baldwin himself) at the time as an old-fashioned, even poisoned and unhealthy vision of no-win moral choices, appears in hindsight as insight into, as well as a way of being in touch with, unswervable (if tragic) existential stakes. Baldwin saw it then. He observed the black power generation opposing American life with increasing intensity, but also in terms far more American than had previous, reputedly less healthy, generations. He addressed the generation then in charge of "the nature of change" and suggested—even though he doubted it himself—a counterintuitive blues-based constant to, if not celebrate, at least acknowledge as part of the revolutionary design. Baldwin's call to remain in touch with the complex existential texture of "the blues" would be largely cast aside by the revolutionaries in the moment.

Those, such as Amiri Baraka, who survived and others, such as Toni Morrison and Gayl Jones, who were positioned to emerge in the early 1970s, would come around to acknowledge the necessity of those complexities in their own ways. As we saw above, as he'd put it in *James Baldwin from Another Place* (1970), "Storms are always coming." But, according to his conception of time above, storms could arrive (even "avenge") from any direction. That dynamic would shift again when, in July 1969, with the FBI following his every move,[38] Baldwin flew to Istanbul to join his lover Alain and his long-time friend and mentor Beauford Delaney in an attempt to step off the stage of direct political engagement and cultural intervention in the United States. *That* change, he hoped, would allow him to reconnect with his sense of his own private life and allow him to survey where he'd been and figure out what the next phase of his work would entail.

## Of Generalized Disasters, Loose Garments, and Miracles of Recognition: James Baldwin, *Poet* (1972–1979)

In a way as immediate as breath itself, it seems, Baldwin needed a renewed approach to himself, his life, the world, and his work. It was no longer merely a question of acceptance and struggle, nor was it possible to simply retain the constants, apprehend the changes, and identify the chimeras. The kaleidoscopic storm was too complex, the nature of time too multidimensional. There had to be a way to address, even attack, generalities without succumbing to them, to address widespread violence and oppression without losing touch of one's intimate experience. In the shadow of disastrous generalities, at this point more than ever, people needed new ways to recognize each other, address each other, and touch each other. The polarities thwarting confessional gestures—ones that he'd described as "the impossible" at the close of *The Fire Next Time* in 1963—however, had radically intensified by 1970 (*CE,* 346). In short, resonant confessions had become both more impossible and more necessary than ever.

In his first book from the 1970s, which would be his account of the previous era, *No Name in the Street,* he intended "to avoid generalities as far as possible" (*CE,* 355). "What I am now attempting," he wrote, "dictates this avoidance." He began the book describing how his eight brothers and sisters entered his life, each a unique, private particularity, no two babies being remotely alike. Confronted with "this breathing miracle," he continued, "you begin the extraordinary journey of beginning to know and to control this creature" (355). More than anything, he fell back upon the act of listening. And when each baby, "without knowing what a miracle it's accomplishing . . . exercises its lungs," one recognizes an anthology of nuance, an infinity of detail: "You know the sound—the meaning—of one cry from another; without knowing that you know it. You know when it's hungry—that's one sound. You know when it's wet—that's another sound. You know when it's angry. You know when it's bored. . . . You come or you go or you sit still according to the sound the baby makes" (355). In the end, from this undeniableness, this intensity of nuance and the necessity of recognition it entails, he concluded, one had two choices: "you have either grown to love it or you have left home" (356). In his life, he'd done both.

From sifting textures at the borders of his earliest memories, even reaching back to the time when he "thought that an 'idea' was a piece of black velvet," in the early pages of *No Name in the Street*, he came upon a new paradigm, one of recognitions. The basic conflict was between generalities to be resisted and outwitted, and particulars to be recognized; according to the kaleidoscopic times, it was a paradigm of miraculous particularity and disastrous generality. The task was poetic; one must get back to the texture of things as if, indeed, an idea *was* a piece of black velvet. There's more than a glance at the early modernist poetics, no ideas but in things, but socialized to focus on the texture and tone of people. He wrote, "Incontestably, alas, most people are not, in action, worth very much; and yet, every human being is an unprecedented miracle" (*CE,* 357). The acceptance of reality and the struggle against injustice (1955) had changed into the celebration of constants and the apprehension of change (1963). By 1972, Baldwin struggled with the simultaneous necessity to "treat [all people] as the miracles they are, while trying to protect oneself against the disasters they've become" (357).

At the core of this necessity was a faculty of recognition that linked back to "the shock of identification" in the 1940s and the secret place "where only truth can live" in the early 1950s. Survival required the ability to recognize the timbre of sound that carried the nuance of possibility, as in the singular signature of a baby's cry. It was almost a physical sense of touch, a willingness to be touched, to be present. It's at this point that the lyrical, poetic valences in Baldwin's writing became crucial to following *where* he was headed, and *why*. And, one had to hone that faculty until it could operate even under the pressures dictated by widespread, often lethal, disasters in the world. Baldwin's sense was that elite—even mainstream—literary audiences, the so-called privileged, hadn't honed those skills in their lives. They didn't think they needed to listen like that. He knew that survival among black families and communities had required exactly that. In October 1975, Baldwin wrote to his brother saying that all life, at that moment, seemed to be "a matter of recognitions." As usual, the key guide was musical.

Baldwin encountered his initial model for his point of view in the 1970s, a few years before he'd had the chance to examine and explore it; before he'd felt his dire need for it. In March 1968, living in Palm Springs, California, in a house paid for by Columbia Studios, Baldwin, running out of cigarettes, sat up late one night working on the screenplay for the Malcolm X film. He was listening to Aretha Franklin's 1967 album, *Aretha Arrives.* In the sound of her voice, he thought, he heard the way he needed to approach Malcolm's story. In a detailed letter to his brother David and sister Paula, then living in London, he explained what he heard. Noting specific lyrics as they appeared in song after song, what he found was that Aretha's voice was capable of doing revolutionary and artistic work at the same time. This meant her songs addressed the people as well as the person. He didn't recognize it in one of her bravura anthems in a soaring, high register. Listening to Aretha's searching and tender ballad, "I Wonder," he heard a sound that could save the world, or maybe it was a sound that could save one person. At bottom, he decided, it amounted to the same thing. It was a matter of recognitions. In Aretha's voice, at once intimate and public, and in which he heard each syllable somehow distill the lyric and epic modes of language, Baldwin found more than just the "shock of identification" in an inward and outward point of view. He recognized a technique that could collapse the private artistic and public revolutionary impulses. It was a mode of confession, a textured, cross-dimensional voice in which he heard what he'd long been after: "a power which outlasts kingdoms" (*CE,* 279). *That,* he thought, was black power. He would soon find that Columbia Studios would not allow him to translate all what he heard in Aretha's "I Wonder" into his portrait of Malcolm X.[39] But, listening to "I Wonder" now, one hears how her sound guides the version of Malcolm that appears in *No Name in the Street*: "the truth about Malcolm: he was one of the gentlest people I have ever met" (*CE,* 410).

The question was how to deal with disastrous generalities without destroying one's sense of particular possibility and, at the same time, how to deal with particulars (not all of which are miraculous) without foreswearing all attention to general phenomena (not all of which indicate disaster)? Believing that artists dealt with the bottomless mysteries of the person in particular and revolutionaries attended the real interests of the people in general, and having heard Aretha pull it off in "I Wonder," Baldwin sought a point of view that fused the two endeavors. In *No Name in the Street*, now, *he* wondered about the "relationship of the odd and disreputable artist to the odd and disreputable revolutionary" (*CE*, 459). Considering the relationship between the public and the private, he suggested that the revolutionary aids the person by focusing on the people and that the artist does the reverse: "But I think that it is just as well to remember that the people are one mystery and that the person is another. Though I know what a very bitter and delicate and dangerous conundrum this is, it yet seems to me that a failure to respect the person so dangerously limits one's perception of the people that one risks betraying them and oneself" (459–460). Baldwin tested his emerging paradigm in his description of Huey Newton. Joining the work of the revolutionary to the personal/impersonal vantage point of the artist, and directly quoting the title of Aretha's song, he wrote: "Watching Huey [while Newton was being held on capital charges], I wondered what force sustained him, and lent him his bright dignity—then I suddenly did not wonder. The very fact that the odds are so great, and the journey, barely begun, so dangerous means that there is no time to waste, and it invests every action with an impersonal urgency" (462).

Prompted by the music, the shifts on the page were more organic than constructed. It wasn't as much a point of view created to explore subject matter as an emerging vantage point on an experience summoned by Baldwin's sense of what the changing times—and, he sensed, the changed nature *of* time—demanded. In a 1972 interview, he described the process: "It doesn't change from the top; it changes from the bottom. If it's not an organic change, it's simply a gimmick."[40] For Baldwin, "organic" referred to "change in the depths" (*CE*, 339), the development, emanating from the way an artist internalized the world in experience and later encountered it via the connection between his craft and his interior life. Inside himself, an artist contained a mirror image of the world; craft was a way of recognizing those images, renewing pride and avoiding vanity, of dealing with the optics of that vision. One looked inward to see out. Or maybe it was a way of looking both ways at once? Means made necessary by the changed demands of a time that "passes backward and it passes forward and it carries you along . . . through an element you do not understand into an element you will not remember" (365). The escape from "the prison of [his] egocentricity" forced him to accept that he wasn't in complete, conscious control (273). It was a matter of being two places at once, of not succumbing "to the apathy of cynical disappointment" nor rising "to the rage of knowing, better than the people do, what the people want" (459–460). He'd given up on prose articulations that explained the world to mainstream—which for Baldwin meant an elite literary culture in—America. In a way, he'd given up on understanding, as such. His new voice would have to be *recognized* from a listener's (or reader's) experience; to be known at all it would have to be incorporated into a compatible, existing rhythm, a *style* connected to change in the depths.

Rather than a matter of understanding, what readers "felt, and, sometimes, discerned" in Baldwin's work from the 1970s depended on the angle, or the style, of their recognitions; their response depended on their point of view almost as much as it depended on his (*CE,* 536). In "In Search of a Basis for Mutual Understanding and Racial Harmony" (1976), he traced the issue to its roots:

> Everyone, for example, is born into a language: a *particular* language, there being no general ones. Languages are—or reveal—various ways of looking at the world. Language is the word made flesh, and reveals the root human necessity of ordering, or making coherent, the chaos of experience; language is a way of controlling the specific reality into which one is born.
>
> Clearly, then, what is east for England cannot be east for China. Columbus, looking for a passage to India, discovered what is now called the West, and sometimes the Far West—or, depending on one's stars, the North. Well, we are certainly west of something; everybody is. We are also south, east, and north of something; everybody is. One is neither inferior nor superior to a language. One learns a language by exposing oneself to the assumptions of this language. These unspoken assumptions contain the key to the people who were born into this language, who live it, who form it every day and who are being formed by it every day; thus one begins to glimpse something of the way in which one is oneself endlessly forming and endlessly being formed.[41]

For his part, Baldwin was mapping a language of flexible intensity capable of joining revolutionary political scope to liberal artistic techniques in ways that connected private, familial, and political levels of experience. Even more than they had been when he was embarking on his career in the New York literary world, as in the case of Aretha above, his most immediate models were musical. His readers, and those who heard him speak, would have to approach the words in a way similar to Sonny's brother coming to hear him play at the end of "Sonny's Blues."

In the 1970s, Baldwin used the novel to explore the musically inflected poetics of his encounters with the world, a disciplined looseness capable of recognizing miracles under the pressure of disaster. Late in *If Beale Street Could Talk* (1974), he described what recognition entailed for Fonny, a young, politically conscious black sculptor, when he learned that his case (a charge for the rape of a Puerto Rican woman) was probably lost. His pregnant fiancée, Tish Rivers, described his reaction to the news: "something quite strange, altogether wonderful, happens in him."[42] Fonny's counterintuitive reaction, at first, seems like the stuff of fantasy, or even madness. In Baldwin's hands, however, the image offers a glimpse at what a poetics of recognition entails. Tish says: "It is not that he gives up hope, but that he ceases clinging to it."[43] By the time he wrote that sentence, Baldwin was nearly fifty. Fonny's embrace of hope mirrors Baldwin's turn to poetic recognitions in place of prose articulations. It's significant that the character's name connects with precisely tactile and musical dimensions of Baldwin's personal world. Fonny is a sculptor, a tactile craft; his legal name is Alonzo Hunt, recalling Baldwin's longtime friend, also a sculptor, named Lorenzo Hail. It's also a musical invocation; the name echoes another decades-long friend, Alonzo Levister, called "Lonnie," an accomplished jazz composer who had worked with the likes of Charles Mingus, Lorraine Hansberry, and Oscar Brown Jr. Baldwin's approach to recognitions invoked a world of fluctuating, overlapping phenomena, it was still a world of disciplined spontaneity, but it wasn't the white-knuckled world of prose articulation. In *The Devil Finds Work* (1976), he discussed the implications: "Identity would seem to be the garment with which one covers the nakedness of the self: in which case it is best that the garment be loose, a little like the robes of the desert, through which robes one's nakedness can always be felt, and, sometimes, discerned. This trust in one's nakedness is all that gives one the power to change one's robes."[44] As its title would suggest, *Beale Street* turned to the blues as Baldwin rethought literary technique "in an age," as Jo Durden-Smith put it in his 1971 interview with Baldwin, "in which it is felt that fiction is merely fraudulent."[45] The connection between politics, music, and Baldwin's poetics in *Beale Street* is precise in its looseness. In "The Uses of the Blues," Baldwin had written: "It's this passionate detachment, this inwardness coupled with outwardness, this ability to know that, all right, it's a mess, and you can't do anything about it . . . so, well, you have to do something about it. You can't stay there, you can't drop dead, you can't give up, but all right, okay, as Bessie [Smith] said, 'picked up my bags, baby, and I tried it again'" (*Cross*, 59). At the close of the novel, Fonny's father, Frank Hunt, and Tish's father, Joseph Rivers, echo Baldwin's thoughts about the blues approach to experience nearly verbatim. Frank: "They got him. . . . And ain't nothing we can do about it" (188). And, Joseph: "We *got* to do something about it" (189).

Contrary to the style of much black arts movement theorizing, such as Mulana Karenga's "Black Cultural Nationalism" (1968), that repudiated the blues as old-fashioned, self-defeating, and counterrevolutionary, Baldwin connected the blues sensibility directly to the revolution. He was anything but out of touch; he'd met and had written about the Black Panther leaders, grappled with Malcolm's legacy in *One Day, When I Was Lost* (1972), and adapted George Jackson's prison letters, *Soledad Brother*, into a screenplay for director Costa-Gavras. *Beale Street* includes echoes of Jonathan Jackson's armed attempt on August 7, 1970, to free his brother from politically motivated incarceration. Frank: "And if they don't give us bail?" Joseph: "We get him *out*. I don't care what we have to do to get him out!"[46] The pragmatic urgency echoes Baldwin's support for prisoners and cases involving well-known people such as Angela Davis, Huey Newton, George Jackson, and others as well as personal friends including Tony Maynard. It also involved unpublicized support such as proceeds from speaking tours donated to the Black Panther defense funds and his personal, financial support of the Conspiracy, an organization run by Susan Sontag and Kathleen Cleaver in support of the Chicago Eight, including Bobby Seale.[47]

Baldwin's novels of the 1970s made radical politics a private, indeed, a family matter. The first steps in this direction occurred in *No Name in the Street*. His description of his first meeting in the fall of 1967 with the Black Panther leaders pivots on two encounters: first, and famously, he and Eldridge Cleaver measured each other in a way that echoed the way he and Norman Mailer circled around each other when they first met; and, second, in a way no one mentions, Baldwin's sister Gloria instantly hit it off with Huey Newton: "as I remember," he wrote, "they scarcely talked to anyone else" (*CE*, 458). Later, in a blues-inflected image of passionate detachment, when informed of Newton's arrest on charges that he killed an Oakland police officer: "Gloria's reaction was, first—'That nice boy!' and then a somber, dry bitter, 'At least he isn't dead'" (460).

As always, the immediate energies of his experience crossed in subtle ways into the fiction. The masculine intensity and even the sexual danger he associated with his friend Alonzo "Lonnie" Levister—whose energy and biography was closely woven into Rufus Scott in *Another Country* and with whom Baldwin had had a glancing erotic encounter in Los Angeles in June 1973—Huey Newton, and other figures echoed in and around Alonzo "Fonny" Hunt from *Beale Street*. Much in the novel and the world around it strongly suggests Fonny is not guilty of the rape charge. Convinced of his innocence, Sharon Rivers goes to Puerto Rico to confront Victoria Sanchez, his accuser. After Sharon claims to know because she's "known him all his life," Victoria replies: "If you knew how many women I've heard say that. They didn't see him—when I saw him—when he came to me! They never see that. Respectable women like you!—they never see that. . . . You might have known a nice little boy, and he might be a nice man—with you! But you don't know that man who did—who did—what he did to me!"[48] The novel never comments on the private authority of Victoria Sanchez's statement. What she said stands. Fonny's company in the world of Baldwin's life doesn't bear upon the legal fact of whether he's guilty or not guilty. But, with the statement above, it certainly removes him from the category of the "innocent" that Baldwin viewed as dangerously sentimental. It also underlines the way that Baldwin resisted making a romance out of the politics of the private.

The connection between the private and political worlds supported Baldwin's need to convert his literary approach into a revolutionary engagement without sacrificing the core structures that, to him, made art *art*. In his 1974 conversation with Margaret Mead, Baldwin described his aversion to the terms of American success: "One of my brothers was in trouble, and I was at this cocktail party and a very famous American intellectual—I wasn't talking about my brother because I don't do that; I was trying to say something about my country, and he said to me, 'What are you crying about Jimmy? You've made it.' . . . and I walked out and never went back and never will. Because something in me despises that level of ambition. Made what?"[49] The values implicit in the "American intellectual's" comment could scarcely have differed more drastically from Baldwin's developing sense of his writing's purpose. As he explained to his brother in June 1972, he understood that his self-described endeavor to lay foundations for a new morality through writing would depend upon an existing but misunderstood—even feared—kind of power and energy. His aim was no longer to make that energy understood; the task had developed into a matter of smelting the energy into a form that could be recognized and put to use and not necessarily in that order. More likely, he thought those already in motion would recognize his lyrics. Actors. In his conversation with Nikki Giovanni recorded on November 4, 1971, he said: "After all, baby, we have survived the roughest game in the history of the world—You know, we really have. . . . And we got this far by means which no one understands, including you and me."[50]

He didn't mean that they didn't understand it *yet*. Tracing his development shows that, to him, the "means" noted above—the black energy of survival and success, *real* success—wasn't the stuff of understanding, as such. Power was in evidence all around him, as were the struggle against it and the struggle for it. Baldwin had positioned himself in the middle of a volatile, often violent, and complex power struggle. His role in it and route through it were far from clear. He suspected that the energy needed was akin to morality but didn't operate according to existing moral categories, possibly not according to *any* categories. The garment was looser than that. In *A Dialogue*, he suggested his suspicion of categorical approaches to morality: "these categories—to put it simply but with a certain brutal truth—these categories are commercial categories."[51] For Baldwin, such categories inevitably led black people, or someone, back to the auction block even if success in American terms could make a few of them into buyers and sellers.

The *energy* that Baldwin had in mind had, in large part, been about stealing power from existing structures. "The relationship between morality and power is a very subtle one," he told Giovanni, "Because ultimately power without morality is no longer power. . . . You can't call Franco a powerful man. He's got a whole nation in jail, but that's not power."[52] Moving full circle, he reached back toward an alternate sense of what morality can be and has been. He concluded: "we have, out of a terrifying suffering, a certain sense of life, which everybody needs. And that's morality for me. You know, you use the word 'morals'; I would use the word 'energy.'"[53] Baldwin set out to explore his sense of a *black energy* that could counter destructive versions of American—including certain formulations of black—power. In *No Name in the Street*, echoing his conversation with Giovanni, he wrote: "For power truly to feel itself menaced, it must somehow sense itself in the presence of another power—or, more accurately, an energy—which it has not known how to define and therefore does not know how to control" (*CE,* 406).

By 1973, he could see that laying the foundations for a new morality meant making an old energy newly recognizable, and usable. According to what he knew about that energy, he could see that black survival in the West would continue to be an indirect, angular endeavor. He also knew it would be important to people who didn't identify with the black struggle at the moment. It would be equally askew to journalistic "facts" as it was to the arbitrary signifiers and insularity of mainstream postmodernism then emerging as a force in 1970s literary culture. He was beginning to accept that it would be a long-term struggle. In letters he meditated upon his contribution to an energy, to a process, the results of which he wouldn't live to see. Since the 1950s, he'd watched a series of revolutionary catastrophes as new nations emerged from colonial subjugation and fell under military dictators with neocolonial allegiances. The colonial structures and categories, associated with what he'd described in *The Fire Next Time* as "the authority with which white men walk," had proved themselves to be at least incapable of recognitions and, at worst, murderous in and of themselves (*CE*, 331).

In 1970, Gil Scot Heron first recorded his song/poem "The Revolution Will Not Be Televised" for his album *Small Talk at 125 and Lenox*. Baldwin agreed with Heron's criticism of the way ostensible revolutionary action could perpetuate oppressive structures, but his sense of agreement was grounded in his apprehension of the relationship between morality—energy—and power. The revolution Heron foresaw wouldn't be *televised*; and, the excavation and praxis of black energy that Baldwin intended wouldn't—indeed couldn't—be *articulated*. Baldwin explicitly marked the distinction as that between prose, which sought to articulate, and poetry, which intended to figure and signify. In *A Rap on Race*, he told Mead: "Now in the 20th century we are going to find only two terrible facts: the fact of prose, on every single level from television to the White House, and the fact of the hope of poetry, without which nobody can live."[54]

In his turn to poetry, Baldwin sought an operation of language more deeply and fully involved with experience and feeling, one that led beyond limits of language oriented to rationality and fact as mobilized by existing structures of power. Echoing the music, lyrical language, he thought, reached into deeper, less controllable dimensions. Those dimensions couldn't be communicated by prose articulations in the way he'd attempted to do during earlier stages in his career, such as in 1955, when he'd described his tool as "the disastrously explicit medium of language" (*CE*, 8). By the early 1970s, he was no longer resigned to *that* disaster. He'd learned that none of this could, in any conventional sense, be articulated and understood. He'd found that people, *in general*, who didn't have the lifestyles, the lives and styles, to accompany the looseness of the garment couldn't accommodate the texture and rhythm of miracles. And, as he'd long known, those who did have the lives and styles, in the main, didn't read. With the furious need for another approach pulsing in his

voice, arguing with Mead, he arrived as closely as he ever did to convey-
ing a point that, by then, he knew he couldn't articulate, one he'd long
resented having to explain:

> MM: Well, wait a minute! Brains are a little useful every once in a
> while. The estimate is that the greatest brain has only used one
> tenth of its available potentiality. So we've got nine tenths to go
> for the—
>
> JB: We're foundering here in the morass of language. I don't know
> what the brain means. I'm a very bright cat, I'm told, but I don't
> trust that at all. If I'm bright at all, and that's debatable . . . and
> I'm not kidding when I say that. I'm not being coy or modest
> when I say that.
>
> MM: It's not very debatable.
>
> JB: It's very debatable to me.
>
> MM: Well, permit somebody else to do the debating.
>
> JB: I never learned anything through my mind. I learned whatever
> I've learned through my heart and my guts.
>
> MM: I don't think it matters where it starts so long as it goes through.
>
> JB: But without a certain passion, and passion has no mind, with-
> out a certain love that—how can I put it, baby? Something has
> happened here and you have to feel it in your heart and your
> guts, and you have to feel a discipline to build that pipeline that
> brings it up to your mind.
>
> MM: Yes.
>
> JB: But if it doesn't start down there it doesn't mean anything. The
> world is full of bright people who are entirely irrelevant, and
> most of them are wicked.[55]

One can hear Baldwin hearing Billie Holiday singing into a complex
register, "Don't Explain." The issue is how the energy of experience
related to American conceptions of intelligence. Baldwin had written his
greatest prose from the mid-1950s through the mid-1960s in attempts to
translate these issues in a way that the American intelligence could understand. From the mid-1960s to the late 1960s—amid a critical chorus
proclaiming his decline—he'd reduced those articulations into forms that
could be engaged by people who didn't have time to read all the time and
could be avoided—by those who did—only by outright refusal to engage.
The American literary establishment largely *did* refuse. Baldwin watched
the responses and concluded that, in fact, the American intelligence—
possibly all intelligence—was, in large part, a mechanism of avoidance,

which led him to ask whether understanding itself was a mechanism of avoidance. He rightly felt that American intelligence, for most of history, had certainly avoided recognizing the realities of black life.

Mead's idea that we wait while humans develop the next tenth of their brain capacity was of no use to Baldwin's experience. First, he'd been waiting long enough. Furthermore, he was as likely to assume that that next tenth would be used in ways that resembled how the first tenth had been used. With his note about the wickedness of bright people, he suggests that those results could be *more* dangerous than ever. Set in opposition to established modes of rationality, his idea of "poetry" served as a felt "discipline to build that pipeline," a method of engaging dimensions of experience, a connection between the brain and what he called "your heart and your guts." Crucially, it was also a way for him to imagine how his work might connect with people whose sense of experience and intelligence *weren't* socialized according to assumptions of the *New York Review of Books*, *The New Yorker*, the *Nation*, and *Harper's*. In the years since the early 1960s, he'd sensed—experienced—that many people who read much less than his critics were quite capable of hearing, and *acting* upon, what he was saying.

As mentioned earlier, in *No Name in the Street*, Baldwin had noted "a very different intelligence" among people who were not guided solely by mainstream American mythologies and lifestyles (*CE*, 431). In a 1972 interview with John Hall for *Transition*, Baldwin elaborated on the possibility, or necessity, of addressing another audience, another structure of knowing and being. He described a key to his development in the idea of being at home in "Harlem, where people know what I know, and we can talk and laugh, and it would never occur to anybody to say what we all know."[56] But, the notion of being in a place where the new approach resonated wasn't strictly speaking an issue of home, or Harlem, or color, or of any one thing that everybody knew: "in Europe, . . . I can talk with people I know, and we both know the same things. Laughing and talking, not about civil rights, anything in particular. Just enjoying each other, you know, meeting on a journey and wishing each other well."[57] The things in Harlem "where people know what I know" and in Europe where "we both know the same things" obviously weren't the *same* things. They probably weren't things at all, which is the whole point. The categories are distractions, false witnesses. Baldwin was trying to use an energy that was available to all even if it seemed some feared it. It was an energy that didn't rally around the auction block wondering who was up for sale next.

As Baldwin told Hall, the development directly involved with the writing occurred in ways that an artist cannot articulate, even to himself: "This sort of thing involves the writer's sensibility on a level at which he can't defend himself."[58] Describing changes in the interior dimensions of his experience, he said:

> My next book, and books to come, will certainly be different, I hope, and certainly the form will change ... and the only thing one can do is work within one's own limits, one's own sights, and do the work one can do. Maybe it will last for five minutes, maybe it will last forever. Nobody knows. But if you begin to think about those things, like the form being conventional, you can't work at all.... I think real changes in form just occur, and I doubt if one's contemporaries are able to see a change when it does occur. The very people who clamour for new forms are also people who do not recognize them when they come. Since this is so, the only thing I can do is to work, and see where my experiments lead me.[59]

On the other hand, no matter the form or level of change, Baldwin wasn't about to withdraw from the terrain of literary—and financial—success. Auction blocks, he knew, couldn't simply be avoided; they had to be at least outwitted if not defeated. In his 1970 anthem, "The Other Side of Town," Curtis Mayfield sang, "the need here is always for more." As a kid from the other side of Harlem, "the Hollow," Baldwin felt that need acutely. The needs were complex, but they always involved money. An important part of the tension in Baldwin's career, therefore, stems from his dynamic understanding of mutually antagonistic needs. Both the antagonism and the needs were real. His development was telling him to be a poet of black energy telling a story the half of which can't be more than half-told. At the same time, he was in the midst of a dangerous, legally dubious—and, by the evidence, more than morally defensible—battle with his publishers over paternalistic informal and contractual relationships and large sums of money. The flash point was the quarter million dollars that he needed to buy his house in France. The purchase figured in his role as elder, eventually—and amid the violence, no one knew how soon—as an ancestor, who could secure a place, land, and an asset around which to further the vision of a revolutionary "tribe" without which he felt the work had no meaning.

Everyone advised Baldwin against this political, financial, and professional battle. The Dial Press said his work wasn't worth what he suspected. Offers in the mid-six figures for unwritten novels from other firms suggested otherwise. In the early 1970s, he was in the middle of a dizzying power struggle, which he'd seen coming for many years. While he was a high school student, Baldwin interviewed Harlem Renaissance poet Countee Cullen for his high school magazine the *Magpie*. Cullen had worked as a teacher at Baldwin's middle school in Harlem. He took Cullen's views on the restrictions of poetry and its limited power in American publishing as warnings that he would need to do something else if he wanted to develop himself and his gift, engage the world, *and* save his family.[60] He knew getting publishers to pay hundreds of thousands of dollars to a radical black "poet" was about as likely as stepping off of a peer in Nice and walking to Tangiers. Passing himself off as a mainstream literary success and a public celebrity, while shape-shifting his work into a radical poetics of black energy—that's just about what James Baldwin was attempting to do. At times it appeared he was out there, standing on the surface of the Mediterranean, beckoning. In his works from the late 1970s, the water would deepen even further.

The dynamics of Baldwin's work from the later 1970s were collective and collaborative. The explicitly gospel-inflected dimensions of this world, its music and rituals, emerged in newly assertive ways. The important complexities were as much—or more—between people as they were within people. In *The Devil Finds Work* (1976) and *Just Above My Head* (1979), Baldwin found locations—the theater and the church—capable of supporting the poet's "recreation of experience,"[61] or the actor and audience's labor of "recreating each other" (*CE,* 501). It wasn't exactly a miracle when it worked—and often it didn't—but it was close. Conscious avoidance of such recognitions and recreations surely led beyond bankruptcy to disaster. In *The Devil Finds Work*, Baldwin described one such successful, personal and impersonal recreation of experience in Orson Welles's all-black performance of *Macbeth*: "For, [the black actors] were themselves. They could be *Macbeth* only because they were themselves: my first real apprehension of the mortal challenge. Here, nothing corroborated any of my fantasies: flesh and blood was being challenged by flesh and blood" (504). And precisely thus, the 1959 "poetic trick, so to speak" (614) of the literary talent as Baldwin apprehended it via decades of his own work, by 1976, had become "the mortal challenge" (504) that bound artists and audiences together. This, Baldwin thought at the time, was how people *develop* the ability to bear the *dynamic* of pride and despair and to celebrate *and* change the constants of experience. This, he held, was how people summoned miracles, averted disasters, and changed each other. Collective action and mutual recognitions, he'd learned, were crucial to any practical "change in the depths."

While some forms were more resistant than others, the dynamic energy could emerge in any form or genre: movies, theater, novels, essays, blues, soul, jazz, or gospel. If one lost it in one location, there were others: "I'm not talking about literature at all."[62] If the mutual, "recreation of experience" ceased in one venue or genre, "the true believer goes elsewhere—carrying, as it happens, the church and the theater with him, and leaving the form behind" (*CE*, 501). In *The Devil Finds Work*, he continued: "If this seems to be saying that the life of the theater and the life of the church are dependent on maverick freak poets and visionaries, I can only point out that these difficult creatures are *also* our flesh and blood, and are also created by our need and out of an impulse more mysterious than our desire" (501). This joy was a fluid, not a categorical, reality; it was more about energy, black energy, than it was about morality. And, it was a reciprocal energy, a mutual force, and the real substance— one so often betrayed by the form—of power. One certainly *wants*, but it was not exactly *desire*. It involved a "true believer," but belief did not mean simple sincerity or earnestness; it was a resolutely personal and impersonal pipeline between dimensions of people athwart conventional structures. Confessions.

In "In Search of a Basis," Baldwin wrote:

> The basis for human harmony cannot be established by denying or forbidding to the human being the right to *be*—which means the right to discover—who he or she is. This being said, it must be added—a crucial matter—that people's right to be themselves does not necessarily imply that they have any desire to be themselves: the self is a journey which many, perhaps most, are reluctant to make. But no one knows enough about this mystery. Certainly I do not.[63]

This fluency required motion propelled by a mysterious force. Desire wasn't enough. Baldwin called up an image of the decadence produced by making a fetish of desire in the political sphere: "When I was young I, like many others, battled on the side of labor unions and would never have dreamed of crossing a picket line. The hunted labor organizer of that hour has evolved into a fat, racist, neofascist bureaucrat, and the grateful rank and file are defending their rights against all comers, especially the niggers, and slobbering into their television sets . . . a vivid illustration of human desire."[64] As for a fetishized private desire, the results were equally disastrous. In his 1985 essay "Freaks and the American Ideal of Manhood," he wrote of people who fled McCarthy-era politics and sought salvation through personal pleasure: "I sensed then—without being able to articulate it—that this dependence on a formula for safety, for that is what it was, signaled a desperate moral abdication. . . . The people who leaped into orgone boxes in search of the perfect orgasm were later to turn to acid" (*CE*, 826–827). "No hiding place down here," sang the gospel song Baldwin quoted often in his letters. The path to salvation connected the personal and impersonal to the private and political; in other words, salvation entailed the labor of "flesh and blood being challenged by flesh and blood" (504).

The final page of *The Devil Finds Work* is dated July 29, 1975, but correspondence shows that Baldwin was completing his draft of the book in late April 1975 when the United States withdrew from Vietnam in defeat (*CE*, 572). At dawn on April 20, he wrote his brother from St. Paul de Vence that the end of his new book was now being written on the front pages of newspapers around the world. Clearly disturbed by the vision, he joked (maybe) about being burned at the stake. Baldwin recast the overriding structure of the American "state of mind" as an overtly racial, *explicitly* political, and openly international dynamic. The structure, he thought, prevented the message about the changed nature of power from registering in American lives. In movies as in the American apprehension of experience, on one side was the delusion that experience could be *only* personal: "the white chick is always, somehow, saved or strengthened or destroyed by love—society is out of it, beneath her: it matters not at all that the man she marries, or deserts, or murders, happens to own Rhodesia, or that she does: love is all" (564). Meanwhile, the other side is *only* social, "the situation of the black heroine, to say nothing of the black hero, must always be left at society's mercy in order to justify white history and in order to indicate the essential [social] validity of the black condition" (564). Baldwin knew the riven terrain between the social reality, coded black, and the private one, coded white, must be crossed; the realities and fantasies that took shape in people's lives trapped within that structure must be confessed. Until persons situated in that terrain were *able* to confess their realities *and* fantasies, and to each other, *in* fact, nobody could really be sure what's real and what's fantastic, what's a fact and what's not, where public and private dimensions of life converge and where they depart. The late 1970s offered few venues for flesh to challenge flesh in that way. The 1980s would be worse.

By 1976, Baldwin's survey had drawn a map delineating possible paths. He meant his work to explore a version of black privacy, of how black people "re-create each other," and participate in the energy of their experiences in the West. In his 1979 speech at Berkeley, he said, "We can't hit the streets, because they're waiting for us." By this he meant that, indeed, the revolution wouldn't be televised; it would, he believed, be forged in a *privacy* capable of bearing social weight of history and in social spaces alive with those private energies. And, he knew what goes on in private was unavoidably connected with Rhodesia,[65] with explicitly oppressive political and colonial forces across the globe. He knew that because that was the (untold) story of people like Dorothy Counts and Elizabeth Eckford and the black freedom struggle which, he also knew, had taken root in church services and in bedtime prayers and at breakfast tables long before it became visible to photographers and TV cameras positioned in the streets of Charlotte, North Carolina, and Little Rock, Arkansas, in 1957. This is what Baldwin meant in 1961 when, in describing young people like Counts and Eckford, he said: "That child has been coming for a very long time. She didn't come out of nothing."[66]

The force of such images of black private (including social and intimate) life was derived from poetic suggestion more than prose articulation. Such images bore a certain *style* that could thwart the delusional structure and unleash the energy: "To consider this forbidden [black] privacy is to violate white privacy—by destroying the white dream of the blacks; to make black privacy a black and private matter makes white privacy real, for the first time: which is, indeed, and with a vengeance to endanger the stewardship of Rhodesia" (*CE,* 564). Political disasters like apartheid in Southern Africa and Nixon-era backlashes in the United States took root, he thought, in private needs that paralyzed millions into complicity with forces ultimately destructive to themselves as well as to the oppressed. Such an image of black privacy, the complex, often counterintuitive energy of the world of negotiation between black *persons*, he thought, "conveys, too vividly, how that victim, the black, yet refuses to be a victim, has another source of sustenance" (564). After scripting a scene which could not have been included in the existing film version of Billie Holiday's autobiography, *Lady Sings the Blues,* he concluded: "Billie's morality at that moment, indeed, threatens the very foundations of the Stock Exchange" (564). Possibly echoing the Isley Brothers' 1975 "Living for the Love of You," Baldwin could sense if not "see a new horizon, slowly, coming into view."

Baldwin then described a "source of sustenance" in the recreative black energy capable of communicating with other people and thereby of threatening "the foundations of the Stock Exchange." In *A Dialogue,* Nikki Giovanni remarked the power of ritual and music over "theology" in her experience of the black church. Baldwin responded, "Baby, what we did with Jesus was not supposed to happen."[67] In *The Devil Finds Work,* he connected the black troupe's work with themselves and *Macbeth* to the church ritual. Tracing the power to ritual energy rather than "morality," he wrote: "The blacks didn't so much use Christian symbols as recognize them—recognize them for what they were before the Christians came along—and thus reinvested these symbols with their original energy" (CE, 566). Recognitions. Echoing as it does Billie Holiday's lyrical skill, this recreation of experience empowered people to transform the reality of *what* they were to each other as well as *who* they were for themselves. It all turned upon images that had to be *recognized*. Dialogic soul.

Thus, as a poet, guided by what the music witnessed in experience, Baldwin traced the vital action that made the people a group of persons and made the person a vehicle of transit between the personal, the "who," and the social, the "what," of identity and back again. As I explore further in Chapter 6, on July 1, 1973, in "The Hallelujah Chorus," performing with Ray Charles in Carnegie Hall, he listened to Ray do exactly that. When the song ended:

> JB: *That's* a trip. How did you endure—that trip?
> RC: Well. It's really the same for everybody, man. Hell. . . . Okay. I been down in the valley.
> JB: Where you couldn't hear nobody pray.
> RC: *Hell-o!*[68]

The result was a collaborative poetic model designed to empower, to create power, black power, by connecting the self to its "selfless totality" without reenacting the oppressive structures in the mirror. Echoing John Grimes's experience at the end of Go Tell It on the Mountain, those who tapped into the ritual of the church shared the energy of travelers who "plead the blood" and pulled for the soul in transit. In such motion, one was both utterly alone and not alone at all. In The Devil Finds Work, he wrote:

> One is confronted with the agony and the nakedness and the beauty of a power which has no beginning and no end, which contains you, and which you contain, and which will be using you when your bones are dust. One thus confronts a self both limited and boundless, born to die and born to live. The creature is, also, the creation which is both the self and more than the self. One is set free, then, to live among one's terrors, hour by hour and day by day, alone, and yet never alone. (CE, 566)

This is the energy whereby a prisoner like Fonny in Beale Street could more deeply engage an energy such as hope by ceasing to cling to it. Loose garments. He continued: "So, you, the custodian, recognize, finally, that your life does not belong to you: nothing belongs to you. This will not sound like freedom to Western ears, since the Western world pivots on the infantile, and, in action, criminal delusions of possession, and of property" (566). More auction blocks. In his 1972 conversation with John Hall, Baldwin connected the personal and impersonal as well as the collective dynamics of the church with his developing sense of who possessed what and what belonged to whom:

> What is important about my work, which I realized as a little boy, partly from the Church perhaps, and whatever happened to my mind all those years I was growing up in the shadow of the Holy Ghost, is that nothing belongs to you. My talent does not belong to me, you know; it belongs to everybody. It's important only insofar as it can work toward the liberation of other people, because I didn't invent it.[69]

This approach was subversive in ways that extended far beyond the relative health of the individual or the community's point of view. At whatever level, the private reality had its social reality and the social world operated in private and intimate spaces. Baldwin, poet, but sounding just as much like a singer, was deeply embedded in a lyrical exploration of the basis for a living conception of black power, the energy of a self the structure of which had yet to be determined, already existed in action, and could not be understood.

In *Just Above My Head*, translating the "mortal challenge" taken up by the black actors in *Macbeth* into the life of a politically engaged singer, he wrote: "Niggers can sing gospel like no other people can because they aren't singing gospel ... when a nigger quotes the Gospel, he is not quoting: his is telling you what happened to him today, and what is certainly going to happen to you tomorrow."[70] Recognitions. Or not. Emphasizing the implications of the contrast between a socially fluent black privacy and a bunkered, apolitical white one, not to mention shocks in the New York Stock Exchange and to the stewardship of Rhodesia, he continued, "it may be that it has already happened to you, and that you, poor soul, don't know it. In which case, *Lord have mercy!*"[71] In "In Search of a Basis for Mutual Understanding," focusing on a dire lack of recognition, he described what an American glimpse of black privacy could reveal while underscoring the danger of not looking and not seeing. By thwarting confessions within and between people, the false image of black people propagated by the culture "has prevented [white people] from realizing that they themselves are treated no better than the niggers."[72] A dynamic engagement similar to "what we did with Jesus," Baldwin thought, could show white people that "their neighborhoods are always being destroyed ... that their government has deliberately placed them in their dreadful position, and manipulates every hour of every day they live. The truth is that the poor whites are absolutely indispensible for the maintenance of the status quo, and madly forge the chains which bind them, imagining that these chains are for blacks only."[73] Without such witnesses, and lacking the energy to *bear* experience and re-recreate each other, people would be reduced to futile and dangerously degenerate, in the end violent, means to claim "that they are free, freedom being a matter of getting the other fellow before he gets you."[74]

The images created in the spaces where black energy achieved its fluid forms—and power—always involved human encounters within and between selves. The threat was the foreclosure of such connections, the ceasing of those dynamics. Seeing the rituals from a distance that brought him closer to the essentials of the energy than he had been as an actual member of a congregation, he wrote in *The Devil Finds Work*: "In our church, the Devil had many faces, all of them one's own. He was not always evil, rarely was he frightening—he was, more often, subtle, charming, cunning, and warm" (*CE,* 567). Hell is the self trapped outside of who it is, or inside of what it's not, or outside of who it's not and inside what it is: "In short, the Devil was that mirror which could never be smashed" (567). Baldwin concluded this thought with one of his most precise evocations of the lyrical dynamics of black energy: "To encounter oneself is to encounter the other: and this is love. . . . For, I have seen the devil. . . . It is that moment when no other human being is real for you, nor are you real for yourself. This devil has no need of any dogma—though he can use them all—nor does he need any historical justification, history being so largely his invention" (571). Recreating that living reality required confessions across boundaries (identities) set up by the world as it said it was. Like the devil in his church, the unreality of other people began in a stifled fluency between one's own self and "its selfless totality."

In *Just Above My Head*, describing the mirror-smashing, liberating sound of black recognitions and recreations at the heart of gospel music, he wrote: "Everyone must cross this bridge, or die while he still lives—but this is not a political, still less, a popular apprehension."[75] By *not political*, Baldwin means that contemporary Western or American political discourses and practices couldn't (and can't) accommodate these dynamics. That's why the energy meant curtains for the "stewardship of Rhodesia." Nor could mainstream consumer culture absorb those moments, "still less, a popular apprehension." Even if it's on television, it still can't be televised which is why it *can* shock the stock exchange.

But, in *Just Above My Head*—despite *this* apartheid separating people from their living sense of themselves and each other—resonant recognitions were still socially fluent dynamics that drew directly on private realities: "*Oh, there wasn't no room,* sang Crunch, *no room! at the inn!* He was not singing about a road in Egypt two thousand years ago, but about his mama and his daddy and himself, and those streets just outside, brother, just outside of every door, those streets which you and I both walk and which we are going to walk until we meet."[76] The politics and culture will continue to fracture people's experience of themselves and each other according to all the usual suspect commercial categories—race, class, color, gender, sexuality—until the inside finds a way out, and the outside finds a way in *or*, failing that, until the commercial possessions—including identities and rooms of one's own—people use to evade experience are taken from them. At that point, people are left with only their own mirror images, ones they themselves can't possibly recognize. Those kinds of culturally coded, blind mirrors can only be—and will certainly be—smashed by someone else who, often, is simply announcing their reality in terms that can't any longer be ignored.

This vision obviously conflicted with the conservative politics resurrecting the myth of a cynically revised version of "self-reliance" in thrall to the god of profit. It also ran counter to the identity politics that would dominate progressive American life in the 1980s. Although he recognized Reaganism as the disaster it was, by the time Reagan had arrived in Washington, Baldwin had already rejected all approaches that simplified either the person or the people and most American popular vocabularies simplified both. In *The Devil Finds Work*, Baldwin wrote: "The question of identity is a question involving the most profound panic—a terror as primary as the nightmare of the mortal fall" (*CE*, 537). Baldwin's work of the 1970s insisted on an energy, a *black* energy, which would loose *all* identities. He knew that in order to do this, one must disturb *every* moral—and at bottom commercial—category as well.

*Anyone* stuck in the mirror of identity will evade the terror necessary to what Baldwin considered a *living* experience. Indeed, they must. The identity mirror cannot provide ways into actual lives, out of them, nor routes between: "This question can scarcely be said to exist among the wretched, who know, merely, that they are wretched and who bear it day by day . . . nor does this question exist among the splendid, who know, merely, that they are splendid, and who flaunt it, day by day" (*CE*, 537). Social forces, however, could make the private need for confessional traffic undeniable: "an identity is questioned only when it is menaced, as when the mighty begin to fall, or when the wretched begin to rise" (537). But, only a personal and impersonal, private and political energy can move between identities: "when a stranger enters the gates, never, thereafter, to be a stranger: the stranger's presence making you the stranger, less to the stranger than to yourself" (537). This was health, growth. It depended on energy created by people driven to come out of their identity foxholes and confess, live, make lives, across their differences.

In *A Rap on Race*, he summed up his position on social and private identity: "What I am trying to get at is if any particular discipline ... does not become a matter of your personal honor, your private convictions, then it's simply a cloak which you can wear or throw off."[77] As mentioned earlier, in *The Devil Finds Work*, he elaborated: "Identity would seem to be a garment with which one covers the nakedness of the self: in which case, it is best that the garment be loose, a little like the robes of the desert, through which robes one's nakedness can always be felt, and, sometimes, discerned. This trust in one's nakedness is all that gives one the power to change one's robes" (*CE*, 537). That trust, he knew, was an energy uncontainable within any categorical morality no matter its specific claim to power. The energy was dangerous, tapping into forces impossible to control physically or rationally. It was rooted deeply within persons but, equally, it needed to be routed between people. Nonetheless, he believed, such forces must be trusted. In *A Rap on Race*, he wrote:

> One of the elements that makes a history, is the reaction of human beings to their situation. And that reaction, when it is a real re-action, is always excessive and always a little blind. You simply find your situation intolerable and you set about to change it, and when you do that, you place yourself in a certain kind of danger: the danger of being excessive, the danger of being wrong. That is the only way you ever learn anything ... the only way the situation ever changes."[78]

Built in response to years of listening to Billie Holiday, Aretha Franklin, Ray Charles, and so many others, Baldwin's poetics were accompanied by an embedded musical score. He rarely wrote *about* music because he was writing a kind music all along—lyric. In his 1979 essay, "Of the Sorrow Songs: The Cross of Redemption," he wrote:

> Music is our witness, and our ally. The "beat" is the confession which recognizes, changes, and conquers time.
>
> Then, history becomes a garment we can wear, and share, and not a cloak in which to hide; and time becomes a friend. (*Cross*, 124)

Clearly we're in trouble trying to read this as prose. It's also much more than lyrical rhetoric. The preceding discussion provides a partial guide to what Baldwin meant in the three-sentence "poem" above. The improvised timbre of each key term sounds out of refracted assumptions Baldwin had added to the American definitions of the words. In the 1970s, his work charted and explored a personalized politics of nonidentical identities and impersonal privacies for which, he knew, there could be no full script; the garment needed to remain loose. Such identities took shape in excessive, partly blind, reactions to circumstances; they were always endangered. The risks were as enormous as the needs were mutual; constants could be celebrated only insofar as the mirrors could be trusted. And there was always something wrong in recognizing, and responding to, the message emanating from "the heart's nearly impenetrable secret place, where the truth is hidden and where only the truth can live" (*ENS*, 152).

But, of course, and in a way Baldwin was done trying to explain, keeping it loose absolutely didn't mean anything goes. As much as in 1959, spontaneity still depended upon discipline. And, as he'd stressed to David Leeming in his letter from the mid-1960s, turning inward didn't mean turning away. In "Of the Sorrow Songs," he emphasized the difficulty of describing—much less enacting—the dynamic, confessional action: "Go back to Miles, Max, Dizzy, Yardbird, Billie, Coltrane: who were not, as the striking—not to say quaint—European phrase would have it, 'improvising': who can afford to improvise, at those prices?" (*Cross*, 121). It was mostly up to the listeners, in any case. As Gil Scott-Heron intoned in the title track to his 1974 album, *Winter in America*, the leaders had mostly been murdered. In his UC Berkeley speech in April 1979, discussing the state of American schools in terms of a collective, decentered black tradition of rebellion he called "non-cooperation," Baldwin said: "One's got to start somewhere . . . there are other things I have in mind but I'm not really a tactician I'm a disturber of the peace. I want you to think about it. Because I know what can happen if you *do* think about it."[79]

To the sensitized eye, or ear, Baldwin's work in the 1970s radiates a black energy capable of operating in—but not succumbing to—a mainstream American context, without appearing to "leav[e] the form behind" (*CE*, 501). Reviewers *thought* they were reviewing novels. Editors thought they were commissioning essays. Meanwhile Baldwin was almost singing on the page. The language was certainly more miraculously lyrical than "disastrously explicit." No ideas but in song. As he wrote to David upon finishing *Just Above My Head*, what Baldwin had in mind was a printed language that he hoped, and doubted, could be "equal to the song" he heard in music and witnessed in black actors performing. In *The Devil Finds Work*, he described the black actor as a black energy trafficker: "What the black actor has managed to give are moments—indelible moments, created, miraculously, beyond the confines of the script: hints of reality, smuggled like contraband into a maudlin tale, and with enough force, if unleashed, to shatter the tale to fragments" (554). These actors supplied Baldwin with models for his writing. Like them, he was smashing mirrors and creating images that resonated with the dynamics of the testifying and witnessing, the pleading of the blood, on the floor of the church:

> The moments given us by black performers exist so far beneath, or beyond, the American apprehensions that it is difficult to describe them. There is the close-up of Sidney Poitier's face, for example, in *The Defiant Ones*, describing how his wife, "she say, be nice. Be nice." Black spectators supply the sub-text—the unspoken—out of their own lives, and the pride and anguish in Sidney's face at that moment strike deep. (*CE*, 555)

The action of recognizing someone else's face in your mirror was crucial to communication at all levels. As if confirming his thoughts in "On Catfish Row," written just after Billie Holiday's death, persons incapable of recognitions and confessions will find themselves "doomed to an unimaginable irreality" (621).

Whether in listening to songs, or watching films, or even by looking in the bathroom mirror, people who couldn't or wouldn't "supply the sub-text" out of *their* lives, who lived at a distance from that level of experience, would miss such moments. Baldwin knew they would have to find a way to *bear*—rather than reject or endure—their lives *without* such levels of experience; a task he believed impossible: "I do not know what happens in the breasts of the multitudes who think of themselves as white: but, clearly, they hold this anguish far outside themselves" (*CE*, 555). He'd pulled long and hard at that string, trying to convince people to face up to this reality. By 1976, Baldwin's attitude was: good luck with that. But, the "unimaginable irreality" wasn't just a white thing. Race—retreating into whiteness or romanticizing blackness—was of no use to the "mortal challenge." That was a problem he saw in the "so-called black films" of the era whose "entire purpose . . . is to stifle forever any possibility of such moments—or, in other words, to make black experience irrelevant and obsolete" (555). Casting himself as a *poet* of sentences and paragraphs, or maybe as a singer of prose, he sought to structure such moments of energy, lyrics for the recognition and use of people who *did* have the subtext.

*Just Above My Head* is Baldwin's most profound exploration of the loose garments of black energy. One of the novel's crucial scenes illuminates how moments such as Poitier's "she say, be nice. Be nice" work in musical fiction. A teenage Arthur Montana and a twenty-something singer in the quartet, Crunch, have found ways of connecting the energy of the gospel songs to their lives offstage; they were in transit, in love, in all locations. Their shady and ineffectual manager, Webster, missed most of what was happening in the songs, but had a salacious interest in what was going on in their lives. True to his name, fixated on definitions and categories, and mistaking physical sex for the living transit between loose garments, for flesh challenging flesh, Webster asked, "What's going on between you two?"[80] Crunch's oblique responses forced Webster to state what was on *his* mind. So, Webster attempted an ultimatum: "I might want to do it, too. . . . Or—I can always make you change rooms."[81] After he made it clear that Webster's secrets imprisoned *him*, not them, Crunch made Baldwin's point about how the poetics of black energy—of things that are themselves and not themselves when they're actually things at all—operate: "Anyway, you *can't* do what we do, brother. You can't sing."[82] As in *The Devil Finds Work*, if the song—the word—wasn't part flesh and the flesh wasn't part song, the matter at hand becomes "sterile and irrelevant, a blasphemy, and the true believer goes elsewhere . . . leaving the form behind" (*CE*, 501).

From the depth of Baldwin's poetic excavations of black energy in the 1970s, he saw most of what went on in American culture as oil on the surface of a shallow pool. In interviews, he appeared to fire from the hip, but the aim was often dead on a target much of the culture hadn't even seen. In a 1974 interview with the *Washington Post*, Baldwin was asked about the vaunted rise and success of the black middle class. Baldwin answered with his view of American ephemera on a treadmill masquerading as renewal, a disaster masquerading as a miracle, of finances (instead of dues paying) as buttresses against bankruptcy:

> Well, it doesn't change my perception at all, because the middle class, the white middle class, is an illusion. The black middle class is a copy of an illusion. The white middle class is an illusion because they don't believe in anything but safety. They don't believe in anything else. They think money makes them safe. And ain't none of them got no money. They ain't paid for their swimming pools,

they ain't paid for their cars. It's true. It's true. It's an enormous group of people who live subtly and desperately beyond their needs. I mean there is a certain group of cats living in Scarsdale who didn't live there before and they have bank accounts that they didn't have before. But the bank is shaky. And what are their aspirations? Whatever those aspirations are, those aspirations are menaced by two things at least: they are menaced by the actual statements of the society, the actual literal statements. The banks may fail tomorrow. And they are menaced by their children, who don't accept their aspirations, whatever they may be.[83]

It's no surprise that Baldwin was reluctant to greet with confidence news of the increasing numbers of black people arriving to the above state of mind. Asked about black entry into the American middle class, Baldwin pointed out the nature of (surface) change:

That happens every hour on the hour, in every generation. It really does, you know. I'm forty-nine years old and every seven or ten years I've heard the same things all the years I was growing up. What is overlooked is that the middle class itself is a different middle class each time you talk about it. . . . The middle class you're talking about now is not the middle class represented by Sugar Hill and Strivers Row when I was a little boy in Harlem.[84]

As if welcoming him into the new decade, in a 1979 article—patronizingly titled "The Fire Still Burns: Black America's Cassandra of the 60s is Foretelling Gloom in Race Relations in the 80s"—Hollie West elicited Baldwin's thoughts on a range of issues. By way of generalizing, Baldwin returned to his familiar constants/changes and surface/depth paradigms: "A great deal has changed on the surface. But nothing has changed in the depths. A great deal has changed in Atlanta, but nothing has changed in Georgia."[85] As for recognizing the disaster masquerading as Atlanta, as I discuss in the next section, he would get to that in the early 1980s. West asked Baldwin about the high-profile work of (and controversy over) black feminist writers such as Michelle Wallace and Ntozake Shange whose "prickly, negative view of black male-female relations has drawn capacity audiences all over the country for two years." Baldwin responded:

I hazard that [the sexual tension and the controversy are] symptoms of black middle-classdom. I doubt very much that the women I grew up with, my sisters, my mother, I doubt very much that that is their complaint. I think—and I'm talking about the women I knew—they had a very difficult time dealing with their men, their husband or lover, brother, nephew, son. . . . And though their relationships were very stormy, they were also very real. . . . The inevitable tension, fury always erupts against the one closest to you. But they understood that. That had nothing to do with our manhood as such. The anti-male thing which is now beginning seems to me to be one of the offshoots of the American dream as ingested by blacks.[86]

While the popular format of these comments didn't allow for anything like an adequate follow-up and certainly lacks a sense of nuance, his comments stress how one dimension of our lives always draws upon (often silent, even unconscious) assumptions in other dimensions. Baldwin's high regard—and public praise—for works such as Gayl Jones's *Corregidora* and Louise Meriwether's *Daddy Was a Numbers Runner* show that he was much more willing to listen when he thought the class assumptions of "making a 'hit'—the American dream in blackface" were on—and not under—the table (*Cross*, 231).

He concluded his comments to Hollie West with this: "It's impossible for black women to expect a black man to become Rockefeller or to be safe in this society, or not to be in some way at war and some way divided. It's simply part of the price."[87] Using Rockefeller, signifying money and power, as a guide to standards of masculinity, Baldwin stacks the deck in his conclusion. But, it's worth noting that he's critiquing black America's (here, black middle-class women's) adoption of standards of the American dream by which to judge their relationships. Many of these same standards, of course, were promoted as "health" by the male-centered black nationalist movements of the 1960s and 1970s. If a black man is unlikely to live up to the myth of Rockefeller, it's as unlikely that he'll live up to the myth of Shaft. With an eye out for the irreality created by foreclosed confessions, his comments anticipate, at least, contemporary debates about the nature of American and black American masculinity.

In the chaos of the kaleidoscope, and no matter one's social position, Baldwin still thought it all began with recognitions deep in the human interior. Twenty-three years after *Go Tell It on the Mountain* was published, Baldwin's 1976 comments to a group of women prisoners at Riker's Island State Prison in New York echo John Grimes's connection to a tradition borne in his mother's heart:

We all got here through many dangerous toils and snags. Our fathers had to go through death, slaughter, and murder—things we still see around us. But there is more than that behind us. If not, we wouldn't be able to walk a single day or draw a breath. I'm only trying to say that one can change any situation, even though it may seem impossible. But it must happen inside you first. Only you know what you want. The first step is very, very lonely. But later you will find the people you need, who need you, who will be supportive.[88]

Three years before that, he concluded his conversation with the *Black Scholar* saying, "The world begins here, entrusted in your head and in your heart, your belly and your balls. If you can trust that, you can change the world, and we have to."[89] The miracle of recognition under pressure of disaster makes way for Baldwin's last, in many ways his deepest, most resonant, engagements with the core American chimeras, his most crucial recognitions which, by 1980, he knew would need to be reflected and refracted.

## Bonding Refractions, Attaching Reflections: Self and Other (1980–1986)

Baldwin's sense of lyrical, half-never-told recognitions in the late 1970s quickly became a matter of necessary reflections and refractions, a complexly connective social and personal optics. By 1980, he was convinced of two things: Americans' most important access to history was through the present-tense texture of their lives, presence-sense; and, that experience of history's presence-tense depended upon a neglected—even avoided—presence-sense, people's *actual* relationships to each other. In 1973, he said: "History was someone you touched, you know, on Sunday mornings or in the barbershop. It's all around you."[90] Any meaningful maturity depended upon the development of a fluent sense of relationships across the divisions (individual, class, race, sexual, generation, and region) that had structured the nation's history. Introducing the image that would provide the focal point for his final and, in many ways, most important works, in *The Devil Finds Work*, he wrote: "To encounter the self is to encounter the other: and this is love" (*CE*, 571). Finding its fictional form in *Just Above My Head*, images of mirroring at every level of interaction from social and political to private, intimate, and erotic pattern Baldwin's 1980s vision of an ever-fluctuating, evolving, threatening, and enlivening sense of past and present, world and self. As he'd written to his brother David, while still in the early stages of writing *Just Above My Head* and allowing the possibility that only a black Westerner at that point in history could say it, Hell was "*not* other people."

As far as Baldwin's actual, youngest brother was concerned, the mirrors reflected an intensified focus, refracted a sense of surprise he knew he could trust. In the 1982 documentary *I Heard It Through the Grapevine*, the directors filmed the two facing each other and, at times, finishing each other's sentences.[91] Several scenes were shot at Mikell's, a jazz club at 97th and Columbus Avenue (now a Whole Foods store) where David worked as a bartender. Discussing their father's white brother, Robert Baldwin, "a brother grandma had by the master," Baldwin interjected an off-the-cuff quotation from Meridian's speech in *Blues for Mister Charlie*, "What a light, my Lord," and David picked up the image without a pause: "is needed to conquer so mighty a darkness. This darkness rules in us, and grows in each and every one of us alike, black and white."[92] Improvising on the play of mirrors, light to Lord, brother to brother, black to white, father to son, past to present, David concluded the scene off-script: "Bounces back, keeps bouncing back." As for mirror visions, as far as David went, while filming in Newark, Baldwin said: "I'm very lucky at least my youngest brother is my best friend. At least one person from whom I have nothing to hide."[93]

The refractions and reflections of this many-dimensional mirroring form networks extending to every level of our social and psychic lives. The experience of those ever-shifting relationships, for Baldwin, was the key to maturity, to social and psychic health; it was a practical, practicable, conception of a real-life salvation. In one of his final published pieces, "To Crush the Serpent" (1987), he wrote:

> Salvation is real, as mighty, and as impersonal as the rain, and it is yet as private as the rain in one's face. It is never accomplished; it is to be reaffirmed every day and every hour. There is absolutely no salvation without love: this is the wheel in the middle of the wheel. Salvation does not divide. Salvation connects, so that one sees oneself in others and others in oneself. (*Cross*, 164–165)

These weren't new ideas for Baldwin, of course. Privacy had long been a sense of self that was capable of living connection to other people. Salvation didn't imply safety anymore than privacy meant secret, any more than turning inward meant turning away. One was saved in, or by, moments of connection to others. Ezekiel's wheel in the sky had appeared to John Grimes over the Harlem rooftops at the close of *Go Tell It on the Mountain*: "Out of joy strength came, strength that was fashioned to bear sorrow: sorrow brought forth joy. . . . This was Ezekiel's wheel, in the middle of the burning air forever" (*ENS*, 211). The image recurred in most of his major works. By the 1980s—following the exhaustive refinements in *No Name in the Street, If Beale Street Could Talk, The Devil Finds Work,* and *Just Above My Head* I've traced so far—these dynamics had achieved a maturity and centrality all their own in his work and in his life. Most of what he said and wrote in the 1980s was really being *sung*; it was improvised according to confessional assumptions he'd lyrically recreated in the 1950s, 1960s, and, most of all, in the 1970s.

For Baldwin, the enemy was clear: the energies of separation; the forces that enclosed the self with itself; the mirrors that refused to reflect, shift, challenge, and distort; the deforming logics of American history and the West that based itself on property and insisted on considering itself "white." Races, social classes, metaphors such as masculinity, were designed to confine, to stop the wheel and thwart the living disturbances of actual human encounters; they were social—at bottom, commercial— concoctions designed to prevent recognition of strangers, make Yes-men or No-women out of the mirrors of reflection and refraction. Removed from the possibility of such connections, from "the shock of identification" (*Cross*, 24), such mirrors froze, became one-way glass, deadly masks. Describing how the disease of segregation changes windows into mirrors then morphs mirrors into masks, in *The Fire Next Time*, he wrote:

> A vast amount of energy that goes into what we call the Negro problem is produced by the white man's profound desire not to be judged by those who are not white, not to be seen as he is, and at the same time a vast amount of white anguish is rooted in the white man's equally profound need to be seen as he is, to be released from the tyranny of his mirror. All of us know, whether or not we are able to admit it, that mirrors can only lie, that death by drowning is all that awaits one there. It is for this reason that love is so desperately sought and so cunningly avoided. Love takes off the masks that we fear we cannot live without and know we cannot live within. (*CE*, 341)

Any mirror could be made into a mask, a slogan, of course. In *A Dialogue with Nikki Giovanni,* Baldwin discussed "legends ... such as 'black is beautiful.' It is beautiful, and since it's beautiful you haven't got to say so.... It's a very dangerous slogan. I'm very glad it came along. But I don't love all black people, you know."[94] Until the end, Baldwin would resist the disastrous temptation to make hiding places out of insanities such as color; he would refuse to freeze lyrics into slogans, to make masks of mirrors.

No matter its limitations, fears, and failures, and despite whatever

James Baldwin in the Newark projects in *I Heard It Through the Grapevine.*

backlash the 1980s had in store, Baldwin thought that the so-called civil rights movement—what he called "the last slave rebellion"—had released an unprecedented sort of mirroring in black America; it had changed the optics of black self- and mutual regard. This was a complex, mysterious traffic of the senses, *not* the work of slogans. It had not been and could not be *televised*. It was a complex wealth of presence no ideology could vouch for. Revealingly, in *Just Above My Head*, Hall Montana returns from the war in Korea to find that his friend, Sidney had joined the Black Muslim movement and had begun to see the world according to that doctrinaire point of view. In their first real conversation, Hall remarks the costs of the racial essentialism. It's not even that he necessarily disagrees with the political point, but something's missing from his friend. Hall feels it in himself: "I could say nothing. I listened to his voice, I watched his face—or, really, I could almost say that I listened to his face and watched his voice. I was beginning to hear, or see—to perceive—in another, new, very troubling way. It was as though one of my senses, or possibilities—sight, for example, or motion—had just been denied me, had just been stricken from me."[95] Attempts at synaesthetics, however, still won't cover the missing pieces of Sidney's lost presence. Only for a moment, in laughter, does the missing person reappear from the forfeiture, "Then Sidney laughed, thank heaven, and my normal senses were returned to me, not quite, however, as they had been."[96] With Sidney unable to bear presence in the world sans a (stand-in) sense of racial and ideological certainty, the two friends part at the end of the evening. Hall realizes that his friend has disappeared: "I knew that I would never see him again, not as I had."[97] It was, of course, a sense of other people Baldwin had long been acutely aware of and in touch with. In February 1962, he had written to his agent, Bob Mills, about the cost of racial orthodoxy, about those for whom "the prison of color" had become a "hiding place" (*Cross*, 198). Sidney in *Just Above My Head* becomes one of *those* many thousands gone. So the dynamic was obviously nothing new. The decades between the historical position of Hall and Sidney in the plot and the writing of the novel had, at least for Baldwin, clarified the stakes.

In Baldwin's mind, black music was indispensible to the authority of a black self and mutual regard that had been, in effect, smuggled through and refined in contention with American history. In *I Heard It Through the Grapevine*, after driving through Newark with Amiri Baraka, Baldwin toured the Newark projects. Voiced over images of him strolling while surrounded by kids from the looming, half-vacant project towers, he addressed Ronald Reagan's social vision for inner city America that was, essentially, if you don't like it leave. The documentary moved from the sounds of the kids' voices in Newark to Richard Tee's piano in Cornell Dupree's quartet. Sitting with David at the bar in Mikell's, and with his voice in a syncopated whisper, Baldwin said: "I would like to indicate to the president-elect, who says you can 'vote with your feet' in this country, I dare him to go to Newark and tell the people in Newark that they 'can vote with their feet in this country.' I dare him to tell all of those trumpet players, honky-tonk pianists, all those gospel singers, and their mamas and their papas, that you 'can vote with your feet in this country.'" In that sense, a revolution—one so close to the senses that many scarcely were conscious of its radical nature—*had* taken place, a miracle of transformed textures, an infinity of possible recognitions to refract. If white people had refused to alter their images in (and as) the mirrors of the world, that was their problem. The same went for black folks or anyone else looking for slogans to hide behind. The work was ongoing, of course, but he saw, and heard, that a new phase had begun. So, he pressed on.

So hell was an "unimaginable irreality" (*CE,* 621) taken root, the absence of the fluid, fluent possibility of reflective and refractive practical salvation, the eclipse of freedom "that burns away illusion" (208). Recalling Sonny's conversation with his older brother in "Sonny's Blues,"—"I know I did awful things, those times, sometimes, to people. Or it wasn't that I did anything to them—it was that they weren't real" (*ENS,* 858)—Baldwin abstracted Sonny's self-enclosed, mirror-masked self at the end of *The Devil Finds Work*: "I have seen the devil. . . . It is that moment when no other human being is real for you, nor are you real for yourself" (*CE,* 571). The one irreality mirrored the other, inextricably. Refusing to encounter the troubling mirror of oneself in others was, in effect, to go blind. In "Notes on the House of Bondage" (1981), the reality of that unreal mask had become a kind of mass blindness: "When white Americans look out on the world, they see nothing but dark and menacing strangers who appear to have no sense of rhythm at all, nor any respect or affection for white people; and white Americans really do not know what to make of all this, except to increase the defense budget" (801). From bedrooms and bandstands to the theaters of international politics, as he wrote in *The Devil Finds Work*, "the Devil was that mirror which could never be smashed" (567).

While no single volume published in the 1980s can stand with major works of previous decades, Baldwin's voice hadn't diminished in power. His writing was more direct and no less complex than it had been previously. His essay "Atlanta: The Evidence of Things Not Seen" (*Playboy,* December 1981)—published in expanded (if somewhat diluted) form as *The Evidence of Things Not Seen* in 1985—examined a subtle and lethal sickness in American life generally effaced by commercial interests and media hype. The serial murders of twenty-eight black children in Atlanta in the space of two years had brought a social illness into view from behind the commercial media mask. The essay turns upon Baldwin's sensitivity to the dangerous American dilemma—in Atlanta, itself a vaunted commercial miracle masking a disaster, it had turned deadly— of children who grow into a world in which adults lie about basic facts kids sense every day. When adults failed to face the reality of the world as it surfaced in the immediate textures of their own lives, they left children—who were, on a visceral level, unable to live in a lie they hadn't yet learned to reproduce in their own image—in a disaster with nowhere to go. It was more than homelessness; it was even more than the speech-lessness, "speechless in the most total sense of the word," he thought had confronted captive Africans traveling west into the middle passage (*Cross*, 79). From Baldwin's 1980s point of view, American children inherited a kind of utter worldlessness—even will-lessness—from their elders. In "Atlanta: The Evidence of Things Not Seen," he wrote:

> Except for a ruthless animal cunning (which is capable of getting a child into as much trouble as it is incapable of getting him out of), children have no defenses. A child believes everything; he has no choice. That is how he sorts out reality. When a child retreats and can no longer be reached, it is not that he has ceased to believe; it is that we, who are all he has, have failed him and now he has no choice but to die. It may take many forms, and years; but the child has chosen to run to death.[98]

This is very difficult to contemplate. But, again, Baldwin was exploring the god of profit that swept the nation in the 1980s and had, he thought, penetrated deeply into the interior and private reaches of human rela-tionships.

It was an era of terror and violence at many levels of American life during which sociologists such as William Julius Wilson, Douglas Massey, and Nancy Denton depicted levels of racialized poverty and isolation never before seen in American cities.[99] In December 1983, at Hamp-shire College in Amherst, Massachusetts, Baldwin recorded a five-hour conversation with the radical black lesbian–feminist poet Audre Lorde.[100] Baldwin described the sense of contemporary American life he'd gained from his time teaching at Bowling Green State, Ohio, and the Univer-sity of Massachusetts Amherst, as well as lecturing at universities across the nation. In his experience, young people were bewildered having—by their elders' failures to remake it—been left a world that can't be lived in. He told Lorde that, deep down, in all kinds of inarticulate ways, young people feel that this means that they've never been loved. Baldwin said that he was obsessed with his (and other adults') failure to reach young people who then inflicted that American silence, and acted out a conse-quent, incoherent American rage, on themselves and each other. Set in this context, all the technology and media of the contemporary era, to Baldwin, amounted to a very flexible and dangerous trap.

Discussing her approach (one that included phantom newspapers and efforts to disrupt network television broadcasts) to the task of breaking through to young people lost in the numb worldlessness of the American inheritance, Lorde echoed Baldwin's sense of the need to create a quality of time in which people can see, hear, and feel their own lives:

> It is maintaining vision. Maintaining a sense, a looseness, an openness and at the same time project after project and sometimes there are projects with no foreseeable end except in the achievement of the time that we believe we are helping. I have no certainty that this stuff is not going to detonate. I also know that if I don't work at it, I will be dead tomorrow because I know that is part of the force. It keeps moving and that's the thing that comes across even when you break into WINS even for 10 minutes. That's when you can get those kids maybe to watch a television program that doesn't constantly destroy any semblance of their blackness, their selfness, their humanness, their maleness, their womanness. Pick any name you want, as long as it's human it's under attack.

The two writers shared a profoundly embattled sense of the Reagan era in American life. For Baldwin, the task was really a matter of recreating people in such a way that they couldn't be destroyed by the contemporary American scene and the panic and rage it provoked around the globe. Lorde responded: "When I say that we need to speak words to our children that no one else will say to them, I guess I'm talking about something very grounded in war." Baldwin asks if he heard her correctly. And, Lorde: "In war! WAR! WAR!" So, Baldwin urged her to continue. She then described the battle she saw and the immediate need for tactical action grounded in renewing people's ability to use their own sense of themselves and each other to begin to rebuild an actual, inhabitable, experience: "I'm talking about being able to construct the vision of a livable future and it will entail terrible pain and terror at this point where we are. That's the closest I can come to thinking about empowerment if I had to use the word. It is being able to recognize fear, pain, love, hate, anger; deal with it and continue to move. Not to be immobilized." Baldwin then asked how one would begin that effort, and Lorde responded:

> For instance, raising my two children and the kinds of things that went down . . . the kinds of learning processes, all right. What does it take to . . . to get across to my son growing up in a household with powerful women that the women don't exist to do his feeling for him. I mean on that level. To be able to say to kids, that shit you're seeing on TV is shit. . . . I don't make a case for the happiness of my children's childhood. But I do make a case for the fact

that they're stronger for it. . . . I think that dual knowledge of both feeling and action, feeling and the ability to move, the ability to make an effect somewhere, somehow is how children very early on interpret power. Children interpret power by being able to act.

Lorde's sense of power and the ways to act differed from Baldwin's. Lorde said: "Jimmy, we don't have an argument," and Baldwin answered, "I know we don't."[101] And Lorde: "But what we do have is a real disagreement." Baldwin offered, "We are behind the gates of a kingdom that is determined to destroy us."[102] Lorde insisted on clarity about how and when black men became perpetrators—maybe surrogate perpetrators—of violence against black women. In that paradigm, she declared her right to self-defense even if, in effect, it meant killing the messenger: "if my blood is being shed, at some point I'm going to have a legitimate reason to take up a knife and cut your damn head off, and I'm trying not to do it."[103] In ways far more clear in the whole conversation than it is from the excerpt published in *Essence* magazine at the end of 1984, a year after it had actually happened, the two shared a sense of the importance of sensual presence in daily, personal, and public life. Such resistance entailed a tactical and widespread dismantling of mainstream American cultural and political structures of thought, feeling, and behavior. Concluding the published excerpt of the conversation, Lorde said, "let's start with that and deal."[104] Lorde's statement echoes a tactical riff Baldwin repeated over the years, in public and private: "patience, and shuffle the cards."[105]

In 1979, describing his own coming of age at a time lacking viable narratives for him to enter, Baldwin told Kalamu ya Salaam, "In a sense I was born in the nightmare of the white man's mind."[106] In *I Heard It Through the Grapevine*, in a question-and-answer session with Chinua Achebe, he elaborated: "I had no identity, I had no language, I had no songs, I had nothing except what Europeans said I had, a very terrifying inheritance."[107] In "Atlanta: The Evidence of Things Not Seen," Baldwin argued that the children of Atlanta had been born into a repudiation of what many, including himself, had dredged out of their heads and hearts, and out of American history, since the early 1950s. Part of the repudiation had to do with a black self-fashioning in the radically untrustworthy mirror of the American dream, an image with a deep, complex, and dangerous history:

The black middle class were the only people in the city of Atlanta (there being, effectively, *no* black middle class in the state of Georgia) even to be remotely considered or consulted in this matter. It is also worth pointing out that in a country as desperately and socially incoherent—paranoid—as the United States, no one has the least idea of what class means, especially when it is preceded by the word black. In the American polarity, one is looked up to or one is looked down upon; there is nothing in between. When the word *class*, which is a mystery, is preceded by the word *black*, which is anathema, Americans simply become spiritual basket cases and head for the nearest cliff, needle, swastika or cowboy.[108]

As it became obvious that the serial murders of black children in Atlanta weren't the work of white supremacists who were white—no white man could possibly have passed without notice in these neighborhoods before or after they'd gone on alert—a grisly feature of black American subjectivity appeared, undeniably, in the mirror: the danger black people posed to each other. It had to be recognized. Mediated by an "American" state of mind, by that numbness and hatred and incoherence, who knew just what black people might be capable of doing to each other? It was a core dilemma of the 1980s. Dusting off Malcolm X's "Message to the Grassroots," Baldwin wrote:

> The terror in Atlanta begins to alter, or to reveal, the relationships among black people. The black middle class of Atlanta believes itself to be the oldest and nobelist in the South—which means the nation—and it probably is; and who cares? I mean, who gives a flying fuck about all this genteel house-nigger ancestry if it cannot save our children or clarify a town? I have always contended that mammy had far better things to do with her time than to fret over the utterly intolerable Scarlett O'Hara, who needed only a fine ass kicking and a job and a man.[109]

What happens when black culture, led by American, pseudo–middle-class aspirations, begins to evade—an evasion that had always already begun, of course—its own reality checks?

Embedded in the Reagan-era refashioning, whitewashing, of the 1960s and 1970s, the city of Atlanta presented itself as a kind of—black, commercial—exception in the American South. And, in some ways it certainly was. In *I Heard It Through the Grapevine*, of his return to Atlanta in 1980, he told his brother: "It has probably done the most extraordinary, spectacular makeup job in the history of the world." Describing the super freeways and the new city skyline which boasted the tallest hotel in the world at the time, he distilled a new point of view that radiates into the information age of the twenty-first century, "you can see *all* of it, from a tremendous height, and you haven't got to be involved in any of it if you don't want to be." In Baldwin's mind, that image of progress intensified the sense of worldlessness that had imperiled the city's black children. Finally, it didn't really matter what Wayne Williams—who had been tried and convicted of two murders and blamed for twenty-eight—did or didn't do. For Baldwin, the danger to the children of Atlanta had no more specifically to do with Williams than the murder of Martin Luther King Jr. had, singularly, to do with James Earl Ray, Malcolm X's with the Nation of Islam, or Medgar Evers's with, as Baldwin put it, "the *one* lunatic in Mississippi, at that time, [who] happened to have a gun somewhere, and in some odd coincidence, unbelievable, shot Medgar Evers in the carport of his home within the sight and hearing of his wife and his children."[110] Conceiving situations such as these as matters of individual culpability was delusional; such narrow legalities could only further obscure the massive and insidious criminality naturalized by American culture into the world as it is. Considering black progress to be a matter of financial indicators and profit—glossed by whatever version of middle-class values—was a recipe for an insidious bankruptcy.

Mainstream American culture in the 1980s had repatriated to its most chimerical images of safety located somewhere in a foggy misremembering of the white, suburban 1950s. Most of the living veins of American life went underground into subcultures, many—but not all—of which were almost as segregated as the mainstream and—in the years before the Internet—largely invisible to each other. By now a veteran witness to over forty years of evasions and attempts at underground evasions of the evasions, Baldwin wasn't about to be forced into a "sub-culture" in his late fifties. In the conversation with Lorde, he understood the stakes: power rooted in the Western myths of white, masculine models had shown, plainly, its cards. It was finished but for the final flailing.

*I Heard It Through the Grapevine* includes footage of the moment when racists interrupted Baldwin during his opening remarks at the African Literature Association conference in Gainesville, Florida, by tapping into the Holiday Inn public address system. At first it sounded like static and Baldwin smiled and said he thought it best to ignore it. When a male, Southern voice said, "You're going to have to cut it out Mr. Baldwin, we can't stand for that kind of going on," Baldwin's brows dropped as he instantly recomposed himself for a different kind of encounter. He said:

"Mr. Baldwin is nevertheless going to finish his statement. And I will tell you now, whoever you are, that if you assassinate me in the next two minutes, I'm telling you this: it no longer matters *what* you think! The doctrine of white supremacy on which the Western world is based has had its hour—has had its day. It's over!" Rolling his neck to punctuate the last syllables, Baldwin stood eye to eye with what he didn't know. He didn't duck, run, or stutter. But, in that instant, he said what he had to say, confirming all of what he'd written to David and his family in 1974 concerning determination not to be controlled by fears (his or theirs) for his life. Fontaine's footage is real-time proof that he'd meant precisely what he wrote. He would sooner risk—and on a moment's notice was prepared to confront—betrayal than surrender to paranoia. He didn't want to die, he told David, but he would sooner be killed than hide. At least, he told David to tell his family, if he were killed, it would be an act by a real person; allowing fear to control his behavior would amount to hiding from ghosts. He refused to do that.

Maybe white supremacy *had* had its day, but the infection was bone deep and there was much work to do. Both Baldwin and Lorde knew, for one, that *all* people's subconscious investments in these now failed myths were profound. Real change would be avoided by most, feared at some level by *anyone* with any functional sense of himself or herself. That's why Lorde said, "it will entail terrible pain and terror at this point where we are." Later in the conversation, Baldwin mused that the decrepit actual state of white morale, despite their glossy images and vaunted privileges in the culture, is a terrifying paradox for black people in places such as Harlem. Most of Baldwin's writings and speeches of the era sought to collapse the veins of his thought into more and more lyrical utterances, improvised songs, really, of the irreducible interdependency and complexity of human life and the unavoidable need to recast its myths and structures at the deepest levels.

In the process of assessing the infection of white supremacy and the naturalized racism and violence ingrained in people's lives, Baldwin knew that social isolation created deeply untrustworthy mirrors. In "The Discovery of What It Means to Be an American" (published in *Nobody Knows My Name* in 1961), he had compared the mobility and fluidity of his experience in France to his life in the United States:

> I was born in New York, but have lived only in pockets of it. In Paris, I lived in all parts of the city—on the Right Bank and the Left, among the bourgeoisie and *les miserables*, and knew all kinds of

people, from pimps and prostitutes in Pigalle to Egyptian bankers in Neuilly. This may sound extremely unprincipled or even obscurely immoral: I found it healthy. I love to talk to people, and almost everyone, as I hope we still know, loves a man who loves to listen. (*CE*, 140)

In his best single piece from the 1980s, "Freaks and the American Ideal of Manhood" (1985), Baldwin moved between autobiographical lenses achieving a sparkling analytical clarity to describe the American male prison. Illuminating a sense of masculinity at least as confined in its worlds and in itself—and constrained especially *between* selves—as he had been in the New York of his early life, he wrote:

> The American *ideal*, then, of sexuality appears to be rooted in the American ideal of masculinity. This ideal has created cowboys and Indians, good guys and bad guys, punks and studs, tough guys and softies, butch and faggot, black and white. It is an ideal so paralytically infantile that it is virtually forbidden—as an unpatriotic act—that the American boy evolve into the complexity of manhood. (815)

Confined in those containers, American boys were sentenced to growing old and dying without ever becoming men, without, in fact, having lived at all. Imprisoned in adolescence, the American imagination created "freaks" for use in fantasized encounters with a range of experience that lay beyond the confines of the life—so-called—it had accepted.

The dynamic between the person imprisoned in their allegiance to supposedly safe, dubiously stable containers of (non)existence and (false) identity and "freaks" of whatever kind was inherently violent. Because "the awakening of desire fuels the imagination," the nature of the violence perpetrated by the imprisoned is *always*, at some level, sexual. So, then, at least for men:

> The American idea of sexuality appears to be rooted in the American idea of masculinity. Idea may not be the precise word, for the idea of one's sexuality can only with great violence be divorced or distanced from the idea of the self. Yet, something resembling this rupture has certainly occurred (and is occurring) in American life, and violence has been the American daily bread since we have heard of America. This violence, furthermore, is not merely literal and actual but appears to be admired and lusted after, and the key to the American imagination. (815)

Violence—"the American daily bread," the tissue of American (false) communion—was the sacrament consecrating stillborn relationships. In his portrayal, American culture violently sundered all American men from who they really were, privately, "in the secret place . . . where only the truth could live," in every venue of their daily lives. No American man made it from the shower to work and back home without running that gauntlet.

As Baldwin remembered his brief sojourn in the gay subculture in Greenwich Village in the 1940s, he affirmed the possibility, the reality, that just as power dominated transactions between so-called men and so-called freaks, it coded relationships between and within the so-called freaks themselves. In a 1984 conversation with Richard Goldstein, Baldwin said that it "may sound harsh, but the gay world as such is . . . a very hermetically sealed world with very unattractive features, including racism."[111]

In his letters to his brother David, and in his public writing over decades, Baldwin had made his dissent from that prison of asymmetrical violence clear enough. Wherever he encountered it in the world, that hermetically sealed male prison—coded white in the American imagination no matter what image it took in the "obscenity of color" reigning in one's perceptions of life—was incompatible with his first-person experience: "I had absolutely no fantasies about making love to the last cop or hoodlum who had beaten the shit out of me. I did not find it amusing, in any way whatever, to act out the role of the darky" (*CE*, 824).

In "Freaks," Baldwin exposed how the "American Ideal" had sprung back and entrapped those it was theoretically designed to keep safe from the perils of experience. Instead of an ideal, it had become "the imposed ordeal" (*CE*, 824). Picking up his image of the always-personal devil from *The Devil Finds Work*, he continued: "The object of one's hatred is never, alas, conveniently outside but is seated in one's lap, stirring in one's bowels and dictating the beat of one's heart" (824). The American imagination, imprisoned in the containers of a commercial morality and assiduously delimited in or as racial and sexual identity, was incapable of experience in the first person. Consequently, Americans, mutely no matter the volume and passively no matter the calisthenics, endured a brutal exile from themselves, from experience, and from each other, achieving only a lonesome, painful—ultimately lethal—state of mind that somehow passed for security, even privilege: "If one does not know this, one risks becoming an imitation—and, therefore, a continuation—of principles one imagines oneself to despise" (824). In "To Crush a Serpent"

(1987), he described the most recent Christian revival—Jerry Falwell, the Moral Majority, and Pat Robertson—as the latest American mob charged with sanctifying the containers, the cultural violence, separating Americans from human selves (not only their own and each others but any human reality around the globe). Members of such mobs were incapable of living: they could only imitate life. And the imitations were forced to find a way back to—and to rehearse again and again—the violence of their separation from actual life. The result was a culture obsessed with violence and infinitely repeated images of death. Baldwin wrote:

> This accounts for the violence of our TV screen and cinema, a violence far more dangerous than pornography. What we are watching is a compulsive reliving of the American crimes; what we are watching with the Falwells and Robertsons is an attempt to exorcize ourselves.
>
> This demands, indeed, a simple-mindedness quite beyond the possibilities of the human being. Complexity is our only safety and love is the only key to our maturity.
>
> And love is where you find it. (*Cross*, 165)

The 1980s were a time of widespread conservative social, racial, and political retrenchment in the United States. The mainstream wanted to be clean, white, and safe again. Ronald Reagan was the no-clothes-having emperor, par excellence, and Americans were eager to pay billions to join in the peep show. In his 1981 satire of a haunted, white state of mind rapidly clotting into the Reagan era, poet-bluesman and proto-rapper Gil Scott-Heron broke it down in terms that echoed Baldwin's. Signifying in his best bluesy baritone, Gil Scott mimicked the voices of retrenchment in his song "B-Movie": "Born again. Civil rights, women's rights, gay rights, it's all wrong. Call in the cavalry to disrupt this procession of freedom gone wild. Goddammit. First one wants freedom, then the whole damned world wants freedom." This parade of liberation had to be stopped, "Someone always came to save America at the last moment. Especially, in B-Movies." Baldwin had already seen this feature presentation. After *Go Tell It on the Mountain* had been accepted in 1952, he returned to the United States and found many people he'd known from the Village running for cover from the McCarthy-ites. He encountered many people who had abandoned the search for resonant confessions and retreated to the underground, this time "to Wilhelm Reich . . . in orgone boxes" (*CE*, 826). Of those who, in order to avoid the hostile political terrain, had traded a socially fluent wonder for (fantasies of) a transcendent, personal pleasure, Baldwin wrote: "The people who leaped into orgone boxes in search of the perfect orgasm were later to turn to acid" (827). Again and again, Baldwin had declined invitations into subcultures organized against, while often—he found—rehearsing roles designed in accord with, the mercantile containers of the mainstream world. Still, the mainstream in the 1980s was worse. In *I Heard It Through the Grapevine*, he summed it up while talking to Chinua Achebe in St. Augustine, Florida's "Historic Market" which had been a slave market: "The meaning of the morality in a consumer society: endless inventions to protect you from reality."

Baldwin had been thinking about it and *living* his critiques for decades. In *Another Country*, a trying-to-be-interracial-heterosexual Vivaldo faced off with a bi-sexual-for-the-moment Eric. Eric said: "Maybe I'm crying because I wanted to believe that, somewhere, for some people, life and love are easier—than they are for me, than they are. Maybe it was easier to call myself a faggot and blame my sorrow on that" (*ENS*, 668). In an early image of reflection and refraction in socially discordant mirrors, Baldwin continued: "There was a great question in Eric's eyes and Vivaldo turned away as though he were turning from a mirror and walked to the kitchen door. 'You really think it makes no difference?'" (668). And, raising the relevant relative issue: "I don't know. Does the difference *make* any difference?" (668). Eric, an actor, suspects that acting as if the difference makes a difference likely *does* make a difference. But, Baldwin's *puritan* (his term) streak didn't allow him to settle for half-measures, and "making words *do* something" required a certain pressure. In pieces such as "Dark Days," "Freaks," and "Atlanta: The Evidence of Things Not Seen" (and, possibly most of all, in the unpublished play "The Welcome Table"), Baldwin's elegant sentences continued to do their trans-difference, socially fluent "dirty work." But, the breach with the retrenching mainstream, subcultures, and the emerging, professionalizing academic enclaves was real. Intellectual and academic debates about this were often intense, at times viciously so. And, locations in inner cities in the United States had become war zones, at times more dangerous (to Americans) than Vietnam during what the Vietnamese called the American War.

Baldwin refused to stand still while prevailing social visions obscured the reflection and refraction between brothers in the mirror. The cost was global, universal, and, as ever, a very particular part of Baldwin's inheritance from his father. With Audre Lorde, Baldwin presented the conundrum of masculinity in American politics as a racialized, commercial endeavor that operated on autopilot where people chose politicians in exactly the same terms and by the same means as they chose which toothpaste to buy at the grocery store. The result was a politics peopled by abstractions instead of men. At which point, Lorde interceded: "But Jimmy, That's right I'm interrupting. It is that hypothetical definition of masculinity and men that is the root of the structure that needs to be questioned as well." After the interjections, Baldwin said that the situation was more historical than hypothetical. Finally, for him and for everyone, it was personal and political: the country was white only because it said it was. In fact, it wasn't white; no one could prove it had ever been white. In order to sustain the mythology, whiteness had become a metaphor for all kinds of illusions. In the end, skin color wouldn't cover it. That politics required massive lies and endless deployments of military force. Skin color wouldn't suffice in personal terms either; the personal delusions of whiteness, finally, required some kind of narcotic. Baldwin connected the distortions in the mirrors of American manhood to the racial opacity of people's thwarted mutual regard. The inheritance isn't hypothetical at all; it was one written into the skin by historical—often family—violence. He related that history to Lorde in terms none could describe as hypothetical.

Elaborating the story he and David referred to in *I Heard It Through the Grapevine*, Baldwin told Lorde about his grandmother, Barbara, who was born a slave and lived with his family in Harlem late in her life when he was a little boy. Barbara had fourteen children. Some by her white owner and some by her black partner who, he explained, laws and customs prevented her from actually marrying. So, Baldwin's father had white brothers and (perhaps) sisters. One was named Robert Baldwin. He described seeing a photo of Robert Baldwin and the family resemblance to his father. But for skin tone and hair texture, in their facial structure, eyes and cheekbones, the two men were very clearly brothers; because of law and custom, because of American politics, they denied the connection. From that family history, as he often did in his writings, he concluded something general about American politics and culture: it forced men to deny their brothers, a denial that, in his mind, falsified the moral (for him, specifically, masculine) fabric of American political endeavor. In terms of race as well as gender, Baldwin concluded that American politics entailed the denial of the irrefutable reality that people on different sides of the mythic lines are part of each other. Lorde responded: "That's the reality." Baldwin agreed and added that that would always be the reality.

Like the forever-turning wheel at the end of *Go Tell It on the Mountain*, the mirrors of reflection simultaneously arrive at and distort a kind of mutually adjusted focus. Stilling that motion and operating via whatever kind of truce with the historical material, and out of whatever kind of personal opacity results, turns people (or at least their pleasure) into acid and politics into a "false endeavor." No one pays these dues willingly; no one desires them. This is why the recreative lyricism, and the joyful reality it creates, exists in such a complex and intimate tension with pain. Whether mainstream or alternative, Baldwin regarded efforts at accommodation to the blind mirrors of American life with similar distrust.

Richard Goldstein's 1984 interview with Baldwin for the *Village Voice* is among the most important and instructive interviews on record and situated Baldwin's position vis-à-vis the gay culture of the past and the contemporary gay liberation movements. The asymmetry between Goldstein's identity-based, group-oriented sensibility and Baldwin's insistence on his reflective and refractive point of view inflected the conversation at every turn. Signaling the shifting mix of singular and collective terms, at one point, Baldwin said: "I'm a maverick, you know. But that doesn't mean I don't feel very strongly for my brothers and sisters."[112] Grounded in his connection to his family, the statement echoes the way that racial and familial levels of experience had collapsed in *Just Above My Head*. Goldstein opened the interview asking: "*Do you feel like a stranger in gay America?*" Baldwin answered: "Well, first of all I feel like a stranger in America from almost every conceivable angle except, oddly enough, as a black person."

Tracing his insistence that people act as mirrors to each other back into his first encounters with "gay America," Baldwin recalled: "I was never at home in it. Even in my early years in the Village, what I saw of that world absolutely frightened me, bewildered me. I didn't understand the necessity of all the role-playing. And in a way I still don't." In a subculture laced with such performances, Baldwin wondered what people would be able to mirror of one another and what coherent sense of self and place could possibly result. Remembering his time spent among the roles played in the Village, in "Freaks," he wrote: "perhaps the last thing this black boy needed were clouds of imitation white women and speculations concerning the size of his organ. . . . '*Ooo!* Look at him! He's cute—he doesn't like you to touch him there'" (*CE*, 824). He recalled: "It seemed to me that many of the people I met were making fun of women, and I didn't see why. I certainly needed all the friends I could get, male *or* female" (823). Baldwin sensed a mirroring here that he couldn't trust; his fear of the role-playing stemmed from the fact that he wasn't, in fact, *playing*. At the same time, he knew he was acting. The somewhat too easy (to him arbitrary) masquerading carried with it the scent of mainstream proprieties he knew were hostile to who he really was, the role he wanted to act, and where he wanted to go: "even today, it seems to me (possibly because I'm black) very dangerous to model one's opposition to the arbitrary definition, the imposed ordeal, merely on the example supplied by one's oppressor" (824). Pride.

Goldstein listened to Baldwin's dissents from a standpoint informed by the terminology and the subculture of a newly assertive "gay America" and noted the ironies: *"You're one of the architects of it by the act of writing about it publicly and elevating it into the realm of literature."*[113] Baldwin responded at a confessional angle: "I made a public announcement that we're private, if you see what I mean." Goldstein pushed ahead: *"When I consider what a risk it must have been to write about homosexuality when you did."* And, crossing up assumptions, again, Baldwin responded: "You're talking about *Giovanni's Room.* . . . I had to do it to clarify something for myself." Goldstein: *"What was that?"* Baldwin then restated his refusal to frame himself and his work in terms offered by the culture *or* the subculture:

> JB: Where I was in the world. I mean, what I'm made of. Anyway, *Giovanni's Room* is not really about homosexuality. It's the vehicle through which the book moves. . . . It's about what happens to you if you're afraid to love anybody. Which is more interesting than the question of homosexuality.
> RG: But you didn't mask the sexuality.
> JB: No.
> RG: And that decision alone must have been enormously risky.
> JB: Yeah. The alternative was worse.
> RG: What would that have been?
> JB: If I hadn't written that book I would probably have had to stop writing altogether.
> RG: It was that serious.
> JB: It *is* that serious. The question of human affection, of integrity, in my case, the question of trying to become a writer, are all linked with the question of sexuality. Sexuality is only part of it. I don't know even if it's the most important part. But, it's indispensible.

Goldstein heard what Baldwin said but attempted, again and again, to return to the oppositional—in Baldwin's mind commercial—categories of the political moment. Baldwin listened and recognized that the two men were building a bridge toward each other from different sides of a chasm. Again and again, he echoed what he'd learned from his experience of what happened between people. How did people respond to their mutual needs? The level of denial, he thought, had a lot to do with how dangerous the needs became. But dangerous compared to what? He attempted to connect the bridges with his basic idea of a black energy, the fluency of a noncategorical morality essentially out of sync with the oppressors' arbitrary definitions.

> RG: I don't think straight people realize how frightening it is to finally admit to yourself that this [by *this* Goldstein means: erotic attraction to men] is going to be you forever.
>
> JB: It is very frightening. But the so-called straight person is no safer than I am really. Loving anybody and being loved by anybody is a tremendous danger, a tremendous responsibility. Loving of children, raising of children. The terrors homosexuals go through in this society would not be so great if the society itself did not go through so many terrors which it doesn't want to admit. The discovery of one's sexual preference doesn't have to be a trauma. It's a trauma because it's such a traumatized society.

As was the case with color and race, Baldwin could feel very clearly how the idea of homosexuality, no matter how it was used or by whom, operated as a comfort to people who wanted to avoid risky thresholds of experience, "I think Americans are terrified of feeling anything." Such terrified people attempt to use "others," so designated, to do their feeling, their singing, their dancing, their aging, their fucking, and even their dying for them. It doesn't work. Try as one may with dancing and fucking, one *can't* imitate one's own death. Which doesn't stop people from trying. Focused on the place of sexuality in this lethal American dynamic, he said:

> I know from my own experience that the macho men—truck drivers, cops, football players—these people are far more complex than they want to realize. That's why I call them infantile. They have needs which, for them, are literally inexpressible. They don't dare look into the mirror. And that is why they need faggots. They've created faggots in order to act out a sexual fantasy on the body of another man and not take any responsibility for it. Do you see what I mean? I think it's very important for the male homosexual to recognize that he is the sexual target for other men, and that is why he is despised, and why he is called a faggot. He is called a faggot because other men need him.

After tracing a racial dynamic of precisely this structure in the 1960s, at the close of *Take This Hammer*, Baldwin had addressed the white viewers directly: "I give you your problem back, you're the nigger, baby, it isn't me." The parallel between the issues as he presents them above is so strong, one almost expects him to pause and address the so-called straight, or so-called homophobic, reader: "you're the faggot, baby, it isn't me." He didn't do that. But the parallel exists and Baldwin was clear about the complex connection between color and sexuality. But, the lyrical, confessional structure of his clarity didn't pretend to explain away the mystery (the miracle) inherent in human experience.

When Goldstein questioned Baldwin about the potential of the gay movement to bridge racial divides, Baldwin was dubious. For him, the facts of black life in America made the stakes of sexuality different than they were for people trapped in the white state of mind, whatever the details of their private lives.

> RG: Didn't people ever call you faggot uptown?
>
> JB: Of course. But there's a difference in the way it's used. It's got less venom, at least in my experience. I don't know of [any black person] who has ever denied his brother or his sister because they were gay. No doubt it happens. It must happen. But in the generality, a black person has got quite a lot to get through the day without getting entangled in all the American fantasies.
>
> RG: Do black gay people have the same sense of being separate as white gay people do? I mean, I feel distinct from other white people.
>
> JB: Well, that I think is because you are penalized, as it were, un- justly; you're placed outside a certain safety to which you think you were born. . . . I think white gay people feel cheated because they were born, in principle, into a society in which they were supposed to feel safe. The anomaly of their sexuality puts them in danger, unexpectedly. Their reaction seems to me in direct proportion to the sense of feeling cheated of the advantages which accrue to white people in a white society.

From his point of view, as long as mainstream standards and categories were used as the basis for measurements, none of the gauges could be trusted. Those mirrors were designed to lie.

Discussing the relationship of sexuality and color with Goldstein, Baldwin departed from this slightly alternative reading of the energy inherent in black relationships. Goldstein said: "When I fantasize about a black mayor or a black president, I think of it as being better for gay people." Keeping both aspects of his perspective in mind, Baldwin responded: "Well, don't be romantic about black people. Though I can see what you mean." Goldstein's next question brought the conversation to the crux of the matter with regard to—and *in*—the dynamic of reflection and refraction.

RG: Do you think black people have a heightened capacity for tolerance, even acceptance, in its truest sense?

JB: Well, there's a capacity in black people for experience, simply. And that capacity makes other things possible. It dictates the depth of one's acceptance of other people. The capacity for experience burns out fear. Because the homophobia we're talking about really is a kind of fear. It's a terror of the flesh. It's really a terror of being able to be touched.

Goldstein's suspicion at Baldwin's lack—or refusal—of specificity and his angular relationship to the politics and terms of the contemporary gay movement continued to resurface.

RG: So you think of homosexuality as universal?

JB: Of course. There's nothing in me that is not in everybody else, and nothing in everybody else that is not in me. We're trapped in language, of course. But homosexual is not a noun. At least not in my book.

RG: What part of speech would it be?

JB: Perhaps a verb. You see, I can only talk about my own life. I loved a few people and they loved me. It had nothing to do with these labels. Of course, the world had all kinds of words for us. But that's the world's problem.

RG: Is it problematic for you, the idea of having sex only with other people who are identified as gay?

JB: Well, you see, my life has not been like that at all. The people who were my lovers were never, well, the word gay wouldn't have meant anything to them.

RG: That means that they moved in the straight world.

JB: They moved in the world.

Goldstein got it. He paraphrased the bridge of their conversation in a way he imagined a contemporary reader of the *Village Voice* could traverse: "You will always come forward and make the statement that you're homosexual. You will never hide it, or deny it. And yet you refuse to make a life out of it?" Baldwin: "Yeah. That sums it up pretty well."[114] But, Goldstein was still hesitant to walk the bridge himself: "That strikes me as a balance some of us might want to look to, in a climate where it's possible." As ever, echoing his statement to the women in Riker's Island, and back to Elizabeth in *Go Tell It on the Mountain*, Baldwin recurs to the heart and refuses to rely on the world for change: "One has to make that climate for oneself."[115] Pride.

In the final exchange Goldstein continued to swerve away from the basic—if also basically *black*—sense of open, personal possibility and sexual responsibility Baldwin described. Holding up one mirror for reflection, Goldstein asked: "What advice would you give a gay man who's about to come out?" Baldwin responds: "Coming out means to publicly say?" Goldstein: "I guess I'm imposing these terms on you." And, Baldwin refracted back straight to the heart: "Yeah, they're not my terms. But what advice can you possibly give? Best advice I ever got was an old friend of mine, a black friend, who said you have to go the way your blood beats. If you don't live the only life you have, you won't live some other life, you won't live any life at all. That's the only advice you can give anybody. And it's not advice, it's an observation."[116] For Baldwin, a living first-person experience required interrogating postures that mirrored the mercantile history, distilling one's sense of the world and self alone and in reflected and refracted connection to others trying to do the same. He realized that the world didn't abound in people eager to embark on such journeys, but he also knew that there would always be those out there trying, searching for persons within reach hidden amid multitudes of people most of whom, in fact, didn't want—but also desperately needed—to be touched.

Looking tired, and even a little bored, on December 10, 1986, Baldwin addressed the National Press Club in Washington, DC. Even, so to speak, in the belly of the beast, the pleasure Baldwin took in and the energy he derived from reflections occasionally flashed to life. Refracting would-be reflections, disturbing the peace, from a point of view he then called, lyrically, "the view from here," he concluded his remarks: "We are living in a world in which everybody and everything is interdependent. It is not white, this world. It is not black either. The future of this world depends on everybody in this room and that future depends on to what extent and by what means we liberate ourselves from a vocabulary which now cannot bear the weight of reality."[117]

A few minutes later, in response to a question, he echoed his comments to Goldstein: "This never has been and never will be a white country . . . and the vocabulary which we are avoiding has got to deal with that." But, it would take people, persons, to do that. With Baldwin's patience visibly thinning and sweat appearing on his forehead, a member of the audience asked a question about "race relations" that seemed to suggest they'd heard nothing he'd said. After a long pause and several deep breaths and imitating his style of engagement from the early 1960s, Baldwin responded: "Well, it's a very difficult question to answer seriously because, well, the question is sincere but it's posed in such . . ." and then the past-tense stand-in for James Baldwin vanished and the real, presence-sense actor appeared once more to answer the mortal challenge of the theater; flesh challenging flesh, he said:

> Let me . . . you know . . . what I would like to do, what I would really like to do? It's an idea which maybe we could take hold of in this room. I want to establish, a modest proposal, white history week [*and smiling*] because the answer to these questions is not to be found in *me*, but in that history which produces these questions. It's late in the day to be talking about race relations, what are you talking about!? And as long as we have "race relations" how can they deteriorate or improve? I am not a race and neither are you. No. We're talking about the life and death of this country. And one of the things, I'm not joking when I talk about white history week, one of the things that most afflicts this country is that white people don't know who they are or where they come from. That's why you think I'm a problem. But, I am not a problem, your history is. And as long as you pretend you don't know your history you're going to be the prisoner of it. And there's no question of your liberating me, because you can't liberate yourselves. We're in this together. And, finally, when white people, quote unquote white people, talk about progress in relation to black people, all they are saying and all they can possibly mean by the word progress is how quickly and how thoroughly I become white. Well, I do not want to become white, I want to grow up and so should you. Thank you.

The final question of the day: "Mr. Baldwin, which of your books do you consider the best, and why?" He answered:

> I think every writer has two answers to the question. And the first answer is, "the next one." It's true. And, if any author has a favorite

among the books he's published, he's always a little afraid to say so. But, I'm going to take a chance. And the reason an author has a favorite book, very often is because the book was so badly treated. It's like having a child of yours badly treated, unjustly, you know, you shouldn't have treated him that way. And the novel I'm thinking about which was so badly treated, is *Tell Me How Long the Train's Been Gone*. Thanks. [*Exits podium laughing.*]

If we go with Baldwin's answer that the next book is the favorite, two of Baldwin's favorite books from the 1980s have yet to be published. "The Welcome Table," set in his house in St. Paul de Vence, was finished to an extent that might make it publishable. One day, I hope it will be. Baldwin, however, wasn't able to complete a viable draft of "Re/Member This House: A Memoir by James Baldwin."[118] Intended to be a biography of Malcolm X, Medgar Evers, and Martin Luther King Jr., as he remembered knowing them, little more than an introduction exists. The manuscript has its indelible moments, however; among them, a revealing collision between Baldwin's images of his first and last encounters with Robert Kennedy. The first meeting happened on April 29, 1962, at the White House dinner for writers, 173 of them, honoring Nobel Laureates. The last time he saw Kennedy alive was at Martin Luther King Jr.'s funeral on April 9, 1968. Of the first meeting, remembering over 30 years hence, he recalled Kennedy with a cigar clenched in his teeth that made him seem dangerous. Since he felt afraid, Baldwin forced himself to engage the US attorney general about federal intervention into Southern racial violence. Baldwin's image of the young, dangerous Kennedy was that he carried an FBI file cabinet in his brain in which Baldwin could almost hear himself being filed. Charting Kennedy's evolution in the years after they had met, and also, acknowledging the lethal price he paid—was to pay a few months after King's funeral—for his public engagement with American madness, Baldwin's dreamlike, second image clearly places Kennedy in the pantheon of martyrs. He describes seeing Kennedy standing on a low hill near the church with a bright smile on his face and wind in his hair. Without a hint of irony, Baldwin completes his image-homage: Robert Kennedy, surrounded by black children rushing toward him, to touch him.

During its last decade and a half, Baldwin's quest had found its sense of place. In a piece published just months before his death, "The *Architectural Digest* Visits: James Baldwin," he narrated the winding journey toward St. Paul de Vence. Recounting the litany of his ad hoc attempts at residence,

Baldwin remembered the locations and vectors key to the itinerary of his life and work:

> A loft and an apartment on New York's lower East Side, for ex-
> ample, when I was very young and a big West Side apartment in
> New York when I was not so young: and, in between, my various
> dwelling places around Paris . . . the Hôtel Verneuil, where . . . I fell
> very ill my first winter in Paris—1948/49—. . . a series of hotels,
> a flat in Clamart some ten years later, a house in London in the
> sixties, a couple of apartments and a summer house on the Bos-
> phorus in Istanbul, and a house I rented in Corsica in 1956, the
> year I decided to return to America. . . . I had bought a building in
> New York. I did not live in this building for very long. . . . Martin
> Luther King, Jr., was assassinated on April 4, 1968, while I was
> living in California. That devastated my universe and was ultimately
> to lead me to this house. . . . I wandered around after Martin's
> death—directed a play in Istanbul, for example, visited London,
> visited Italy. For some reason, I don't know why, I avoided France.
> I collapsed physically several times and when I came back to Paris I
> collapsed again. Friends then shipped me, almost literally, out of the
> American Hospital to Saint-Paul-de-Vence. . . . A friend of mine
> came down from Paris to look after me, and was so outraged at my
> hotel bills that he packed me up and moved me here, to what was
> then a rooming house. I was forty-six years old then, which means
> that I have been here for sixteen years. It is far from certain that
> I will live another sixteen years, and so I consider that the house
> found me just in time.[119]

It was a serious itinerary, blown by winds at each level of life, but, in the fall of 1970, Baldwin's personal world had found its mooring, a space in which he could pursue the last phase of his life and work: "It is, also, a very old house, which means that there is always something in need of repair or renewal or burial. But this exasperating rigor is good for the soul, for it means that one can never suppose one's work is done. And perhaps I have reached the age at which silence is a gift, and the vineyards in which one labors a rigorous joy." Baldwin's death early in the morning of December 1, 1987 (though it was still the evening of November 30 in New York) passed the craft of disciplined spontaneity by which changes, constants, and chimeras are apprehended, trusted, and revealed, and by which disastrous generalities are reflected and refracted into miraculous sounds, to the next generations. No ideas but in song. His work charts a dynamic engagement over four decades. The preceding has been my attempt to trace a lyrical, musically resonant version of its most turbulent and demanding course, one that offers a wealth of charts for further spontaneous, disciplined—dare I say—improvisation. There's much left out here. But, there's a spine of crucial reckonings linking these eras of Baldwin's life and work, an itinerary of distilled presence and engaged work of the highest order.

# BOOK II

## The Uses of the Lyric
### Billie's Quest, Dinah's Blues, Jimmy's Amen, and Brother Ray's Hallelujah

When I say poet, it's an arbitrary word. It's a word I use because I don't like the word artist. Nina Simone is a poet. Max Roach is a poet.... I'm not talking about literature at all. I'm talking about the recreation of experience.

—*James Baldwin,* Black Scholar *interview (1973)*

# 4

# Billie Holiday: Radical Lyricist

> There is the area of Lyric—the area in
> which one is absolutely convinced that one's
> emotions are an insight into reality.
>
> —*George Oppen, "Daybook I"*

> Poetic imagination or intuition is never
> merely unto itself, free-floating, or self-
> enclosed. It's radical, meaning root-tangled
> in the grit of human arrangements and
> relationships: *how we are with each other.*
>
> The medium is language intensified,
> intensifying our sense of possible reality.
>
> —*Adrienne Rich, "Permeable Membrane"*

**S**tarting from the earliest moments of his publishing career, as early as the opening of his 1951 essay "Many Thousands Gone," James Baldwin measured the capacities of writing, his and that of other writers, against the depth and complexities of black music. The list of musicians and singers he used in measuring his own voice is long. High on this very long list, and among those he listed himself, are Bessie Smith, Fats Waller, Louis Armstrong, Miles Davis, his decades-long personal friend Alonzo Levister, Nina Simone, Ray Charles, Edith Piaf,[1] Mahalia Jackson, Abbey Lincoln,[2] and Aretha Franklin. None of these singers, with the possible exception of Charles, appears as often in or as centrally to Baldwin's conception of artistic voice and possibility as Billie Holiday. In his September 1959 review of MGM's film opera *Porgy and Bess*, Baldwin considers Holiday and Smith as emblematic images of black freedom stolen from an American mainstream unwilling to, even incapable of, imagining their lives. Noting Holiday's death from liver failure, while she was under arrest and guarded by police in her hospital bed, on July 17, 1959, he wrote: "Billie was produced and destroyed by the same society" (*CE*, 616). Anticipating the outcry, he placed himself among the audience, "We are altogether too quick to disclaim responsibility for the fate which overtakes—so often—so many gifted, driven, and erratic artists." In a comment which clearly echoes the fate of Rufus Scott in *Another Country* (1962), the novel Baldwin was attempting to complete at the time, he wrote: "Nobody pushed them to their deaths, we like to say. They jumped. Of course there is always some truth to this, but the pressures of the brutally indifferent world cannot be dismissed so speedily."

Almost twenty years later, in *The Devil Finds Work* (1976), Baldwin's criticism of *Lady Sings the Blues*, the 1972 film version of Billie Holiday's autobiography (written in 1956 with William Dufty), picks up where he left off in 1959: "She was much stronger than this film can have any interest in indicating, and, as a victim, infinitely more complex" (*CE*, 562). It has to be this way, he thought, because "when the prisoner is free, the jailer faces the void in himself" (563). Noting the same dynamic, nearly twenty years earlier, in "On Catfish Row," he wrote: "It is simply not possible for one person to define another. Those who try soon find themselves trapped in their own definitions" (620). Black artists and audiences bore a serious danger in all of this of course but, at least in Baldwin's mind, the contrasts were clear enough so that black listeners and viewers could readily—collectively if at times subconsciously—free the images from the jail of mainstream perceptions and projections. The creative action implicit in that freedom was a very powerful, private resource, one crucial to Baldwin's understanding of history as well as his own cultural and psychological life.

This action, widespread in the daily lives of black people, of stealing images—even lives—back from the mainstream frame was lyrical. The model for that relationship to the world was most profoundly conveyed in black music. In *The Devil Finds Work*, imagining a scene from Holiday's book that was inadmissible in the film, as it appears, and would have been opaque to mainstream viewers in any case, he describes the structure of that power:

> Billie's account of her meeting with Louis McKay is very simple, even childlike, and very moving. Louis is asleep on a bench, a whore is lifting his wallet, and Billie prevents this, pretending that Louis, whom she has never seen in her life before, is her old man. And she

gives Louis his wallet. Anyone surviving these mean streets knows
something about that moment. It is not a moment which the film
can afford, for it conveys, too vividly, how that victim, the black,
yet refuses to be a victim, has another source of sustenance: Billie's
morality, at that moment, indeed, threatens the very foundations of
the Stock Exchange. (*CE*, 564)

In "The Uses of the Blues" (1964), Billie Holiday also appears: same
scene, different role. This scene clarifies the power and—from mainstream
points of view—ambiguity of this redemptive action:

People who have had no experience suppose that if a man is a thief,
he is a thief; but, in fact, that isn't the most important thing about
him. The most important thing about him is that he is a man and,
furthermore, that if he's a thief or a murderer or whatever he is,
you could also be and you would know this, anyone would know
this who had really dared to live. Miles Davis once gave poor Billie
Holiday one hundred dollars and somebody said, "Man, don't you
know she's going to go out and spend it on dope?" and Miles, said,
"Baby, have you ever been sick?" (*Cross*, 64–65)

That sense of discernment was crucial to black people's sense of themselves and each other, and also represented a rare opportunity for
American culture itself to steal its own image back from the prison of an
impossibly narrow and willed conception of human experience. Baldwin
concluded his 1959 thoughts on *Porgy and Bess* relying on that faculty of
discernment, fearing its diminishment: "If the day ever comes when the
survivors of the place can be fooled into believing that the Hollywood
cardboard even faintly resembles, or is intended to resemble, what it was
like to be there, all our terrible and beautiful history will have gone
for nothing and we will all be doomed to an unimaginable irreality"
(*CE*, 621).

The role of music, of lyric, in the culture—exemplified by Billie Holiday and other musicians—was an essentially interactive one. In October
1973, a few months after his historic performance with Ray Charles at
Carnegie Hall, Baldwin identified this interaction at the crux of what
art was all about. Again, Billie Holiday appears at the center of his conception:

I'm not talking about literature at all. I'm talking about the recreation of experience, you know the way that it comes back. Billie
Holiday was a poet. She gave you back your experience. She refined

it, and you recognized it for the first time because she was in and out of it and she made it possible for you to bear it. And if you could bear it, then you could begin to change it. That's what a poet does. I'm not talking about books. I'm talking about a certain kind of passion. A certain kind of energy which people produce and they secrete in certain people like Billie Holiday, Nina Simone, Max Roach because they need it and these people give it back to you and they get you from one place to another.[3]

With that interactive energy in mind, one that Baldwin thought "threatens the very foundations of the Stock Exchange," I propose the following short trip through Billie Holiday's career as a singer, which is also to say, to listen to a few moments of the artist's articulate life: "My Mother's Son-in-Law," recorded on November 27, 1933, Billie Holiday's first recorded song for Columbia; followed by the first song featuring lyrics she had written herself, "Billie's Blues," recorded on July 10, 1936; after that, "Long Gone Blues," featuring another set of Holiday's lyrics from March 21, 1939; then, a subsequent version of "Billie's Blues" from January 1944 in which key lyrics from "Long Gone Blues" reappear; a rehearsal recording of "I Don't Want to Cry Anymore" recorded at Artie Shapiro's house in Los Angeles on the afternoon of August 22, 1955; and finally two songs from her Newport Jazz Festival concert on July 6, 1957, "Willow Weep for Me" and "My Man." Seven songs. A lyric life. An autobiography in thirty minutes. A lifetime of listening.

The point is to unlock our hearing of Holiday's work and by that energy unmoor very basic questions about what's what from their anchors in what Baldwin called the American "state of mind." It's to travel with her, guided by the sound and rhythm of her voice as it arced across its career of utterance. There's no path like that careening career in which Holiday distilled our language's capacity for emotional acuity and communication. As is the case with all real lyrics, hers is no report to observers, one hears—cannot hear without hearing—her voice as it emanates out of *our*, as well as *her*, experience. Ultimately, as with much art, the questions lead to further questions. Summary conclusions to the side, the lyric *I* in Billie Holiday's music twists and turns, changes timbre, tone, and shade. She thereby communicates a brilliant palette of emotional durability and flexibility. She performed all this in tandem with her life, lyrically tangent to ours, never separate, never identical. In her first recordings, Billie Holiday rarely was a featured voice. She began as an instrument in the group, often taking the second or third "solo" in the song, using the sixteen or thirty-two bars to solo within the lyrics of songs inherited from Tin Pan Alley and Broadway. She began playing almost as one of the boys. Nevertheless, from the start, she testified to nuances, pressures, and pleasures of her experiences as a woman.

Her first known recording, "My Mother's Son-in-Law" (November 27, 1933), fits the early mode. Playing with an all-white band featuring Benny Goodman, Billie Holiday appears midway to take her choruses, and reappears, after similar solos on trombone and trumpet, to close the song. It's not great writing, not a great song; stock swing, but it's a start. Holiday's urbane, buoyant force as a vocal instrumentalist shows through in fine relief. She attacks the verses straight on, giving them a force and confidence: "You don't have to sing like Bledsoe / you can tell the world I said so. Can't you see you've got to be / my mother's son-in-law." The distinctive quality that shines through more than anything else is the almost total clarity of the conception and delivery of her solo. She hits notes dead on the mark, dead on the beat. And, most of all, her diction is razor sharp and impeccable; listen to the crisp shape of lines, delivered at a racing tempo, like: "You don't have to have a hanker / to be a broker or banker," or "Needn't even think of trying / to be a mighty social lion." Holiday holds to the words' pronunciations so tightly that she refuses colloquial phrasings necessary to retain the rhymes in the lyrics. Declining to pronounce proper as "proppa," Holiday sings, "Just wish you'd make it proper, to call my old man poppa." Holiday's precise diction placed syllable by syllable and (as far as my ear tells) dead center on the notes actually contrasts markedly (if later recordings are any guide) with her speaking voice offstage and the fine solos that follow hers in the song itself.

What we know about the personnel in the studio that day is that John Hammond set up the date, Benny Goodman played clarinet (presumably other instrumentalists are from his orchestra), and all the players were white. Jack Teagarden's trombone solo after Holiday, like Goodman's solo that opens the song, slips and slides and stretches around and between the notes and the tempo. In ways appropriate for the lyrics themselves, Holiday's voice and *I* in the song evoke a persona of great personal power, precision, and control. It was 1933, after all, and, contrary to mainstream mores at the time, the woman here is really proposing to the man. In its tonality, rhythm, and diction, the voice sounds almost *too* in sync and clear.

Biographers' accounts and interviews with those present at the date indicate Billie Holiday wrote "Billie's Blues" on the spot to fill studio time left over after the set recording schedule was finished. The group plays a standard blues march and Holiday records the first lyrics for which she's the lyricist of credit. To be sure, we can recognize the singer—the precision, the confidence—from "My Mother's Son-in-Law." But the story is blues. The figure's in a troubled relationship but she's handling it and not afraid to announce it: "Lord, I love my man tell the world I do / I love my man tell the world I do / but when he mistreats me makes me feel so blue." The clarity is there. The lyrics of understated pain in "Billie's Blues" tell a more complicated story. And she's begun to bend the words. The first "do" stretches upward between two notes. The bent pronunciation whispers a question or conditional nuance beneath the plain-stated fact. The result is a hint of dramatic tension. Holiday's tone embodies tension in every syllable of the song.

The second *I* (in contrast to the first, which is a pure, one-beat note) that begins the B line of her AAB verse drags into several syllables;[4] Holiday makes space for that *I* by removing "Lord" from the beginning of the second line. The words are basically the same, but, as is the case in standard AAB form, the repeated line challenges and comments on the first. There's a brilliantly improvised, warped twinning here between line one and its bent mirror in line two. Concluding, Holiday tilts the second "do" downward in almost perfect symmetry with the first upward-arching "do." It's subtle, angular and balanced all at the same time. The tempo is slower than in "My Mother's Son-in-Law," and Holiday sounds freer to move inside the rhythm.

In "My Mother's Son-in-Law," she meant it when she sang, "you can tell the world I said so." "Billie's Blues" puts the laundry in the street in plain view: "My man wouldn't give me no supper, wouldn't give me no dinner, squawked about my supper and put me outdoors. Had the nerve to lay a matchbox on my clothes. I didn't have so many but I had a long long ways to go." It's private trouble made public. Holiday's character's voice is not trapped in domestic space or in silence. As verse two shows, she and her story are in the world. In the struggle between blues content (pain) and blues lyrical form (joy), the song's energy leans toward vocal prowess, as well as the clarity of the account, and the ultimate freedom of the figure. The *I* in "Billie's Blues" (focused on that second *I* in verse one) hurts. Openly. She also sees and reports clearly on the pain. And when she concludes with "I didn't have so many but I had a long long ways to go," one wonders if she's talking about clothes (cursed or even burned by a raging man) or men. Clarinetist Artie Shaw and trumpeter Bunny Berigan take solos afterward. They're both great players, but their solos sound oblivious, as if they're deaf in one ear to the tonal and verbal narration, that is, the story itself. They both sound as though they're playing to the listener but not talking to Holiday's character. In other words, they sound as though they're missing the point.

In verse two of "Billie's Blues," Holiday comes back in the persona of a single woman free in the world and astutely aware of how she's seen and the multiple selves she has in the eyes of men: "Some men like me 'cause I'm happy / some 'cause I'm snappy / some call me honey / others think I've got money. / Some tell me / 'baby, you're built for speed.'" The emotionally awake, suffering *I* in the first verse is still there, but the bounce and pop in the delivery puts the speaker squarely in charge of the play of identity (in what would later be known as the 'male gaze') going on in the social world (as opposed to the domestic space) that she finds herself in. Finally, the last line of the song lands us back in an emotional control close to that of "My Mother's Son-in-Law." She takes all the partial and motivated versions of herself in the eyes of men and winds them together concluding: "Now if you put that all together makes me everything a good man needs."

Heterosexual marriage, and the emotional terrain that pulses in and around it, is the idiomatic home of Holiday's lyrical quest. It's an inherited idiom and within it and its emotional economy, Holiday considered the options and conditions of her character's corner of human existence. As biographers have made clear, Holiday's life offstage traversed racial, gender, and sexual borders. But in keeping with the times, and in contrast to her actual life, rarely do her onstage personae explicitly challenge the normative (intraracial, heterosexual, monogamous) assumptions in the ways a contemporary lyricist might. Subtly, however, while rarely specifying their race, Holiday's characters experience themselves and each other in a recognizably black world. Despite the limitations of the performed idiom, and in ways due to the intraracial assumptions carried by her stories—and evinced in the performances themselves—"Billie's Blues" declares a strength and transpersonal force (of voice, body, and spirit) imbuing Holiday's lyric *I* with the guts to feel the experience and the power and acuity to tell the truth she feels about it to the world.

In 1939, two years after "Billie's Blues" was recorded, "Long Gone Blues"—also written by Holiday—told a markedly different story of intensified intimacy and deepening trouble. It's a different register of experience, several orders of magnitude closer to the skin of the experience, and the power of the lyric *I* remains—at least—undiminished. Holiday delivers the verses over silky ensemble horns, no longer a public oration; this is a conversation in close emotional quarters. It's a manifesto masquerading as pillow talk. Holiday's persona begins: "Talk to me baby / tell me what's the matter now. Tell me baby / what's the matter now?" The first "baby" invites a lover into an honest, eye-to-eye, almost nose-to-nose, conversation. The repetition of the line challenges the interpersonal parity. The voice in line two hovers over the lover's reluctance to communicate (and thereby face) the truth. The repetition of "now" suggests a kind of chronic recurrence of the conversation and implies the lover's silence in the face of Holiday's character's directness. Closing the verse, the speaker begins the conversation on behalf of the lover: "Aw you trying to quit me baby but you don't know how." There's an unmistakable power differential here. Let's assume (within the historical idiom) Holiday's figure addresses a man. If so, the woman's emotional toughness, insistence upon truth, and ability to articulate not just her own but *his* perspective outmatches her lover's abilities in all respects. Once more, in contrast to the power of the single woman in the world in "Billie's Blues," the portrait here is of a man trapped by his emotional weakness, strung out on an addiction to a kind of emotional obliquity if not unavailability. If there's something of a loverly, motherly caregiver in the first verse, Holiday's second verse draws the line in a dare routed in an epic vein of rage.

"Oh Freedom" is a traditional African American spiritual song from the eighteenth and nineteenth centuries that contains the famous lines: "and before I'd be a slave, I'll be buried in my grave / and go home to my Lord and be free." Verse two of "Long Gone Blues" dips directly into "Oh Freedom" and adapts the militant slave logic to a contemporary, intimate space. Without changing the tonal register of the song or backing away from the intimacy much at all, Holiday delivers the following message to her character's man: "I've been your slave, ever since I've been your babe. I've been your slave / ever since I've been your babe. But before I'll be your dog, I'll see you in your grave." It's the stereotyped slave's song with the mask torn off. Making sure we know exactly whose grave we're discussing, Holiday's tender character changes the existential stakes of the spiritual from suicidal to homicidal. The way Holiday hits the front of each note and slides off the back while shifting the historical and political to the contemporary and personal, and switching the suicidal to the homicidal is subtle and radical at the same time. It has the effect of hitting someone with a sledgehammer in a way that registers the full impact of the hammer but leaves no scar on the surface. Verse two of "Long Gone Blues" goes off like a silent bomb.

Following the stark clarity in verse two, Holiday concludes "Long

Gone Blues" with a beautiful lyric of intimate ambiguity. Her tone shuttles around shadowy corners in the private life where love's complex connections make rational distinctions between pain and pleasure, self and other, right and wrong, notoriously difficult to sort out. Holiday sings: "I'm a good gal, but my love is all wrong. I'm a good gal, but my love is all wrong. I'm a real good gal, but my love has gone." The verse sounds one way if "my love" refers to the lover and, subtly, it sounds a very different way if "my love" sounds self-reflexive. The complex plot and tone of the song warn against choosing either option and suggest that the various alternative meanings overlap. Among the meanings, I hear an indictment of the rigid terms for the romantic, monogamous, and heterosexual idiom itself. In one voicing, the figure is a "good gal," but her love, the emotional reality of her life, doesn't fit the mold. It's a sharp knife in a silk sheath.

In contrast to her work with Shaw and Berigan, the solos by Tab Smith and Hot Lips Page signal that someone was listening. Closely. Page's trumpet and plunger mute response to Holiday's tour de force almost literally speaks back to Holiday's character. It's not clear exactly what he is saying on the trumpet, but it's safe to say he was listening, he gets it, and he's none too happy about what he's heard. Call it counterdissent with plunger mute. The song initiates a stage in Holiday's recording career in which she engages in lyrical conversations about the ambiguities of human existence—in the emotional idiom of the blues—with many of the finest instrumentalists of jazz history during the 1940s: Lester Young, Buck Clayton, Roy Eldridge, Johnny Hodges, and Ben Webster, among others. The record of *that* conversation is another story, likely as sophisticated a discourse on the experiential textures of black modernity in the United States as exists.

On January 26, 1944, Billie Holiday performed "Billie's Blues (I Love My Man)" at an *Esquire Magazine* awards concert at the Metropolitan Opera House in Manhattan. The band was magnificent: Roy Eldridge (t), Barney Bigard (cl), Art Tatum (p), Al Casey (g), Oscar Pettiford (b), and Sidney Catlett (d). The better known of only two recordings with Holiday and Tatum together, it's a live performance taken at a *slow* tempo stretching the song out to nearly double its former length. Along with the tempo, Holiday changed verses to bring them closer to spoken syntax, added new ones, and spliced the "Oh Freedom" verse from "Long Gone Blues" into the song. The length of the song postponed its release for twenty years (Holiday would already be dead). As it is, it's my pick for the single greatest performance she ever recorded. Among other things, it gives us a glimpse of the truly conversational nature of the idiom among the performers. The band isn't just listening to the tonal narration of the performance and playing into the conversation, but Sid Catlett is literally (and audibly to Holiday *and* the audience) talking to her, even arguing with her, as she sings.

By 1944, Holiday was the center of attention on her stages. She'd seen plenty in Baltimore and Harlem while surviving the reform schools, brothels, speakeasies, and clubs of her childhood and adolescence. As an adult, she'd been hastily led off stage (while touring with Artie Shaw) and out of town in Kentucky after calling a white man (a would-be admirer who'd called out "let the nigger gal sing") a motherfucker from the stage. While touring with Count Basie, in Detroit, she'd had to perform in blackface so as not to be mistaken for a white woman from a distance and thereby upset white racist lovers of Basie's music in the audience. She had been ushered to the freight elevator and instructed not to mingle with white patrons between sets at the bar in New York City's segregated, upscale Lincoln Hotel. She'd served a year in federal prison for narcotics possession and had been banned for life from New York clubs serving alcohol. Effectively, one could say the Lady had seen it all. Hilariously (or not), on the recording the MC of the awards ceremony introduces her as "the all-American girl singer Billie Holiday." Center stage in the spotlight and (if the MC's perspective is any guide) simultaneously invisible, there she was. Wasn't? On the recording, she's there *now*. The band accompanies her. Eldridge and Tatum play behind Holiday filling in windows she leaves open in the vast expanse of space created by the slow tempo. Eldridge announces the song and slides into the slow tempo with a soaring solo; Holiday follows with the first verse of "Billie's Blues" translated a little closer to spoken (black) speech:

I love my man, I'm a liar if I say I don't.
I love my man, I'm a liar if I say I don't.

The tempo and tone go directly to the neck and the back of the head. It's swinging hard, slow as a pendulum in a long arc. Somehow, beneath the languid take, there's a great, implied (later in the song, explicit) velocity. Holiday enters the song almost a full beat early and stretches the first *I* out over about three counts. Her by then signature vibrato appears at the end of each held note. Same in line two—*both* times. The former "I love my man, tell the world I do" becomes "I love my man, I'm a liar if I say I don't." The third line follows with equal clarity and drastically rewrites the narrative of the song. Where Holiday used to end the first verse

"But, when he mistreats me, makes me feel so blue," the 1944 version concludes the first verse, "But, I'll quit my man, I'm a liar if I say I won't."

Next, Holiday folds in the "Oh Freedom" revision from "Long Gone Blues." The duration of each line stretched by the slow pace leaves Art Tatum space to add a modern, multiangular, eerily beautiful and lush accompaniment to the personal declaration washed in historical militancy. She goes through the "airing laundry" verse (breakfast, supper, etc.) over stop time that leaves almost a whole line a cappella.

The next verse is totally new and begins with Holiday holding a quavering "I" over more than six counts. It's one of her finest sketches of the lyric self. It's an epic *I*. Crucially, before the celebratory, single-woman-and-in-the-world-and-in-the-eyes-of-men verse, Holiday adds this verse about her character's *own* self-regard. The verse openly searches for an alternative source of feminine power. Beginning with the most drawn-out, various, and ambiguous *I* she'd recorded to date, Holiday sings: "I ain't good looking, and my hair ain't curls." After the first line, Catlett at the drums is barely audible saying, "I wouldn't say that." When Holiday repeats the line, Catlett's ready and repeats his commentary much louder, "I wouldn't say that, Billie, I wouldn't say that," followed by laughter and a bit of applause in the audience. Holiday makes it clear that beauty in the mirror or in the eyes of men (including Catlett) isn't her point. She closes the searching verse: "But, my mother she give me something / it's gonna carry me through this world." It's a black woman's epic. For his part, Catlett, if one listens very closely, can be heard agreeing ("It's true, it's true") as the next verse begins. Naming the implied velocity beneath the slow-swaying tempo, when Holiday finishes the "in the eyes of men" verse with the line "Some say Billie, baby you're built for speed," Catlett chimes in one last time, "Now *that's* the truth." Musically and verbally, Holiday's assertion of militant self-possession sounds not only within supportive earshot and musical cooperation, but also in *literal conversation*, with the men on stage.

Holiday closes the song with the triumphant, "Now if you put that all together makes me everything a good man needs." At just over four minutes, the song sketches a tonal epic of women's emotional strength in the face of its challenges. The crawling blues tempo and the close attention to vernacular phrasings ("I'm a liar if I say I don't / . . . my mother she give me something / . . . it's gonna carry me") sound an intensified performance of blackness in the song. The strength, in personal terms, is inherited from the slave tradition and from her character's mother; it signifies backward (against the suicidal options in the nineteenth century), and, in contemporary terms, it rebuts the normative standards of beauty in the 1940s. At the same time, Holiday's work in the first person, especially the way she draws out that ambiguous, quavering "I" in the mirror of the line ("I ain't good looking"), confidently contrasts the song's narrative. Holiday's lyrics rupture multiple discourses, bind up the ruins into a coherent, communicable utterance in dialogue with history, in concert with black women's counterhistorical discourse of survival, and in instrumental and verbal conversation with the black men around her on stage. That's a lot.

But there's another important dimension to Holiday's brilliant lyric work in the 1944 "Billie's Blues." Even among her good friends and fellow artists on stage, and in relation to the tradition in the song, Holiday's drawn-out "I" is alone in a modern way that was new in her work. The ambiguity would increase throughout her career. This dimension of the story had been there for years. It is most subtly and intricately audible despite the most virtuosic and empathic accompaniment by key players from the Basie Band (Buck Clayton, Lester Young, Freddie Green, Jo Jones) in the jaunty 1939 version of "Travelin' All Alone." Riding the rhythm of the band, she sings, "Who will see and who will care," of her modern shadow, "'bout this load that I must bear? Travelin', travelin', all alone." Eventually, the shadow—an existential solitude and an experience-bruised fatigue—seemed to eclipse her songs until more than a few listeners wished she would stop. Several obituaries greeted Holiday's death with relief. But she didn't stop. Instead, as the 1944 "Billie's Blues" highlights, her lyricism continued to accompany a hard life lived and a life lived hard.

One afternoon in 1955, at bassist Artie Shapiro's house in Los Angeles, Holiday, Shapiro, and pianist Jimmy Rowles tried out songs for the recording date to follow the next day. Shapiro set up a microphone and let the tape run. The result is an amazing, real-time record of Billie Holiday slipping in and out of character, trying on verses of songs as if deciding which coat to wear while Jimmy Rowles (and at times Shapiro) follows along. Among the songs recorded are "Please Don't Talk About Me When I'm Gone" and "I Don't Want to Cry Anymore." Holiday moves between her spoken voice, sings out of key (at one point in "Please Don't Talk About Me When I'm Gone" she pauses to ask, "[What] the fuck key I do it in?") in a raspy, backstage growl and, here and there on certain phrases, lets her silken performance voice slip into the rehearsal. At the close of a rehearsal version of "I Don't Want to Cry Anymore" split between two key signatures, Holiday explains her approach to the lyric: "You know I have to live with my tunes. When I sing a song it's got to mean something to me. I got to live with it. Otherwise I can't sing." The rehearsal tape offers a vivid glimpse of Holiday's methods of trying on different *I*'s and perspectives on their experiences.

Rowles and Holiday slip into "I Don't Want to Cry Anymore" and improvise their way through a few verses until Rowles asks, "What's the name of this tune?" That neither Holiday nor Rowles knows the song by title suggests something of Holiday's lyric method as well as their approach to finding and rehearsing material. It appears that Holiday would simply light upon phrases and scenes that attracted her attention and Rowles would move in behind her with chords until he found the key in which she was singing. Holiday begins the unnamed song with a scene in which one lover passes by the house of the other. During the rehearsal, she visits this scene three times. The first time, she sings: "Each night, just about sunset, you'll find me passing your door." The second time through, she sings: "Each day, just about sunset, I watch you passing my door." Both times, Holiday's voice changes from her rehearsal rasp into her smooth, performance silk at the phrase "just about sunset." It's as if the visual image itself draws her voice into its matching color and tone. Equally as revealing of her approach to the lyric is the way she switches the scene so that (in the first take) the singer is outside passing the lover's door and then returns to the scene from an alternate perspective in which she is inside watching the lover pass outside her house.

We see here in real-time terms how Holiday (whether consciously or not) is drawn to emotional, even visual, scenes in the music that she, in ways not unlike a film director, approaches from varying angles and points of view. Near the end of the rehearsal, Holiday comments to Rowles, "You only got one part that's kind of puzzling you, and it's hard, Jack, this is a hard tune, that's why don't nobody fuck with it." They repeat the end of the song and Holiday recalls the title midway through the passage: "It's all I can do, not to run to you, but I don't want to cry, that's the name of it, anymore. No I don't want to cry anymore." Finally, after singing through to the end of the song, Holiday explains her interpretation: "I want that son of a bitch jumping because you know everybody else would make it pretty. You know I want to tell that cat 'I don't want to cry. It's all I can do, every time I pass by your house, to keep from throwing a stink bomb into that son of a bitch [*laughing*].'" The next day, Holiday put the stink bomb on the shelf and sang the song with beautiful emotional availability, her voice a tonal dance in a state of threatened grace.

As is well known, Billie Holiday's late-career live performances and recordings drew many complaints and, since her death, have been a point of controversy. Some claim that her late recordings were rich with pathos and emotional power, her skills as a singer and storyteller keenly matched to the last chapters of her story. Others argue that they're portraits of a broken artist whose instrument has gone to seed. But the latter version seemed in the majority in years contemporary with her late life and immediately subsequent to her death. The former perspective has gained momentum with each decade since. Consider the following positions. Of the late recordings, John S. Wilson wrote: "We hear a singer who is more diseuse than jazz singer, who is depending largely on mannerisms to carry her through tempos which are often killingly slow for a limited voice.... She seems reduced to a ragged, wavering ghost of the inspired singer she once was, straining for the remembered effects that she can no longer achieve."[5] Of the same records, Miles Davis said: "I'd rather hear her now.... Sometimes you can sing words for five years and all of a sudden it dawns on you what the song means. I played 'My Funny Valentine' for a long time—and didn't like it—and all of a sudden it meant something. So, with Billie, you know she's not thinking now what she was in 1937, and she's probably learned more about different things. And she still has control, probably more now than then."[6] Buck Clayton, among others, sided with Miles on the matter: "She is greater than she was before because Billie continued to grow. She continued to improve with time until the time when she expired. By then she had done the whole thing.... People say that Billie could barely stand up when she made these records and maybe she couldn't. But she sure could sing."[7]

No matter the verdict, none can miss the shift from the threatened grace in "I Don't Want to Cry Anymore" to the bent character in Holiday's later versions of "Willow Weep for Me" and, finally, the utterly shattered figure (now only short-breath lines and brief twists in phrasing away from Holiday herself) in "My Man." Eventually, Holiday's personal lyrics, like her life, collapsed into a tightened tangle in relation to which listeners and reviewers had a difficult time knowing what do. They were confessional performances. Existential in that death sits in the room, measuring its distance from every line. Much of the listening public had always been deaf (listening to the all-American girl singer, wherever *she* was) to much of the substance of what was happening in her music; her late style makes that kind of happy, oblivious listening difficult if not impossible. Like Catlett on stage in 1944, Miles and Buck Clayton and innumerable others had been listening (and playing) along from a vantage point radically different than that of her mainstream audience.

If some of the songs in the songbook, especially the upbeat ones, sounded out of reach for Holiday in 1957 and 1958, "Willow Weep for Me" and "My Man" sound more than within her grasp. The songs allow Holiday herself to slip, sans mediating persona, inside their structures. She wears the music like a translucent gown. Audiences could seemingly see straight through the gown to an aching, tired, interior life in a woman who, "built for speed" as she sang in "Billie's Blues," had arrived at her early forties seeming as if she were closer to seventy. Unable to blindly see her as the all-American girl, mainstream audiences and reviewers didn't know *what* to see or where to look. Many turned away.

When she sang "Willow Weep for Me" and "My Man" at the Newport Jazz Festival in July 1957, the songs were still crafted illusions on Holiday's part; they were still performances, but the effect was a true-to-life, confessional appearance of, at times, disturbing power. "Sonny's Blues" first appeared, in *Partisan Review*, that same summer in 1957. Listening to Sonny play, his brother confesses: "All I know about music is that not many people ever really hear it" (*CE,* 356). If one attends closely to Holiday's performances at Newport that July, the result *isn't* happy listening. But none can deny that Holiday's in control of "Willow Weep for Me," steering the song into collisions with where she'd found herself during the last two years of her life. She sings, "Willow weep for me / bend your branches down / along the ground and cover me . . . gone my lovely dreams / lovely summer dreams / gone and left me here to weep my tears along the stream / sad as I can be / hear me willow and weep for me." The song is deep blue, yet also somehow flesh-toned, a palette well beyond what one would imagine given the lyrics. Steeped in lyric fluency, as the wood from the willow bends, so do we; its strained branches become our bones.

Holiday takes in her breath and makes the rhymes swing. Remarkably, the arcs are shallower but the effects are deeper. She matches the lyrics to the state of her life: "Weeping willow tree, weep in sympathy, bend your branches down along the ground and cover me, listen to my plea, hear me willow and weep for me." The total command of rhythm and pitch of phrase contend with the near-desperate portrait of the character in the song. It's not a bravura command; such virtuosity would have been as impossible for her as a lie. Holiday almost never did that. She never used music as a balm or disguise; her method of lyrical utterance was a lens of enlivening, at times threatening, focus. It's therefore nearly impossible to find even a moment of vanity—which is dependent on its disguises—in her music. Her work always rode close to the rhythm and texture of her life. That's the truth of her approach, the fluency of her communication.

Her songs lived with her. Her lyric characters were her twin sisters. Audible between verses is a loud, at times boisterous, noise coming from the audience out on the lawn that sound nearly oblivious to the narration taking place on the stage. The effect magnifies the solitude and pathos of the singer.

While the Newport crowd munches sandwiches and clinks wineglasses, Holiday closes the song, repeating "Willow ... Willow ... Willow" in ways that make it almost seem as if a tree itself can bleed. She finishes the song with "weep, for, me," drawing "me" out into a portrait of torn and damaged flesh. Accompanied by Mal Waldron's tragic, thunderous chords at the close, the performance seems to span the distance between her insinuated idiom of emotional and physical love and the overt racial politics of "Strange Fruit." This falling "me" sounds the tragic destiny of the epic *I* in 1944. Her pronunciation of "me" at the close of "Willow Weep for Me" at Newport in 1957 gathers pieces of the self together from a brutal, personal history. It's the sound of a broken window sweeping itself back together. The sound of someone falling down the soul's stone steps in the rain, or maybe in the hail, and getting up to describe it.

Holiday's "My Man" follows directly and, while it doesn't seem possible, makes the previous version of "Willow Weep for Me" sound almost carefree. "My Man" originated as "Mon Homme" in France where it had been a hit as early as 1916. Ziegfeld Follies singer Fanny Brice introduced it in English in 1921 and it became part of the American songbook of standards. Holiday recorded it several times: a bouncy 1937 version for Brunswick and two slower versions for Decca in late 1948. In the Decca versions, her good friend Bobby Tucker accompanies on piano. In the recording, for most of the song, the band lays out setting Holiday and Tucker against an empty background of studio silence. She'd quoted the lyrics to close her autobiography *Lady Sings the Blues* (1956). In 1949, after a jury of six women and six men (all white) acquitted her of possession of opium which she said belonged to her manager and lover John Levy, she nearly quoted the song while describing the case in the papers, "My man makes me wait on him not him on me."[8] The truth was, more likely, my man set me up. In any case, as an artist and as a woman, even as a legal defendant, she'd lived with the song for over twenty years. She'd lived in tangled tandem with its lines; in performances she ordered the tangle, she *lined* her life.

The tempo of her "My Man" at Newport in 1957 is torturously slow. Holiday gets the message across: this is how it is, maybe it shouldn't be this way, but it *is* this way and there's no way out. Or, maybe there's one way out. Death hangs behind the song like a heavy, silent curtain. The balance between her character's vitality (blues voice) and her struggles with love qua existence (blues content) has tipped wildly in favor of the struggles. The character sounds nearly completely defeated but still, in a show of confounding strength, utterly refuses any consolation or possible amelioration of the condition. Holiday's delivery sculpts a Janus figure in which strength and weakness switch masks until we lose track of which is which. Holiday's "My Man" uses the romantic idiom to arrive at the existentialist's unswerving conclusion about human destiny.

She dispels any whisper of fairy tale romance right off: "He isn't much on looks, he's no hero out of books." It's the voice of endurance as it nears the end of the journey: "I don't know why I should / he isn't true / he beats me too / what else can I do?" We've come a long way from "before I'll be your dog, I'll see you in your grave." "My Man" is a song of soul-bondage—of fate—seemingly beyond the reaches of mother wit and the epic strength of the slave ancestors. The trouble's too modern for tradition, too deeply personal for inherited balms. Avant blues.

In this performance more than any other, Holiday's idiom reaches deep into a perilously impersonal version of an intimately personal struggle. The character is one-on-one with an indifferent existence and, at this point, it's a mismatch—a rout. But achieving a voice for the full extent and horror of the beat down, Holiday's performance seems to say, "This is where it's at and I'm not about to start lying now." She sings: "What's the difference if I say / I'll go away / when I know I'll come back on / my knees someday. / For whatever my man is / I'm his / forever more." We might not want to accept the brutal constraints of Holiday's song, but if she's right about them—her experience vouches for her acuity if not for her understatement—there would be no more powerful way to put it across. A soul or gospel singer could play with the pronouns, feign metaphysics, switch out man for God or love, and get away with it. For Holiday and her earthbound blues, there's no exit.

This isn't the only quotient into which one's life divides, I hope, but it was hers and she had it nailed. At the end as in the beginning, and in a stunning string of instances in between, Billie Holiday lived her own lyrics (and ones she'd made her own through interpretation) bending her portrayal of her characters in a fluctuating symmetry and asymmetry with what she knew (which it seems is *how* she knew) about her own life. In the rehearsals of "I Don't Want to Cry" she explained it in so many words and offered us a backstage glance at her method and approach. In the songs in front of audiences and in the studio, her work (evinced in the seven songs I deal with above and in many, many more) shows precisely why I consider her America's greatest twentieth-century lyric writer and performer. Listen to these seven songs once. You'll want to listen again and again. You'll want to travel their depths. You'll find echoes of your own in them. Keep these Billie Holiday lyrics with you and no matter where you are, whom you're with, and even when listening by yourself, you'll never know if you're alone or not. If, according to Adrienne Rich, radical means "root-tangled in the grit of human relationships and arrangements," Billie Holiday is certainly one of our most radical lyricists.[9] For these reasons as well as others, Baldwin returned to her work again and again placing her high on the list of his guides as to what it meant and what it didn't mean to recreate experience; no matter the prices she taught him that, at bottom, improvising meant living the lyric and lining the life.

# 5

# Dinah Washington's Blues
# and the Trans-Digressive Ocean

> I had more fun doing this album, and, pain.
> It was a good pain.
>
> —*Chaka Khan, "Funk This"*

In "Book Two" of *Another Country* (1962), Vivaldo, a little high, lies on his back on a Manhattan rooftop with a few downtown hipsters he's just met. On the roof, he realizes that he likes them better than he did in the bar they'd come from, "at the same time he knew . . . that none of them, really, would ever get any closer to each other than they were right now" (*ENS*, 645). He stares into the sky above, which mirrors this benign informality he feels with his hip, white companions which itself is a reflection of the sterility of the American myth: "The sky looked, now, like a vast and friendly ocean, in which drowning was forbidden, and the stars seemed stationed there, like beacons. To what country did this ocean lead? for [*sic*] oceans always led to some great good place: hence, sailors, missionaries, saints, and Americans" (645). Hanging out with what the world would consider his peers, Vivaldo also senses, looming, a thick curtain between himself—under that sky—and his black friend, Rufus, now dead by suicide, and his girlfriend, Ida, who is Rufus's sister and who is also a singer. He knew that both Rufus and Ida descended from families for whom that ocean wasn't as friendly, having been prevented from accepting the myth of the "great good place" to which it had led their ancestors and having not found it in their own lives.

Whether it is reflected in the ocean or the sky, when familiarity can't become intimacy, talk will change the subject. Or at least try. Turns out, the hip kids also know Ida. Talk turns to her and Vivaldo sees a new sky suspended in his memory of Ida singing "a song [she] sometimes sang, puttering inefficiently about the kitchen":

**149**

Just above my head,
I hear music in the air.
And I really do believe
*There's a God somewhere.*
    (*ENS,* 646)

Vivaldo's no fool but he's not omniscient either. His dead friend's leap from the George Washington Bridge had left a shadow in the American myth, one he could neither erase nor accept. Somehow he senses that attempting to love Rufus's sister will allow him to deal with his friend's death and with the "un-American" sky under which that death happened. Under the remembered sound of Ida's voice, he wonders: "But was it *music* in the air, or *trouble* in the air?" And, the song changes:

Trouble in mind, I'm blue,
But I won't be blue always,
'Cause the sun's going to shine
*In my back door someday.*
    (*ENS,* 646)

Trying to find a familiar geography for the troubled music in the air, he thinks maybe of some distant, segregated social architecture and wonders, "Why *back* door?" Baldwin had marked that structure hovering before John Grimes in *Go Tell It on the Mountain,* and not in the South, where he wrote: "For him there was the back door, the dark stairs, and the kitchen or the basement" (*ENS,* 34). John's fate appears before him to refute the song's vision of possibility: "he could try until the sun refused to shine; they would never let him enter" (34). But, across the metaphoric tracks in that symbolic terrain the back door is also the personal, intimate meeting place, the unusual door. Back in *Another Country,* the question places Vivaldo, or so he thinks, beneath a different sky that "now seemed to descend, no longer phosphorescent with possibilities, but rigid with the mineral of choices, heavy as the weight of the finite earth, on his chest" (646).

Vivaldo's trying. But, he doesn't realize that it's impossible to hear a song—a lyric—that's exclusively about someone else; it's impossible to listen without one's own ears. One can't *observe* a lyric. He's confounded by the way a lyric operates according to geographies, and under skies, which can't be accounted for according to racially exclusive homelands. When he realizes that, then, he'll have to begin to deal with the signs hanging in that mutually riven sky, nonetheless. For the moment, that's an ocean he doesn't know is there, certainly isn't prepared to risk drowning in. Instead, he wonders about Ida's ears, thinking that it's *her* privacy in which the musical keys to the troubled sky will appear:

> What in the world did these songs mean to her? For he knew that she often sang them in order to flaunt before him privacies which he could never hope to penetrate and to convey accusations which he could never hope to decipher, much less deny. And yet, if he could enter this secret place, he would, by that act, be released forever from the power of her accusations. His presence in this strangest and grimmest of sanctuaries would prove his right to be there. (*ENS*, 646)

It's pretty clear that Vivaldo is not totally paranoid, that Ida *is* complexly attacking him partly for his passive role in her brother's death, partly to protect herself from the grief-stricken song in *her* ear. But, she is also attacking him for not knowing anything about the sky and ocean of a lover, a best friend, a million strangers who live, technically, in the same city that he does. And, finally, the song attacks him because he is sharp enough to sense the outrage in attempting to listen to a song with someone else's ears, of looking for shelter under someone else's sky, for mistaking privacy as a secret one keeps from someone else, and for solitude as something that respects individual autonomy. Ending their 1961 interview, Studs Terkel asked Baldwin the title of his forthcoming novel; Baldwin replied, "*Another Country*. It's about this country."[1]

"Trouble in Mind" was written by Richard M. Jones. Interesting. We know Baldwin's mother's name was Jones when he was born. And, John Grimes's biological father in *Go Tell It on the Mountain* was named Richard. Thelma La Vizzo first recorded the song on May 15, 1924, a few months before Baldwin was born on August 2. When Baldwin was working on *Another Country*, hit versions of the song were in the air. Dinah Washington had released a version in 1958 that echoed her hit (no. 4 on the R&B charts) with a studio recording of the song in 1952. And, Nina Simone's version of the song from the Newport Jazz Fest in July 1960 was also popular at the time.

The passage in *Another Country* made me wonder about an updated, citified blues that turns lyric phrases on dropped dimes. And, I heard Dinah Washington in *my* ear singing over Wynton Kelly's accompaniment at once elusive and present. In verse one, a redemptive black sun comes around the house and enters the back door. In verse two, after Ben Webster takes a chorus on tenor saxophone, the figure imagines escape, how else, via the railroad. The blues' knowing and sardonic take on the romance of escape:

> I'm going to lay my head
> On some lonesome railroad iron
> Let the 2:19 train ease my troubled mind.

I checked. Twenty-seven days after James Baldwin was born in Harlem, Ruth Jones was born in Tuscaloosa, Alabama, on August 29, 1924. By the time she was fifteen, she had moved with her mother to Chicago and was singing in blues clubs on the South Side. By the time she was nineteen, she had been renamed Dinah Washington and had gone on the road with Lionel Hampton.

"Trouble in Mind." Listen to Dinah Washington sing this song recorded on January 18, 1952. Baldwin was holed up with a few records by Fats Waller and Bessie Smith in Switzerland, finishing *Go Tell In on the Mountain* in a village where, he said, the villagers "really thought I had been sent by the Devil."[2] Baldwin was living with Lucien Happersberger, a Swiss man playing the role of wife in the domestic scene which Baldwin (if not Lucien), in a steely or even brutal way, understood could not really come down out of the mountains.[3] Working under a somewhat different sky, let's add the narrative element that Dinah Washington sang en route through six marriages in her forty-year life. But, no matter the specific minerals in the sky, this record is virtuosic lyrical precision. Listen to her put single notes on one-syllable words: the "two," of that "2:19," and "e" of that "ease." Then listen again and consider how she balances single notes against one- and two-syllable melismas that flutter under "iron" and "troubled." Arpeggiated syllables over Wynton Kelly's right hand coming down like the first bright drops in a sun shower. I would suggest these as instances of precisely the techniques, the basic tonal and rhythmic ingredients, at work in the lyrical point of view with which Baldwin credits the blues. As for this sky's lyrical minerals, call it part cinder block, part ripple effect.

In "The Uses of the Blues," a 1964 essay for *Playboy*, James Baldwin wrote that the blues comes from an impulse at the core of (and is itself a constituent element in) experience. He explicitly leaves behind discussions of generic boundaries: "The title, 'Uses of the Blues,' does not refer to music: I don't know anything about music. It does refer to the experience of life, of the state of being, out of which the blues come. . . . I'm using them as a metaphor—I might have titled this, for example, *The Uses of Anguish* or *The Uses of Pain*."[4] But, as Baldwin knew, the blues aren't reducible to the experience itself, they're not received passively (as in "I've got the blues"); the blues are active. They depend upon formal expertise and, simply put, a level of toughness, guts. Baldwin writes: "I want to talk about the blues not only because they speak of this particular experience of life and this state of being, but because they contain the toughness that manages to make this experience articulate. I am engaged, then, in a discussion of craft or, to use a very dangerous word, art."[5] This articulation is a lyrical endeavor; he argues that joy is simply lyrical pain. This might be what Joyce's Stephen Dedalus meant when he said, "Song is the simple rhythmic liberation of an emotion."[6] But it also echoes Pound's image, which he described as an "intellectual and emotional complex in an instant of time,"[7] and which was really the human, or modern, liberation of a fact. Such a lyric method, then, was a musical mode of animating facts, of investing them with existential authority for singers and poets in just the way that independent corroboration gave a fact authority for historians. Methods.

The blues carries an existential mandate emanating from beneath the intellectual and cultural buttresses of the modern self. It's no accident that the method of the blues comes from a modern community that lived for many generations without the philosophical and civic consolations of modernity (citizen's rights, individual autonomy, due process, etc.). A few months before "The Uses of the Blues" appeared, Baldwin, in the documentary *Take This Hammer*, said, "The only way to get through life is to know the worst things about it." In *Playboy* of all places, he wrote that such encounters offer a way to "walk away from the TV set, the Cadillac, and go into the chaos out of which and only out of which we can create ourselves as human beings."[8] Craft, lyric method, intercepts illusions and delusions that create the manifold dissociations of American life. To craft and art, Baldwin could have easily added work and labor to the short list of evaporating ingredients in a functional American self. As he saw it, a person "who has somehow managed to get to, let us say, the age of 40, and a great many of us do, without ever having been touched, broken, disturbed, frightened" is a dangerous character (*Cross*, 64). Aware that no one actually eludes these elements of experience, Baldwin argued that American culture prompted people to avoid internalizing them, to avoid creating, as it were, an experiential sense of self and world. One can then assume no authority and must forfeit the ability to take oneself seriously. Is this one result of American citizenship? In unassuming terms, the blues method suggests we think about that. Baldwin's essay underscores the suggestion already there in the music.

In "Sonny's Blues," Baldwin provides the contra fact to the cultural mandate for an even-keel, abstract sense of life in America. The narrator asks the very American question of what to do with the scars of experience if we can't always avoid or forget them. Sonny responds that the effort is to "keep from drowning in it, to keep on top of it, and to make it seem—well, like *you*" (*ENS*, 856). This is Vivaldo's dilemma on the rooftop. He has no name for *that* sky. This amounts to the deeply un-American tautology: one's lived life should bear some resemblance to the life one lives. Living experience. For Baldwin, the blues operates on tandem logical premises: first, "you can't know anything about life and suppose you can get through it clean"; second, that the "most monstrous people are those who think they are going to" do just that.[9]

It's interesting that about the same interval between their births, twenty-something days, separates the appearance of Baldwin's "The Uses of the Blues" in *Playboy*, January 1964, and Dinah Washington's death by overdose in Detroit, December 14, 1963. They were almost forty at the time. In "The Uses of the Blues," Baldwin "suggests that the anguish one finds in the blues, and the expression of it, creates also, however odd this may sound, a kind of joy."[10] This short sentence comes directly from what he had learned from art, in this case music, and sounds a pithy obituary for our hopes on behalf of a rational, emotional (one where divisions between pain and pleasure, good and bad, strength and weakness abide) foundation for our behaviors.

In so many words, he'd written this before. Baldwin's characters that learn anything learn this. In *Go Tell It on the Mountain*, we leave John Grimes exactly with his first first-person confrontation with the connection between joy and anguish. In "Sonny's Blues," Sonny and his brother come upon this wisdom from opposite directions; Rufus (possibly Baldwin's most densely interesting character), who is "alone and dying of it," seems to both encounter and avoid this truth at a pitch of deadly intensity; in *Just Above My Head*; Hall, Julia, Arthur Montana and his fellow Trumpets of Zion all learn this basic lesson in their own ways. All of Baldwin's characters pay a price for this wisdom. Some live it out, some don't.

Baldwin's phrase "the anguish one finds in the blues, and the expression of it, creates also, however odd this may sound, a kind of joy" sounds the indigestible precondition for living and learning in Baldwin's fictional worlds. In "The Uses of the Blues," he follows the link between anguish and joy with the following, somewhat brutal, categorical statement: "Now joy is a true state, it is a reality; it has nothing to do with what most people have in mind when they talk of happiness, which is not a real state and does not really exist" (*Cross*, 57). The lyrical slip—and the authority that comes from it—between joy and pain is the precondition, then, for *real* life and *real* learning. For Baldwin, happiness devoid of risk and pain is a fantasy. It isn't real, it cannot teach, learn, or love. With these two sentences, it strikes me that Baldwin is also naming key ingredients involved in the modern alchemy we know as "experience." He's talking about art and its inextricable but never identical relationship to life.

When Baldwin and the former Ms. Jones, by then Dinah Washington, were almost twenty, she recorded "Evil Gal Blues." She was only nineteen and by this time had already been on Chicago's most serious stages for nearly five years. The song ends with her indigestible:

> If you want to be happy,
> Don't hang around with me.
> Hmm I said if you want to be happy,
> Don't hang around with me.
> Cause I'm an evil gal and I want to set you free.

Just technically, for now, for a handbook on the manufacture and uses of joy, a study of what Dinah Washington did with the second A line (here and elsewhere) in the AAB lyrical structure of her blues recordings would be hard to beat. She states the basic anguish in the first line, a lyrical truth, a surprise. That's the first person. It's what Ralph Ellison called the "autobiographical chronicle" of the blues.[11] But, if the first line is the first person, who follows? Who arrives on the next beat, free enough to retrace the line (usually a description of personal torment) for the simple pleasure of it? And what Joyce called the "simple rhythmic liberation" of it?[12] The not-so-simple pain-pleasure of it. It's Jazz. The key is that second line, the unrepeated repetition. The slip between the first person and its mirror image. That anonymous, singular place between the first person and whomever follows. Me and my shadow blues. As background to the cover story on Baldwin for *Time* magazine published in May 1963, Roger Stone, who was traveling with him on a Core-sponsored speaking tour early that month, reported the following from the San Francisco Bureau:

> James Baldwin . . . is fond of telling a beautiful story with a quick twist. One of his current stable is about how he was walking along a quiet street in a pretty town on a sunshiny day. As he strolled along, he suddenly saw, on a quiet patch of green lawn, a father swinging his tiny, pretty daughter in the air. "It didn't last for more than a

second," says Baldwin. "But it was an unforgettable touch of beauty,
a glimpse of another world. Then I looked down and saw a shadow.
The shadow was a nigger—Me."[13]

Baldwin lived with Washington's lyrics, too. In his 1982 letter to his
friend David Moses, he concluded the first paragraph, "I got *bad* news,
baby, and you the *first* to know!"[14] Langston Hughes said, "the blues ain't
nothing but a good man feeling bad." In her second lines, as in "Evil Gal
Blues," Dinah Washington shows the blues is also about a *bad* woman
feeling good. Damned good. For now. And then what? In 1945, "Blow-
top Blues."

> I've got bad news baby and you're the first to know
> Yeah, I've got bad news baby and you're the first to know.
> I've discovered this morning that my top is about to blow.
>
> I'm a girl you can't excuse, I've got those blowtop blues.
>
> Last night I was five feet tall, today I'm eight feet ten.
> And every time I fall down stairs I float back up again.
> When someone turned the lights on me it liked to drove me blind
> I woke up in Bellevue and left my mind behind.
>
> I'm a gal who blew a fuse, I've got those blowtop blues.

In "The Uses of the Blues," (after citing Bessie Smith and Billie Holiday) Baldwin writes: "I'm trying to suggest . . . a triumph here—which
is a very un-American triumph . . . they were commenting on [experi-
ence] a little bit outside it: they were accepting it. . . . It's this passionate
detachment, this inwardness coupled with outwardness" (*Cross*, 59). As
discussed in Book I, this is the most crucial goal of Baldwin's aesthetics:
an imagined balance, which allows things, *real* things, to come and go.
The basic phase change (from pain to joy) of lyricism: solid pain made
fluid. Joy. He thought by that motion experience became active, transformed from an inert thing, a dead weight one had to endure into a living
something one could bear, and then change. It's a way of handling ambiguity, a condition high on Baldwin's list of key American repudiations.
But, that's art. Lyrics. They are tangent to experience. Strictly speaking,
one can't, as it were, live there. The lives of all the artists Baldwin cites (of
course, including his own) clearly demonstrate this. For many artists, the
measured control they demonstrate over this key lyric alchemy (pain and
joy) sits in drastic contrast to the way they flail wildly in their experience.

The flailing in life, of course, is what artists have in common with
most (all?) people. The uncommon things are the lyrics of surprising,

coherent clarity. This seems obvious but, as discussed in Chapter 7, American culture often concludes the opposite, holding scandals of artists and performers up to the would-be coherent opprobrium of public, common sense and avoiding the deep sense of the lyrics. Is this an accident? Hardly. It's the meat and potatoes bait and switch in a consumer public's neurotic relationship, or thrall, to popular culture. But there's an irreplaceable energy in the chaos of connection as well.

In *Another Country*, Vivaldo wants to lie beneath the sky of Ida's song. The only route to her sky, he's beginning to fear, is dealing with the minerals in *his* sky, the same *and* different from hers. Lyricism like that of the blues is the art it is, in fact, exactly because of the steady stream of the failures at acceptance of experience. We don't consciously internalize our lives. Strictly speaking, none of us live where we are if for no other reason than we all occupy several (only partially overlapping) places at once. We can't, therefore, fully accept anguish or anything else. That's but one key to the dangers and delusions of American innocence. As far as anguish goes, it strikes me that if we do accept it, and to this exact degree, it ceases to deserve the name, anguish. So, (nearly by axiom) no one accepts it, let's accept that. "No one," as Baldwin says in *Take This Hammer*, "pays their dues willingly." We all craft our approaches to experience as it crafts its superior approach to us. No one is smarter than one's own life. In "Sonny's Blues," Sonny says, "Nobody just takes it!" In the blues, there are no gurus. As Baldwin wrote in his letters to his brother, in this sense, life can't be known and so must be trusted. Every word unsays half of what it says and then says something else. Dialectics, at least. But, that it's ambiguous doesn't mean it can't be clearly (as clearly as possible) put. Which doesn't, of course, ensure it'll be heard. But, as with Holiday and Catlett, Miles, Page and others, we see that it *can* be both said and heard.

During much of the 1960s and 1970s, while he excavated the culture and wrote and talked about facing facts, I wonder how many hours Baldwin logged in airplanes in flight from his immediate reactions to events (public and private) in his own life? This is what Elia Kazan meant when he told Alex Haley that "Jimmy is a slippery fish. I don't mean he's fishy, I mean he's slippery."[15] Kazan knew that, if the Malcolm X project had any hope at all, he and Haley would "have to turn Jimmy around and point him to the table with the typewriter on it." It can't be work if one really wants to do it. It can't be art if one isn't at least a little afraid of it. Experience is that way. Family. In a way propelled by the realization that he would never work again as a drummer, Rufus rides straight through Harlem on his way to the George Washington Bridge. He's "alone and dying of it," but he won't stop and talk with his sister, Ida. That's one mineral in Ida's sky she's trying to hold over Vivaldo's head. Dues *she* won't pay willingly. Ida's ace—and also her most serious risk—is that cast of characters in *Another Country* largely lack the authority to call her on it, to help her face it. If Vivaldo, who seems for much of the novel to get younger by the hour, ever grows up, he might help. No such white American figure, however, ever appears in Baldwin's subsequent novels.

As mentioned earlier, in a 1987 piece for *Architectural Digest,* Baldwin traces the slippery route by which he came to live in St. Paul de Vence (where among other things, incidentally, his writing studio was once the studio of Georges Braque), Baldwin wrote: "I wandered around . . .— directed a play in Istanbul, for example, visited London, visited Italy. For some reason, I don't know why, I seem to have avoided France. I collapsed physically several times and when I came back to Paris I collapsed again. Friends then shipped me, almost literally, out of the American Hospital to Saint Paul de Vence. It was grief I had been avoiding, which was why I had collapsed."[16] As he writes about these kinds of failures at acceptance, this avoidance (itself failed as well, of course), in "The Uses of the Blues," he concludes simply, "we all do this all the time, of course"; the point of which has a whole lot to do with the inimical quip a few lines above when he writes, "When I say Negro, it's a digression. . . . I'm not talking about a people but a person" (*Cross,* 60). By this distinction, Baldwin signals an open-ended, private calculus behind any public drama or issue. A wheel of *who* questions inside the wheel of *what* issues. He maintains that there's always an unknown shadow behind anything standing in the light of day.

"Negro . . . a digression," yes, but an important one. Baldwin insists on the importance of race in thousands of places. In others he argues that it's a ruse, a digression. In a 1961 symposium that included Baldwin, Langston Hughes, Lorraine Hansberry, Alfred Kazin, Nat Hentoff, and Emile Capouya, Hughes says that he considers Baldwin "one of the most racial of our writers, in spite of his analysis of himself as otherwise on occasion."[17] Both objecting and accepting Hughes's observation, Baldwin responded, simply, "Later for you. (*laughter*)."[18]

"We all do this all the time," but which *we* is this? In "The Uses of the Blues," Baldwin sketches the "Negro experience of life" and the "American dream or sense of life" and admits that it would "be hard to find any two things more absolutely opposed." Ray Charles and Doris Day, here as elsewhere in Baldwin's work, stand in as emblematic figures of this difference. That particular feature of apartheid didn't last. It's precarious to imagine that the clarity (at least in hindsight) such stabilities offered weren't inextricable from lethal forces of mass economic and social violence. And Dinah Washington often performed with one foot in each world (as had Billie Holiday).

Nonetheless, after the image of cultural apartheid, of cultural codes "absolutely opposed," Baldwin returns to a transracial statement in "The Uses of the Blues": "We all do this all the time." Just beneath that, the perspectives (black and white) diverge when he writes: "He [the negro] doesn't want anything you've got, he doesn't believe anything you say" (Cross, 61). Clear (if impossible) enough. Immediately, and ambiguously, following, he writes: "I don't know why and I don't know how America arrived at this particular point of view." Precisely because Baldwin's collective "America" teeters here between twin (white and black) racial digressions, it's tempting to paraphrase this as an open-ended query into the origins of the passionate detachment, the inward outwardness, of the blues itself. Critics have argued that Baldwin's American we—in essays such as "Many Thousands Gone"—is written in the voice of white America. But, understandable as that is, that's really Vivaldo's delusional sky. Baldwin's deployment of pronouns—to say nothing of the transracial cultural stakes of American life—is far more complex than that. Through this racial-ish shifting of personae and perspective, Baldwin suggests that, in America, everything is both always and simultaneously never about race. If so, a provisional answer that conserves the basic ambiguities closes the paragraph. Returning to the (can I say?) transdigressive we, Baldwin writes: "We came from Europe, we came from Africa, we came from all over the world. We brought whatever was in us from China or from France. We all brought it with us. We were not transformed when we crossed the ocean. Something else happened. Something much more serious. We no longer had any way of finding out, of knowing who we were" (Cross, 61). Baldwin's trans-digressive we is a point of view that didn't exist but said it did. He made it up as a riddle for those that said they existed but didn't. It's from exactly this point of view, pushed to extremes, in No Name in the Street, that he wrote, "there are no Americans yet" (CE, 358).

Now, when Baldwin concludes as he does many, many times (possibly most powerfully in the dialogue between Guy and Arthur in Just Above My Head) that "our history is each other," this is what he means. This is not a Hallmark slogan. He means that we, in each other's eyes, are the only evidence left. In this way, it's arguable that Americans mean things to each other with a unique kind of intensity. I think it also implies the (otherwise inexplicable) force of black music's obsession with interpersonal relationships. When the verse of the song says, "the little girl's all I got" it means something to a black man (an American) that it might not mean to anyone else on the planet. It's a beautiful and terrible burden for people to carry for each other and that pressure really does explain something about the smiling faces singing songs of pain and the painful faces singing songs of love and togetherness. And it also explains a lot about all the people listening over each other's shoulders. This blues triumph, the rare statement ("here I am, here we are") appears in and through the technical and existential complexities of Dinah Washington's phrasings above. This confounds the oceanfront sky view of the Vivaldos of the world. It torments the Idas of the world and has killed many Rufuses. By now, we all have all those minerals in our skies. In our eyes.

In life I think this is also the very bottom of why most Americans don't look at each other or why we see (and don't see) what we do (and don't) when we look. And, as D. H. Lawrence noted in the 1920s, why we fear each other possibly in ways (in shallows and depths, alone and in a crowd) unlike any other people.[19] It's also a clue as to why such basic things remain so mysterious and unacknowledged in American life. In 1960 Baldwin told Chicago journalist Studs Terkel that the key to understanding the antics of all these, what he termed, "success-ridden" American lifestyles is our failure to accept the following insight: "Life is difficult, very difficult for anybody, anybody born."[20] He credited the clarity to a conversation he'd had with Ingmar Bergman in October 1959. It seems obvious. But, one cannot know this about one's transcendental life. This isn't a matter of contemplation but of life lived in real relation to real people; if you can find any. But, to find real people you've got to *be* one. And, no one does that willingly. No one can do it alone. Paradox blues.

In "The Uses of the Blues," Baldwin concludes that people who can't accept this basic rule become "the most monstrous people" (*Cross*, 65). Without the blues, your enemies *are* your friends. One's strengths (to feel and accept the ambiguities of life) are regarded as weaknesses and one's weaknesses (one's repudiations) become signs of strength. One needs the repudiations. It's an addiction. From the distance of this addiction, the world appears, at first belated glance, opaque and terrifying. Other. Finally, Baldwin leaps to conclude "The Uses of the Blues" with the claim that the "fantastic disaster which we call American politics and which we call American foreign policy . . . is an exact reflection of the incoherence" produced, in private, by the American failure to accept the most basic facts of life. And it makes an elegant sense. What other people ever declared wars on basic human givens like poverty and terror? Doesn't this echo precisely armies in Herodotus wielding swords and marching against the desert winds? What other people claim, fantastically, that human life can be made to be happy, clean, and safe? Can't we easily imagine people gripped in this delusion going to war against "terror" and or trying to stab a sand dune to death?

All this does indeed, as Baldwin admits, "[claim] a great deal for the blues." It claims a lot for the lyric. I guess the question this leaves me with is: What does it mean, really, to depend upon lyrics, on the gap between the person and what the person sees when they look in the mirror? On surprises? To see one's own sky with other people's stars, an ocean that reflects other people's journeys and one's own journey in ways that aren't labeled like Birmingham drinking fountains in 1955. In "The Uses of the Blues," Baldwin suggests that the conflict between the "negro experience of life" and "the American sense of life . . . thus give[s] [a black man] his freedom" (*Cross*, 60). That's a lyric space. So in Baldwin's thought, the widespread foreclosure of American charades of happy, clean, and safe lives (of "whiteness") to black people brought on a historical kind of anguish that, when clearly—lyrically—grasped, ushers in the possibility of *joy*. No wonder, in 1949, he focused upon the deadly business of "becoming more American everyday."[21] How different, then, does Dinah Washington sound when, at nineteen, and in the persona of the *evil* gal, she casts happy people to the side and claims the aim to set you free.

I'm told that it's an inescapable fact of the postmodern that all truths are partial. More than just partial, the facts of life are in conflict. This is nothing new and it's really not post-anything other than a certain American innocence. Baldwin's joy, at times he calls it freedom, is a matter of finding a fluid, lyric tension in the conflict. Joy is pain (chaos) ordered, made fluid and rhythmic, in a lyric. In "The Uses of the Blues" and elsewhere, Baldwin's self-lacerating intelligence shows this in surprise after surprise. Like Dinah Washington's second lines, even the repetitions are new. With that sense of razor-edged lyricism, it's time to have a close listen to Baldwin's time onstage with the male singer whose voice meant the most to him, Ray Charles. And, we'll listen to what reviewers heard and didn't hear as they listened over their shoulders.

# 6

## "But Amen is the price"
### James Baldwin and Ray Charles in "The Hallelujah Chorus"

Lights dim.

Shortly after 6 PM on July 1, 1973, the audience in Carnegie Hall heard Ray Charles's solo piano lilt out the opening, brightly lit and darkly toned choruses of his classic "Sweet Sixteen Bars." A brilliant, seemingly effortless contest between simplicity and complexity, between joy and sorrow, invention and tradition, played out as Ray touched the keys. That sound bore musical witness to how a deft sense of simple touch can signal a basis for complex human presence. A political complexity. It carried clues to how history exists in the present tense of presence-sense; how the past happens, between people in the ways they touch, stay in touch, and in the ways they fail and fall out of touch in everyday life. Standing behind the curtain while Ray played was the slim figure of James Baldwin, the most famous black writer in the world.

Such a complexly veiled and engaged sense of music informed the core of Baldwin's life and work. In one of his earliest essays "Many Thousands Gone" (1951), Baldwin wrote that it was "only in his music . . . that the Negro in America has been able to tell his story. It is a story which otherwise has yet to be told and which no American is prepared to hear" (*CE*, 19). Twenty-two years later, there he was sharing one of the nation's biggest stages with his favorite singer in "The Hallelujah Chorus," a performance he had designed to explore who was prepared to hear what.

After a few minutes, the curtain would rise to reveal Charles, aka "the genius," sitting at a concert grand piano, flanked, as was customary, by

Ray Charles and James Baldwin (and the Raelettes to the right) onstage in Carnegie Hall performing "The Hallelujah Chorus." (Courtesy AP Photo / J. J. Lent.)

his orchestra on one side. On the other, stood the Raelettes behind microphone stands in concert-length, matching gingham dresses. Nothing unusual there. For Ray Charles, rare brilliance of sound and presentation had come to pass for normal, maybe even *natural*, in the minds of his critics and his audience. It was the unofficial opening of the the Newport . Jazz Festival-New York, performed at venues across the city between June 29 and July 8. Including popular black acts such as Donny Hathaway, the Staple Singers, Stevie Wonder, and Aretha Franklin, the aim was to extend the reach of "Newport Jazz" to black audiences in the city. All seemed normal enough at the outset even if the music Charles opened with cast its arm back to his jazz and blues recordings of the 1950s. Something was bound to be different about this concert. The audience had come out that Sunday evening, after all, to be witness to: "JOS. SCHLITZ BREWING COMPANY SALUTES 'THE LIFE AND TIMES OF RAY CHARLES' as written and narrated by James Baldwin and featuring Ray Charles and Cicely Tyson."[1]

## Curtain

Downstage at a podium, or, as it was, in the pulpit, listening to, or *washed* in, the rhythm of Charles's somehow intensely languid sound, stood Baldwin. Since July 1969, when he left Hollywood and returned to Istanbul—aborting his attempt to adapt Alex Haley's *The Autobiography of Malcolm X* to the screen with, or against, Columbia Studios—Baldwin had become increasingly reluctant, angular, and unpredictable as a spokesman for black America; in addition to being a famous writer, he was a cultural celebrity, whose public profile was, at the time, turbulent. Many thought then that Baldwin's relevance was fading, that his profile was in decline. In fact, he'd been shifting his methods in a mix of conscious determination and unconscious intuition. As he often put it, he was flying by radar.

Since his exploded visibility propelled him into a position as a kind of prophetic celebrity in 1963, Baldwin had interrogated and confronted the terms of his own success. On June 26, 1972, looking back on his career, he told George Goodman of the *New York Times*: "I myself began as a kind of dancing dog. There are still some people who think poets can be safely accommodated within the system."[2] Owing to his shifting approach to engagement with the page as well as with his life and the stage, Baldwin's reputation as a literary genius was under some mix of dispute and attack. Responding to conscious and unconscious needs, he crafted his public persona into a lyrical mix of mystery and confrontational clarity. In ways unlike most of his high-profile friends and colleagues who were entertainers (Sidney Poitier, Lena Horne, Marlon Brando, Harry Belafonte, Ava Gardner, Ray Charles, and others), Baldwin had positioned and repositioned his life, his image, and his work so that it seemed to be many things, but never normal and rarely natural.[3]

The controversy associated with his career, especially as it might affect his family, had tormented Baldwin from the beginning. By 1973, they all knew that they would have to accept it. Baldwin would even argue that their dangerous *fate* must be embraced. In his latest book, *No Name in the Street*, released in May 1972 to stormy and mixed reviews—reviews which, Baldwin told his brother, were consciously and unconsciously motivated to hurt, even to destroy—about his audience, and even some of his friends, he had concluded: "I had to face more about them than they could know about me, knew their rent, whereas they did not know mine, and was condemned to make them uncomfortable" (*CE*, 365). As a basic frame, Baldwin wrote in his 1964 essay, "The White Problem": "In this country, for a dangerously long time, there have been two levels of experience. One—to put it cruelly, but, I think, quite truthfully—can be summed up in the images of Doris Day and Gary Cooper: two of the most grotesque appeals to innocence the world has ever seen. And the other, subterranean, indispensible, and denied, can be summed up, let us say, in the tone and in the face of Ray Charles" (*Cross*, 78). In ways that by 1973, he felt, were condemned to be disruptive and in ways that were also on the verge of being simply disregarded, Baldwin clearly hoped to lift the indispensible touch and presence of Ray Charles to the cultural surface such that it couldn't be denied by everyone. The response to "The Hallelujah Chorus," in fact, presents a detailed chart of the ways critics displaced disruption with disregard, or even ill regard, when it came to Baldwin's work of the era.

It was a performance billed by renowned jazz producer and founder of the Newport Jazz Festival, George Wein, as "a unique experience in theatrical concert presentation"[4] and described after the fact by *Jet* magazine as "a bit of theatrics, a touch of oratory and some righteous jazz music."[5] Authored and directed by Baldwin, the performance spliced together a conversation between himself and Ray Charles, solo and ensemble performances by Charles, and dramatic presentation of excerpts from "Sonny's Blues." Three actors performed: Baldwin's brother and principle confidant, a professional singer and actor himself, David Baldwin; Baldwin's close friend, actor, his preferred barber in Los Angeles, and a model for the character of Joseph Rivers in Baldwin's next novel, *If Beale Street Could Talk* (1974), David Moses; and the then recently Oscar-nominated (*Sounder*, 1972) actress, Cicely Tyson. Described as the opening show for the festival in New York, "The Hallelujah Chorus" was performed twice (6 PM and 10 PM) as the near-ninety degree afternoon heat cooled into evening. As it happened, it was a show jazz critics weren't prepared to hear. And, it was a performance even Baldwin's most assiduous critics and biographers have almost totally ignored.

The reviews of "The Hallelujah Chorus" may or may not have been meant to destroy, but they would hurt.[6] And, they most certainly would challenge any connection a general audience might have been inclined to take away from the confluence of Ray Charles's "natural" musical genius and James Baldwin's prophetic insurgency in American culture. In remarks about the concert, jazz critic Whitney Balliett wrote that Charles and Baldwin "were born poor, black, and gifted, but beyond that they have little in common."[7] In the end, opined Balliett, "trying to weld their alien souls didn't make sense." The performers, on the other hand, had a sense of connection that refuted the perspective of the jazz critics typified by Balliett's comments. In an interview for the *New York Times* printed the day before the show, Baldwin said, "I come out of the church and so does he. . . . That's the basis of his sound, and it's the sound I was born hearing."[8] Whatever the critics meant to do, their dismissal of "The Hallelujah Chorus" attacked the possibility of the touch and presence it meant to convey and did what it could to erase any serious contemporary consideration it may have provoked. In the forty years since its high-profile debut, the piece has totally vanished from the record. One wonders what we might hear, now, if we cast our listening back and bring Baldwin's urgent, even insurgent, sense of Ray Charles's touch and presence into our hearing and serious consideration. In his novel *Molloy*, Samuel Beckett's afflicted traveler informs, "I began to think, that is to say to listen harder."[9] So, listening, now, both to and with Baldwin, let's see what *we* can hear.

## Toward Fluent Presence, a Sense of Healthy Touch

Baldwin was born in Harlem in 1924 and left New York in 1948 for Paris. In the decades that followed that first big move, he constantly traveled between venues, from New York to Tallahassee to Selma to San Francisco to Stockholm, from Jerusalem to Nairobi to Dakar, and from Broadway to Hollywood, where he could directly experience and *engage* a rapidly politicizing and internationalizing American culture. And, from positions in and around Paris, from Fire Island to London, from Ibiza to Istanbul, he searched out locations where he could hole up and *write* about his experiences dispatching articles, essays, interviews, novels, and plays that circulated across the globe but were almost always designed, as he would put it, to "*do* something," to hit home, at home.

The peregrine structure of his experience had shown Baldwin that the lives of those people he most wanted to save, namely his family and friends, were inextricably linked to each other and, moreover, connected to others in complex networks and circles of expanding circumference. Manhattan connected directly to Charlotte and Macon, Chicago to Jackson and Birmingham, Los Angeles to Shreveport and Houston, Paris to Freetown, Tunis, Algiers, and Saigon. These and other kinds of networks connected people all over the globe. On levels and in ways for which there was no available vocabulary, Baldwin sensed, these lives touched each other. These connections, for him, were historical and political, not mystical. The nonetheless ineffable links between people created social presences, experiential realities that were not under the control of any individual, nor were they intelligible from any one of the connected realities alone. Absent sufficient discourse, these realities, effectively, had no name. The result was a sense of connection that, he had observed, provoked profound fear, even panic, within and between persons, within and between peoples, and even within and between nations.

On other levels and in other ways, as numerous commentators observed at the time, American life in the postwar years threatened to reduce people to cogs in a mechanical wheel. Rationalization. Racial divisions and sexual taboos policed the borders between the resulting, so-called rational, stratifications between a capstone of successful, if neurotic, elites, a thin, anxiety-ridden middle band of undetermined qualification, and the broad-based tenuousness of working-class and poverty-ridden sectors of the American geographical and economic pyramid. All levels, but especially those at the top, Baldwin observed, in *No Name in the Street*, were plagued "by an emotional poverty so bottomless, and a terror of human life, of human touch, so deep, that virtually no American appears to be able to achieve any viable, organic connection between his public stance and his private life" (*CE, 385*). The violence inherent in the situation manifested when mythologies about *what* people were supposed to be thwarted connections between *who* people actually were and, at the same time, when other, more private fantasies about *who* people were supposed to be were impugned by the so-called facts of *what* people actually were. The result, Baldwin thought, made Americans uniquely reluctant to experience experience itself. Having lived on four continents of the U.S., D. H. Lawrence observed: "I have never been in any country where the individual has such an abject fear of his fellow countrymen."[10]

In general, Baldwin's call from the Carnegie Hall stage would be familiar to anyone who had heard him speak recently. One must say amen to life, forgo delusions of personal safety, and accept the twists and turns of experience in attempts to remain in touch with others doing the same. A denied experience *can't* be changed; from a sense of connected presence, however, serious and meaningful personal and political change was possible. What wouldn't have been known was the radical nature of Baldwin's own amens at the time. His life in 1973 was far too *political* to qualify for what most Americans would consider *personal*, and, at home and abroad, the FBI surveillance alone prevented any sense he might have had that people would have recognized as *privacy*. Whatever he said or did, he assumed, was already "on the wire." Nonetheless, even by his standards, the life he *did* have was uncommonly intense during the months of 1973 bracketing the performance of "The Hallelujah Chorus."

In April 1973, his closest friend and mentor, the painter Beauford Delaney, then living in Clamart-Seine outside of Paris, experienced acute psychological lapses requiring Baldwin to step in as Delaney's legal guardian. Baldwin had recently found an agent he trusted, a young black American woman living in Paris named Tria French. Unlike his representation in the states, she was game to work with him in an intensifying, years-long, quasi-legal, international battle with his American publisher, the Dial Press, over existing and future contracts. The battle was tumult enough. But, tragically, also in April, Tria French died suddenly of a cerebral hemorrhage leaving Baldwin grieving, financially strapped, legally vulnerable, and, for a period, in charge of her two young children.

Baldwin's intimate life at the time was likewise complex. However, he was learning, firsthand and for the first time, the extent to which human touch and presence involved an erotic life laced with confrontation, revelation, *and*, something new to him, surrender. In vivid ways, in enabling and disabling ways, he could sense how public and political fears and desires found their way into intimate and erotic reaches of life and vice versa. His experience then centered on what he thought of as a marriage to an Italian painter, Yoran Cazac, who was also married to a woman with whom he had two children. The "marriage" between Baldwin and Cazac—which included a visit in April 1973 (on Easter Sunday) to Cazac's home village in Italy for his son's baptism where Baldwin was named the child's godfather—would propel Baldwin toward a new point of view. What he learned from his connection to Cazac would directly inform his 1979 novel, *Just Above My Head*, his most fully and explicitly musical novel and his most deeply realized and profound exploration of human erotic, moral, and political experience.[11] Much of the energy of their relationship is likewise visible in Cazac's dazzling illustrations for Baldwin's 1976 children's book based on one of his beloved nephews, *Little Man, Little Man*.

Meanwhile, politically related uncertainties jeopardized Baldwin's permanent resident status in France, status necessary to complete his purchase of the residence where he'd been living in St. Paul de Vence—the money for which purchase depended upon his winning the war with the publishers who were at the time (fraudulently, he believed) controlling his income. Amidst these intrigues, in early June 1973, internationally known fugitive Eldridge Cleaver had begun to contact Baldwin seeking assistance. Ultimately, about two weeks before returning to the United States to meet Ray Charles and rehearse "The Hallelujah Chorus," Cleaver's messenger arrived at Baldwin's house in St. Paul de Vence with a tape-recorded request for ten thousand dollars. Under multiple kinds of pressure and, essentially, not trusting phones, his mail, or anyone outside his family and a very close-knit circle of friends at the time—what he called his "tribe"—Baldwin sent the messenger away with a vague commitment. He concluded that Cleaver was either extremely politically naïve or desperate, or that he'd become little more than a hustler or even an agent. It was from a maelstrom containing these pressures among others that Baldwin reentered the United States—during an era of widespread political violence—to say "Amen," to implore people to be present in their lives and works in ways that go beyond the taboos and divisions. And Ray was there to depict, in sound, what it meant to say "Hallelujah" in response.

Baldwin's creative vision, ca. 1973, of a society "in touch" with itself and present across its differences was widely resisted then and is often misunderstood—or simply avoided—now. The vision then was as demanding as his personal life was complex. Neither the demands nor the complexities were totally new, of course. In his 1959 essay "The Discovery of What it Means to Be an American," he wrote: "I was born in New York, but have lived in only pockets of it. In Paris, I lived in all parts of the city—on the Right Bank and the Left, among the bourgeoisie and among *les misérables*, and knew all kinds of people, from pimps and prostitutes in Pigalle to Egyptian Bankers in Neuilly. This may sound extremely unprincipled or even obscurely immoral: I found it healthy" (*CE*, 140). From his point of view, in 1973, the anxiety-ridden upper classes, their brokers in the middle, the tenuous workers, and the poverty-ridden oppressed were all connected; their sense of themselves depended upon their sense of each other. Until the nation achieved some form of fluency with itself across those divisions, that is, until people became able to envision mobility in terms other than the mythic-schizoid fracture between a hopeful *upward* and a paranoiac *downward*, Americans' sense of human touch and mutual human presence would be unhealthy, menaced—and so, in turn, menace all it did touch—at every level of experience from intimate and personal to international and political.

"The Hallelujah Chorus" came together in Baldwin's mind in precisely these terms, an exemplification of healthy cultural presence, of the sound of being in touch. In the interview for the *New York Times* published the day before the concert, sitting in his Plaza Hotel suite, Baldwin described his time with Charles in Los Angeles the previous week. Being in Charles's midst, Baldwin sensed how the singer defied Americans' poverty-of-presence and their dangerously *out-of-touch* way of being in their lives and in the world: "I just hung around a lot, watching him playing and talking. What struck me was his sense of touch, of presences entering or leaving a room, his fantastic ear."[12]

In Baldwin's mind, American culture was dangerously lacking in presence and touch at many levels. *No Name in the Street* documents the sexual and political violence that follows alienation at various levels of experience. The narrative depicts how former friends and acquaintances had become strangers from connections, especially family, connections in their lives that he considered basic facts of life. A few months before the Carnegie date, in February 1973, Baldwin had traveled to Germany where the Stuttgart branch of the NAACP was to be inaugurated. Describing the event that took place in the Mozart Saal of the Liederhalle for *Stars and Stripes*, Ed Reavis wrote: "A white man stands up ... and asks how, and in what direction, he should turn to seek a new identity in a culture that is not exclusive."[13] From forty years in the future, we can plainly see how Baldwin's response frames both his vision in "The Hallelujah Chorus" and the critics' resistance to it:

> Your history is not your fault. But there it is. I'm not trying to put you down but give you a sensible answer. Now, for all practical purposes, your situation would be very different, and your question would scarcely exist if America had a culture. Now, having said that, I mean, the Americans as a nation cannot be considered to have a culture, as no one can discover what it is that they have in common or respect except things, and that does not make a culture. They also have in common a certain terror and a certain hidden shame and despair, none of which makes a culture, either. Now, what you have to do with all that in order to free yourself from what I referred to as your history is, first of all, accept that history. Learn to accept, for example, that the American people never honored a single treaty that they made with the Indians, not one. That means that you are the issue of a very dishonorable people. Now, if you can get that far, you can also see that to condemn a culture is not to condemn a nation nor all the people in it. If you can get that far, you can see that American Slavery had two faces and still has two faces. One of them is visible, and that's my face, because the Americans imagine that I am their slave, but that other face is your face and that's the keystone to American slavery: what is happening to you. Now, it's not a matter of your fighting for my liberty, it's a matter of your contending with your parents, with your leaders for your life![14]

Baldwin's advice that the man reorient himself to his familiar frames of reference, the reality of his racial identity—a reality largely unexamined among white people frozen by associated guilt and blinded by what is termed "privilege"—among them, in fact, has a complex and contested career of its own. In 1962—in a letter from Loèche-les Bains, Switzerland, to his agent, Bob Mills, eventually published in *Harper's* (1963)—Baldwin had written: "There is a very grim secret hidden in the fact that so many of the people one hoped to rescue could not be rescued because the prison of color had become their hiding place" (*Cross*, 198). In the early 1960s, Baldwin could see Americans furnishing enclaves of color in which—from his perspective, that is from the perspective of the kind of touch and presence an actual culture entails—the principle differences among projects, condos, and prison cells were essentially matters of décor. Writing to Mills, he continued, "I have said for years that color does not matter. I am now beginning to feel that it does not matter, *at all*, that it masks something else that *does* matter" (198). His comments to the white man in Germany trace a route through precisely this terrain. One must, in essence, *accept* the false door, a door nonetheless made real by the lies and violence of American history and present-day sociological, so-called, reality, in order to contend at all with the harder, durable truths of human life. Functional reckonings with real human questions were impossible from *any* one position within the "prison of color" fundamental to existing cultural, personal, and psychological experience. Such was the American dilemma, positioned in uncomfortable proximity to a blues-laced version of the human condition, in Baldwin's view at the time.

In the 1960s, in dispatches from four continents, Baldwin moved through these options and their implications with an analytical ferocity few could follow intellectually and very, very few could actually attempt in their lives. In mainstream terms, people's would-be sense of *who* they were, as he had observed in his letter from Switzerland, was largely hiding out, obsessed with its particular choice of curtains, within the—unasked—question of *what* they were, a question involving everyone directly with the "prison of color." Of course, black people's sense of these dimensions of identity had, basically always, been undeniably tangled. The protest movements in the South were, among many other things, an attempt to untangle—but not to detach—these questions so that the relationships could be acknowledged, and then *changed*. The American twin fantasies of individuality and transcendence simply couldn't answer the realities. By 1973, in saying "American slavery had two faces," Baldwin was signifying his awareness that the dissonance between *who* and *what* people were in American life involved everyone. In order for a white man to be free, he would have to confront *what* the world—the white and nonwhite worlds—saw when it looked at him. And that confrontation was and is almost meaningless in strictly individual terms.

This unnamed dissonance had been brewing in Baldwin's work and mind since at least the mid-1950s. As discussed in Chapter 3, in July 1961 a breakthrough seems to have occurred when he was asked, pointedly, both *who* and *what* he was during the same visit to Chicago. We have evidence of the first question. It came from Studs Terkel who interviewed Baldwin for Chicago Public Radio during a publicity tour for his second book of essays, *Nobody Knows My Name*. At the close of a searching conversation, after detailing Baldwin's career—and after asking, hopefully, if his first novels were still in print—Terkel opts for a personal ending: "Perhaps one last question, James Baldwin, who are you, now?" And, Baldwin, in concert with the depth of the conversation, pauses thoughtfully, and responds with a kind of gentle precision: "Hm. Who indeed?" After seconds of open air, he continues: "Well, I may not be able to tell you quite who I am. But I think I'm discovering who I'm not."[15] Letting his punctuated last syllable sound into an audibly deep breath, he changes his approach. He tries going back to the 1955 "Autobiographical Notes"—an author's questionnaire—from his previous book of essays, *Notes of a Native Son*: "I want to be an honest man. And I want to be a good writer" (*CE*, 9). But, even his actor's sense of timing and heartfelt inflection can't save it from its rehearsed, bygone ring; so, he tries again and, in so doing, shifts the terms of the question: "And, I don't know if one *ever* gets to be what one wants to be." In a way that almost emphasizes the music, again, he gets out of the scene: "I think you just have to play it by ear, and pray for rain."[16]

Evidence of the second question comes from Baldwin's most high-profile single piece, "Down at the Cross," published in the November 17, 1962, issue of *The New Yorker*. During the same visit to Chicago where he had talked with Terkel, sitting at dinner in the Hyde Park home of Elijah Muhammad, head of the Nation of Islam, Baldwin recounted his failure to answer Elijah's religiously and politically inflected question, "And what are you, now?" (*CE*, 327). Unable to accept Muhammad's rigid racial expectations, and conscious of the irrelevance, at least in this setting, of the personal responses available to him as a *writer*, Baldwin's most high-profile essay records his defeat in debate. Leaving his rhetorical chin—for Baldwin, improbably—wide open, he finally responds, lying, "I don't, anyway, . . . think about it a great deal." Muhammad seizes the opening in front of his followers at the table, "I think he ought to think about it *all* the deal" (327). The conversation then culminates in an impasse that left the famously articulate Baldwin speaking without speaking:

"(I said to myself, but not to Elijah) ... isn't love more important than color?" (327). Even his literary persona ca. 1962 knew better than to ask this question out loud at Elijah Muhammad's house in Chicago, on the South Side, with "a million in captivity—stretching from this door step as far as the eye could see" (321). Baldwin could feel that what, or rather *who*, his writer's mind had on its mind wasn't relevant to Elijah Muhammad's resolutely social and starkly racial concerns. Nor, when he thought about it, was it relevant to the "million in captivity" themselves, "they didn't even read ... don't have the time or energy to spare" (321).

But, in saying it to himself, Baldwin asked that question of his readers in *The New Yorker* as well. And, by the time the essay was in print and the book version, *The Fire Next Time*, was in its place—call it captivity, the "dancing dog"[17]—at the top of the nonfiction best-seller's list in 1963, Baldwin could sense the answer to his parenthetical question on behalf of "liberal" America, at least. For these readers, insulated from questions of *what* they were, say, in the eyes of history, love was, indeed, more important than *their* color—the power of which would operate in an unexamined, even unconscious, silence in their lives—but not more important than *his*, a visible symbol of the danger their lives must avoid. Carrying the weight of history by itself, in these terms, the importance of *his* color would continue to dominate his readers'—not only his white readers'—choices in love, real estate, politics, and education and alter the operation of all major US institutions.

By 1963, Baldwin could feel a kind of burning wind-sheer between the subtle and supple role and power of his color in his life and in the lives of his family and friends—that is, in the question of *who* he was—and the power of that color in the white American world—in the question of *what* he was—and, for that matter, in the world of international politics. At the close of *Take This Hammer*, a documentary film shot in San Francisco in 1963 and aired on KQED television in 1964, Baldwin faced the camera and addressed the wind-sheer directly:

> Now, in this country we've got something called "the nigger," which doesn't in such terms I beg you to remark exist in any other country ... white people invented it. ... I've always known that I am not the nigger. And if I am not the nigger, and if it is true that your invention reveals you, then who is the nigger? ... But you still think, I gather, that the nigger is necessary. Well it's not necessary to me. So he must be necessary to you. So, I give you your problem back. You're the nigger, baby; it isn't me.

Sitting for the film's final scene on director Richard O. Moore's couch, exhausted by the filming but revived by a bubble bath and a few fingers of scotch, Baldwin recast his vision ca. 1963. In an America without a culture, without a sense of fluent presence across its divisions, lies about *what* people were trapped the connective and shared truths of *who* people were. The two levels of experience were, nonetheless, inextricable. Therefore, Baldwin urged, one must accept the American duty to enter history through the false door created by the lies that rule one's psyche and the world around it, which acceptance invests a person with a new relationship to experience and the world. That shift releases one from the terrifying (no matter the curtains) and destructive (no matter the lies about so-called advantages of privilege) prison of that history and into another, less isolated, level of experience. Such acceptance, he thought, made available a different set of encounters with human reality involving, first and foremost, a fuller, more various sense of touch and presence with other people. Coherent, fluent social presence, Baldwin held, was better than privileged isolation and certainly better than segregated oppression. Absent that sense of touch and presence in the world, a person caught in either form of isolation, Baldwin thought, could not reliably find out anything meaningful about their experience, or anything else that mattered. Any person willing to make connections beyond the position accorded to them by the system could accomplish this. "But," as he would insist from the Carnegie Hall stage ten years later, "Amen is the price." And, as Baldwin had experienced, many people in the world depended upon the world's divisions for their sense of reality and identity. Many, therefore, resist such shifts and the world they suggest, and, at times, will try to punish the disruptive amens.

However impossible it might have been, Baldwin imagined "The Hallelujah Chorus" as a kind of crash course in the pleasures and demands of a radical set of repositionings such as he had outlined to the viewers of *Take This Hammer* and as he had recommended to the audience in Germany: of music from its role as entertainment into a window from which one reencounters one's life in the world; of the human joys and dangers that operate behind the false veil—however real—of *race* in American life; and, finally, a newly enlivened, more challenging but far less terrifying, sense of what goes on within and between people. He thought America's racial (often masquerading as rational) realities menaced and thwarted any and all elements of experience. "The Hallelujah Chorus" would present black music as a kind of phenomenological Virgil guiding people back to a living sense of themselves and each other. It led to a sense of life instead of being prisoners to the confines of class and color, a sense he thought was our only access to history, to an American sense of experience. Absent such a radical reorientation, as he had written in *No Name in the Street*, he thought, in fact, "there *are* no American people yet" (*CE*, 358). Of this peculiar and particular American pressure, in *Just Above My Head*, he would write: "Our history is each other. That is our only guide. One thing is absolutely certain: one can repudiate, or despise, no one's history without repudiating and despising one's own."[18] The most sophisticated record of all this was, again, available in the music. He concluded the thought: "Perhaps that is what the gospel singer is singing"[19]

## Toward Subversive Fluency, a Nonmurderous Revolutionary Presence

Baldwin introduced "The Hallelujah Chorus" into an immediate world where violence was intense, widespread, and commonplace. Historic levels of labor unrest marked the era in which the AFL-CIO began to veer toward catastrophe. In *Stayin' Alive*, Malcolm Cowie notes that 2.4 million workers were on strike in 1970 alone. During the summer of 1973, conflict between the Teamsters and the United Farm Workers over contracts with growers led to dozens of shootings and multiple fatalities on the West Coast.[20] Urban crime rates were extremely high. New York City Police Department statistics list over 2,000 murders and nearly 5,000 "forcible rapes" in the city in 1973.[21] Apart from street crime, domestic violence and labor's internecine maneuvers, organized political violence was also rampant. Christopher Hewitt's *Political Violence and Terrorism in Modern America* lists over 70 incidents of organized political violence across the nation in 1973, including kidnappings, bombings, bank robberies, racially motivated murders, and targeted attacks on police. Even by Baldwin's standards, violence between police and citizens was shockingly common at the time. A spectrum of black militant organizations such as the Black Liberation Army, the Death Angels, the August 7th Guerilla Movement, the Black Guerilla Family, the Symbionese Liberation Army, radical leftists such as the Weather Underground, together with the American Indian Movement, the Secret Cuban Government, the Frente de Liberación Nacional de Cuba, the Chicano Liberation Front, the Palestinian group Black Spring, and the Puerto Rican nationalist Armed Independence Movement carried out dozens of politically motivated robberies, shootouts with law enforcement, and racially motivated reprisal killings that year. Between October 1973 and April 1974, for instance, more than a dozen seemingly motiveless murders of white people—known as the "zebra killings"—were directly linked to the Death Angels in San Francisco.[22] The police, the FBI, and other law enforcement agencies intensified tactics of surveillance and control leading to widespread and increased tension and violence between police and nonwhite communities nationwide.[23] During the spring of 1974, fearing for his life amid racist death threats, Henry Aaron approached and eclipsed Babe Ruth's homerun record in major league baseball. The racial-rational schisms in modern American life had become politicized borders as numerous as they were deadly.

For years, thinking his fame would make him a prime target in the conflicts, Baldwin's family had advised him to minimize his time in the United States. The question of revolutionary action, of course, reached beyond the nation's borders. In his February appearance in Germany, Baldwin addressed the issue of political violence directly. After his remarks, a "tall black youth with a proud Afro" asked, "Mr. Baldwin, what is your opinion of armed revolution?" Obviously tired of engaging what he considered macho-militant fashion, Baldwin sardonically signified his response saying, "I'm not a general," and turned away. He was speaking on a US Army base, after all. Not dissuaded, the young man caught up with Baldwin and confronted him on his way out, "You're not a general? What the hell does that have to do with my question?" Engaging the confrontation, Baldwin responded instantaneously: "I mean, if I tell you I'm for armed revolution, it would mean very little. Because I'm over 50, and you are the one that's going out there to get killed. I could say I'm for picking up the gun, but anyone in his right mind ought to know that the cops are not going to let you get three blocks."[24]

Owing to the intricate tangle between so-called racial and would-be rational thought in American life, Baldwin also knew how difficult it was to maintain one's "right mind." The violent kaleidoscope of American life in the 1970s amplified this basic American psychological and intellectual dilemma. In ways that he sought to resist but not to deny, Baldwin knew much of the physical violence linked back to psychological violence inherent in manufacturing false realities such as race, privilege, power, and danger out of skin color. Linking racial typing directly to physical violence in his previous comments, he concluded, "You cannot treat another man as a human being if you first of all think that man is black or that you've got to treat him a certain way because he is in some way benighted, or that you know something he doesn't and that you have to teach him. The man is certainly going to resent it, or kill himself, or you. And that hasn't changed either." The effort to keep or attain one's "right mind" amounted to *accepting* the reality of the lies and then *defeating* that reality in pursuit of the joyous and challenging, even tragic, human truths they obscure. In this, he thought, the complex yet basic sense available in black music was one's best bet.

As the "The Hallelujah Chorus" performance date loomed, Baldwin, armed only with his experience of black music's powerful guide to historically resonant touch and presence, was set to enter the fray and return to the United States. In early June 1973, in what was by then a customary commuter routine for him, as well as a mission crucial to his sense of his work, Baldwin traveled (supported by a subsidy from Pan Am Airlines obtained by promoter George Wein) from his home (which he had yet to pay for) in St. Paul de Vence, a village on La Côte d'Azur in France, to New York City. He installed himself—courtesy of expenses paid by the concert's sponsor, Schiltz Brewing—in a suite at the Plaza Hotel just in time to leave for Los Angeles. Between June 15 and June 25, he would re-side—courtesy of expenses likewise paid by Schlitz—at the Beverly Hills Hotel and Bungalows. He had gone to Los Angeles to meet Ray Charles so the two could refine and rehearse their plan for the performance. While in Los Angeles, he also reconnected with his long-time friend, pianist and jazz composer Alonzo Levister. Stirred by a brief erotic encounter with Levister, and owing to a uniquely fluent circulation of comings and goings between people he had felt in Ray's midst and in Ray's touch on the piano, "of presences entering or leaving a room," Baldwin had clarified the content and structure of the performance.

I had read about "The Hallelujah Chorus" a few times. The title recurs in Baldwin's correspondence over the years in ways that tantalized me as I studied the life he recorded in his letters to his brother David. I searched the biographies for information about the performance but found only one very general reference to it. For years it had occupied its position in my mind as a minor, perhaps even regrettable, footnote to Baldwin's career. Then, while searching through unrelated materials in the Harvard University archive, I discovered David Baldwin's copy of the script in a box.[25] Recognizing the title, I knew what it was immediately. Or, so I thought. And, then, when I began to read the script, I recognized immediately that this was no minor footnote. I felt a sharp regret that the performance had been hidden for all these years. When I began to research the reception of the performance by critics, my sense of regret morphed into a strange sensation: I was shocked but not surprised. I had witnessed, in print and in life, this brand of resistance to Baldwin's work, usually disguised as attacks, often enough. Clearly "The Hallelujah Chorus" had unearthed connections between music and experience, connections that were political and personal, to which people, at least reviewers, weren't eager to say amen.

## Toward a Politics of Being in Touch, a Sense of Touch Revisited

With the possible exception of Aretha Franklin, Ray Charles was the contemporary singer that meant the most to Baldwin in the 1970s. His published praise of Charles's music appeared as early as 1964 and Baldwin invoked him often as a resonant instance of the energy and clarity he identified with artistic excellence. As discussed in Chapter 3, in his 1968 address to the World Council of Churches, "White Racism or World Community," Charles figures directly in Baldwin's thought about the danger of people living, as he put it, having "put themselves out of touch with themselves" (*CE*, 754). He wrote: "the Christian personality split itself in two, split itself into dark and light, in fact, and is now bewildered, at war with itself, is literally unable to comprehend the force of such a woman as Mahalia Jackson, who does not sound like anyone in Canterbury Cathedral, unable to accept the depth of sorrow, out of which a Ray Charles comes, unable to get itself in touch with itself, with its selfless totality" (754). When, during their 1971 conversation, Nikki Giovanni said, "personally, I hate critics," Baldwin responded: "Actually, I love critics, but they're very rare. A real critic is very rare," continuing, "I will be able to accept critical judgments when I understand that they understand Ray Charles."[26] For Baldwin criticism itself was a kind of mutual, musical recognition, a fluency between presences who move when we move; in other words, it was personal and impersonal, it was part of a culture. Giovanni, twenty-eight years old at the time, cast the possibility aside, "It'll never happen." Playing the elder, Baldwin left the door ajar, "When that day comes . . . we'll play it as we see it."[27] Well. It's been over forty years; but, possibly, we can replay it now as we might have seen it then.

The script shows how the performance proceeded at the time, the logic holding it together, at least in the performers' minds. With the Carnegie Hall curtain still down, the audience heard Ray Charles's solo piano version of his "Sweet Sixteen Bars" which was actually an instrumental version of "A Fool for You," a soft blues into which he folded equal parts modern, subtle jazz technique and a relaxed, gospel feeling. In his liner notes to the 1956 release of *The Great Ray Charles*—the pianist's first jazz sessions, which included "Sweet Sixteen Bars"—Gary Kramer quoted Charles on the connections between black musical idioms. Charles's words directly echo Baldwin's sense of the artists' connection quoted earlier, a connection refuted by the critics. The common ground lay in the force of an experience recreated in the music of the church:

> All music is related. Gospel music background is important to a jazz musician, for it draws out feeling. What you speak of as *soul* in jazz is *soul* in gospel music. The important thing in jazz is to feel your music, but really feel it and believe it—the way a gospel singer like Mahalia Jackson obviously feels and believes the music that she is singing, with her whole body and soul. And if you feel and believe in your music, that conviction carries over to the public. You can create a very strong emotional bond between yourself and your listener that way.[28]

In conversations with his brother David about having been in Jimmy Carter's hometown, Plains, Georgia, not far from where Ray Charles was born, Baldwin described having been stunned that the "white" people of the South bore mostly similar complexions while "black" people of the South carried complexions that ranged across the spectrum from light and bright to ebony dark. Reacting to the denied truth of cross-racial connections in Southern life, ones made perfectly obvious simply by people's appearance, Baldwin said: "No lie can live forever, and the truth about America is to be found on the porches of the South."[29] It was but one truth made invisible, certainly unspeakable, by the reality lent to the lie of race in American "culture." At the same time, it was a truth lived out intimately—if rarely discussed openly—in black families and communities across the nation. Black communities' ability to say amen to this historical American diversity, absorbing it into their families, formed the central drama of Baldwin's unproduced, unpublished screenplay from the early 1970s, "The Inheritance."[30]

According to the script, the Carnegie Hall curtain rose to reveal a "Single spot on Ray, alone on stage," playing "Seems Like I Gotta Do Wrong," an image of black people framed by American culture's selective blindness to its history and its present: "Nobody saw me walking/And nobody heard me talking/Seems like I gotta do wrong gotta do wrong gotta do wrong/before they notice me." The opening montage of music in "The Hallelujah Chorus" combined the deep roots where faith and trouble (gospel), pain and clarity (blues), and constant change (jazz) reconnect. The selections sounded the core of the tradition with which modern black life, as Baldwin would put it from the podium/pulpit, "descend[s] into the valley" of racism in America. It was a national tradition, "the truth about America." The anthem of that tradition, *that* nation, followed: "Then, lights up completely for *Lift Every Voice And Sing*." Following Charles's version of the Negro National Anthem which was also the opening track from his 1972 album, *a message from the people . . . by the people . . . and for the people*, Baldwin's script reads: "As this song ends, we discover the narrator, (JB) alone, downstage." Doing at least as much translation as narration, Baldwin read his opening testimony:

Amen.

This testimony service tonight is called The Hallelujah Chorus, which, as you know, is the name given to the final movement of Handel's The Messiah, which is a relatively popular Christmas tune.

The hallelujah, however, to which this testimony service refers—and out of which it comes—is not a matter of the seasons. It testifies to a movement and a mystery in the soul.

I have observed that not many of us can say, or sing: hallelujah. Perhaps it is because one first [must] descend into the valley, where one learns to say: Amen. If one can find in oneself the force to say, Amen, it is possible to come to Hallelujah. But Amen is the price. The black experience in the valley of America remains, my friends, America's only affirmation. We have sung the Lord's song for a very long time, in a very very strange land.

One of the realities which has made this land so strange, and which has bequeathed it so striking a torment, is the invincible sound of those voices, rising from the valley, where—the song says—I couldn't hear nobody pray.

Having had to accept Amen: and learned to sing Hallelujah: some of us know that love is the key to life and that life is stronger than death. We know that because we have had to teach our children that. Perhaps we can suggest to you, then, during this testimony service, that love and life and death and children are more real than all our illusions of safety; that perhaps we lose our lives and our loves and our children, and come to a waking, a walking death because we are afraid to say, Amen.

Perhaps that is why so many like to say that only black people can sing the blues.

But I am here only as a witness, to say, Amen. The right Rever-
end Ray Charles is testifying, singing Hallelujah:
Listen.

The political and personal intensity and the high stakes of what such
an amen, what all the amens at all the levels, meant to Baldwin himself
during that time obviously underscores the pathos of his call.

The script then calls for more music, "RC: *I Won't Leave.* And *When I
Stop Dreaming,*" after which Baldwin, having moved from a podium to a
stool placed in the curve of Charles's piano, recasts Charles's testifying in
a complex personal/impersonal, inside/outside poetic idiom. He charts
how any art recreates experience transforming it from an inert thing received into a living something that one can accept, *bear,* and therefore
change:

Tell me—tell *us*—a little bit more about—what you're saying—
about yourself, as music, because *that* is what you are—and also
about yourself, as *you.* I am aware that by this time, certainly,
they—the music and you—may be the same. But music, let us say,
is an abstract reality. *You* are a reality, but you are *not* abstract. You
are a man, and a man is never abstract. Tell us about the wedding:
between you and you.

In the scripted dialogue, Charles recasts Baldwin's conceptual statement
in more visceral terms; he describes his origins in the music and the
origins of the music in him:

Music was like a rib. I mean, it was in me before I got here—like
your heart or your liver or your lungs. Those are things you're
born with. Listen. I remember a gentleman—Wiley Pittman was his
name—well, he lived next door, and I used to listen to him play his
boogie woogie piano all the time. All the time, man, all the time.
I just used to listen. And he used to let me sit and play with him.
Now, you know, I wasn't no more than three years old—something
like that, maybe a little bit older—and, so you *know* I wasn't playing
nothing. But he used to play with me, and I could play his piano
anytime.

Of the orchestrated asymmetry aligned by Baldwin's script and typified
by this exchange, John S. Wilson wrote in his *New York Times* review:
"Mr. Charles responded in such a natural and engaging manner as to

underline the pomposity of Mr. Baldwin's approach."[31] Apart from re-aligning what's natural and who is pompous, from our position in the present, one can easily discern the connection between the two statements; the two passages read as anything but statements by men who possessed, as Whitney Balliet had put it, "alien souls."[32] Near the end of the performance, naturally or not, in a moment no reviewer noted, Charles asks at least one clearly political, blues-informed question at the center of his own autobiography, "Like, man, I also know, being no fool, that I didn't really have to go blind—in the richest country in the world? How come?" The script for Baldwin's and Charles's performance ends with a note about the necessity that people be in touch with their own lives if they're to know anything about each other by way of "presences entering or leaving," according to the rhythm of amen and hallelujah:

> RC plays *Hey, Mister.*
> and
> *America, America*
> JB: The valley—where you couldn't hear nobody pray. You want to tell us some more about it?
> RC: If you know—if you really *know*—about *your* valley—then, you know about mine.
> RC plays
> *My God And I.*
> Finale

Closing the act in Italian might well invoke a subtle sense of Yoran Cazac's presence into the performance.

The next section of the performance featured dramatic vignettes from Baldwin's story "Sonny's Blues." Now acknowledged as a classic Baldwin work, "Sonny's Blues (a long story)" was first published in the summer 1957 issue of *Partisan Review*, an influential left-leaning literary review of the era; the issue also featured poems by Theodor Roethke, John Hollander, Stanley Kunitz, and Carolyn Kizer. The issue was released just as Baldwin was preparing for his first trip to the American South. With the title character partially based on one of Baldwin's most important early lovers, an aspiring jazz drummer and percussionist named Arnold, the story depicts the relationship of two estranged brothers; one an unnamed high school math teacher attempting to achieve a *normal*, middle-class American life, the other, Sonny, an aspiring jazz piano player. Owing to his unwillingness to say amen himself, the older brother suffers alienations Baldwin thought were typical of mainstream American lifestyles. Sonny suffers the early terrors associated with the "recreation of experience," or "the wedding: between you and you," key to artistic craft of any kind in Baldwin's mind. Sonny also suffers the archetypal accompanist of jazz performers in the popular imagination during the 1950s—heroin. The story ends in an unnamed downtown jazz club where Sonny plays with his brother in the audience, each man, we imagine, saying his own amen to the turbulent risks Baldwin thought came along with a life lived in touch with living presences, historical and present day.

In the first scene on stage, David Moses, playing the unnamed brother (named Robert in the script), talks to his mother about the risks facing Sonny. In the course of the conversation, the mother, played by Cicely Tyson, informs her son of an uncle—his father's brother, a guitar player—who had been run down on a country road in the South by a car full of white men. Onstage, Tyson describes the cost of that racial trauma to her husband, the boy's father: "Oh, yes. Your Daddy never did really get right again. Till the day he died he weren't sure that every white man he saw was the man that killed his brother."[33] Collapsing the history into the contemporary message to her son, and simultaneously connecting the mid-1950s setting of the story to the early 1970s, Tyson concludes her speech: "I ain't telling you all this, to make you scared or bitter or to make you hate nobody. I'm telling you this because you got a brother—And the world ain't changed." In the "long story," the final, italicized, note of the scene accents the politics of personal presence. The mother concludes her talk with her nameless son: "You may not be able to stop nothing from happening. But you got to let him know you's *there*."[34]

In the two scenes that followed, David Moses plays Robert, the older brother, and David Baldwin plays Sonny. Scene 2 depicts a conversation early in the brothers' attempts at reconciliation. In the role of quasi-parent counseling practicality and security, of Sonny's musical ambitions, Robert asks: "Doesn't all this take a lot of time? Can you make a living at it?" Urging his brother to accept Sonny's determination to be passionately present in his own life and work, Sonny retorts, "Everything takes time, and—well, yes sure, I can make a living at it. But what I don't seem to be able to make you understand is that it's the only thing I want to do." Scene 3 opens with David Baldwin reading a letter from Sonny, in prison, written to Robert. At the close of the letter, Sonny questions the authority of Baldwin's own sermon about the old-fashioned necessity of acceptance, of saying amen to what life brings, from the outset of the performance with Charles: "I wish I could be like Mama and say may the Lord's will be done, but I don't know it seems to me that trouble is one thing that never does get stopped and I don't know what good it does to blame it on the Lord. But maybe it does some good if you believe it."[35] From his comments on the gospel origins of his sound, the importance of believing with one's "body and soul,"[36] it is clear that Ray Charles agreed; in the musical marriage of "you and you,"[37] at least one of the intra-personal spouses better be a believer. The scene concludes with Sonny and Robert's attempts at coming to terms with the inevitability of Amen as the route to a resonant, mutual Hallelujah.

On the page in the script upon which James and David Baldwin's alterations appear, written in felt tip and ball point respectively, Sonny and Robert discuss the role of music, drugs, faith, and skepticism and finally conclude that a sense of touch and presence between people is the only way of living with the reality that there is no final cure for life's turbulence, no sense of safety upon which any community or individual can depend. After a passage in which Sonny's drug addiction stands in for a generalized, universal sense of risk, the dramatic performance ends on a note that clearly mirrors the violent political reality of the early 1970s:

> ROBERT: All right, so it can come again. All right.
> SONNY: I had to try and tell you.
> ROBERT: Yes, I understand that.
> SONNY: You're my brother.
> ROBERT: Yes, yes. I understand that.
> SONNY: All that hatred down there, all that hatred and misery and love. It's a wonder it doesn't blow the avenue apart.

The script ends with Baldwin's handwritten note:

> R.C. Full Choir If I Had My Way

## Can I Get an Amen? [Silence]

In a sense, in her 1971 conversation with Baldwin about critical understanding, when she said, "It'll never happen," Nikki Giovanni had a point.[38] To say the very least, the day for critical recognitions of the politics of touch and presences Baldwin, Charles, and the actors presented onstage in "The Hallelujah Chorus" wasn't soon forthcoming. Few critics seemed to realize that the actors were reprising scenes from "Sonny's Blues." The *Jet* reviewer assumed that the "sketches were related to Charles's real life problems with dope addiction and to his genius as a musician."[39] Balliett wrote that a "couple of meaningless dramatic interludes . . . followed (one was taken from James Baldwin's short story 'Sonny's Blues')."[40] The *Chicago Defender* printed a review, which merely reprised the press release. Confirming little other than the fact that the reviewer hadn't been present, the short piece informs that the performance "featured poet and author James Baldwin and actress Cicely Tyson, reading from 'The Life and Times of Ray Charles.'"[41] In the *New York Times*, jazz critic John S. Wilson opened his review noting his shock at the "molehill that this mountain of talent produced."[42] Apropos the dramatic scenes, Wilson wrote: "Mr. Baldwin also wrote four brief sketches concerning a mother and two sons that seemed, in a general sense, to relate to Mr. Charles's problems with drugs without really providing any enlightenment about Mr. Charles himself."

Reviewing for the British music magazine, *Melody Maker*, Richard Williams rehearsed the contemporary pre-1963 rise and post-1963 fall version of Baldwin's career—a narrative still inflecting mainstream perception of his career—and went out of his way to mock and criticize what he deemed "Baldwin's somewhat erratic literary form in recent years."[43] In presenting scenes from "Sonny's Blues"—a now-classic work from the era of Baldwin's career most associated with his meteoric rise—in a contemporary forum, Baldwin, knowingly or not, created something of a blindfold test for the critics. Not able to resist the bait, Williams's review compares the would-be contemporary, "erratic," Baldwin unfavorably with the previous high quality of his work. Fooled by the a-chronology of the evening's dramatic material, Williams, in effect, compares "Sonny's Blues" unfavorably with itself: "The actors were adequate, the material was not. Baldwin once again parodied the emotional directness of his early work, and left us with overblown platitudes. Only the choir's performance of the traditional 'If I Had My Way' made any impression."[44] Reviewing for the *Boston Evening Globe*, Ernie Santosuosso called the performance a "prolonged stretch of dreariness" and, after "a series of embarrassingly contrived song cues by the celebrated author," seemed confused that the performers "walked off despite the sustained standing ovation with it's [*sic*] request for an encore."[45] Santosuosso solved the impasse between his disapproval and the New York audience's appreciation concluding, improbably, "standing ovations come comparatively easy in this city."

In 1951, Baldwin had written that the story told in black music about black experience in America was a "story no American was prepared to hear."[46] Much closer to the date of the performance, in 1969, giving a speech at the West Indian Student Center in London, Baldwin had revisited the politics of listening to black music: "And if I discover that those songs the darkies sang, and sing, were not just the innocent expressions of a primitive people, but extremely subtle and difficult, dangerous and tragic expressions of what it felt like to be in chains. Then by one's presence simply, by the attempt to walk from here to there, you've begun to frighten the white world."[47] Baldwin's radicalized sense of the politics of hearing and responding to black music resonates powerfully against the critical reception of "The Hallelujah Chorus" and echoes throughout the poetics of his later career.

Apropos critics, in 1971, Nikki Giovanni said that such a politically engaged and resonant listening would never happen. When it came to the musical and conversational portions of the show, responding mostly through conscious and unconscious abuse of the performers, if the critics didn't prove both Baldwin and Giovanni right, they certainly didn't prove them wrong. Calling the performance "virtually a disaster in artistic terms," *Melody Maker*'s Richard Williams signaled one source of dissonance preventing mutual, musical critical recognitions at the time. Recoiling from both the sense of touch and presence Baldwin had hoped to convey with Charles, Williams observed, "Baldwin blew a good chance to create something worthwhile with his faggoty mannerisms, both literary and personal." In attempts to warn readers away from associating Baldwin further with the music he supposedly valued, Williams forecasted that further work by Baldwin in connection to "major jazz artists ... would do more harm than good."[48] Jazz critic Whitney Balliett wrote that the musical portion of the show struggled because Baldwin and Charles "have little in common ... Charles remains a canny, tough, pinewoods primitive, and Baldwin is a delicate urban visionary."[49] In contradiction to his overall impressions, Balliett noted that, late in the show, however, "a strange and moving thing had begun to happen"; it was a thing, moreover, that owed directly to the presence of Baldwin and Charles onstage together. Balliett wrote: "Apparently, Baldwin had suggested to Charles that he abandon his regular show, with its pop tunes, gospel numbers, and country-and-Western songs, and concentrate on his old blues. Charles did and the results, in blues after blues, were superb."[50] In his memoir, George Wein wrote, "Although Jimmy and I grew very close in the ensuing years, I never told him that I had been disappointed with the concert."[51]

Since the reviews of the performance, historical commentary has been minimal. No mention of the performance appears in the 2004 biographical film, *Ray*, starring Jamie Foxx. Charles's complex and directly told autobiography, *Brother Ray*, written with David Ritz, makes no mention of the date either. Apart from Bob Stumpel's useful detailing of the program in May 2010 on his blog, *Ray Charles Video Museum*, commentary amounts to exactly five words.[52] David Leeming, the only Baldwin biographer to note the event at all, restricted his comments to logistical details leading up to the performance and, paraphrasing the *Chicago Defender* reviewer who wasn't there either, concluded "the overall effect was moving."[53] And that, as it's said, was *that*.

But, not for Baldwin. After the first performance, "The Hallelujah Chorus" presented, at least to *his* imagination, another opportunity to engage directly with American politics and the issue of prisoners in particular. He also entertained the possibility of a TV program or a commercial tour. But, the prison tour was obviously where his commitments solidified. Baldwin's experience with police, prisons, and prisoners, which began in his childhood, had been deepened by his recent work directing the hit, 1969–1970 run of John Herbert's prison play, *Fortune and Men's Eyes*, in Istanbul. His attitude had been radicalized by his experiences with the imprisonment of his one-time personal assistant and long-time friend, Tony Maynard, and by his connection to widely publicized political prisoners Angela Davis, Huey Newton, George Jackson, and many others. Just weeks after the performance, on July 21, 1973, he wrote to his brother David about his intentions to organize, and fund if need be, a tour of the performance in American prisons. Determined to break the silence and invisibility surrounding American prisoners, he explained his intention to force the reality of prisons on the American public awareness and asked, in case David was pragmatically skeptical, his brother to have faith and go with him on the idea. While personally attracted to the Plazas and Beverly Hills Hotels of the world, and professionally willing to pursue deals in the popular culture (TV, national tours), he made it perfectly clear where his real priorities lay. He concluded his thoughts about "The Hallelujah Chorus" in the prisons saying that he realized it meant that nobody would make any money on the tour, but that there were more important things. He said they would all worry about the money later. George Wein, who would later write that Baldwin's notorious recklessness "when it came to finances . . . was one of the traits that endeared him to you,"[54] and maybe Ray Charles, whose financial discipline was legion, too, might well have been inclined to worry about it sooner.

In the end, "The Hallelujah Chorus" didn't produce a lucrative commercial tour or television program nor did it succeed in casting light on the plight of American prisoners. The contemporary abuse of critics, more than anything else, demonstrated that they couldn't tell the suppos-edly *good* old Baldwin from the notoriously *bad* recent Baldwin any more than they could focus very well on the "natural," "pinewoods primitive" (one can now but wonder why?) genius of Ray Charles when it operated in association with Baldwin's explicitly political, if "faggoty" and "er-ratic," prophetic, celebrity-poet persona. From the present, we can see the outrageous numbness and prejudice embedded in the critics' points of view. Read today, at least in my view, critics confess their resentment at how "The Hallelujah Chorus" had taken Ray Charles hostage sundering him, and music in general, from its natural, politically neutral—basically, white—environment. Sadly, apart from that, there has been scarcely any comment at all on the vision the brothers Baldwin, David Moses, Cicely Tyson, George Wein, and Ray Charles intended to cast from the stage of Carnegie Hall on July 1, 1973. The critical abuse of "The Hallelujah Chorus" at the time, and the vacuum surrounding it since, testifies viv-idly to a profound American—and, in the case of Williams, British—dis-trust of what goes on in the work, to say nothing of in the lives, of our greatest artists.

Forty years after the fact, indeed, even from just the script and scraps of sound—such as those available to vinyl-philes on the 1974 Buddah Records release, *Recorded Live at Newport in New York*—capably set in the context of Baldwin's career, we can, now, finally, begin to excavate some of the pressure and power, to say nothing of the pleasure, of the engaged vision they made available then.

It's a vision of the things, many of which aren't things, made visible by the presences that come and go in real music. And, it's a sense of touch made possible by that presence—namely, ours—made available only in the work of our best writers. There's no other window open on those dimensions of what we are. But, finally, as Baldwin noted again and again in his writings, speeches, and in performances such as "The Hallelujah Chorus," and in ways that still trouble the critics today, the presences in music and what touches us in the literary work are painfully incomplete if they remain locked onstage, carved in vinyl, laser printed onto pages or up-loaded into the cloud. In order to have our Hallelujah in life, we've got to say our amen in the world. And, that amen has to be said to each other, addressed to the truths of who we are and in defiance of the lies about what we are. In this, we must acknowledge *what* the world takes us for and is trying to make us into, as well, *and* deal with our own, per-sonal delusions in *who* it is we think we are supposed to be; because—whether we take the sentence from the *good* Baldwin in *Partisan Review*

(1957) or the *bad* Baldwin in Carnegie Hall (1973), from Gaza to Cambridge, MA, to Istanbul, from Aleppo to New Orleans, from Mombasa to Maiduguri—the world where our Amen counts is still so full of "hatred and misery and love" that it's ever a "wonder it doesn't blow the avenue apart." And, of course, it *does* blow many avenues apart, even as I type.

Some of the schisms are visibly invisible. As I sit here in Cihangir Mah, Istanbul, on July 1, 2013, forty years to the day after "The Hallelujah Chorus" was performed in Carnegie Hall, CNN International blazes images of Cairo across the television screen over my shoulder. I think, "has anyone been to Cairo, IL, lately?" The town in Southern Illinois looks as if it has taken artillery strikes. A week ago, amid protests, clouds of tear gas blew down this very street in Istanbul. Other schisms are numbly untouchable; locate your own address on Google Earth and see how close you can get before the image breaks apart. Been *there* lately? There are, indeed, still many songs few are prepared to hear and presences abound, many within arms reach, that even fewer are prepared to touch.

Someone cue Ray, or maybe let's substitute Georgia Ann Muldrow, for "If I Had My Way." She could do it as a hallelujah duet with Oumou Sangare or Thandiswa Maswai. Or, hell, Jhené Aiko. In Madison Square Garden. They can open for Bruce Springsteen. Or Kendrick Lamar. The house will be packed. Truth is, there are a lot of singers who could give us such a Hallelujah. We're hurting for writers—and publishers—who can do a credible job at what Baldwin had in mind with Amen. For those that are, well, amen to that. And, hallelujah.

# BOOK III

## "For you I was a flame"
### Baldwin's Lyrical Lens on Contemporary Culture

Was this because, for the portrait of Lady Barb, I felt appealed to so little in the name of *shades*? Shades would be decidedly neither of her general world nor of her particular consciousness.... It was Jackson Lemon and *his* shades, comparatively, and his comparative sense for shades, that, in the tale, most interested me.

—*Henry James,* "Lady Barbarina"

Shades cannot be fixed; color is, eternally, at the mercy of the light.

—*James Baldwin,* Just Above My Head

As long as we are forced to go from black to white, with the first of these abstractions providing something like a point of support for the eye as much as for the brain, we flounder.

—*Paul Cézanne,* The Letters of Paul Cézanne

# 7

## On Camden Row
### Amy Winehouse's Lyric Lines in a Living Inheritance

In his introduction to the 1984 edition of *Notes of a Native Son*, Baldwin described his beginnings as a writer and the twin aim of discovery and avoidance he encountered: "If I was trying to discover myself—on the whole, when examined, a somewhat dubious notion, since I was also trying to avoid myself—there was, certainly, between that self and me, the accumulated rock of ages" (*CE*, 809). A cultural-political obstruction thwarted his efforts at discovery: "This rock scarred the hand, and all the tools broke against it." At the same time, he sensed someone, almost someone else, whom the world couldn't see or hear: "Yet, there was a me, somewhere: I could feel it, stirring within and against captivity" (809). As with the beginnings of any lyric sense in the world, Baldwin felt a particular inheritance stirring. But he found all the world had taught him about who and what he was stifled it. He found his inheritance was unique to him, his and his alone, yet if he could get beyond his own fear and the obstructions (first and foremost: racial and sexual taboos associated with the American myth), he sensed there were links between that inheritance and the world around him. He referred to that universalized particularity, that lyricized self, as a "birthright."

The bridge, Baldwin found, between a person's own sense of world and self and a broader set of connections was counterintuitive and indirect. He didn't have to deny things particular to himself in order to connect to the world and other people. He did the reverse: "When I began, seriously, to write—when I knew I was committed, that this would be my life—I had to try to describe that particular condition which was—

is—the living proof of my inheritance. And, at the same time, with that very same description, I had to claim my birthright" (*CE*, 810). There was no map to that sense of a fluent, connected particularity that was key to what Baldwin meant when he mentioned privacy. One holds one end, an inherited end, of a living connection and follows that energy to where it leads. Poets and musicians have described what that entails. Audiences have observed the frequent wreckage. Listeners balance what they hear against what they observe in their own attempts at discovery. No recent singer preformed a more intricate and powerful version of that quest than Amy Winehouse during her brief, brilliant career. Meanwhile, in response to her tumultuous, by turns brilliant and flailing, transit between living inheritance and birthright, critics often played the role of the rock of ages.

By far the most nuanced and considered corpus of writing about Winehouse's work appeared after her death at age twenty-seven, on July 23, 2011. It seemed that her death created a kind of quiet against which culture writers were able to listen again. They did listen, again, to Winehouse's songs and, I think, also heard their own voices against a new sense of the stakes. No longer were they writing against a deafening screen of 24/7 cyber chatter, the backdrop was the end of a life.[1] The existential nature of Winehouse's voice had been made unavoidably clear. Also, in a way, the sense seemed to be that the danger was over. A storm had passed. The signals of a postponed close listening laced the articles. Jess Harvell noted Winehouse's ability to "turn personal anguish into songs more pleasurable than painful . . . writing singles that sound buoyant and strong-willed until you unpack the lyrics."[2] Bill Wyman heard the retro production of Winehouse's second album, *Back to Black*, conjure the Motown image of cleanliness and the comfort of historical prizes safely framed and protected from contemporary contingency. "But then," he wrote, "you notice an odd minor note in the jauntiness, and then an unprintable phrase in the second line."[3] These were but a few very subtle dimensions in which Winehouse's voice crashed the familiar codes.

One after another, within days of her death, critics noted a multi-leveled script of disruption in Winehouse's work. In possibly the best single piece written after the singer's death, Laura Barton wrote:

> Pop music had often cast women as sweet, bright creatures, but Winehouse's lyrics revealed something mulchier, messier . . . not in the eccentric mad woman in the attic mould of Kate Bush or Björk, but a woman who chose to live a little wild, follow her heart and

sing of the simple stew of being female ... not the squawky, shrill sexuality of *Sex and the City* and Ann Summers, but something truer, more physical, more serious. She sang about the ache of the body, the need for emotion, the distracting allure of men's shoulders, shirt, underwear.[4]

Barton recast the lyrical terrain of Winehouse's music in terms that resonate with Baldwin's musically inflected paradigm of constants and changes from *The Fire Next Time*. The trouble was that the celebrated constants and apprehended changes couldn't find a livable coherence.

> She gave you an image and then quickly swiped it away, a honeyed love scene soon dissolved into wretchedness; over the course of an album it gave the impression of a life of instability, lived from one ramshackle lurch to the next. But there were constants—namely addiction and passion, the flaming five-storey fire of love she always returned to ... the ferocious proprietorial female strength ... fogged by drugs and love and desire.... The other constant presence was self-recrimination and remorse.[5]

In the music, the volatility bore the energies of a living inheritance. And, over two albums, Winehouse summoned the strength and skill to stay in lyrical touch with it. As Barton observed, something in her was skilled and tough enough to make those twisting constants fluent: "She had a special knack in her lyrics, a twist that made her songs startlingly truthful; each composition would contain at least a line, an image, a turn of phrase that seems to shuck the song open."[6] Recasting the crux of lyric work, this opening of language invited a wide-range of listeners to come inside the sound and hear themselves in Winehouse's voice. That's what lyrical language is all about.

Even among capable commentators listening in the pause of her death, however, the commentary broke down where the clichés and stereotypes of (constants *not* to be celebrated in) the mainstream consumer culture collided with what Baldwin detailed in "The Uses of the Blues." Commentaries tended to assign mystical and transcendental duties to a blues/jazz continuum that, in the ears of another audience, is actually quite brutally realistic and pragmatic. Randall Roberts wrote that, on *Back to Black*, "the music is so buoyant and life-affirming that it tempers the message and makes one believe that magic can overpower despair and addiction."[7] As Baldwin pointed out almost forty years before Winehouse appeared on the scene in 2003, the sense of joy and possibility, "however odd this may sound," that comes from the blues isn't magical; it's directly linked to the craft, skill, and "the toughness that manages to make this experience articulate" (*Cross*, 57). Amplifying the trouble, Nitsuh Abebe wrote that Winehouse's lyrics were "soaked in fatalism" that "says there's no point fighting sadness so you might as well leap heedlessly into self-obliteration."[8] But, heedless leaps don't lace songs with images that shuck the language open. There's always something brutally sober and clear in that labor. In "The Uses of the Blues," Baldwin echoes Beckett's no-win existential stakes in saying that the blues accepts difficulty, even impossibility, and then goes on ahead with an "ability to know that, all right, it's a mess, and you can't do anything about it . . . so, well, you have to do something about it" (*Cross*, 59). Still less do open lyrics and performances originate in the stereotyped (often racist) images audiences have projected onto historical black performers; Abebe nonetheless contended that "the most 'retro' thing about *Back to Black* turned out to be not its period styling or vintage detail, but that streak of woeful resignation borrowed from the old jazz records."[9]

In confused observations that actually resemble heedless leaps much more than did Winehouse's keenly honed and deftly deployed lyrical images, critics writing after her death did, at times, arrive at useful and illuminating observations. Abebe aptly notes the impossible poles of misunderstanding to which listeners and critics often tie the songs and stories they encounter: "At one end of the spectrum are those who see art as being about artifice . . . that needn't have any literal connection to the way an artist actually lives. . . . At the opposite end are those who are desperate to see life and art as the same thing: music as memoir."[10] So, when Baldwin argues that it's a paradoxical "passionate detachment," an "inwardness coupled with outwardness," that accounts for the ability to somehow watch one's most difficult experiences "with eyes wide open," he's signaling a point at which the two poles of formal control (artifice) and experiential reality (memoir) collide. All artists know something about this vexing and necessary territory. Most critics either miss it altogether or overinterpret it in ways that, really, prove very difficult if not impossible to actually trace. Almost in spite of himself, however, Abebe ends his reflection with clear evidence of Winehouse's skilled use of passionate detachment. "She could be wickedly good at using her brain and her expertise to create music that really worked," so that "what you tend to take away is good humor, odd clarity, and flashes of actual bravery."[11] Likewise, following echoes of Mavis Staples and Billie Holiday, Julianne Escobedo Shepherd places Winehouse's phrasing exactly at Baldwin's lyrical crossroads: "It's rare to find lyrics as raw and yet so dispassionate about one's own predicament."[12] Noting the unstable twinning at the crux of lyrical labor, and echoing Rita Dove's meditation on Billie Holiday in her classic poem, "Canary," Lidija Hass concluded that despite the overexposure in the contemporary publicity mill, Winehouse "still appeared mysterious, as if she was disguised as herself."

Now, all this finely tuned aesthetic and intimate experiential business about lyrical fluency and inwardness coupled with outwardness frames one level of Winehouse's career and its profile. But, that she was also a young, attractive, white, British woman operating in a basically black idiom has to be noted in terms as it happens in life, beyond the songs, too. And, often, racial politics operate with their own force of disruption and obliteration. If Winehouse had been simply another "blue-eyed" mimicker and diluter of black style or if she'd been obscurely or even moderately successful, it would have been one thing. But, that didn't happen. Looking back on the eve of her death in the *New Yorker*, Sascha Frere-Jones sketched the artifice of the dilemma as if it was a kind of urbane curio somehow dangled athwart an American racial etiquette: "Winehouse made American soul a viable category, even though many American singers had already been working on that. Welcome to the World Series of Awkwardness: Winehouse had a genuinely interesting take on black American soul, yet she was a white British woman. So what to do?" Other critics took the racial stakes of Winehouse's lyrical profile in the culture far more seriously.

In possibly the most important single piece written about Winehouse's image during her life, scholar and culture critic Daphne Brooks's 2008 essay, "Amy Winehouse and the (Black) Art of Appropriation," sounded alarms that dangerous (maybe sacred) air space had been infringed upon. As the then-burgeoning Internet publicity machine coupled with the mainstream media (Grammy Awards, etc.) to make images of Winehouse's turmoil-ridden life nearly inescapable, Brooks stepped into the fray and upped the political ante to deepen the historical sense of the scene. In a sardonic tone reminiscent of Baldwin's dissents in the popular culture from the mid-1960s through at least *The Devil Finds Work* (1976), and with a sense of racial cross-over politics/economics borrowed from Public Enemy's "Fight the Power," Brooks argued that Winehouse's image soiled a hard-won legacy of black women singers from the 1960s freedom movement era. Echoing another of Baldwin's most important ideas from "The Uses of the Blues," she argued that the importance of black music wasn't really musical at all:

And while some might get caught up in debating whether Winehouse is merely a hack black-music ventriloquist, the most troubling aspect of her routine is rarely discussed. The real travesty of Winehouse's work is the way that her retro-soul draws from and yet effaces those black women—from Diana Ross to Aretha Franklin to Tina Turner—whose experiences helped ignite the rock and soul revolution of our contemporary era.[13]

Brooks's essay lambastes Winehouse, her producers, and her audience for, in effect, dancing on the grave of a principled and dignified cultural edifice, the surface of which they misunderstood and the depth of which they degraded. The original draft of this chapter, in fact, comes from my own signified response to Brooks's essay that, at the time, I thought heaped scorn on a talented, young poet and performer who was clearly in serious trouble. Granting the cross-over racial violence exerted in how Winehouse's image was created and disseminated—which for some is, understandably, because life is short, the end of the matter—I also thought that Brooks's essay had not been sufficiently "caught up" in the lyrical dimensions of Winehouse's work nor in the contemporary—if mulch-y and messy—importance of her voice. Respectfully, and in some keeping with the signifying tradition out of which Brooks's essay itself comes, I'll touch upon various points she made from a point of view informed by the musical, political, and lyrical tradition from which I thought Winehouse's career came and to which I heard it contributing a daringly new voice. If her voice was dangerous—and I think it was in ways that all lyrical work is dangerous—I thought, at least, she never pretended to exempt herself from the perils in the shadow it cast. But, that alone shouldn't be expected to impress anyone, either. Today, revising this essay, I found myself thinking about Sterling Brown's great (1932) poem, "Ma Rainey," and how Brown scripted a subtle and near-sacred reciprocity between the singer and her audience. Immediately after her performance leading the audience in the recreation of their experiences, the great artist then becomes the follower, "An Ma lef' de stage, an' followed some de folks outside."[14] And, I think through the responses in print to Winehouse's work and how far it seemed she was from anything resembling that kind of reciprocal knowing and trust. We'll glance back at this thought at the end of the essay. But first here's some of what I heard in and around Winehouse's voice while she was alive.

"I keep thinking about the lessons of the human ear / which stands for music, which stands for balance," writes Adrienne Rich in "Meditations for a Savage Child," from *Diving into the Wreck*.[15] She's meditating on the role of the ear, of hearing, and of language in trafficking between and charting levels and terrains, a kind of terraced sense, of who we are. She considers the physical structure of the ear: "the whorls and ridges exposed / It seems a hint dropped about the inside of the skull / which I cannot see."[16] As one pushes one's listening back into the interior, the identifications and distinctions between self and other (between whole grammars of this and that) begin to bend, flex, and warp. This listening echoes the "Freefalling, weightless" voyage and vantage in Robert Hayden's paradigmatic lyric poem "The Diver," first published in Rosey E. Poole's 1962 anthology, *Beyond the Blues*. It also sounds in Rich's own paradigmatic, second-wave feminist poem, "Diving into the Wreck." This lyric fabric is subtly and powerfully, at times surprisingly, connective tissue. In fact, late in her career, Rich herself would trace the consciously forgotten (but lyrically remembered) importance of Hayden's poem to her own account of diving in marginal notes she'd made in her well-worn copy of *Beyond the Blues*.[17] These are the intimate pressures that signal a living, lyric inheritance. At a point, they veer into what Baldwin called a "birthright" beyond one's own life and individual personality. In "Meditations for a Savage Child," Rich concludes the section observing: "go back so far there is another language / go back far enough the language / is no longer personal."[18] Those spaces contain possibility and danger, the relationship between which can, probably must, be ambiguous. Rich wrote: "these scars bear witness / but whether to repair / or destruction / I no longer know."[19]

At bottom, the lyric pulls back these kinds of layers (in language, memory, experience) in the socially constituted "rock of ages" or suddenly pierces through them. Lyrics provide a way of charting and summoning buried structures and putting them into social circulation. Obviously, various borders, which can be concrete in one level of experience or voice and which can become porous, and even *vanish*, in others, are blurred and crossed in this lyric process. These dynamics can be informing, even freeing; they can also be disruptive and disorienting. They can be lethal even when the world of "prose" and "facts" and so-called history says none of it is real. But, what happens if the lyric traveler and the audience operate in proximity to sacrosanct, historically volatile borders? The results could be even more confusing, dangerous, and deadly. This chapter charts just such lyric dangers and disruptions, possibly, some that offer a sense of growth and repair, emanating from and swirling about the career of Amy Winehouse. Possibly, considering her work in close relation to its lyric pulse and in relation to multiple lyric traditions with which she is aligned might enable a new glimpse at what she did, what she undid, and what she provoked in response to her "lessons [for] the human ear." And that can address the rock of ages in us all.

Winehouse's lyrics—in the tradition of *lyricists* like John Keats, Billie Holiday, Hart Crane, Sylvia Plath, John Berryman, Dinah Washington, Marvin Gaye, Yusef Komunyakaa, Lauryn Hill and others—involved frayed edges of her life and psyche. Even more conspicuous was Winehouse's rare gift for living the line in performances that dangerously blurred the border between life and art in a way that communicated a turbulent, simultaneous sense of living and artistic flux at the threshold between becoming and unbecoming. So, this is an essay about art and the rough, largely interior, but not necessarily personal, waters it swims on its way to us. Before that, some ground to clear.

The "rock" that obstructs communication between a living inheritance and a birthright, especially when the search happens in the popular culture, isn't a passive object. It's made of people. And, many of them resist the connections. At times, in the years between 2005 and 2011, when the Internet blogosphere was busy creating what Lidija Haas called "a culture of unprecedented over-exposure" in which Winehouse was "one of the most exposed," commentary on Amy Winehouse's lyric quest and career presented a formidable distraction.[20] It had been a while since a performer of such talent had provoked such a stomping from the critical commentators. But, still, amid it all, I knew, could hear, that Amy Winehouse was a uniquely skilled lyricist. One of the best I'd heard. And, as happens in all real lyrics, registers of experience collide and the results in life can be as ugly as the results in song can be beautiful. The "recreation of experience" Baldwin thought was the crux of artistic labor is a very serious enterprise.[21] Certainly, there were things to pick at about Amy Winehouse as she enacted that enterprise. And it was and is easy to dart the barn-sized board of popular culture. Even easier than that is to deconstruct historical popular culture where we don't share the blind place in the contemporary chaos that the performers occupy. And, critics in contemporary popular culture are often as publicity crazed as the performers. In this, let's acknowledge that the commentators aren't taking the same lyrical risks as the performers; and, often, the performers are much younger than the commentators.

Critique of performers in the popular culture isn't enough. Pinning sources of brilliant, surprising lyrical writing (and performance) is difficult and it takes a kind of time disallowed by the pace of information flow in (that is) the contemporary market culture. But, even with the kind of time required for the repetitive rhythms of lyrical attention, finding the source of lyrical brilliance might be impossible. It didn't take too long for the sociologists to appear casting obstructions between Winehouse's living inheritance and her birthright in racial terms. Attempting to account for subtle, lyrical connections in brutal sociological terms, Daphne Brooks opined that Winehouse wanted "to be a black man."[22] By which she meant, I think, that Winehouse's lyrical recreations crossed the color and gender line. Dangerous lines to straddle, to be sure. But, still, why the motivated attention to her behavior and to the production and publicity apparatuses to the relative exclusion of her own work as lyricist? I wondered had anyone wondered to what extent Amy Winehouse's turmoil related to her very private attempts to coexist with her powerful verbal and vocal lyrical gifts? As the lives of Billie Holiday and Dinah Washington show plainly, coexistence with intense lyrical talent has a well-earned reputation as risky, even more than risqué, business and an MO that matched Winehouse's short life along the ever-blurrier line between on and off stage. Critics and the FBI had obsessed themselves with Billie Holiday's lifestyle, too. Maybe, in both cases, people were just scared that such lyrical connections between living inheritance and birthrights don't obey social structures created and maintained for their security? T. S. Eliot wrote about a would-be lyricist, another love singer, "disturb[ing] the universe." When we listen to Winehouse and consider the reactions she provoked, are we in that territory a century later? Let's cover a little territory and then get back, briefly, to what was so overlooked about Winehouse's music—namely, her voice and, most of all, her writing. And then let's give a moment's attention to the pulse-under-razor in some of her lyricism.

Obviously, features of Winehouse's style were begged, borrowed, and stolen. Everyone knew that. She named "Ray" Charles and "Mr. Hathaway" in her biggest hit, "Rehab."[23] Was that a new thing? Seems to me as I look around the University of Georgia campus where I work, young "white"—they and some of the world may think they're white, Baldwin would say otherwise—men wouldn't even be able to say hello and shake hands without the guidance of black culture telling them to chin up and find a way to touch hands while staring through instead of into each other's eyes. Cross-racial lyric gestures? Am I supposed to be mad at that? Ironically enough, I used to be mad at that! Maybe, on a bad day, I still am. But, if they'd come up with surprising poems and songs about it, I'd be less mad at it. I think. But, it doesn't matter; the fact is that if you live on earth and have electricity (or someone you know does), you've been touched by the rhythms and gestures of black life in America. The question is: then what?

Further furor occurred with news of a video where Winehouse sang racist ditties to the tune of "Heads, Shoulders, Knees, and Toes." I hadn't heard it. It didn't surprise me. I don't want to hear it, really. We all seem to carry around brains full of racial slurs about "our own," whatever *that* means, and other races, sexes, in our heads. Do we really imagine that each individual conjures them up themselves? Is that the inheritance or the birthright? Likely, it's neither. It's the obstruction. When a slurring addict like Winehouse, or a repeat offender like Jesse—"cut his nuts off"—Jackson, or a Spanish—"chinky-eyed"—basketball team lets out in public, or whatever the most recent or next incident is, it's offensive.[24] There's utterly no question about that. It propagates a poison that is, finally, lethal to real people's lives. Even so, me, loyal inheritor of Chuck D's "Elvis, was a hero to most," I sensed very clearly that Winehouse was operating in a different atmosphere, out of a sense of *who* she was being poisoned by that racist venom and, so, chanting in a kind of twisted effort at self-inoculation.

And the hoopla, politics, dope, and money swirled about Amy Winehouse in ways I'd seen before, too. The political substance of Brooks's criticism that Amy Winehouse desecrated the dignified behavior of performers who crafted images of black people compatible with Dr. King's vision of a racially inclusive America, and upon whose musical legacy she borrowed, appears here. She borrowed heavily, no question. But, what's this about desecration? I think everyone really knows that we cannot honestly look at sources of lyrical brilliance for models of good behavior. Maybe the Motown girl groups. Maybe. But, let's not look to Dinah Washington and Billie Holiday or Mahalia Jackson for our models of personal behavior, ok? Is this why Whitney Houston, Chaka Khan, Natalie Cole, Phyllis Hyman, Alicia Meyers, and so many others are left off the well-behaved list used to advance such obstructions? Did they desecrate the dream, too? In "Baby Get Lost," Dinah Washington nods to the moral sense, but she's too busy to follow through. She sings: "I'd try to stop you cheating but I just don't have the time. Cause I've got so many men that they're standing in line." Don't keep listening, one of the men is a seven-foot tall dentist named "Long John."

Speaking of the "rock of ages" obstructing the living inheritance, was it really, again, the role of music to affirm black dignity through respectability? First, as W. E. B. Du Bois noted in horror, and as Billie Holiday noted from *her* childhood in Baltimore—and in a way that echoes many scenes in my own life—many "respectable" black folks might not have been eager to rub elbows with someone like Amy Winehouse. No home training. Second, I doubt members of this critical moral minority would tolerate, say, an upload of twenty hours worth of day-in-the-life, real-time footage of Billie Holiday in action. F and N bombs for all, she'll make your toenails curl up. And before we go washing Barry Gordy's feet in hot oils, now, if the Motown men and women were prodded into respectability (the ambiguities about which obstructions poets like Melvin Dixon, Cheryl Clarke, and others have long had lots to say) for the Dream, and they most certainly were, no doubt, they were also prodded—flipped hair, pearls, diction lessons and all—that way for the cross-over cash. Why else move the operation to a city named for *los angeles* and dedicated to covering the globe with celluloid delusions.

Cross-racial heresy and the poisoned privacy meets media frenzy dilemma are all old friends of pop talent, aren't they? Billie Holiday did a year in federal prison for it. No, scratch that, she did life—*and*, death. The contemporary spectacle was a friend of the agents and record labels while their eyes were watching the ten-second news cycle. Some artists handle it better than others. And, some make a lot of money for someone while it happens. It's probably obvious that (the mistaken for) *white* train wrecks do make a lot more money for someone than the black ones do. Legions and generations of black blues and jazzmen and women who were geniuses and train wrecks, and some who lived dignified anonymous lives and some veering from one to the other and back, did it basically for free! Some lyric brilliance coexists with obscurity for decades; Samuel Beckett and Thelonious Monk were in their forties before many people paid much attention to their work.

But, after the protests and indignation on cable news and in the blogosphere, none of this seemed new—much less news—to me at all. At bottom, it was an unavoidable ebb and flow, like sunrise and sunset, in a fundamentally delusional culture. Except that there were lyrics of rare quality being delivered in Winehouse's work, I found that lyric work was obstructed by the conversation among commentators.

If her actual voice and music were often absent from the conversation, was it just the buckets of money, media play, and the way her private demise was made pornographically public? So, why Amy Winehouse? Well, what about *talent*? Signaling an impasse between the public mode of culture critique and the intimate shades of a musician's craft, Brooks, wrote: "Winehouse has been lauded for essentially throwing [Billie] Holiday

along with Foster Brooks, Louis Armstrong, Wesley Willis, Megan Mul-
lally's Karen on *Will and Grace*, Moms Mabley and Courtney Love into
a blender and pressing pulse."[25] This is, indeed, quite a brilliant, hybrid
observation in its own right. However, it obscures the delicate and dangerous texture of lyrical labor. The precarious vulnerability of poets in
that condition is a subject best dealt with elsewhere; the crucial point at
present is that, when the chips are down, a *person* achieves the passionate
detachment of lyrical clarity and invention, not a blender. And during the
key moments when it happens, they're as good as deaf and blind. Interviewed in 1969, Baldwin told *Transition* magazine that questions about the
depth at which lyrical craft is actually developed and deployed "involve
the writer's sensibilities at a level at which he can't defend himself."[26] If
there were buttons to push there would have been a million Amy Wine-
houses. There aren't. And, in the legion of imitators (Adele and many
others) one can easily and immediately tell which is which.[27]

When we say culture, sometimes, we are also talking about art; and
music. So, why were aesthetics (sound) and lyrics (writing) and lyricism
(apt performance) so missing from the discussion of Amy Winehouse
while she was alive? It may have been that simple, her lyrics made it unavoidably obvious that she *was* alive. Millions heard that. Or, they heard
something. A living inheritance was morphing into a birthright.

Aesthetics. Granting all the politics of identity, yet and still, shockingly,
frighteningly, like Billie Holiday, Amy Winehouse was able to write it
out and then *live a line* in a song. "Inwardness coupled with outwardness" (*Cross*, 59). It's about how to sing with one foot in the song and
one foot in the world and be both places and neither at the same time. In
other words, you have to be who you are *and* who you are *not* in prideful
contest with *what* the world thinks you are and aren't. In *The Devil Finds
Work*, remembering his encounter with Orson Welles's all-black *Macbeth* troupe, Baldwin glimpsed something similar to this lyric exchange;
he said it was "because [the actors] were themselves" that they "could play
Macbeth." In other words, they could be who they were and who they
weren't. And, then, between the performers and the audience, at least for
him, it amounted to "flesh challenging flesh" (*CE,* 504). It's tough to do
that. It's tough to know that the bottom of who you are has little pre-
dictable to do with whom you think (let alone *what* other people think)
you are. That's the lyric: language astraddle indeterminate facets of what
makes, and keeps, us human. The identity containers, some imagine, reinforce the hierarchies and keep them safe. But it only feels safe, if it does,
if you enjoy your (or, maybe someone else's) place in the pyramid. Lan-

guage, therefore, that causes the walls to shake will be, at least, as difficult to accommodate for some, as it is necessary for others. Baldwin told Studs Terkel: "That's what the Blues and Spirituals are all about. It's the ability to look on things as they are and survive your losses."[28]

Joyce's Stephen Dedalus said, "Song is the simple rhythmic liberation of an emotion."[29] It's a complex simplicity and, from the evidence, a liberation—like so many—with deeply ambiguous consequences. Rich wrote: "these scars bear witness / but whether to repair / or destruction / I no longer know."[30] In other words, it's a real risk. On the other hand, if you don't know you can survive your losses, you're not free, not free enough to take the risks that freedom requires. In this it helps to be able to distinguish real losses from pseudo-forfeitures in which we cunningly cover our own losses by trying to pay someone else's dues. Sometimes it feels like a strict accounting of whose is whose, exactly, would solve the impossible, interpersonal tangle. But, it won't; this is because the rational grid of homelands of which racial identity is but one dimension cannot map a human reality.

And, this doesn't mean one does—or can do—any of this alone. That key lyrical point is often missed. Like Baldwin wrote of his days in the pulpit, allowing for all the preparation and self-deceit involved: "In the middle of a sermon, I knew that I was somehow, by some miracle, really carrying, as they said, 'the Word'—when the church and I were one. Their pain and their joy were mine, and mine were theirs" (*CE,* 306). We reach a language somewhere hidden in us that, as Rich writes, is "no longer personal." But, by this point we can clearly see that that's not quite it, either. The lyric voice routed through the "living inheritance" is, indeed, beyond the personal. At the same time, it's not *not* personal, either. Is there a word for that? In my experience, when the beyond but not *not* personal blurs inter- versus intra-racial dynamics into each other, well, there's a word for *that*—trouble.

Such complex traffic is the crux of the living lyric tradition, a map of the immediate simultaneity of otherwise divergent interior and public lives. Tangents. Lyrics. Ever looked at a Francis Bacon triptych and seen your portrait? Millions have. It's the opposite approach to an epic condition. It's the same with Kara Walker. Baldwin found, surprisingly, that the route to the universal, the birthright, leads through things that aren't things about the most intensely *private* reaches of our beings. The counterintuitive, lyrical logic goes like this: if you can touch that private thing that's so private it's a secret from yourself, that seems like it's yours and yours alone, and if you can voice that thing, other people will see themselves there. The language will shuck itself open to the reader. A listener will overhear something of yours, now, in *their* name. Something that isn't them appears in their image. That is to say, if you can really get alone, you realize you're not. Go figure. And, then get ready for what becomes possible, and impossible—and whether in repair or destruction one isn't usually sure—when the lyric makes the divisions between identity containers into permeable membranes.

And, yes, and with all the well-founded critiques of Amy Winehouse, with all of it, the child could summon that lyric space and communicate it. She did do that. Not every performer can do that. No one really knows how he or she does that. Smokey Robinson went into Marvin Gaye's house while he was writing *What's Going On*. Marvin said, "Smoke, this album is being written by God, and I'm just the instrument that he's writing it through."[31] Maybe, maybe not. But it wasn't really "Marvin," either. And Marvin knew that and it was tough for Marvin to know that.

All lyric origins aren't quite so intensely metaphysical. Still, it's tough to pin them down. On July 10, 1936, during her first recording session as the featured artist, with studio time left over and a scheduled song that no one liked, Bernie Hanighen asked Billie Holiday if she would record an extemporaneous blues. Reluctantly, she agreed. The first version of "Billie's Blues," her first copyright, was recorded on the spot.[32] In 1940 during the ASCAP strike that prevented broadcasters from airing songs copyrighted with them, Arthur Herzog recalled that "the only things that got on the air were things like 'Jeanie with the Light Brown Hair,' things in the public domain."[33] Herzog wasn't an ASCAP member and knew that BMI had begun to license music during the strike. Looking to get a song on the radio, he met up with Billie Holiday on a night off. Herzog's story echoes Billie's version from *Lady Sings the Blues*. Both stories illuminate how lyrics can originate in collective dynamics and—together with concentrated focus—enlist the periphery of the writer's attention. Herzog:

> I said to Billie, this is the idea I've got, and I want you to give me an old-fashioned Southern expression that we can turn into a song. . . . She scratched her head and came up with nothing. . . . We turned to conversation about her mother, Sadie, and about how she was opening up an after-hours illicit joint, and wanted money from Billie, and how Billie didn't want to give it to her, didn't have it, and in a moment of exasperation she said, "God bless the child." And I said, "Billie, what does that mean?" She said, "You know. That's

what we used to say—your mother's got money, your father's got money, your cousin's got money, but if you haven't got it yourself, God bless the child that's got his own." And I said "That's it Billie." And the song took twenty minutes to do as it stands today . . . we took it down to a publisher, and the publisher snapped it up because Billie had the authority to record it.[34]

But the saying *is* not the lyric. Billie Holiday had had the saying in her life, a conversation about something else brought it up. Herzog recognized it. She pinned the saying to a floating moth of a melody and injected it with . . . well, with what? Voice, sure. But, what's that? Roland Barthes said it's when the reality of the body—by which he meant as yet unwritten history—comes out of someone's mouth.[35] That's closer. From here we can say that the lyric voice—here in Billie's creation of "God Bless the Child"—carries something unknown (to her) in herself, something inherent in her that she didn't own or consciously control, something without an exact name. By naming that dimension, the lyric adds a name to history. Herzog said that Billie Holiday had the "authority to record it."[36] At bottom, as discussed in Chapter 4, her authority comes from the way she handled this dimension of the lyric. By living it and lyricizing that. A great lyricist makes it difficult to tell which is it and which is that, where one thing (the song, for instance) stops and another (the listener) begins.

There's no map to the origins (although it seems to be close to some pain center in the brain of the gifted and afflicted) of this talent and there damned sure isn't an etiquette guide for how to handle that gift. Baldwin called his workspaces torture chambers. In them he worked as if even *he* didn't know his name. A list of lyric writers from John Keats to Marvin Gaye to Ms. Winehouse's Mr. Hathaway and many others won't necessarily produce a viable group of people to run for Senate or to affirm anyone's respectability. Then again, neither will any other one hundred randomly selected people (including, obviously, the present senators). *That's* the key delusion in the obstruction. At some point, in dealing with people room has to be made for persons. That's what Baldwin thought Amen meant.

The lyricists affirm plenty: we're here; this is who we really are. They leap into the dark and say, "if it's there in me, it's there in us all." Is there any real dignity—never mind respectability—without that affirmation? Baldwin told Studs Terkel, "my responsibility [to readers] is to try to tell the truth as I see it—not so much about my private life, as about their private lives."[37] By the 1980s, Baldwin had learned the difference between pride—a search for and assertion of the "first person"—and vanity, an ego-driven defense or assertion of selfhood. The difference, he thought, was that vanity depended upon disguises while pride searched for a way beyond any mask of the moment. Pride was, therefore, deeply inclined toward the collective, beyond the confines of the individual, beyond what Baldwin, in 1961, called "the prison of my egocentricity" (*CE*, 273). It was dangerous business not the least because, when privacy inclines toward not away from other people, one quickly "finds oneself tampering with the insides of a stranger" (272). Intimacy with strangers? In 1961, Baldwin allowed, "one probably has no right to do [that]." Rights or not, that's the lyric reality; by 1979, in *Just Above My Head*, "Our history is each other."[38] Billie Holiday sings in her lover's ear in "Long Gone Blues": "Aw, you trying to quit me baby but you don't know how." How she knew this is one question. But, how do *we* know she's right? Lyric truth. The routes it travels often don't seem to exist at all. That's why it's *lyric* truth. If easy math and newspaper prose could get one there we wouldn't need lyric. We wouldn't need poets.

Lyric. Repair and Ruin. In 1983, at the NBA All-Star Game, Marvin Gaye sang the United States as close as it's ever been (in my ear) to a truly "lyric anthem" of itself. It was as if he'd been possessed by the ghost of Lester Young—who was always in touch with the presence of Billie Holiday and vice versa. Try listening to Marvin's anthem against Lester Young's "I'm Confessin'." You'll hear the connection. Marvin showed up late to the Spectrum. But, when he did arrive, he was *very* respectable. Well dressed, clean, with dark shades on to hide how hopelessly fucked up he was. In his voice, the nation—this is Reagan's America—actually sounded like a place to live, not a prison, not a napalm strike, not a suburb, not a cliché or an abstract "homeland" to be defended through the extermination of "terror" and other murderous, delusional objectives to achieve. I listened then and I listen—via YouTube—now and I think, I could live *there*. And I watch Marvin's chin bump the microphone and see his knees buckle to near-collapse and his face crack open into a vague plea when he belts "La-and of the free." I think, shit, I *do* live there.[39] And, I wonder what color flashed behind those shades when he whispered "Oh lord" (just off the mic) at the close of the song. And he did it in Philadelphia, where Billie was pinned to the narcotics charge that sent her to federal prison. She came out nine months later in March 1948, banned from New York nightclubs and broke two box office records at Carnegie Hall before the year was over. Almost sixty years before Winehouse's "Rehab," after beating narcotics charges in 1949, the first song she recorded (on August 17) was "Ain't Nobody's Business If I Do." "Listeners," wrote Steven Lasker, "considered it her anthem."[40] She never played in a New York City jazz club again.[41] Life. It's nobody's business. In 1967, New York City Mayor John Lindsay ended the regulations that had Holiday (and many others) banned from performing in clubs. She had been dead for eight years. As for Marvin, after the All-Star Game appearance, he was dead in less than a year.

So, yes. That racial apartheid American-style and the sheer terror of life on the denied territory athwart Thomas Jefferson's disease-and-genocide depopulated, slave-state dream of a tabula rasa with inalienable rights has forced some black folks to *show out*, perform, dress well, and behave better than that no matter the hell inside marks an important line in the sand. It's a valuable principle of coherence for black culture with its own dissident tradition. It's why people like Robert Williams, Malcolm X, and Baldwin weren't on stage at the March on Washington. So, was it the point that Amy Winehouse should put that part of the culture in the mix too? Sure, why not? If she'd lived long enough to have grown up, she might have. At the peak of her contested visibility, she was twenty-five and living a very high-velocity life.

Lyrics. Aesthetics. Why do it? I've listened to a thousand singers and few of them *live a line* in a song like Ms. Winehouse did. The pulse of her lyrics traversed and blurred the color line. She was describing her life; at bottom, it was autobiography. But, strictly speaking, maybe it wasn't just *her* life she was living in these songs; that's true of every autobiography we have. These stories are *imagined*. Lives come apart and come back together in the turbulence of an imagination. Alberto Giacometti would spend hours sculpting or painting his model's face (his brother, his wife, a lover, friends) and then go to dinner with them (usually around 3 AM) and claim that he didn't recognize them at all. Things get loosed in a lyric, that's why we need them. And, why we fear them. And, I think, it's part of why the critics sought to obstruct the route between Winehouse's sense of living inheritance and her birthright. The self asks the self: have we met? Beckett found the voice in the murmurs and stirrings of silence, put the words into novels and plays, wrote the best of them in French, and then translated them back into English and often into German. Asked by Charles Juliet about his early difficulties publishing, Beckett said: "It doesn't matter if you're not published. One does it to be able to breathe."[42] Of that conversation in October 1973, Juliet recalled: "I tell him how surprised I am that he has been able to keep faith in writing and communication. . . . He too finds it surprising. He calls it a 'mystery.' I move on to the universality of his work, which has enabled thousands of people throughout the world to discover previously unknown parts of themselves. He nods. 'That too is a mystery.'"[43] Lyric sub-fluency. Identities loosed, borders be damned. Stevie Wonder is (and isn't) Steveland Morris. Yusef Komunyakaa isn't (and is) whomever he was by whatever mismatched name growing up in Louisiana. Ruth Jones in Alabama, Dinah Washington in Chicago. Some little black, Irish Catholic girl in Baltimore by the name of Fagan, someone *else* (and not) sings "Moanin' Low" with Lester Young whispering to her in *our* ear. Who are they when they sing what they sing? Who are *we* when we hear them? Because if they're not exactly who they are, then are we? This lyric business *can* disturb. It's describing things that aren't what they are. Maybe that's why lyric is left out of the culture wars. It won't choose sides. It won't *represent*.

Racial, ethnic borders in a riven, violent world imperil and protect people's lives. Destruction and repair. Which is which? In what ways is who protected and in what ways is who imperiled? Under lyric pressure the abstract guides aren't enough. In *Doubt*, Viola Davis's character tells the concerned sister-principal played by Meryl Streep: "You know the rules maybe, but that don't cover it. . . . You accept what you gotta accept and you work with it."[44] In "The Blue Ghazals," Adrienne Rich held out for the rigor (and terror) of lyrical empiricism: "They say, if you can tell, clasped tight under the blanket,/ the edge of dark from the edge of dawn, your love is a lie."[45] No matter, the imagination won't obey the rules and identities bend, fracture, and tangle in creative work. At that pressure, one can't defend oneself. That vulnerability is the closest thing to safety the lyric world offers; there really isn't any being one traveler. The myth of "one traveler" is the American innocence, again; in *The Fire Next Time*, Baldwin wrote his nephew: "It is the innocence which constitutes the crime" (*CE,* 292). As Du Bois knew way back when and as Michelle Cliff's brilliant book, *If I Could Write This in Fire*, shows again and again, being what George Oppen called "numerous" in America is ever an interracial, fraught, reality. All artists aren't well studied in matching one dimension of experience (of a life) to the others. But, their skill and foibles and guts illuminate otherwise invisible lies and perils and, hopefully, otherwise invisible boons and pleasures and truths. As an artist, while one is busy tripping the invisible beams of the alarms (which is never the point of a piece, much less a life, really), it's hard to tell which is which. Enter, critics.

In the end, who knows just whose life (or lives and how many) sounded in Amy Winehouse's voice? But, in the lines she lived, she had made it hers (and, and by *lyric*, so, she made it ours) better than crowds and crowds of others. Here and there on the records it happens. The critics and audiences know this. And by obsessing the obstructions, it seemed the audience and critics had as much trouble dealing with her gift as she did. T. S. Eliot wrote that the perfect critic must first submit to the work; get eye to eye and toe to toe with the art. Were critics doing that while Amy Winehouse was alive? Many in her audience were. When I do that, it's moving and scary. How, for instance, did she learn to differentiate between real human connection that leads us beyond our masks signaling needs (existential, political) beyond narrow desires and the pseudo-attractions between people that mirror our vanities and reinforce the prison of egocentricity? In "You Sent Me Flying," my pick for her single-greatest recording, Winehouse sang, "A simple attraction that reflects right back to me / So, I'm not as into you as I appear to be." She was nineteen when she sang that. Standing there, next to that moment, one can see the incredible wealth that comes with having some sense of what to do with that apprehension, of where it leads. And, about the origins of that sense, say, in an audience, of what to do with attractions that refract outward, a musical angularity that sounds beyond the ego prison of the narcissist, the solipsist and the masochist.

Moments at the threshold of apprehensions like that litter the records. I find them, however, most densely present in two performances available on YouTube, solo vocals with acoustic guitar accompaniment. Black men accompanied on guitar in both cases: "Love Is a Losing Game" and "Stronger Than Me." To Femi Temowu's joyous, in a way even protective, accompaniment, "Stronger Than Me" works in the blues-signifying tradition over gender roles. Echoes of "Long Gone Blues" and "Baby Get Lost," and even something twisted out of Aretha Franklin's "Respect," sound out of Winehouse's delivery. The woman's voice tells the man he should be stronger than she is while she—showing, if not always explicitly telling, strength—distills her needs and voice into crystal clear beams of being. The lyrics twist and reverse gender roles in which it's the man who always wants to discuss his feelings. Meanwhile, thirsty for physical intimacy, the woman in the song wants the emotions on the shelf. She taunts the man for his passivity. She curses the curse of the superwoman myth and riffs on race informing her lover that she "pales" when compared with who he takes her for. She dips into the American songbook quoting, "You Don't Know What Love Is," but instead of the mutual romance of being lost in the unknown, she demands he get it together and get a grip. Dinah Washington sang, "I'm a girl who blew a fuse." Billie Holiday: "Ah, you're trying to quit me baby but you don't know how." In "Stronger Than Me," Winehouse openly questions whether the source of a man's strength is, indeed, masculine, and if so then, she demands, what gives? She echoes the ancestry and ironies of this search in the voices that preceded her. I would love to hear Hot Lips Page with a plunger mute filling in windows with Ms. Winehouse. Keep the Dap-Kings. I prefer the music solo without the retro-production, the pseudo-sixties, and the stage spectacle. This gives her lyrical precision the spotlight-space and attention it deserves and rewards.

Going under. At the Mercury Awards in 2007, her version of "Love Is a Losing Game" is classic concert songstress lyricism. The tune swims in the whirlpool like a bird with a broken wing. Afloat, for now. And, Ms. Winehouse behaved herself even if her tattoos didn't. Maybe it's borrowed straight from Billie Holiday at La Scala? Or stolen. She stands at the microphone like Sade's shadow figure. Because he was there at those pianos with Billie Holiday at the end, I'd love to ask Mal Waldron what he hears in this performance. That "no longer [but *not* not] personal" birthright that lives in those lines through Amy Winehouse's inherited voice probably didn't announce itself when it appeared. Likely, like any inheritance, it knew her before she knew it. Could she have handled it better? Yes. Who knows? I don't. Would I have? Am I stronger than Amy Winehouse? Was I when I was twenty-five? These questions are meaningless. Or maybe they're not. But, they shouldn't overshadow the brilliant lines the woman lived in her work.

Take a few reads through the lyrics of "Love Is a Losing Game." Then dial up the Mercury Awards performance and listen again. Where did she get *that* lyrical ground to stand on? I know she didn't pour it out of anybody's blender. And, what *did* that cost? Cost who? If she stole it upfront, she paid for it soon enough. With interest. In "Love Is a Losing Game," she sang vocal equivalents for what memories do when they tear through the mind, and she ripped the word *m-i-n-d* apart and into the sound (if it makes sound) of tearing flesh. If tearing flesh didn't used to make a sound, it does now. As Adrienne Rich put it in "Meditations for a Savage Child," another "lesson of the human ear."[46] Lyric brilliance. Always dialogic, always ours. That *is* new. Like Pound said about real poetry, it's news that stays news.

And, watch with your ears or (via YouTube) listen with your eyes as Winehouse, echoing Sade's "Is It a Crime," marks the intricate and intimate lines between what we should do and shouldn't do to and for a lover. She marks them the only way they can be marked, by crossing back and forth and surviving the losses. As I've mentioned before, Baldwin, in "The Uses of the Blues," recounted a story about Miles Davis giving an addicted and broke Billie Holiday one hundred dollars. And someone said to Miles, "man, you know she's going to go buy dope with it." And Miles responds: "Baby, have you ever been sick?" (*Cross*, 65). Which, in whatever imperfect way, was Miles saying two things: first, the crux of the lyric dynamic, "don't fool yourself, it could be you"; and, the compassion born of experience, "go easy on her, ok?" I wrote the first draft of this essay in 2008 in response to what struck me as obstructive critiques of Amy Winehouse's life and work while she was alive. I could see she was in a terrible position tangled up between rare talent and real trouble. I was hoping she would survive and I was hoping that her work would find listeners who could use it to seek their own living inheritance en route to a sense of birthright that enlivens the world. And, really, it was her talent that was rare. Her troubles were actually very common. So, I wondered, why focus on the common? Maybe it's just a plain old distraction.

Baldwin himself could be very abrupt and hostile when he thought the tradition of black musical exploration and witness was being trifled with. His sense of those politics was sensitive but at times the metaphorical "rock of ages" drew his wrath in ways that shocked those who knew him. In the fall of 1969, months after leaving Hollywood and giving up on the Malcolm X project with Columbia Studios, he trashed an outdoor café in Istanbul because a Turkish singer's rendition of the blues struck an ill-chord. The hope borne in lyrical pursuits of the living inheritance that traverses whatever terms of cultural apartheid travelers encounter, nonetheless, glimmers throughout Baldwin's work and life. And, the next day, Baldwin brought flowers to Zeynep Oral, the young journalist who he had terrified with his outburst in Istanbul.[47]

Against looming shadows in *If Beale Street Could Talk* (1974), one resonant instance appears when Sharon Rivers goes to Puerto Rico to confront the woman who had accused her future son-in-law, Fonny, of raping her. Waiting to speak with the accusing woman's husband in a nightclub, she watches a rock band working with a blues and gospel tradition with which, according to Ms. Rivers's ear, they had but superficial experience. A former singer who grew up surrounded with the energies of the gospel and blues, Sharon listens with one ear and, with the other, hears black music, black lives, being imitated. The scene travels through a moment of distant recognition: "That song is Birmingham, her father and her mother, the kitchens, and the mines . . . this is the song, which, to different words, if words indeed there are, the young people on the bandstand are belting, or bolting out. And they know nothing at all about the song they are singing: which causes Sharon to wonder if they know anything at all about themselves."[48]

Rock of ages. Watching and listening to the young people's song, the American song sprung from black roots in gospel and the blues; Sharon hears what she hears and listens for what she doesn't: "*My gal and I!*" cries the undernourished rock singer, whipping himself into an electronic orgasm. But no one who had ever had a lover, a mother or a father, or a Lord, could sound so despairingly masturbatory."[49] Through his character, however, Baldwin does not simply tune out the sound. Instead, Sharon Rivers watches them on the pivot: "For it is despair that Sharon is hearing, and despair, whether or not it can be taken home and placed on the family table, must always be respected. Despair can make one monstrous, but it can also make one noble: and here these children are, in the arena, up for grabs."[50] The band finishes the song and Baldwin signs off on what he's heard: "Sharon claps for them, because she prays for them."[51] *Something*, a thin thread of a living inheritance, was being recognized. Baldwin doubted it would extend to any mainstream American collective but, he was committed to promoting living quests over obstructions, black energy over chaos and entropy, and to helping those who might try. Meanwhile, as he knew, not everyone—at times not even he—listened like Sharon Rivers.

Often lyrical attention discovers historical convergences in action. Lyric time is time copiously made of other times. "Inter-viewing" *Take This Hammer* and Barry Jenkins's brilliant 2009 film, *Medicine for Melancholy*, offers a unique perspective on racial and social terrains of the twenty-first century traced in relation to fifty years of gentrification in San Francisco.

# 8

# Speechless in San Francisco
## "A somewhat better place to lie about": An Inter-View

U pon entering her new acquaintance's one-room Tenderloin district apartment, Joanne Hardwicke sees the following: a surplus fixed-gear bicycle, a bed that takes up half the floor space of the apartment, an aquarium, and a framed poster of text with "LIES" stenciled in block letters over it. The camera approaches the poster over Hardwicke's shoulder. As it pans down, we read:

> SAN FRANCISCO is now developing programs to correct blighted and congested conditions and to deal with an accumulation of housing that is continuously aging and deteriorating faster than it is being rehabilitated or replaced. The study area contains an estimated 1008 residential structures, many of which are in various degrees of deterioration and in need of rebuilding or replacement. More than 50 percent of the structures are past middle age with an estimated average of sixty-seven years. It is this condition which results in neighborhood blight and calls for both major public improvement and private rehabilitation and reconstruction.

> Leonard S. Mosias for the San Francisco Redevelopment Agency,
> "Residential Rehabilitation Survey Western Addition Area 2,"
> July 1962

The poster explicitly links the world in Barry Jenkins's 2009 film, *Medicine for Melancholy*, with the politics of urban renewal and gentrification at the center of Baldwin's historic visit to San Francisco in *Take This Hammer*

**215**

Joanne in front of the 1962 housing rights poster linking Jenkins's film to the
politics of "redevelopment" explored in *Take This Hammer*.

(1963).[1] While touring the city, Baldwin's guide, Orville Luster, points
to a neighborhood "slated for redevelopment." Baldwin: "When you say
redevelopment?" Luster: "Removal of Negroes." Baldwin: "That's what
I thought you meant." In *Medicine for Melancholy*, upon reentering the
scene from the bathroom, Micah asks Joanne, "Are you familiar with
that?" A short exchange ensues:

J: Um, kinda, I'm a transplant.
M: Born and raised. My folks lived out there. Imagine the Lower
    Haight, nothing but black folks and white artists.

J: Hm. But why would you put it on your wall? I know you're not supposed to forget but it's not like you would forget without seeing it everyday.

M: Oh no no, it's not like that. You know people just walk around this city like everything's so perfect and it's all good and everything and I don't know this just reminds me that poor folks still got it hard like you look at Mission Bay and this poster's still relevant.

Fearing his politics will kill the vibe in the moment, Micah dissembles: "I'm just saying," lightens the mood, and goes to make tea. The conversation concludes:

J: Do you even like it here?
M: What?
J: It seems like this city just pisses you off.
M: Naw I love this city. I hate this city but I love this city.

Then the film cuts away to a montage of color-saturated vistas of San Francisco that look like footage from a 1960s-era home movie shot over a basso nova–style score by the group Total Shutdown. Over this cut-away, Micah elaborates his ambivalence:

I mean the hills the fog. Any man that can find himself a street corner has got himself a view. San Francisco's beautiful and it's got nothing to do with privilege. It's got nothing to do with beatniks or yuppies it just is. You shouldn't have to be upper middle class to be a part of that.

Baldwin agreed. In *No Name in the Street*, of time spent with Huey Newton's brother Melvin in 1967, he described how he loved "simply walking through the streets of San Francisco, by far my favorite town— my favorite American town" (*CE*, 464). Nonetheless, *Take This Hammer* opens with a young black man, Famous Bell, comparing San Francisco to Birmingham, Alabama:

I'll tell you about San Francisco. The white man he's not taking advantage of you out in public like they doing down in Birmingham but he's killing you with that pencil and paper, brother. When you go to look for a job, can you get a job? [*Gesturing to another man in the crowd*] Can you get a job Winkle?

The text in Micah's poster in *Medicine for Melancholy* provides exhibit A for what this speaker in *Take This Hammer* means by "killing you with that pencil and paper, brother." *Take This Hammer* then cuts to James Baldwin sitting with the group of young people. Baldwin: "This is the San Francisco Americans pretend does not exist. They think I'm making it up." Later in the opening moments of the film Baldwin's comments echo the young man immediately above and then provide a script that Micah's ambivalent speech in *Medicine for Melancholy* comes close to paraphrasing. Baldwin's comments connect directly with the message "LIES" stenciled over the text in Micah's poster:

> What is really crucial is whether or not the country, the people in the country, the citizenry, are able to recognize that there is no moral distance, no moral distance, which is to say, no distance, between the facts of life in San Francisco and the facts of life in Birmingham. And there's no moral distance, which is to say no distance, between President Kennedy and Bull Connor because the same machine put them both in power. One's got to tell it like it is and that's where it's at. . . . I imagine it's easy for any white person walking through San Francisco to imagine that everything was at peace. Cause it certainly looks that way on the surface. San Francisco's much prettier than New York. And, it's easier to hide in San Francisco than it is in New York because you've got the view you've got the hills and you've got the San Francisco legend too which is that it's cosmopolitan and forward-looking. But it's just another American city. And if you're a black man that's a very bitter thing to say . . . but this city's a somewhat better place to lie about. Which is really all it comes to.[2]

As is the case, then, with so much in contemporary life, art, and culture, if one moves through it having seriously attended how James Baldwin's work aligns different dimensions of experience, one has the sense that Baldwin had already been here. And, knowing something about the difficulty of finding what he found there when he *was* here, one apprehends the present with a deeper sense of what it is than, at times, it appears, the present is capable of containing on its own. One has then, in short, a sense of history, a usable past, which, speaking of America to Studs Terkel, Baldwin said "is precisely what we don't have here."[3]

The connection between the two films is actual as well as geographical and conceptual. Barry Jenkins had *Take This Hammer* and Baldwin in mind during the writing and shooting of *Medicine for Melancholy*. The director claims Baldwin as a central influence. Neither film is widely known. *Take this Hammer* is an obscure, historical documentary. *Medicine for Melancholy* made the usual tour of festivals, garnering its share of nominations, reviews, small awards, and limited release distribution in major cities in 2009 and 2010. Jenkins's first full-length film ostensibly portrays a two-night, one-night stand. It features two characters: Micah, a black aquarium designer (played by Wyatt Cynac) who lives at Geary and Leavenworth, and Joanne Hardwicke, a twenty-four-year-old, unemployed black woman (played by Tracey Heggins) with vaguely gender-conscious artistic ambitions (she's currently designing T-shirts with the names of women film directors) who lives with a successful (white) curator in San Francisco's fashionable Marina neighborhood. Both films succeed in their own right. But they benefit from encounters with each other. *Take This Hammer* provides *Medicine for Melancholy* a usable past to gauge what's medicine and what's melancholy, and *Medicine for Melancholy* offers *Take This Hammer* a glimpse of its future. The combination offers contemporary viewers crucial terms to rethink certain racial and post-racial contours of our lives.

An inter-viewing of these films reveals how such demographic redevelopment exiles whole spectrums of physical and verbal energy, intensities of movement and real-time arabesques of imagination. Baldwin's film documents a brilliant diversity of devotion and anger as well as analysis and confrontation in San Francisco's black neighborhoods, anthologies of energy swept by "history" out of the city and across the Bay. In *Medicine for Melancholy*, Jenkins remaps the terrain using subtle, lyrical, visual, and musical angles of articulation to resuggest the war between abstractions of *black* and *white* and the ways they cover up (and depend upon) endless near-imperceptible contests in shade, tone, and texture. Jenkins's characters walk through a largely whitewashed urban space while the film restores myriad gradations of nuance without which actual human social and intimate life suffocates.

By constantly shifting the chromatic saturation of the film's visual palette—from stark black and white to maximal color saturation and by degrees in between—and by using a skillfully deployed and expertly chosen soundtrack and score as a tonal backdrop and narrator, Jenkins invokes ineffable and subconscious dimensions of his characters' experiences as black people in a white city. Of the fluctuating color palette, Jenkins wrote:

It's a thing that tracks along with the characters and is very deliber-
ate ... it's more to do with the characters relating to one another,
as the only two people of color in a film that's pretty much out and
about in a significant city. . . . We tried to be subtle with it, it's not
speaking directly to the point but it's there for anyone who wants.[4]

Not only is it not the point, the film shows that the range of subtlety is
nearly impossible to make conscious, to bring into focus in conversation.
Whenever these two young people open their mouths, the abstractions
emerge in ways that obstruct their connections to themselves and each
other. The resulting "rock of ages"[5] makes one wonder if all the subtle
beauty and possibility surrounding them isn't a delusion, a make-believe
indulgence, even a mask for oppression.

## Tonal Narration: Songs in the Key of an Indie-American Make-Believe

Part of the brilliance in *Medicine for Melancholy* lies in Jenkins's attempts
to position the characters in a twenty-first century "indie" landscape
where racial (musical, biographical, even visual) identifications operate
in aggressively angular and asymmetrical ways. Indeed, Jenkins's *blipsters*
(my students in Athens, GA tell me this is—or *was*—the term for young
black people who identify with the indie rock scene more than—or in a
sense undifferentiated from—urban R&B or hip-hop culture) appear to
live in a world distant from the sledgehammers of historical segregation
featured in *Take This Hammer*. They also appear distant from contemporary racial identifications and aspirations (and the clichés that go with
them) with tangible links to the cultural politics of the civil rights era
in the urban North and West and in the South set in place in films by
black directors such as Charles Burnett, Spike Lee, Ava DuVernay, John
Singleton, Theodore Witcher, and Tyler Perry.

*Medicine for Melancholy* signals this distance in musical and geographical terms. Jenkins eschews Perry's Atlanta, Lee's Bed-Stuy, Witcher's
Chicago, Burnett and Singleton's Crenshaw Boulevard, Los Angeles, and
even his own moorings in Miami in setting his film in San Francisco.
Announcing its musical allegiances, the film debuted at the 2009 South
by Southwest music festival in Austin, Texas, the annual mecca for indie
rock bands. Indeed, San Francisco and the film's music function as indispensible supporting characters. Micah and Joanne meet at a party, wake
up the next morning after sex but still don't know each other's names.

They spend the next twenty-four hours walking and riding their trendy bicycles, visiting various San Francisco sites, napping, more sex, making dinner in Micah's one-room studio, and spend their second (we think, last) night together dancing at a decidedly hip, apparently almost (meaning, but for them) all-white, indie-rock club. Throughout the itinerary, we gauge their relationship to each other largely in relation to a sonic make-believe of subtle shades and nuances seemingly unpoliced by social, historical, or racial consciousness.[6] In this, the brilliantly deployed soundtrack of South by Southwest–style bands provides a sense of the characters' experience of themselves, the city, and each other that goes far beyond what they can articulate in conversations with each other. The result places them, and us, out on a limb, involves all in an experience, which can't be translated into language: a lyric condition.

The music in the film watches the characters with the viewer, connects all to the floating scenes of San Francisco, and frequently takes on the role of tonal narrator. The film opens with a song about meeting, "New Year's Kiss," and closes with one about parting, "Tonight Was a Disaster," both written by Owen Ashworth and performed by Ashworth in the solo act, Casiotone for the Painfully Alone. In between, Micah rides his bicycle over Madlib's dub-jazzy "Elle's Interlude"; then the pair ride a carousel over Dickon Hinchliffe's Erik Satie–inspired composition "Le Rallye," make the transition from frantic condom-search to slow-motion, early-evening sex over Gypsophile's "The One I Dream Of," make a second-night-of-a-one-night-stand's dinner over "No One Needs to Know" by the Changes, and head into a slightly-stoned cab ride through the San Francisco night to "Through the Backyards" by Au Revoir Simone singing, "Baby tell me please, is this a dream, spending the night with you." The pitch-perfect match between the indie soundtrack and the textures of black characters' emotional lives found in *Medicine for Melancholy* is unique in American film. Some of this certainly owes to Jenkins and his team—especially James Laxton, director of photography, Nat Sanders, editor, and Greg O'Bryant, music supervisor. And, some of it owes to largely twenty-first century demographic and cultural shifts including the legacy of gentrification in Obama-era American culture.

Mobility in the city that allows the match between the indie tunes and the characters to work in the way it does, of course, is a relatively new and localized—even haphazard—advent in black American life. In *Take This Hammer*, a young man talks with Baldwin about police surveillance that restricts his mobility in 1963 San Francisco. Baldwin asks, "What do you think about the police?" And the man answers:

I think they have a purpose. But, then again the way some of these people do you sometimes when they pick you up, stop you. Like a couple of times you'd be downtown just walking around and they'd look at you and if you look suspicious they would just stop you. Like I was going to the show one night, me and my wife, and we just happened to go around Market Street and we seen this police car go by. All right, and we turned the corner the next corner they stop us, alright, the show starts at 7:45 and we were out there until nine o'clock. And they didn't have an excuse to stop us but they stopped us, searched the car, called in and this and that. Now what was the purpose of that? We weren't doing anything wrong. Nobody was mad.

Then the man turns the questions to Baldwin: "Let me ask you one thing what do the police do when they get mad?" Baldwin: "What do the police do when they get mad?" The man: "Hmm, I mean we ordinary citizens and when we get mad we can do things to hurt people, rob and steal, what do they do when they get mad? Who do they take their steam off on?" Baldwin, smiling, looking as if he doesn't quite believe he's actually being asked: "I think you know the answer to that question." And, the man answers: "Well, I couldn't answer that because the police has never bothered me in that way but I read the newspapers, I've been living around here all my life and I see things that's going on." As if suddenly struck by the man's sincerity, Baldwin, now very serious, answers: "Well, when a policeman gets mad he's got a gun and he's got a club." And, the man: "And they use them too don't they?" Baldwin answers, now clearly perplexed at how this man only hesitantly admits what (Baldwin assumes) he very well knows. Assuming his role of stating starkly and openly things that many people were too afraid to state (or even to know) in direct terms, Baldwin, still in partial disbelief, confirms: "Yeah!?" This conversation, like many others in *Take This Hammer*, sketches myriad subtleties with which black people ca. 1963 partially acknowledged and partially protected themselves from the knowledge of their condition. The film documents a wide variety, in fact, of such lyrical *styles* in which people sifted their sense of the so-called facts of life for a black man in San Francisco, which, in Baldwin's descriptions above, mirror (with "no distance") those in Birmingham, Alabama, and, indeed, bitterly, in any other American city.

In *Medicine for Melancholy*, the mobility of the characters through the city on cue with the indie music's tonal narration of mostly breezily ascending and descending emotional pressures and pleasures invites the viewer into a kind of postracial American dreamland. Origins need not apply, everyone's arrived with sufficient SAT scores and neutral-enough phonemes to the extent that the city becomes a welcoming (at best) or neutral (at worst) backdrop to the personal lives unfolding like time-lapse blossoms in the plot. Via the photography and the music, Jenkins sketches lyrical profiles of black characters (and *not* easily classifiable caricatures) into the liberal dream of an American freedom flowing out of human interiors unobstructed by political coercion or social constraint. This is a world of emotional rhythm-gradients and tonal-social structures (along with the names of the bands providing the sounds), one would guess, largely unknown to the lives and CD shelves (even iPod menus) of most residents in black America and habitués of black radio across the country. One thinks, maybe this is a version (unthinkably futuristic at the time) of the "American dream" that possessed Sonny's nameless brother at the outset of "Sonny's Blues"? When Baldwin told those young men in 1963 San Francisco that the country that elects a black president "will not be the country we're sitting in now," one wonders if Jenkins's vision of his characters' emotional-geographical charting of San Francisco, of each other, and of themselves approximates what Baldwin might have had in mind? Maybe. Baldwin was the same age as Joanne Hardwicke (24) in the film when he left his family in New York City and went to Paris. Was he searching for a version of the freedom Jenkins sketches for his characters via the soundtrack in *Medicine for Melancholy*? Maybe.

## Lyrics and the Door of No Return: Black Speechlessness and Speechless Blackness

Unthinkable in 1963, as Jenkins knows, such a vision of life ca. 2009 still contends nonetheless (if less intensely) with its racialized, historical containers in the world and in the consciousness of the characters. As if mixed by a DJ with the nuances of emotional openness in the soundtrack narration, the two floating black signifiers also move in telescoping proximity to the stark, black and white metaphors and realities of the African American epic. That world is submerged (if not silenced) beneath the soundtrack of *Medicine for Melancholy* but still painfully alive in Micah's mind and in the world submerged (if not exiled) by the role of gentrification in the contemporary, "forward looking . . . San Francisco legend." When the atmospherics of the San Francisco cityscape and the indie bands aren't doing all the talking, the characters (Micah bluntly, Joanne reluctantly) wind up in conversations that search for a racialized sense of themselves in an ostensibly de-racialized scene. When Micah appears at Joanne's door (in a condo owned by her curator boyfriend) to return the wallet she left in the cab home from night number one, the upscale neighborhood instigates the following.

M: [Looking incredulously around the apartment.] So you don't pay rent here? [Joanne shakes her head.] Who does pay rent here?

J: No one.

M: Ok, who pays the mortage?

J: My boyfriend.

M: Your boyfriend.

J: My boyfriend.

M: And, where is he?

J: London.

M: London.

J: Yes. London. Would you stop repeating me?

M: Alright. What's he do?

J: He's a curator.

M: A curator. [*Realizing he'd repeated her again*] Sorry. Sorry. It just seems weird that, as a *curator*, he doesn't really have any art on the walls. Like, none. I mean it just seems like, they've probably got like an extra painting or a sculpture lying around that he could have brought home. Sorry. Sorry. Is he white?

J: Does it matter?

M: Yes and no.

J: Well, what if I told you he *is* white. [*Micah makes the "I knew it" laugh-face.*] And, what if I told you we met in a volunteer program in Bayview. Would *that* matter?

M: Yes and no.

J: Oh, I see, you're one of *those* people.

M: Those people?

J: Yes, *those* people, that think that Black History Month is in February because it's the shortest month in the year.

M: It is.

J: Black History Month is in February because Carter G. Woodson wanted Negro History Week to coincide with the births of Frederick Douglass and Lincoln. Both in the same week in February. [*Micah accepts defeat, Joanne continues.*] Ok, well, thank you for returning my wallet. But, you have to go.

M: Why? We're just getting started.

J: You need to leave.

M: What did I say?

The impasse between Micah's insistence that such questions are, like the poster on his wall, "still relevant" and Joanne's position that such questions lead "those people" who insist upon them to dangerously simplified versions of reality threatens to close down the conversation altogether. As he does in the scene described above with the "LIES" poster, Micah lightens the mood, and this time with a rendition of the Mr. Rogers theme song played on guitar to his "one-night-stand neighbor." The scene above sketches the limits of what can be *said* in connecting the postracial dreamland and the submerged, racialized texture of contemporary life. It suggests that gentrification is a psychological and conversational, as well as a demographic and sociological, situation. Making the dichotomy between racial limitation and postracial dreamland explicit, after singing the Mr. Rogers theme jingle in his best Fred Rogers voice, Micah invites Joanne into the latter terrain: "Hey there, one-night-stand neighbor. Wanna go to the land of make-believe with me and King Friday and all the magical critters and creatures?"

The scene that follows directly involves Baldwin's notion of how diasporic speechlessness emanates out of the particularities of the diasporic lyric condition: the way black experiences in the West elude available discourses, forcing people to improvise lyrics, to think for themselves—and communicate with each other—at all. After avoiding being thrown out of Joanne's boyfriend's condo, Micah accompanies her on a boyfriend-/art-related errand (on bicycles, of course). The trip bears none of the violent challenges to mobility experienced by the speakers in *Take This Hammer*. No police appear. But race nonetheless explicitly brackets Micah's idea (as its lack informs Joanne's) of mobility and options for what to do with Obama-era black freedom. After the errand, Joanne suggests they spend the afternoon at SFMoMA. This leads to the following exchange:

M: I don't want to go to MoMA.

J: What's wrong with MoMA?

M: No comment.

J: [*Sensing a return to the racial landscape.*] Ok, black man. So, what do two black folks do on a Sunday afternoon?

M: Go to church. Eat fried chicken. What do two black folks *not* do on a Sunday afternoon?

J: What?

M: Go to a museum.

After his ironic invocation of the stereotyped options, the conversation ends in another of Micah's contradictory stylings of his black life in contemporary San Francisco.

J: That is not funny.
M: It *is* funny.
J: It's *not* funny.
M: It's funny 'cause it's not funny.

The music on at least part of Micah's mind, however, sounds in stark contrast with the film's indie soundtrack and tonal narrator. Playing a game, Micah asks Joanne to name a contemporary song that samples a historical one (in this case Biggie Small and Lil Kim's "Get Money" using Sylvia Striplin and Roy Ayers's 1980 rare groove classic "You Can't Turn Me Away").[7] Joanne responds, "I don't listen to music like that." One wonders, listen (genealogically) like that? Or, music (black) like that? Either way, the game itself is a kind of subtle parable of tensions between mainstream (or indie-alternative) and racial (and romantic) identification. "Get Money" would be familiar to some pop audiences in a mid-1990s era of rap crossover appeal. A mainstream, white, or indie-rock audience wouldn't nearly as likely know "You Can't Turn Me Away." The older song voices itself in a language almost totally, tonally, different from that in pop music, or alternative rock, from the 1980s. Stemming from an era of intense musical apartheid in American pop culture, Sylvia Striplin's delivery of lyrics such as "don't try, don't try, don't try to turn me away ... when you believe in your heart I'll always want to stay" sounds a simultaneous call to a racial and romantic connection from an era where the two were tightly fused. In 1980s popular music, the alternatives were almost exclusively white, radically whitened, or underground. Later in the chapter, we'll see Micah wondering if anything other than his individual location had changed in the alternative-independent musical culture ca. 2009. Apart from a chorus by Micah and a failed (Micah asks, "Why does yours sound like a farting trumpet?") attempt to mimic the bass line by Joanne, neither "Get Money" nor "You Can't Turn Me Away" appears in the actual film. Rather the contrasting blackness of the sampled song and its tonal exile from the indie culture leads the characters to an even deeper sense of the limits of what they're able to talk about, maybe even what they're able to think about.

Speechlessness. The temporary couple does forgo the visit to SFMoMA; instead they tour San Francisco's Museum of the African Diaspora. A compromise. We watch them approach the museum; we overhear Micah's lyrical "MoAD mama, not MoMA." The characters tour the museum, almost five minutes of screen time, without speaking a single word. The viewer accompanies the couple through several exhibits of diasporic culture. In addition to the silence of the characters, the tour includes a full minute where the screen is nearly black while silhouettes of the characters (and the audience) listen to a reading from *The Interesting Narrative of the Life of Olaudah Equiano, or Gustavus Vassa*. Equiano's narrative recounts his capture in West Africa and experience of middle passage and beyond. The tour also pauses at a photograph of the Door of No Return in the slave fort at Gorée Island, Senegal.

The view from this stone opening facing west over the Atlantic Ocean happens to be the precise vantage point from which Baldwin drew one of his most important, diasporic redefinitions of the American vocabulary. A redefinition which reinforces and deepens our sense of the silence between the characters during their tour of MoAD as well as the impasse that appears in each of their attempts to translate between the indie American dreamland narrated by the soundtrack, the role of the "removal of Negroes" in the postracial cityscape of San Francisco, and the racial epic that permeates their minds (especially Micah's) and surrounds them in their indie bubble. In his 1964 essay, "The White Problem," of looking out through this stone passage to the West, Baldwin wrote:

> Let me tell you a small anecdote. I was in Dakar about a year ago, in Senegal, and just off Dakar there is a very small island, which was once the property of the Portuguese. It is simply a rock with a fortress; from Africa, it is the nearest point to America. My sister and I went to this island to visit something called the Slave House. The house was not terribly large. It looks a little like houses you see in New Orleans. That's the truth. It's got two stories and a courtyard and a staircase on each side, sweeping stone staircases. I assume that the captains and the slavers lived upstairs; downstairs were the slave quarters. You walked through a kind of archway, very dark, very low, made of stone, and on either side of you were a series of cells, with stone floors and rusted bits of iron sill embedded in the walls. This may be my imagination, but it seemed to me that the odor was still there, that I could still smell it. What it must have smelled like, with all those human beings chained together, in such a place. I remember that they couldn't speak to each other, because they didn't come from the same tribe. In this corridor, as I say, there are the cells on either side of you, but straight ahead, as you enter the

archway, or corridor, is a very much smaller doorway, cut out of the stone, which opens on the sea. You go to the edge of the door, and look down, and at your feet are some black stones and the foam of the Atlantic Ocean, bubbling up against you. The day that we were there, I tried, but it was impossible—the ocean is as vast as the horizon—I tried to imagine what it must have felt like to find yourself chained and speechless, speechless in the most total sense of that word, on your way to *where*? (*Cross*, 77)

Whether or not Baldwin's historical sense is totally accurate is somewhat beside the point. In fact, polyglot and linguistically *fluid* as such civilizations were, many such captives could well have spoken to each other to some extent. But, that's not the point. The point is that the other side of the Atlantic isn't visible. From this it struck Baldwin that, no matter the language, the experience awaiting those Africans facing west through that passageway was *unspeakable*. It hadn't happened before. It hadn't happened *yet*. The language, the tone and rhythms of speech and movement, didn't exist. Baldwin imagined an immense silence and, at the time those captives looked over the Atlantic, no existing language or sense of style could cover it. In Baldwin's mind, then, those captives were "speechless, speechless in the most total sense of that word, on [their] way to *where*?" (*Cross*, 77). The captives bore dissimilar—possibly conflicting—origins; now, irrespective of that, they were chained together. The new language would have to articulate that chain as part of the journey as well. "You Can't Turn Me Away." Of the musical, cultural labor of filling that silence, Baldwin's gospel singer in *Just Above My Head*, Arthur Montana, told his brother:

> It's strange to feel ... that you come out of something, and something you can't name, you don't know what it is—something that has never happened anywhere, ever, in the world, before.... I don't know any *other* people learned to play honky-tonk, whorehouse piano in *church*! ... And keep both of them going, too, baby, and all the time grinning in Mister Charlie's face.... Wow. And sing a sorrow song so tough, baby, that it leaves sorrow where sorrow is, and gets you where you're going.[8]

Arthur concludes his thoughts about the alchemy of black speech styles and the epic struggle against being "speechless in the most total sense of that word" by saying "And *that's* the beat."[9] At some point, those captives also vanished from the view of anyone watching from the Door of No Return; the languages on the continent would cease to describe them.

And, the sanctioned languages of the West would spend centuries in attempts (which aren't over yet) to pillory and exile as well as to pillage, imitate, and profit from "the beat" as it attempted to name *itself* and its new world.

That ambiguous reality has, of course, called into being an ocean of music over centuries, the sound of modern music is largely unthinkable without it. Options are endless, but Charles Lloyd's 2010 conversational composition, "The Water Is Wide," comes as close as anything I've run across in recent years to voicing the mix of diasporic risk and the style and even grace (see Audre Lorde's "Coal" for a diagram of such diasporic grace under pressure) that's been made by confronting it. As Lloyd's quartet featuring Jason Moran, Reuben Rogers, and Eric Harland make tangible, moreover, it's a heroic and ambiguous legacy shared by all the descendants of those who came to the West through portals such as the one on Gorée Island.

Framed by Baldwin's sense of diasporic speechlessness, we can perceive Jenkins's characters in *Medicine for Melancholy* navigating a silence far wider than they can speak across, deeper than they can fathom. They are connected exactly by "something you can't name." So, mostly they don't try. They've each been told that they don't have to in myriad ways by a culture eager to evade what it conceives of as its past and in a hurry, therefore, to advertise its avowed openness as "postracial." Joanne and Micah largely eschew the lyric challenge to speak the unspeakable. At the close of the MoAD scene, the temporary couple of speechless diasporants sit silently, Joanne with iPod earbuds in her ears. The shadow tone of the scene as the couple sits amid the random noise of the room and the street outside somehow speaks to that speechlessness. The chain between captives is also there. Maybe it's signaled in the chord of Joanne's earbuds. And, I think, the visual tone of the scene speaks to the sense of how Sylvia Striplin's plaintive, rare groove ballad is also a statement of a veiled, matter-of-fact sense of connection among people in the diaspora both in historical and contemporary terms: "You Can't Turn Me Away." The phrase resonates in several levels of historical and contemporary experience. Maybe the title isn't a plea or even a hope; maybe it's a fact. From MoAD the couple leaves the bikes and walks through the city into the soundtrack's narration of emotional atmospherics described as "make believe" above. Of MoAD, Joanne asks, "Have you been there before?" Micah: "The opening, a few times after that." Joanne, as if wondering at herself: "I didn't even know it was there." Fred Rogers hangs up his cardigan.

Wyatt Cenac as Micah and Tracey Heggins as Joanne in *Medicine for Melancholy*.

Far from speechlessness, viewing *Take This Hammer* adds powerful portraits of a black verbal intensity and dense physical immediacy absent from
*Medicine for Melancholy*. Even more, *Take This Hammer* marks a presence
the absence of which, in *Medicine for Melancholy*, save in Micah's "LIES"
poster, bears scarcely a mark. It's as if the historical film reopens a wound
that the contemporary world has attempted to graft into invisibility. Jenkins's portrait of his characters' emotional and geographical freedom takes
place in a depopulated zone, in a city missing whole spectrums of verbal
energy and styles of dense human presence once palpable in the streets of
San Francisco. At one point, Micah casts his imagination back, "Think of

Famios Bell, nineteen, discussing jobs in *Take This Hammer*.

the Lower Haight, nothing but black folks and white artists." In *Take This Hammer*, nineteen year-old Famios Bell notes bitter ironies in the opportunities for jobs that *did* exist for black men in San Francisco ca. 1963:

> Wait, let me tell you. Now, they talking about better jobs. Jobs out here. Want me to tell you what kind of job they gonna give us? They gonna let us tear down our own homes out here in Hunter's Point. That's the job we getting. [*Even Baldwin looks on stunned by the man's speech.*] And you know what they gone pay us? Let me tell you what they gone pay us. They gone pay you two dollars an

hour, they gone hire you in some kind of apprenticeship deal or something like that. Now, what is that gaining you? It's not gaining you a thing. You won't get anything. You'll tear down your own home. It's a job temporarily. And then what you gone do? Where you gone live? You're not going to live anywhere.

Baldwin then enlists a (thirteen-year-old?) young woman in a discussion about the "removal of Negroes" program at Hunter's Point. In a voice shaded with the music of Southern speech, she talks to Baldwin and Luster about her impending homelessness while holding her own in the crowd of young men who've monopolized the conversation thus far.

> JB: And you live around here too?
> YW: Yeah.
> OL: In temporary housing or ...?
> YW: No, I stay in the projects.
> VOICE IN THE CROWD: [*Taunts.*] That *is* temporary housing.
> YW: It ain't no temporary housing no more they tearing them down! They ain't no more. They ain't going to be no place when they get through. We gone be living out in the streets.
> OL: Does that make you feel bad?
> YW: Yeah it make you feel bad there won't be no place to go we'll be living out here in the streets in tents.
> OL: Well, what part of San Francisco would you like to live in?
> YW: I like to stay up here on top of the hill.
> OL: You would?
> YW: Uh, hm.
> OL: How long have you been living on top of the hill?
> YW: Ever since I been born.

Baldwin knew the idiom he was listening to had been created, precisely, to confront the threat of speechlessness and the reality of homelessness connected to the roots and routes of the diaspora itself. In 1961, Studs Terkel played Bessie Smith's "Back Water Blues" for Baldwin and asked him what he heard, Baldwin responded:

> It is very hard to describe that feeling.... What struck me was that she was singing, as you say, about a disaster, which had almost killed her, and accepted it and was going beyond it. There's a fantastic kind of understatement in it. It is the way I want to write, you know. When she says, "My house fell down, and I can't live there no mo'"—it is a great ... a great sentence. A great achievement.[10]

Girl discusses homelessness in Hunter's Point in *Take This Hammer*.

The force and directness of this young woman's responses to questions about the radical contingency of her life amid the forces of redevelopment surrounding her echoes precisely what Baldwin heard in "Back Water Blues." In the footage, remarkably, the young woman confronts the questions about not having anywhere to live directly. Yet, as if shadowboxing with the dialectics of speech/speechlessness and amputation/gangrene, she chews her gum and almost never looks at anything (the famous writer, the man with the microphone, the camera, the crowd around her) directly for more than a glance. In *Take This Hammer*, Baldwin argues that the core of black style emanates, "has to come out," of "another level of experience that doesn't allow them as much room for make-believe as white people have." In "The Uses of the Blues" (1964), Baldwin returns to black people's (in particular Bessie Smith and Billie Holiday's) style of angular confrontation with what make-believe won't cover:

> And the way they sort of ride with it. And it's very, very tricky. It's a kind of fantastic tightrope. This is what happened, this is where it is. This is what it is. Now, I'm trying to suggest that the triumph here—which is a very un-American triumph—is that the person to whom these things have happened watched with eyes wide open, saw it happen . . . they were commenting on it, a little bit outside it: they were accepting it. . . . So that it's this passionate detachment, this inwardness coupled with outwardness, this ability to know that, all right, it's a mess, and you can't do anything about it . . . so, well, you have to do something about it. (*Cross*, 59)

Not the least in the clips mentioned earlier—in which Famios Bell and other young people address, through styles adept at a direct indirectness and passionate detachment, issues imperiling their lives—*Take This Hammer* documents a blues-driven tenacity and capacity that contend directly with diasporic dangers of speechlessness and homelessness. One of the ugly beauties of *Medicine for Melancholy* is the way it depicts the absence of such energies (from this perspective, they almost appear to be prisoners in MoAD) from contemporary San Francisco. In inter-viewing these films, those voices sound in their silence, become present in their absence. The effect intensifies our sense of both and of the pressures that, exactly by their absence, stifle Jenkins's couple's ability to talk to each other and think for themselves.

On the return leg of their rather improbable three-mile grocery run from Micah's apartment (at Geary and Leavenworth) to the alternative-archetypal Rainbow Grocery (at Folsom and 13th Street), the couple passes a housing issues meeting in a storefront. Jenkins confirms that actual housing activists played themselves. The couple stops out front and the film pauses for almost three minutes as the voices fade in over street noise en medias res before the camera moves in close and focuses on each speaking face:

> And they were like, "our property values and blah blah blah," and I was like, "What? Property values more important than human lives?" And, I think, unfortunately, that's what happened to the Castro, as the upscale people moved in, the attitudes became more the attitudes of the upper class. There is this sense in this town that

we are becoming a city of the very rich and the very poor. We all know people have been pushed out at an alarming rate. . . . They're already building market rate condos in Bayview and you know that they're not going to have market rate condos next to projects. You know what's going to go and it ain't going to be the market rate condos.

The participants are seeing the city's gentrification spiral ahead, they're watching with their eyes open. The leader of the meeting concludes the scene saying that the whole city faces imminent loss of rent control, the result being "all of the great things that we love about San Francisco would be gone over night." All of the speakers (and almost all of the participants) in the meeting appear to be white. Certainly, none of the speakers in *Medicine for Melancholy* address the issues with anything resembling the force and style of those dissenters in *Take This Hammer*. The result of juxtaposing the two narratives of gentrification is the palpable sense of how many of the "great things" about San Francisco are already gone, absent even from the dissents about (absent as are the historical dissidents from) the contemporary issues of gentrification themselves. This pattern, of course, goes on all over the United States in psychic, linguistic, and demographic levels of experience.

What language can speak to what? Whose reality lurks, invisible, making a "land of make-believe" out of someone else's street, home, or life? The action of such misaligned signifiers is in no way arbitrary. It's political. In her 1968 poem, "The Burning of Paper Instead of Children," Adrienne Rich addresses such collapses in the language of dissent itself. Recalling a protest earlier in the day, she writes: "I am composing on the typewriter late at night, thinking of today. How well we all spoke. A language is a map of our failures. . . . There are methods but we do not use them. . . . In America we have only the present tense. I am in danger. You are in danger. . . . The typewriter is overheated, my mouth is burning, I cannot touch you and this is the oppressor's language."[11] The voices of dissent surrounding Baldwin in *Take This Hammer* add a crucial past tense (really a past sense) to the subtle and nuanced attention *Medicine for Melancholy* gives the present. It suggests how the open and universal, if indie-alternative, experience of Jenkins's couple—and our experience as we travel with them—occurs in depopulated territory, in the terms allowed by oppressors who seem themselves to have vanished from the screen as did the captives from view through the Door of No Return. Who is left who can speak to the absence of that presence (or to the presence of *that* absence) that *Medicine for Melancholy* confesses when set in connection to *Take This Hammer*? The way Jenkins ushers his couple obliquely into tangents with these issues suggests *he*, for one, has more to say about it. But that's material for another film, I hope. Jenkins's present film aims to make the (black) reality of his characters' style reckon with the (postra-cial) make-believe of their world.

## When the Speechless Speak: Race Talk in the Era of Postracial Chalk

After dinner and a joint, Micah and Joanne lapse into another attempt to bridge the ocean of speechlessness separating the indie dreamland from the racial epic, a silence amplified by the brutal history of "removal of Negroes" discussed earlier which hovers over their contemporary San Franciscan lives. The conversation begins with the age-old issue of racial firsts. In the comic tones of a History Channel voiceover, Micah recommends Joanne get a fixed-gear bike, saying she'd be like the first black woman to travel in space, "like Mae Jemison, first black woman to ride a fixed gear-bike through the Marina." Well, they *are* high. Joanne laughs. And, back in his own somewhat stoned voice, Micah says: "Hell, you're probably the first black woman *in* the Marina." No laughter. Micah swerves the conversation back to contend with its phantom, festering history of "removal of Negroes."

> M: Hey, you ever think about how black folks are only 7 percent of this city?
>
> J: You have a real issue with race, you know that?
>
> M: Obviously, I'm serious, and this ain't the weed talking. You ever think about how we're only 7 percent of this city?
>
> J: You're not 7 percent. You're Micah.
>
> M: You know what I mean. Like if black folks are 7 percent of this city, and then you take whatever 1 or 2 percent considers itself like punk or indie or folk or, you know, just not what you see on BET, like you ever realize just how few of us there really are?

Joanne obviously doesn't want to have the conversation. Opting out of inclusion in Micah's vision of the "few of us there really are," she rejects the racial point of view. As if searching for a place to reconnect to the direct and indirect black style evinced in *Take This Hammer* and gone from Obama-era San Francisco, Micah attempts to break it all down to basics. But instead of a passionately detached blues "lyric" that Joanne can connect her own angle to, Micah comes up with self-conscious simplicity that pushes her further away.

> M: If you had to describe, you know, your idea of how you see the world, like how would you do it, in one word?
>
> J: That makes no sense. People aren't that simple. How can you define yourself in one word?
>
> M: Easy. Me, I'm a black man. That's how I see the world; that's how the world sees me. But, if I had to choose one, I'm black before I'm a man. So, therefore, I am black.
>
> J: I don't see it that way.
>
> M: Why not?
>
> J: That's your problem. You feel you have to define everybody. You limit them to the point where they're just a definition and not people.
>
> M: How you figure?
>
> J: You just said it. You went from "I am Micah" to "I am black."
>
> M: I'm not?
>
> J: Yes but you're everything else too.
>
> M: That's not how society sees it.
>
> J: Well, who gives a shit about what society thinks?!

Marking a silent line of wondering about the role of gender in the racial markers Micah insists upon and Joanne denies, the conversation lyrically brackets the unspeakable dimension between the American liberal dreamland version of "freedom" ("who gives a shit what society thinks") and a black point of view from which freedom diminishes with dwindling connections between people ("how few of us there really are"). In order to refine the conversation, the two would have to venture into the region of discomfort and ambiguity and neither have the terms with which to go through *that* door. One wonders if such terms as were there have been swept away with the voices of dissent in *Take This Hammer* and replaced by surface-level vocabularies about assimilation in the dreamland where the facts of life need not pose a threat and from where, therefore, blues selves are exiled? In order to speak into *that* space, Joanne would have to find a voice for her postracial isolation, for the things about a freedom—a black freedom, *her* black freedom—that have pushed her into a life trying, as she says, "to figure it out" in the Marina on her own. And, Micah would have to find a voice for his own racial isolation as one of the few (functionally) assimilated black individuals that he finds so poisonous and empty. In finding and hearing these voices, they'd have to call into question the assumptions (what Baldwin called "enemy assumptions") behind all kinds of American terms (success, freedom, life, happiness, blackness, whiteness) that have been force-fed to them by their era. *Medicine for Melancholy* doesn't have the terms for all of this. Seems no one does. But, this is the kind of conversation that Baldwin was desperately trying to instigate and execute in his work.

As happened in their first conversation, Joanne calls it quits: "I don't want to talk anymore. Let's *do* something." Micah: "What you want to do?" Joanne: "I want to dance." Of course, Micah—knowing the stark, racial terms of the conversation lurk in a wide range of American activities, dancing (with the possible exception of church-going and funerals and Tea Party fund-raising) maybe most of all—is waiting for this: "Alright. Black folks or white folks?" It is a two-night, one-night stand after all, so he relents: "My bad." Then, as ever, he lightens (not to say whitens) the mood and the two head off to dance. Incidentally, as the evening's montage of music and frolicking in the indie club shows clearly, the unstated answer to his question was obvious: "White folks."

But, as with the afternoon with the indie soundtrack in the American dreamland, here Jenkins likewise avoids the ironic distance that would seem nearly mandatory for the film to coexist with itself at this point. Not so. That's *my* point of view: amputation. Micah and Joanne party and drink and dance and take photo booth photos. We see that they're probably the only black people in the place, but they don't seem to notice. Rock and roll. After the bar, the two fend off a pair of hilarious bootleg "hydration" merchants peddling organic juices by the taco stand who provide the film's only—if momentary and seemingly unwelcome, at least to Joanne and to the film's viewers who certainly see them as threatening though many will lie about it after the gag is out of the bag—black company to the pair. If, maybe because, the couple participates in the all-white indie club scene without the irony we'd expect (at least from Micah), the experience boils and spills back into the stark racial dichotomies of Micah's questions after dinner. The two walk arm in arm when Joanne's phone receives a text (we—as does Micah—imagine it's her curator boyfriend in London). Micah, at this point, has one word for the whole damned situation. White.

> M: Is it any surprise that folks of color in the scene date outside their race?
> J: Ok-ay?
> M: I mean think about it—
> J: No, let's not.

M: Everything about being indie is all tied to not being black.

J: I don't want to talk about this.

M: Like, everything, is all tied to not being black. Like, friends who are indie, white. Bands who are indie, like, ok you got TV on the Radio but the rest of them are white.

J: Okay!

M: No it's not ok. It's not. Like everything. People call it interracial dating but there's nothing interracial about it. Nine out of ten times, it's somebody of color hanging on to a white person . . . it's always one of us clinging on to one of them. I mean look at you. Why the fuck you got to date some white dude?

J: Why are you doing this? What do you want from me? You think just because I'm black and you're black that we should just be together? We're just one, right? We fucked. And, I didn't even know you. I've been spending the last twenty-four hours cheating on my boyfriend and you think because I'm black and you're black that we should be together . . . fucking crazy.

Pushed to racial extremes in (by?) indie isolation, the two find themselves nose to nose on opposite sides of the postracial membrane of the dream bubble. There's obviously important living experience between Micah's passionate, racial simplicity and Joanne's detached universals, but they don't have the words to go there. Does Joanne's "We're just one, right?" retort ironically slash back at Sylvia Striplin's tone (even more at Frankie Beverly and Maze's song "We Are One" also from 1980) or is that collateral damage, more absent presence, in *my* musical ear? Of course, no one actually lives at those extremes of single-mindedly racial or all-mindedly universal identity, which is the whole problem. The couple, like many (maybe just about all) Americans, is locked out of their own lives by the limitations (willed, imposed, unconscious) in their struggle with speechlessness. It's a verbal jail and the bars are psychic, demographic, and diasporic. This condition, the inability to enter one's own experience and thereby connect to someone else's, actually is the core dilemma in "Sonny's Blues" and in much of Baldwin's best work. In "The Uses of the Blues," Baldwin described the condition imposed by speechlessness, by life sans lyric, by being unable or unwilling to articulate and communicate the actual terms of one's life: "Nobody lives in that country. That country does not exist and, what is worse, everybody knows it. But everyone pretends it does. Now, this is panic" (*Cross*, 65). Baldwin concluded that line of thought stressing that he's not trafficking literary metaphor, "This is not mystical talk; it is a fact" (65).

The beauty of Jenkins's film, in fact, doesn't lie in the vistas of San Francisco and the trendy bikes; it emanates from the brilliant subtlety in his framing Baldwin's (somewhat too brutally put) fact—the fact of functional speechlessness, black speechlessness, as well as the need for diasporic lyrics to sound those oceans within, and bridge those between, persons. Seen in this way, Jenkins returns us to the lyrical, passionate detachment of the blues-lyric impulse at the core of diasporic speech. This echoes the origin myth Baldwin imagined in Senegal in 1962, the pursuit of which he enacted in his work, and the evidence of which he found himself surrounded by in *Take This Hammer*. All that, in Jenkins's film, and he avoids the stock scenes and props that litter so many black popular films. No one flashed a piece or pulled a knife in the kitchen. No one even got slapped. Imagine *that*.

Early the next morning, Joanne leaves Micah's place on her bicycle after make-believe night number two. We watch from above through the bars of his fire escape; she pedals away obscured by the unfocused, purple petals of Micah's potted plants. The audience leaves *Medicine for Melancholy* with a sense that generations of Americans after *Take This Hammer* have lived amid real alterations (demographic, cultural, technological, political) in the racial grain of experience. Despite all kinds of useful ingredients, Jenkins's characters can't articulate a sense of the world beyond that readily delivered to them via the media. They're still sampling. But, he portrays Micah and Joanne against myriad subtleties in the tonal narration and in the city. The intricacies with which he makes the couple surf invisible waves of *Take This Hammer* usher them through the door of what they can't deny and look at each other as if staring at an ocean they *can* see across. But, something in the surf at each shore silences their voices. Evidence suggests Barry Jenkins has a grasp on one end of the equation. And, he's equipped as an artist to make use of voices washed away such as those that surrounded Baldwin in *Take This Hammer*—and Baldwin's own—to guide his audience in tuning their own ears to the tasks which come from far behind us and which we meet, daily, before us on the road.

Joanne and Micah's speechlessness brackets their ability to connect to necessary arenas of experience within and between their lives. They survive anyway. Call it privilege, maybe. But what about diasporic locations, which haven't obeyed the cultural brackets, determined by "removal of Negroes?" For a glimpse of that we'll cross the Bay Bridge and head down 580 East to Oakland.

# 9

## "In a way they must..."
### *Turf Feinz* and Black Style in an Age of Sights for the Speechless

In *Take This Hammer*, Baldwin's guide positions him in San Francisco's Lower Fillmore District across the street from the Booker T. Washington Hotel. As they pass on Fillmore Street, Orville Luster says, "Now, off to our left here's one Negro hotel, that's owned." Baldwin, eyes intensifying, looks across the street from the car.

> JB: The only Negro hotel, and it's called the Booker T. Washington?
> OL: Yes.
> JB: Naturally.

Though at that time Baldwin was a stranger to San Francisco, he recognized the scene as if staring at a stage: "This is the street that all Negroes are born on. The street all Negroes have to survive. The Booker T. Washington, the Baptist church, and the mosque. There's really a great history, a great thing to be summed up in that if one could." Lyrical as Baldwin's stage set is, he leaves out at least one crucial historical detail. In fact, few of the black adults on that street were born there at all (not even metaphorically). If they had been, their parents most likely hadn't. Maybe re-born is the word? While touring the district, just after Luster explains that redevelopment means "removal of Negroes" (a phrase still used to describe redevelopment efforts by many black residents in the Lower Fillmore in the early twenty-first century[1]) he relates: "In other words now the Negroes who came because the Japanese were pushed out are now being pushed out themselves." So it goes in the dreamland. The two get out of the car directly across the street from the Booker T.

Men outside the Booker T. Washington Hotel in San Francisco in *Take This Hammer*.

Washington Hotel (the lounge of which was an important jazz venue in the Lower Fillmore in the years following World War II) and Luster asks: "When you look at this street now . . . what comes to your mind about some kind of music or passage of the Bible that describes this?" Tiring in (if not of) his role as documentary-translator, Baldwin responds by positioning what he sees in relation to the Door of No Return and the predicament of diasporic speechlessness:

> Sing the Lord's song in a strange land? I don't know, I don't know. I'm sure those cats across the street can dance like, you know, like their white counterparts can't. And the reason they can is because

in a way they must. It is . . . it has got to come out somehow. It's got to come out somehow. You know. And the pressure is great enough that it has to come out in a certain kind of . . . Negroes have great style . . . I think this is true even if.it sounds chauvinistic. And white people don't have much style. And one of the reasons that Negroes have a certain style is because they are aware of the conditions of their lives and they can't fool themselves about it. You know. And when a Negro laughs or tries to make love or, or eats, or dances, it's a kind of total action. I don't mean this in the way white liberals are going to think I mean it I don't mean that they're more sensual more primitive or more spontaneous and all this, um, ethnic *jazz*. I mean that they live on another level of experience that doesn't allow them as much room for make believe as white people have.

Midway through the comment above, the documentary cuts to images of a black family dancing on the street. The woman wears a fitted skirt and blouse. The man in dark slacks, white shirt and a tie untied under his collar, dances while holding a baby girl in a Sunday-style dress.

Baldwin is certainly in dangerous water here, and he knows it. He knows he'll be misunderstood; he knows he only partially understands it himself, but he says it anyway. In "Color" (1962), writing for *Esquire* and guarding against the romance and racism that cloud the American imagination of scenes like this, he had noted: "Dancing and love are meant to seem effortless, but are very difficult and dangerous activities" (*CE*, 674). He thought, then, that black people were on the whole less susceptible to this romance, "having seen too many dancers, to say nothing of lovers, swept straight into the madhouse." In any case, working-while-out-on-the-limb is part of the style he's describing, a style he would explore and emulate most complexly in his writing of the 1970s and 1980s. His points about diasporic speechlessness being "speechless in the most total sense of the word" and about black style being "a kind of total action" acted out in relation to a "level of experience" that (a) can't be named according to mainstream American idioms (and the assumptions that guide them) and (b) has relatively little "room for make-believe," frame much about what we can see (but not necessarily easily name) in contemporary black aesthetics. It's a *lyrical* condition in that it must communicate in ways more (or less) directly than conventional conversation and understanding can accomplish. In this, it must also provide cues for its reception and interpretation. Even more, as Arthur Montana says in *Just Above My Head*, such styles often have to lyricize (if not improvise) their articulations and guide their receptions while dissembling *both* to those listening over the shoulders of the target audience. As Arthur puts it, a black artist comes out of an undocumented tradition, comes "out of something you can't name" and steps into a surrounding culture with the power to assign false names, and, finally, must "keep both of them going too, baby, all the time grinning in Mister Charlie's face."[2]

In *Another Country*, published less than a year before Baldwin filmed *Take This Hammer*, he'd gone further than he'd ever go again in describing the complex anthology of deceits and failures that confined his characters in cells of self and mutual isolation. Amid the arguments, violence, and downtown musical frenzies Baldwin describes in the novel, a dance scene in Small's Paradise provides the deepest and most trustworthy image of human fluency the novel provides. Ida has taken Cass uptown to be witness to her affair with Steve Ellis. In the club, Cass watches a "ginger-colored boy dancing with a tall, much darker girl" (*ENS*, 684). Cass marvels at the dancers' manipulation of the space, "sometimes very close to one another, sometimes swinging far apart, but always joined, each body making way for, responding to, and commenting on the other" (684). Observing the nuanced, "impassive," and complex connections the dancers described, she notices how "they followed the music, which also seemed to follow them" (684). Within that space and with the juke-box music leading and, somehow, following the couple, nothing seemed taboo, "the girl was, in no sense, appalled by the boy and did not for an instant hesitate to answer his rudest erotic quiver with her own" (684). It's a resonant instance of flesh challenging flesh; as an image of a tradition that enables people to tell, witness, and respond to a wide array of impulses and angles in themselves, each other, and in the world, the scene provides a bar by which to measure the conversations (Eric and Vivaldo, Vivaldo and Ida, and Cass and Richard) which structure the final forays of the novel's unparalleled, conversational depth. At that time, bracketed by a seemingly inescapable but thoroughly intolerable sense of make-believe in her own life, and surrounded by a world, downtown, designed to keep her there, Cass asks herself in "what sense, and for what reason, and why would it be forever impossible for her to dance as they did?" (684). Talking with Studs Terkel in 1962, Baldwin described a widespread state of mind similar to Cass's as a kind of extended American adolescence: "if you're frozen in this particular way then you can only be lonely because you haven't got any basis on which to operate, on which to be bound to others. You have no dance floor."[3]

Baldwin's notion of a style that emerges because "it's got to come out somehow" positions style between a speechless diasporic situation (lyric) that defies conventional understanding and articulation (Arthur's "something you can't name") and leaves little room for make-believe (blues); it provides a lens through which to rewatch and reimagine *all* conceptions and performances of black style. In such reconsiderations, no recent occasion is more purely to the point than the 2009 video short, *Turf Feinz*.[4] Its debut on YouTube went viral, earning it millions of views.

It's just over nineteen miles from Micah's Tenderloin apartment to the corner of 90th Avenue and MacArthur Boulevard in East Oakland. The trip leaves behind the lattes and croissants at Angel Café & Deli in Micah's hip and fashionable neighborhood. It's about the same distance— plus almost fifty years—from what Baldwin described in the Lower Fillmore to that East Oakland street corner. There, dancers Garion Morgan aka No Noize, Leon Williams Jr. aka Man, Tee "BJ" Stevens, and the video's central character, Darrell Armstead aka Dreal, perform on camera. The quartet of dancers work in a vernacular dance idiom called "turfin," descendant of black vernacular dance styles that date back to before the age of vaudeville. The video of the dance was shot (with a Canon 7D digital camera) and produced by Yoram Savion who was at the time the multimedia coordinator at an East Oakland teen center called Youth Up-Rising. Savion stressed that the dancers worked without musical accompaniment. Having chosen the track before shooting, the video and music was placed in sync afterward. With three partners, Savion also runs an independent film company, Yak Films.

The plot is fairly simple on the surface: A jam session. Ad hoc. A cutting contest. Baldwin's lens on lyric and style contradicts assumptions (improvisation, all that ethnic "*jazz*") and opens on the scene like second sight. The video begins with a pair of young men. One, Man, wears black jeans and a black jacket with the hood of a sweatshirt pulled up over his head. The other, No Noize, wears jeans and an orange hooded windbreaker, hood up with a bandana covering his face below his eyes. The two stand on a street corner in the rain as synth-chimes and a shrill melody float behind the scene. Police pull up. The video cuts to No Noize talking to the police with the bandana pulled down to expose his face. Police drive off. The camera cuts and street signs come into focus through a hard rain in front of wind-tossed trees, MacArthur Blvd. and 90th Ave. The camera pans down to the pair standing beneath a bus stop sign. One early comment on YouTube asked if that was the city of Richmond, California? Someone else wrote back to say that only Oakland has the tree insignia on the street signs. Man finishes a cigarette and flicks it away. The video splices together moments that suggest (via missing intervals) that the first twenty-something seconds we see stand in for a longer period of time. Waiting. Still, all appears to be happening in what the computer age calls real time and according to basic, Newtonian norms of space and place. The two are hanging out, although standing in the rain suggests some kind of motive. Maybe that's what the police thought? Maybe they're waiting for the bus? In fact, they're grieving, but I'll get to that shortly.[5]

Then a bass and snare rhythm appears beneath the wind and rain of synths and chimes, No Noize makes the sign of a cross, and his movements fall from the so-called real time-space Newtonian norms of the street corner. He appears to hold invisible bars for a second. His feet twirl beneath him making him seem suspended from the unseen supports. His hands let go of the invisible bars and he steps into a dance space that seconds before looked like an ordinary East Oakland street corner. In two pirouettes made of tai chi, figure skating, and karate punctuated by hand gestures, in about ten seconds of video time, No Noize refigures the space between the bus stop and the stop light pole. Saddled with an experience "that's got to come out" and that can't be articulated in conventional terms, with relatively little room for make-believe and where "the pressure is great enough," the lyric physics of diasporic presence emerge from the Newtonian norms. Style.

No Noize pauses against the pole and ends his redefinition of space far enough out in traffic that a Cadillac has to arc wide to miss him while making its right turn. Realism. By the time the Cadillac disappears down MacArthur Blvd., Man and No Noize are in the midst of an interactive routine where they watch each other's moves while, at times, gripping hold of each other in such ways that it's impossible to tell if they're holding each other up or throwing each other down, or both. Breaking the supportive and restrictive mutual grip, Man glides out into traffic in a circle that suggests to passersby (pausing in their Jeeps and Pontiacs) that they had not only mistaken a dance for a fight or a fight for a dance, but they had also mistaken a skating rink for an East Oakland intersection. The two come back together, No Noize makes a no-bone-having wave of his arms and a shimmy of his shoulders and the camera moves across the street.

There we find two other young men, BJ and Dreal, in jeans and short sleeves on the corner. The camera frames the pair between a rusted pole holding a Vitamin Water advert at the boundary of the parking lot for Harry's Drive-In Liquor and Groceries on the left and the stoplight pole

Dreal (*low*) and BJ (*standing*) on MacArthur Boulevard in Oakland in *Turf Feinz*.

on the right. In this frame, at the entrance of the crosswalk, BJ has already begun to dance. In twenty seconds, he continues the deconstruction and rebuilding of the space between the poles initiated by the two across the street. BJ's space is far more abruptly percussive than the spaces Man and No Noize charted seconds before. Using snare beats as markers, he dances, at one point—in a way that's supposed to look accidental—losing a folded sheaf of papers from his pocket, as if he has no time for paperwork and an epic of invisible collisions and confrontations to describe in some twenty seconds. Having described the contours of an invisible and brutal labyrinth, BJ freezes on a snare beat cueing the central dancer, Dreal, to step from behind the concrete support for Harry's Drive-In's Vitamin Water pole and into the space. As was often the case for the leader of a jazz quartet, Dreal's solo is twice as long as were those of the other three. He's taller and thinner, and his footwork allows his long angles to float above the *am*-putative ground where ordinary people enter the crosswalk in real time. Dreal time takes over.

He passes left to right and back and forth within the frame while BJ leans against the stoplight pole to watch, although his eyes appear to abstract something fixed that the camera can't deliver. Dreal's dance is cursive script, almost Arabic in its calligraphic grace and complexity. His style converts the frame between the poles into a space in which physical statements chart a dialectic of constraint (gravity, bone, friction, what's up, what's down, etc.) and possibility (concrete acts like ice, feet move in an invisible substance erasing friction, bones and joints flex into rubber, etc.) that, finally, operates in the guise of a mathematical elegance in which all statements and functions, no matter the complexity, have been solved, broken down into their most basic terms. Lyric elegance. Testifying to "another level of experience," indeed, Dreal writes a note into the space as if dancers could burn a graffiti mural on the air in body language strung between the poles. Apparently they *can* exactly because—as Baldwin said of black self-stylers—"in a way they must."

In the first half of the video described above, each of the four dancers summons a unique, invisible realm of condition and possibility into lyric statements framed in the video. As Dreal concludes his first solo, Man shows up in the frame followed by No Noize. In the second half of the video, the dancers trade fours taking a few bars of the song to describe a new move. The others' attention no longer abstracted into their own unseen realms, or into passing cars, now they watch and respond to the soloist and to each other. Man makes his statement, exits the frame slipping through the space between Dreal and the stoplight pole, goes around the back while BJ dances, picks up BJ's papers off the wet asphalt, and stands next to No Noize who hands him his cell phone and replaces BJ in the dance frame. No Noize enters the space in a backward summersault but appears to vault himself to his feet by an action of his neck alone and almost without using his hands. Dreal, BJ, and Man simultaneously agree that something important, unprecedented, and *not* simply made up, has been said. Lyricized pressure. Joy. Dreal enters again as if he's skipping puddles, hopscotch, or landmines, skates his script back and forth through the frame replaced by Man whose few bars of splits and spins call back to James Brown and Prince. The dancers acknowledge the camera in triumph. The short video ends while we watch the four exchange various elaborate handshakes that seem to introduce the realms danced into the

(*Left to right*) Dreal, BJ, Man, No Noize, *Turf Feinz*. (Photo courtesy Yoram Savion.)

frame to the ones in daily life as much as one person to another. We watch as the young men we saw before the dances begin now to talk to each other, listen, and punctuate the statements with glimpses from the realm summoned moments before in the dances caught on video. The men introduce their characters to each other and each other to their characters in a presence dense with each other that—evinced in millions of viewings and thousands of comments—is somehow widely envied around the world. The video shows how lyrics of a living inheritance defy obstacles and engage birthrights in the eyes of millions and across continents. All in under four minutes.

We watch Yoram Savion's video depict the dancers in East Oakland from a vantage point not unlike that from which Baldwin watched the scene outside the Booker T. Washington Hotel in the Lower Fillmore. In a 1979 opinion piece for the *New York Times*, "If Black English Isn't a Language, Then Tell Me, What Is?," Baldwin wrote, "*A language comes into existence by means of a brutal necessity, and the rules of the language are dictated by what the language must convey.*"[6] Diasporic "pressure great enough" is the crux of the brutal necessity; he argued, "People evolve a language in order to describe and thus control their circumstances or in order not to be submerged by a situation that they cannot articulate."[7] His depiction of the "passionate detachment" of the lyric pulse of black language in "The Uses of the Blues" by which people "kind of ride with" the texture of their experiences, "commenting on it," and "accepting it" on a "kind of fantastic tightrope," does more than describe what Savion depicts in his *Turf Feinz* video (*Cross*, 59). It provides terms through which one can look into the scenes, listen to the moves, and look on again and again as the dancers watch each other. And, as is the case with all successful lyrics, one sees and hears the subject speak to an experience as one also hears, as Baldwin notes in "If Black English," to the extent one can "afford to," one's own experience at the same time.[8]

In the rumor and chaos mill of thousands and thousands of YouTube commentaries, one learns a little more about the *Turf Feinz* video. Some of it is true; some of it is not. Rachel Swan's 2010 piece "Turf Feinz Go Viral" sets the record straight.[9] Savion and the dancers know each other through association with the Youth UpRising teen center located a few blocks from the corner in the video. Savion, a French-born, French-Israeli graduate of UC Berkeley, works at the center. According to Swan's piece, the video was shot in December 2009, the day following an auto accident at 90th and MacArthur in which Richard Davis, Darrell "Dreal" Armstead's brother, was killed.[10] Swan explains: "They wanted to memorialize Davis and sanctify the corner where he died." In so doing the dancers created a document that not only honored Dreal's brother and communicated between themselves, but said something to viewers who have added comments to the video on YouTube in over a dozen languages from places as far away as the Ukraine, Mauritius, and New Zealand and as near as (and nearer than) Goofster 510 who wrote, "ay, that's like five minutes from my house." Among the exclamation marks and notes of all kinds in ALL CAPS, the racial slurs and rebuttals, the rumors (false) that Davis had been shot, that Dreal has been killed, one learns that the song behind the video was coproduced by Oakland producer Erk the Jerk and Youth UpRising music students Yung FX and Coop. It's titled "Love in Every Move." That's true.

Baldwin's ideas about the essential role of love in art and life require their own book. The Turf Feinz know, somehow, that sanctifying the location where Dreal's brother was killed is complex, personal business involving all kinds of things well beyond the personal. It's doubtful that they learned Baldwin's translation of the diasporic blues impulse, "the only way to get through life is to know the worst things about it," from anything with a name. But, they *did* learn it. Savion's video over Erk the Jerk's sound depicts more than articulation or explanation of such complexities; it depicts the lyric *communication* of them. The dancers listen to and see each other, face to face; they do seem to get part of it and enough of it to suggest it makes sense to keep on meeting up, talking, and listening. Oh, and dancing. In a radically chimerical, hall-of-mirrors media world, out of which has poured millions of thirsty viewings, that alone suggests something of what is worth *what* to human life in an era of broken gauges and fraudulent markets, of rich people surprised, daily, to find they have nothing in the bank, and of others with no bank accounts at all who, because they are lyrically liquid, make withdrawals and deposits every hour on the hour in a time that is yet to be named, in a space that seems to (but doesn't) appear out of nowhere. For now, let's call it Dreal Standard Time.

The Turf Feinz dancers understand plenty about their profiles in the public eye; in part their dances are stylized confrontations with and deft manipulations of their profiles. More importantly, the dances are a way of staying alive to and in touch with the conditions in their own lives and to those of people in their immediate surroundings. In relation to a voyeuristic mainstream culture, the ability to make oneself seen and felt in these ways, as well as the ability to see and feel other people, is a serious form of power, *interactive being*. When Baldwin told Nikki Giovanni that what she was calling morals he would call "energy," *this* is exactly what he had in mind. In the next chapter, I examine the politics of that energy and the culturally inflected, racially coded privileges that the world thinks can replace it, as well as the costs of thinking that way.

# 10
## "Shades cannot be fixed"
### On Privilege, Blindness, and Second Sight

In the introduction to *The Price of the Ticket* (1985), Baldwin wrote that "part of the price of the black ticket is involved—fatally—with the dream of becoming white. . . . This is not possible, partly because white people are not white: part of the price of the white ticket is to delude themselves into believing that they are" (*CE*, 835). The image presents a portrait of Americans carrying their tickets to destinations that don't exist. Meanwhile, each looks to the other for, or as, evidence that these destinations *do* exist. The web of associations people weave during their daily lives escapes full description and remains largely unconscious. A few common tickets support the structure. In this social theater, seen by black people, white people signify a life of advantage, relative comfort, and a reasonable (if, in part, stolen) access to American happiness, cleanliness, and safety. White people look at black people, as well as others, for images of what white people are not, by turns dangerous and endangered. In white people's eyes, black people become images of social jeopardy from which the so-called fact of racial difference insulates them. Characters in black culture—somewhat more than actual persons—and very often musicians, invest white people with visions of distinctly American freedoms (largely from imagined physical inaction and psychological repression) that float somehow beyond this racial boundary as well. In white people, black people encounter a vista of de facto citizenship that racism prevents them from entering. The resulting traffic jam amounts to a radically unstable and, finally, impossible burden borne by people in each other's eyes, which is to say, in each other's imagined lives. Inquiry into this theater spanned Baldwin's career. Describing this mutual American theater in *Take This Hammer*, he noted the importance of considering that, at once, "there's something real in it and a terrifying invention in it." The terms of the "vacuumed panic" and the nature of "amputation" and "gangrene" discussed in Chapter 1 depend upon this mutual measure Americans take from other people and then apply to themselves as persons and vice versa. Over the decades, such dynamics have played out in international theaters even more drastic and complex.

Chapter 3 mentions that Baldwin listened to Aretha Franklin's album *Aretha Arrives* and heard a way to address the people and the person. What he heard in songs like "I Wonder" and "Baby, I Love You" crystallized his awareness that any human life was a mesh of personal/private and impersonal/public (historical) realities. In the eyes of others and in the functioning of institutions, we are assigned to a "people" directly affected by impersonal, historical power, powers that operate without regard for individual traits and nuances; we're also living personal lives impossible to account for in strictly public, historical terms. These levels of experience are distinct, but not separate. In Baldwin's mind, a conscious life, or a politically engaged art, entailed a nonresolving quarrel between them.

In *No Name in the Street*, Baldwin took his first major step consciously responding to what he heard in Aretha's voice. He painted a black and white portrait to clarify impersonal dimensions of this American scene. In order to do it, he employed starkly two-dimensional terms: *people* advantaged, but also imperiled, by the structures that produced their prosperity and other *people* brutalized, but also empowered, in that same system. Of the perils of the prosperous, he wrote: "not even the people who are the most spectacular recipients of the benefits of this prosperity are able to endure these benefits: they can neither understand them nor do without them, nor can they go beyond them" (*CE,* 406). Meanwhile, "the excluded begin to realize, having endured everything, that they *can* endure everything. They do not know the precise shape of the future, but they know that the future belongs to them" (407). In his two-dimensional portrait of clarity "the victor can never be the victor . . . bound up in a terror he cannot articulate, a mystery he can't read" and the brutalized "begin, almost instinctively, to forge a new morality, to create principles on which a new world will be built" (407). As a chart of how racially articulated power works in American culture, as well as how American power works in international arenas, this portrait offers a crucial, impersonal clarity.

But, Baldwin also knew that power plays out in personal terms as well and most, if not all, persons live complexly astraddle the impersonal chart of people drawn above. Members of a victimized people prey upon persons of that group, even themselves, in ways that echo the structures of power oppressing them all. Members of a politically dominant people identify with their historical and cultural "others," their victims, in all kinds of ways to make sense of their personal and private lives. So, Baldwin knew he would need another portrait in which the impersonal ways that color and power work in the lives of *people* interact with the multi-dimensional nature of power in the lives of *persons*. In addition to Aretha and other musical sources, in creating that portrait, Baldwin would draw on the tools of two very different artistic guides, one impersonal and one deeply personal.

The first was Henry James, a writer that Baldwin read and reread throughout his adult life. In prefacing his interview with Baldwin about Henry James, David Leeming noted that James's grandson had gifted Baldwin a portrait of his grandfather that Baldwin placed "directly above his writing desk."[1] The "picture became a kind of direct link between him and a writer who, as far as Baldwin was concerned, came closer to sharing his concerns than any other." The crux of the connection was Baldwin's reading of James "as the writer who shares with him the one essential theme, that of the failure of Americans to see through to 'the reality of others.'"[2] It's little surprise that Baldwin's most sophisticated fictional account of a white man and a black man trying "to see through to" each other turns precisely on a term borrowed directly from James.

In his preface to the New York edition of his 1884 novel *Lady Barbarina*—the same preface, as I discuss in the conclusion, from which Baldwin took his epigraph to *Another Country*—James accounts for a lack of nuance and depth in the title character when compared to her American counterpart: "Was this because, for the portrait of Lady Barb, I felt appealed to so little in the name of *shades*? Shades would be decidedly neither of her general world nor of her particular consciousness. . . . It was Jackson Lemon and *his* shades, comparatively, and his comparative sense for shades, that, in the tale, most interested me."[3] In *Just Above My Head* (1979), Baldwin asserts the role of "shades" in adding living dimensions to the necessary account of racial power at play within and between persons and people. In a way, shades allowed Baldwin to account for the fact that "color" is not a two-dimensional reality; it's not, after all, solely a matter of black and white. To operate in two dimensions personally is to surrender one's life to the impersonal coherence of his portrait of power from *No Name in the Street*. On the other hand, to imagine one's life in strictly personal terms, terms divorced from that portrait of power, is to retreat to the theater of innocence and incoherence at the root of white-ness and the whole tangled mess.

Baldwin had understood the trap well enough for years. In *Another Country*, Vivaldo marks the impasse when Ida collapses the people into the person addressing her critique of white people to him. Ida concludes: "You're a fucked-up group of people. You hear me? A *fucked*-up group of people" (*ENS*, 616). It doesn't work. In a loving and playful irony, which wasn't (and isn't) enough, Vivaldo marks the shortcoming by agreeing, "I'm just a fucked up group of people" (617). Realizing the absurdity of the reduction, "Ida laughed, helplessly, and he pulled her down on top of him." A few pages later, Baldwin abstracts a warning about taking the people for the person: "God save the people for whom passion becomes impersonal" (636). The companion admonition remains implicit in the structure: You better look out, if you think you can personalize history.

This didn't mean one didn't continue to work in personal terms. Just before *Another Country* was released, Baldwin told Studs Terkel: "You have to impose, in fact—this may sound very strange—you have to *de-cide* who you are, and force the world to deal with you, not with its *idea* of you."[4] In a section of *Another Country* likely written in the late 1950s, possibly in 1959, Eric, a white actor from Alabama, improvises in these jazz-inflected terms. Echoing the extension of the classic AAB form, Baldwin wrote: "There were no standards for him except those he could make for himself. There were no standards for him because he could not accept the definitions, the hideously mechanical jargon of the age ... this meant he had to create his standards and make up his definitions as he went along. It was up to him to find out who he was and it was his ne-cessity to do this, so far as the witchdoctors of the time were concerned, alone" (*CE,* 555). His conversation with Elijah Muhammad in *The Fire Next Time*—which actually took place the same week in July 1961 as the conversation with Studs Terkel—would force Baldwin to confront the fact that one couldn't impose a personal decision upon the world all by oneself. Eric's quest certainly inflects his power as an actor, as a lover, and as a friend, and Vivaldo's irony diffuses the private impasse with Ida, for the moment, but even then the world isn't moved at all. Shades aren't enough.

Baldwin's sense of shades and color also involved his first artistic men-tor, the great African American modernist painter Beauford Delaney. They met when Baldwin was a teenager and remained closely connected until Delaney's death in 1979. Looking back from 1985, Baldwin credited Delaney with initiating him into a newly immediate experience of his senses and surroundings. Arriving for his first visit, he knocked and Beauford, "a short, round, brown man came to the door" (*CE*, 830). When he entered the apartment at 181 Greene Street in Greenwich Village, he recalled: "I walked through that door into Beauford's colors—on the easel, on the palette, against the wall." In 1984, he would recount: "[Beauford] taught me how to see, and how to trust what I saw. Painters have often taught writers how to see. And once you've had that experience, you see differently."[5] Eyes opened to color in a new way, in entering Beauford's place, he also "walked into music": "in his studio and because of his presence, I really began to *hear*" (*CE*, 831).[6]

Senses don't operate in separation; the distinctions between them aren't rational. Early in their friendship, Beauford took Baldwin to a concert to hear Marion Anderson. His newfound sense of color and sound merge in his memory of the evening, "at the end of the concert, in a kind of smoky yellow gown, her skin copper and tan, roses in the air about her, roses at her feet" (*CE*, 832). Something in the way Beauford's loving presence ushered Baldwin into worlds of sound and sight made it clear to him that, in fact, the world was a complex and subtle play of overlapping textures, never strictly a matter of black and white, this and that. Combining "Beauford's colors" and James's "shades," Baldwin scripted his most complex, both personal and impersonal, exploration of racial dynamics between people who are also persons.

Late in *Just Above My Head* (1979), Baldwin's protagonist, Arthur Montana, by then a famous gospel singer, meets Guy, a Frenchman. The two abscond from their lives for a weekend of stolen time. Before they meet, while Arthur sits alone at a café on Boulevard St. Germain, as if to forecast a deepened experience of color, Beauford appears in the scene. He's not named but the resemblance is unmistakable: "A small, round, brown man, carrying a sketchpad and a shopping bag, and wearing a knitted hat, of many bright colors. He is remarkable, even a joyous apparition; Arthur cannot imagine where he was born."[7] Soon thereafter, Guy and Arthur meet initiating a reconsideration of race in painterly terms owing, finally, to Henry James's shades and to the long song of Beauford's presence in Baldwin's career as a hearer and seer of colors, as a connoisseur of human textures.

His time with Guy forced Arthur to reconsider the way he sees, hears, and feels the people around him. In New York, Guy would have been white but Arthur hasn't been able to fix him there. In conversation it doesn't work, his voice, his eyes don't resemble an American white man's eyes. And, intimately, "drinking in each other's odors, each has been astounded by the other's color—how many colors a color has!"[8] After a few days and nights together, Guy and Arthur find themselves in a bar where "there is an American trio playing, and an old blues singer from Memphis, Sonny Carr, is sitting in."[9] Opened to the play of color and texture in a new way, Arthur surveys the Americans, the Europeans, and the Africans on the stage and in the crowd. In the novel, Arthur's brother narrates as Arthur looks out at the white people in the crowd:

> It is necessary to revise the optic through which one sees what has come to be called color. The children from the Netherlands, from Germany, from England, for example, are all, more or less, the same color, and this would not even have been a question, had Arthur found them in New York, or in Boston. In the harsh, democratic light of these metropolises, they would have been the same color whether they liked it or not.[10]

The impersonal (not to say brutal) American frame of racial power, however, isn't in control of what Arthur's sees. Beauford's presence has passed by; Guy's odor is still in the air, as it were; the music keeps the time the men stole; and he's not at home. In that space, at least, he can sense that color (reduced to *race*) isn't the only force in the room. After Beauford's presence, color can't be collapsed into two dimensions. He senses a palette of shades as well:

> But, truthfully, if one really looks at them, though they are, anonymously, the same color, they are not, ultimately, the same shade. Different histories, and different hazards, are written just beneath the skin, these histories and hazards accounting for the subtleties of shade. Some descend from the Viking by way of Constantinople, some from the Turk by way of Vienna, some from the Jew by way of Turkey, some from Turkey by way of the Spanish Jew, some from the Portuguese by way of New England: all from a history, if that is the word we want, which predates what is known as Europe. And these subtleties are in their eyes—if one wished, ruthlessly, to pursue the matter, in their names. They are, therefore, not only what their history has made of them, they are also what they have made of their history.[11]

From his sense of the people around him, Arthur, acknowledging the power of color in history, realizes that the vocabulary it offers isn't enough. The key questions orbit the music: "And what brings them here? So far from the Druid forest? To listen to a trio, piano, bass, and slide trombone, from, after all, let's face it, the Lord alone knows where. One will not find the answer in the color of their skins."[12] Then, he considers the black folks:

> And this is also true of the venerable blues singer, and the Africans who surround him. In New York or in Boston, they would, of course, all be the same color, being seen, necessarily, through the optic of power and guilt—being seen, necessarily indeed, as objects. But here, in this beleaguered capital, and not as far from home as Arthur is, no matter which way he turns, which body of water he faces, or which overland journey, their shades are more vivid than their color. Their shades are mute testimony to a journey which the Netherlands, for example, deny.[13]

Finally, in Arthur's eyes, and in the voice of Arthur's big brother, Hall, Baldwin sets up a painterly optics, one washed in the sound of the trio, which doesn't have to surrender its senses to the racist power of history which—though it must, "necessarily, indeed," be acknowledged—can't be allowed to falsify the textures of the scene, of life:

> It is impossible to know what future can be made out of an alabaster past so resounding, and an ebony past so maligned, but some key may be found in the palette which experiments with colors in order to discover shades, which mixes shades in order to arrive at a color, or color, which, by the time one has arrived at it, and by means of this process, always bears an arbitrary and provisional name. Shades cannot be fixed; color is, eternally, at the mercy of the light.[14]

By this dynamic formulation, Baldwin gives people the power to acknowledge the color of their respective, historical tickets and, also, a guide for assessing the journey obscured by history. That assessment, if communicated by people to each other, can steer the future elsewhere.

Drawing on Ray Charles, Donny Hathaway, Dinah Washington, and others, Amy Winehouse invoked the presence of such a future in each syllable. In many ways, it's precisely this variable palette of the senses, this sense of shades, which the characters in *Medicine for Melancholy* lack. And, it's exactly the kind of subtle, expertly shaded rhythm and style created by the dancers in the *Turf Feinz* video. Next, I'll consider aspects of our contemporary vocabulary for the ways that power, history, and color interact with several of Baldwin's riffs that link him back to the senses he drew, first, from Beauford's presence in his life and from James's influence in his work. Shades, he knew, took on timbre and meaning most profoundly, and most precisely, in the music he loved the most.

*Just Above My Head* was Baldwin's attempt to imagine people who had survived a flood, who had ridden the rise and demise of the freedom movement. As always, he was interested in what American culture would consider the private lives of characters engaged in intensely public struggles with history. In a 1979 interview with Mel Watkins, published alongside John Romano's tepid review of *Just Above My Head* for the *New York Times Book Review*, Watkins attempted to get Baldwin to talk about the book in terms of its impersonal issues: religion, homosexuality, and race. In each case, Baldwin attempted to bridge the gap between the two-dimensional generalities of the question and the play of shades improvised in his work. When the talk turned to what Watkins called "the racial situation," Baldwin's response signals his dissent:

> Well, first, there are few white people in the novel. But it was unconscious. It just came out that way. It perhaps reveals something that is happening to me. It's difficult to get at, as yet. I think the whole concept of race has had its day. Ultimately, to be white is a moral choice. It's obviously a very deliberate challenge to people who think they're white to re-examine all their values, to put themselves in our place, share in our danger.... In any case, [key characters in the novel] realize that white people are irrelevant to their lives, at least provisionally. Not because they're white, but because of the choices that they've made. At the very bottom, it's now the choices we make, we no longer depend on the choices they make. Even they can't depend on the choices they make.... They must get back in touch with reality. They can't avoid it, if they want to live."[15]

For Baldwin, by 1980, it was clear that "whiteness" was an ephemeral state of mind attained only by people who had amputated their connection to a living inheritance. Then, as if to clarify his terminology—an explicit trace of which is there in his thought at least since the letters in *Harper's* in 1963—he added: "I'd like to say that when I say 'white' I'm not talking about the color of anybody's skin. I'm not talking about race. It's a curious country, a curious civilization, that thinks of it as race. I don't believe any of that. White people are imagined. White people are white only because they want to be white."[16]

In *Just Above My Head*, Baldwin reached for characters, his imagined characters, which had avoided moral and existential choices that would—in his mind at least—render them irrelevant. Irrelevant to whom? To what? Well, most of all, to each other and to themselves. And to the mind doing the imagining. And, ultimately, to the history that produced them.

His comments about life and politics operate by this logic. The effort was to avoid being trapped (and rendered irrelevant) by the insidious appeals of whiteness—safety veiled by whatever term of fashion—in American civilization. Baldwin kept on as he did because he understood that one couldn't avoid the trap of whiteness alone. Hell, he would tell his brother David and his sisters, was not other people. He now saw the invitation to engage historical power solely in personal terms as part of the trap laid by Western history. He urged caution as the culture lured people, persons, into thinking about themselves as "individuals." In his 1979 speech at UC Berkeley he argued that one real victory of the freedom movement was the black recognition of the worth and wealth of collective improvisation: "We come out of a history the black people of this country come out of a history that was never written down. The connection between father and son between mother and daughter . . . we forged ourselves out of this fire."[17] All persons were unique, of course, that was the key to the miraculous particularities, but American individuality didn't describe the complex relevance black lives held for each other. The situation didn't allow a formally scripted approach; there was no clear path forward. The course would be improvised and it would be the work of a flexible collective sense of action. It would depend, in other words, upon a multidimensional, musical sense of color and a wide array of shades that still had no name in the street. "I know I ain't got no jobs to give nobody. I know I ain't got no money," Baldwin told the audience in Berkeley, "I know many things must be done and I *know* that I can't do them. But I also know that I haven't got to do them alone. We've never been alone. That's the mystery." Later in this chapter, I'll examine the implications of Baldwin's claim that no white man can prove he's white. For the moment, suffice it to observe that no white man, alone, can prove he's not.

As discussed in Chapter 3, Baldwin's dissents from contemporary debates in each era of his career are rooted in his refusal to accept the (private or public) worldviews implied and assumptions veiled by the terms used in discussions of popular post–World War II fiction, the private world of 1950s literary aesthetics, the necessity of pushing literary art to deal with social issues without becoming sociology, the Black Power movement of the late 1960s, the headlines and class issues skewing the critique of black feminists in the 1970s, all the way up to the Reagan Reaction and the rise of Jerry Falwell's Moral Majority in the 1980s. Throughout his career, he resisted the tendency to use one set of terms to cover for another, deeper, more troublesome reality.

Baldwin maintained that the delusions of the American dream bore costs that its nominal advantages couldn't pay for. In short, Baldwin didn't believe that delusion could be an advantage to anyone. Paying delusional dues led to bankruptcy. In a critical observation to Richard Goldstein about the gay rights movement that could apply readily in many contexts in the 1980s and since, Baldwin argued: "[Many in the gay rights movement] feel cheated because they were born, in principle, into a society in which they were supposed to be safe. . . . Their reaction seems to me in direct proportion to the sense of feeling cheated of the advantages which accrue to white people in a white society."[18] Meanwhile, Baldwin thought that, in reality, there were no (relevant) "white people" and that the United States was not and had never been a white country. Lives measured consciously or unconsciously in comparison to the ephemera of whiteness take place in a vacuum, in a panic. He wondered in relation to what (or whose) standards do we perceive our lives? In relation to what do we judge our health? How, in relation to what assumptions, do we assess the proportions of our risks? Do we make these assessments in relation to the dream of a happy, clean, and safe life? Or do we realize that the facts of life *never* deliver any of this, that the cost of that dream is the colors and shades of human experience itself? Obviously, Baldwin argued the latter. Assertions of "pride" aligned with frustrated attempts at assimilation must necessarily turn to vanity if only to cover the shame accruing from successes and failures, impossible as these become to distinguish from each other. In *Take This Hammer*, touring San Francisco in the director's car, at one point Baldwin paused the talk of class and race and the fact that the term *redevelopment* meant "removal of Negroes," and said, simply, "I'm always struck by a certain blankness in American faces." In his mind, these faces signaled the costs of a bankrupt approach to life.

One of the most consistent features of Baldwin's analysis is his uncompromising sense of what one might call reciprocal damage. He told Studs Terkel: "The human fact is this: that one cannot escape anything one has done. One has got to pay for it." In Baldwin's world, gains made on fraudulent terms bear costs. The costs outweigh the gains. As he would tell his brother, you pay for your life with your life. According to this logic, the so-called winners in a fraudulent system lose in ways the losers never could. Obviously, the losers lose, too. Finally, the difference between winners and losers can never be made coherent or meaningful until people with various trajectories in the terrain are able to tell each other about their lives—which conversations, reflections, would go far toward eliminating *winners* and *losers* as meaningful terms in the discussion—and listen. And trust. But, trust what? This was exactly what Baldwin had attempted in discussing relative health or ill health (and the implications of each conception of health) with the Black Power generation. And, this is the source of his signifying contempt for what he called, among other things, a "black middle classdom" that forfeited the living inheritance in pursuit of success within the mercantile system.

Among other things, Baldwin's developing point of view enables insights into contemporary (early twenty-first century) debates surrounding terms such as *privilege*. The costs of the pathways to privilege—which like happiness is probably not a "real state" in the ways Baldwin would understand it—are never examined, certainly not by those who want it. Paradoxically, as his chart of impersonal power in *No Name in the Street* suggests, one of the features of *privilege* is, most likely, that those who have it can't examine its costs. And, if such a destination as a "privileged position" exists, we've yet to imagine the language by which people who "have it" are able to communicate its perils to themselves much less to people who consider themselves to be without it. And, by *destination* I mean a place to be, to *live* in connection to one's living inheritance, not to simply approximate someone else's supposed entitlement to safety. The problem with saying "privileged position" is that the terms of privilege often vacate any sense of being other than being *on one's way* somewhere else. Maybe it's me, but every time I'm in the company of supposedly— I'm guessing—privileged people, they talk incessantly about places— from St. Moritz to Darfur—other than where they are. From what I've seen, the privileged live in airports.

Most problematically, our contemporary culture's obsession with the term *privilege* collapses discourses about human rights, constitutional law, or citizenship into a (basically bourgeois) anxiety about prep schools and professional pecking orders that operate exactly with the odds of pyramid schemes. It appears privilege is the ticket price of a middle-class lotto scam; the actual cost—forfeiture of a personally and historically engaged experience, a living inheritance—is prohibitive and remains hidden. Seen in this way, privilege becomes part of a dream of paying for your life with someone else's. Of course, in whatever way, people are always trying to do this; the question is in what way, how, and to what effect?

Baldwin invites us to measure our lives against the idea that privileges don't bear upon the constants of human experience, period. This is what he meant by crediting Ingmar Bergman with "recognizing: that life is very difficult, very difficult for anybody, anybody born."[19] He continued: "This is irreducible. And it's true for everybody."[20] He reasoned that the chronic bewilderment of so-called privileged people had to do exactly with the fact that they thought success would mitigate the intensity of human suffering. He touched upon this silent dynamic, too, with Terkel in 1961: "I'm very worried [about this country], I'm not worried about the Negroes in the country so much as I'm worried about the country. The country doesn't know what it's done to Negroes but the country has *no notion whatever*, and this is disastrous, of what it's done to itself. They've yet to assess the price they've paid, North and South, for keeping the nigger in his place. And from my point of view, it shows in every single level of our lives from the most public to the most private."[21]

We would need to have a serious discussion about this whole discourse of privilege and separate what, indeed, is a privilege (driver's licenses to those who abide the rules of the road, for instance) and what's a human and citizen's right (a coherent, affordable system of public transit, for instance). Driver's licenses for those who abide the rules of the road are one thing, possibly a privilege. Basic Fourteenth Amendment equal access to institutions such as schools or the right to *not* be profiled by police, hunted by neighborhood watch personnel, and murdered by predator drones without a trial (see the conclusion) are not privileges. They are rights, and withholding them is a *crime*. Young men profiled by police are not underprivileged. They are citizens upon whom *crimes* are being committed. I would argue the same for any child in a school funded at rates below the national (or at least regional median). I'm aware that there are technical legal arguments against this interpretation of the Fourteenth Amendment but, as we know, all that is a discourse not a stone tablet. Our strange fixation on privilege freezes that discourse by focusing us back into the incoherent, two-dimensional theater of American mutual regard. In that theater white people set the standard and one's health in whatever era is then measured according to the gap between you and the white bar.

Then there are the so-called (at times, strangely self-described) privileged themselves. The terms of privilege have even been brought to bear upon the labor of artistic creation. In *Ordinary Genius: A Guide for the Poet Within*, Kim Addonizio writes: "Because I am a Caucasian-American in a culture that is predominantly white, I have blind spots. Sometimes I know what they are, and I can try to see them in a side mirror. But sometimes, I think, I don't even notice them. I can usually afford not to notice. This is the privilege of my skin color."[22] So, I gather, *blindness* is now a privilege? At least in spots? For an artist!? How? This bizarre line of thought wouldn't be remarkable at all if it didn't represent the core of the contemporary discussion. How far away from the "immunity to bullshit" and "knife-edge of seeing" in Chapter 2 have the false terms of the discussion taken us? On what level of experience can one "afford not to notice" things that happen (or just as importantly, don't happen).

Is that the level of experience against which to measure key terms in our social thought?

In "Disloyal to Civilization" (1978), Adrienne Rich foreswore her entitlement to a related kind of blindness and argued for the work at seeing:

> I used to envy the word "colorblindness" which some liberal, enlightened, white people were supposed to possess; raised as I was, where I was, I am and will to the end of my life be acutely, sometimes bitterly, aware of color. Every adult around me in my childhood, white or black, was aware of it; it was a sovereign consciousness, a hushed and compelling secret. But I no longer believe that "colorblindness"—even if it exists—is the opposite of racism; I think it is, in this world, a form of naiveté and moral stupidity.[23]

In "An Atlas of the Difficult World," Adrienne Rich described a chronic loneliness she perceived in poetry by white men as a "white man's madness."[24] To this, she added, "I honor your truth and refuse to leave it at that."[25] I'd say the same to those whom I perceive as honestly working, though trapped, within this discourse of privileged and underprivileged. The idea of privilege rests on an essentially bourgeois assumption that one can "afford" to not do the basic work (work from scrubbing the tub to perception itself) of one's own experience, the assumption that one can coast, blindly, and "get away with it." I wonder to where these people imagine that they'll get away? Or maybe the assumption is that this work can be done while they remain, somehow mystically, alone? If so, one wonders what people imagine they'll do with this private leisure. It's exactly here that Beckett's Didi asks Gogo, famously, "What do we do now, now that we are happy?"[26] The answer in American life has usually been, I paraphrase, "let's steal back our amputated connection to our happy lives from a song sung by someone who isn't." This is a vexing dynamic for people whose history, as Baldwin insisted, "is each other." All this leads directly to the dynamics of convenience in the American psyche which I discuss in the conclusion.

What are the blind spots of social privilege, exactly? I think we assume that privilege amounts to a certain insulation from the trials of not having privilege. And, although a serious discourse of citizenship rights and responsibilities would indicate otherwise, insofar as the generality of Americans can determine, it certainly does. But, even if it is so, privilege also blinds and numbs people to their *own* risks and experiences. Useful evidence for this exists in a poem by Sharon Olds. Writing of a lynching in "Race Riot, Tulsa, 1921," Olds opens the poem:

The blazing white shirts of the white men
are blanks on the page, looking at them is like
looking at the sun, you could go blind.[27]

Can the sons, wives, and daughters of these men really afford to not
see them and "get away with it." What could that mean? Get away with
what? And, to where, exactly? Olds follows the image of the blind spot
(of history, of the camera, of the eye of the poet) obscuring our view of
the white men who had perpetrated or observed the lynching with the
following:

Under the snouts of the machine guns,
the dark glowing skin of the women
and men going to jail. You can look at the
gleaming horse-chestnuts of their faces the whole day.[28]

This is a good poem, but its most important strength isn't in what it sees
so much as what it confesses that it won't look at. As Olds's images make
clear, the blind spots of so-called white privilege obscure much more
than visions across racial difference. The invisible ones in the poem are
the white men, the ones it hurts or blinds the speaker in Olds's poem to
look at. We might call this the blindness of the liberal gaze.

Are we to assume it hurt Robert Hayden any less to look with such
touching (and so horrifying) nuance and precision at his white human
subjects in "Night, Death, Mississippi"? Hayden's vision intensifies rather
than obscures our encounter with white hatred exactly by linking it to
human constants: wonder, fatigue, and generational love. In the won-
drous memory of an aged nightrider, Ku Klux Klan regalia shimmer
in Hayden's poet's eye: "White robes like moonlight / in the sweetgum
dark."[29] Of the desperate fatigue of a failed ritual, Hayden's white su-
premacist recalls "we beat them . . . / beat them till our arms was tired / and
the big old chains / messy and red." Hayden culminates the horror by positioning the horror itself as part and parcel of generational love. Imagining his own son out on the hunt, Hayden's persona anticipates his return:
"have us a bottle, / boy and me— / he's earned him a bottle— / when he
gets home."[30] Finally, of a previous generation (possibly his own childhood), the persona hears the maternal voice: "You kids fetch Paw / some
water now so's he / can wash that blood / off him."[31] In "Night, Death,
Mississippi," unblinded by the optics of so-called privilege at the chimerical surface, Hayden's portrait still shocks us (openly, somehow, not
closed) because its senses are alive in ways that position violence and ha-

tred in terrifying proximity to the deepest of human constants. This is what, in 1947, Baldwin had called "the shock of identification," that he found missing in the work he found lacking (*Cross*, 240). Hayden's poem links the impersonal terrors of whiteness to the subtle shades of private, personal life.

It is instructive to consider the difference between these two poems as a gauge for measuring the price of being able "to afford not to notice." Possibly, privileged blindness is simply a code word for eyes and nerves averted from certain kinds of risk and pain and consequently from joy and experience, an exile from the living inheritance and the foreclosure of the birthright? If so, no one wins. Period. Can artists or anyone do that with impunity? Obviously not. Isn't the privilege an express lane to the missing bridge? In "Race Riot, Tulsa, 1921" the poetics trace the optics of the camera, but as a result of this conceit, the poem remains nearly as silent as the glass in the lens. The poem ends with an image of darkening vision, the face of the lynched black man: "tilted up / toward the sky, to get the sun on it, to / darken it more and more toward the color of the human."[32] Whiteness is blind to whiteness, but seems perfectly able to look at even gruesome images of black suffering and the supposed nobility that comes from it. *It*? Is that the looking or the suffering? This liberal paradigm persists and is applied with much syrup all over the globe. For his part, Baldwin brutally summed up the crux of it in *Another Country*. Making sure no one would mistake the offense, Baldwin's Leona consoles Rufus: "Ain't nothing wrong in being colored" (*ENS,* 411); and, Rufus: "Not if you a hard-up white lady" (412). Which is about as far as we seem to have gone in the public conversation. Given that one can only guess what goes on, or doesn't, in private.

At this point, it's useful to follow Baldwin's distinction between blackness as a "condition" negotiating between amputation and gangrene and whiteness as a "state of mind" (a phrase he borrowed from Malcolm X) convinced that it is—or that it can be—free to pick and choose its blind spots. In the 1980s, fulfilling one dimension of his long-held views, Baldwin regarded white liberal America in tatters and, confirming another dimension, he could see conservative America turning its back on mountains of moral evidence and priceless social energy summoned by the multiple, interconnected freedom movements during the 1960s and 1970s. In the 1960s, Ronald Reagan was liberal America's joke about California; by the 1980s the joke was on everyone. Baldwin began to amplify and expand his dissent from the racial terminology he had begun in the 1940s and put succinctly throughout the late 1960s.

In a 1968 interview for *Esquire* titled "How Can We Get the Black People to Cool It?" the interviewer asked: "Is there a white man who can . . . ?"[33] Before the interviewer could complete the question about understanding the politics of imperialism, Baldwin cut him short: "White by the way is not a color, it's an attitude. You're as white as you think you are. It's your choice." After cutting the conclusion of Baldwin's thought, the article resumes by picking up on part of the comment edited out. Interviewer: "Then is black a state of mind too?" Baldwin: "No, black is a condition." To gauge the relative nature of a "state of mind" and a "condition," and because he thought Baldwin was in a rhetorical trap, the interviewer asked Baldwin if "the underclass of black people, given an insufficient education, understands the specifics of this imperialism." Baldwin: "We understand very much better than you think we do, and we understand it from the letters we get from Vietnam."[34] This comment clarifies Baldwin's view that education must exist in *connection* to experience (and experience in connection to the world), not in abstraction from it no matter if the code word for such abstraction is whiteness, privilege, or Harvard. Confirming the pedagogical importance of experience and implying the poverty of privilege, the question of learning itself comes up in relation to Robert Kennedy's (then, burgeoning) presidential campaign. Baldwin responded: "The best thing that can be said about Bobby Kennedy, and I'm not trying to cop out on this, was said by Al Calloway in that rather curious issue about Soul that *Esquire* just did. Al said that if Soul could be studied and learned, he'd learn it. He'd study and learn, but it can't be studied and learned."[35]

Far from a privilege, then, for Baldwin, "whiteness" became an index for the attempt to preempt experience itself, the effort to transform one's human condition into a racialized "state of mind." Privilege, it seems is, indeed, a useful device in that bankrupt quest to be present in, but not a presence in, the world. In the 1984 piece, "On Being White and Other Lies," Baldwin eschewed equivocations and attempted to summon another level of reality buried under fraudulent terminology:

> White men—from Norway, for example, where they were Norwegians—became white [in the United States] by slaughtering the cattle, poisoning the wells, torching the houses, massacring Native Americans, raping black women.
>
> This moral erosion has made it quite impossible for those who think of themselves as White in this country to have any moral authority at all—privately or publicly. The multitudinous bulk of

them sit, stunned, before their TV sets, swallowing garbage that they know to be garbage, and—in a profound and unconscious effort to justify this torpor that disguises a profound and bitter panic—pay vast amounts of attention to athletics even though they know that the football player (the son of the Republic, their sons!) is merely another aspect of the money-making scheme.[36]

Rather than for a "race-blind" view of reality, Baldwin argued that perspectives willing to imagine themselves to be "white" take place via false pretenses. Such perspectives, including, or beginning with ones that claim to be "race-blind," announce a thinned, impossibly willed version of experience. Call it self-blind, or maybe life-blind. As a result, he can't imagine how a meaningful engagement with life could accept "whiteness" as part of a serious conversation or a functional vocabulary let alone a considered life. So, when people (poets!) stare at their shoes and speak about the advantages of blindness as a consequence of whiteness—privilege—we can only imagine them to mean the world of experience their delusional "state of mind" has cost them to this day.

But, not so fast. From here, in light of the terms of the forty-year dynamic meditation on the blues Baldwin's work established, we can see that it's not white guilt or even shame that motivates this whole discussion; it's the price paid by people, the lives forfeited (first person vacated, blues foreclosed) in return for illusions of "safety" often indexed in consumer terms. We can also see the multicolored, multinational audiences for these performances made up exactly of those who covet those same illusions. Which, in part, let's face it, accounts for almost all of us in some way save ideologues who risk living personal lives of "the people" and making passion impersonal. That's what Baldwin called "part of the price of the black ticket" (quoted at the beginning of this chapter). As a state of mind, moral choice, or cultural principle, "whiteness"—in the way Baldwin intends it be understood—can't be avoided by anyone. It's woven into a tangle of organic longings in human life and consciousness, among them the longing for safety and for safe passage for one's children. In her 1967 poem, "5:30 A.M.," Adrienne Rich links the dangerous appeal of such truths to impulses rooted even deeper than our species:

No one tells the truth about truth
that's what the fox sees from his scuffled burrow:
dull-jawed, onrushing
killer, being that
inanely single-minded
will have our skins at last.[37]

Sensing and attempting to clarify the point at which self-interest becomes self-destructive, Rich recognizes and rejects the narrowed, bunkered point of view. With Rich, Baldwin, therefore, reasons that, no matter one's skin color, the allure of "whiteness" can't be avoided. It must be clarified, confronted, and defeated. His critique of "black middle class-dom" (noted in the 1970s and 1980s sections of Chapter 3) is clearly Baldwin's attempt to warn against using a version of blackness as a "state of mind" for the relatively "privileged" black few as a measure of social health.

Avoiding professional terminology, Baldwin's critique largely employs language of everyday use. Confusions can arise. Baldwin himself slipped in his efforts to defeat the "enemy assumptions" of the American vo-cabulary and at the same time "expose [himself] to the assumptions of this language."[38] Such exposure was necessary because Baldwin aimed to simultaneously engage (rather than dissect from above) the cultural blind-ness and the dilemmas of the language in a way that didn't make an ivory tower of the conversation. At UC Berkeley, in 1979, he argued that it is impossible to convert a condition into a "state of mind," and then use the latter as the foundation of a national myth: "I want to suggest and it is a very important suggestion, first of all, this is not now, never has been and now never will be a white country. [*Applause.*] There is not a white per-son in this country, from our President to all his friends, who can prove he's white! [*Widespread laughter and applause in the audience*]."[39] At this point, with key terms in this book in the background, one wonders how many in the audience follow what Baldwin meant? How many under-stand the tangled levels of "white" he's referring to: the census mark or the moral choice? Condition or state of mind? Skin color or Cutty Sark? Happy access to privilege or the mute terror of preempted experience? Privileged access to the American dream, or the forfeiture of what it en-tails to know one's self (or anything else) in a first person that's not irrele-vant to other people, persons. And from Chapter 3 we know Baldwin had largely given up on prose articulation and understanding in favor of a poetic-musical mode of provoking recognitions, reflections, and refrac-tions. In the same speech, investing his energy in an open-ended sense of collective improvisation, Baldwin continued to signify:

[*Cutting the laughter short.*] It is absolutely true. [*More laughter.*] The people who settled this country came from many places and where they were before they came here was France, England. In France they were French. In England they were English. In Italy they were Italian. In Greece they were Greek. In Russia they were Russian. . . .

And this means, that we have to consider, first of all, that white, as Malcolm said, "is a state of mind." Because I don't want to be misunderstood as saying . . . I'm not talking about white people. Insofar as you think you're white, you're irrelevant. [*Much laughter then applause.*] We can no longer afford that particular *romance.* [*Laughter.*] We are all, in any case, here.

Baldwin is speaking without a prepared speech, he is riffing his way toward a point about the vocabulary he is using and not using. He employs obvious elisions here and there. For instance, as he knew, many Russians came to the United States exactly because in Russia they weren't *Russians*; they were, for instance, peasants, or they were Jews. Many came from Greece because they were Armenian or Turkish, from Turkey because they were Greek, from Croatia because there wasn't one. Many came from England because they were Welsh or Irish, etc. Many were fleeing from terror made legal in nations or normalized by traditional cultures. Baldwin goes on, lyrically. He's almost singing.

Symmetrical phrasings, "in France they were French," move him to the point where the use of terms (such as white) fractures. His point about the term *white* is perfectly sound; whatever "white" Americans were before arriving to North America, they were *not* white, certainly not in terms relevant to American experience. Those who disagree may frame their arguments in the home language of "whiteness." Nonetheless, with his voice climbing into a shout, he completes the thought before the audience:

I want to point out a paradox. The only people in this country who have any notion of who they are. The *only* people in this country who have any notion of who they are, are the black people of this country. [*Applause, no laughter; then, with anger in his voice.*] And I will tell you why! When the Italian got here or the Greek or whoever, there was a moment in his life when he had to start to speak English, when he became a guy named Joe. And that meant he couldn't speak to his father, because his father couldn't speak English. That meant a rupture, a profound rupture. So some did become a guy named Joe and never found out anything else about himself.

One might think that the accident of being born to parents (or of growing up within arms reach of a couple of aunts, uncles, or neighbors) who have some idea "who they are" would be a certain advantage in a republic, maybe even a privilege. Such a circumstance might have something to do with what the song "To Be Young, Gifted and Black," for example, as sung by Donny Hathaway, celebrates as being, "where it's at."[40] That this point *never* comes up in public discourse reveals the (at least from Baldwin's point of view), at best, ambiguous stakes in the squabble over privilege and its vaunted traction in the American dreamland. Of course, to the extent that one doesn't actually live in a republic (which is also "where it's at"), such inanely single-minded approaches might count as spoils of war, rations of crime. But, with those terms it's already another discussion, one that explains, for instance, much of the militarized popular culture that surrounds us (more on this in the conclusion).

Baldwin's point is certainly sound in one respect: no immigrant leaves home aspiring to the "black condition" in the United States. At UC Berkeley, identifying the point at which the American myth breaks away from the real situation, he nailed the point: "Every white person in this country, I don't care what he says or she says, knows one thing. They may not know, as they put it, 'what I want,' but they know they would not like to be black here." Then, pausing for applause and laughter, and almost chanting a tone poem as much as delivering sentences at this point, he concluded the thought: "If they know that, they know *ev-ery-thing* they need to know. And whatever else they say is a lie! Bear it in mind children, I mean that." No immigrant wants to be black here; it's true. But, after the profound rupture, it's another story for their children. In order to come up with American voices and styles and unable to accept (or afford) the numbness of whiteness, children of immigrants very often internalize very intense encounters with "blackness."

Elsewhere in the speech, after pausing to explain his subterranean use of the term *white* (state of mind, a moral choice), Baldwin argues that some people haven't made such a choice; "black" people (a condition) understand who they are as a function of the reality and history rather than the dream or fantasy of American life. Here, in the speech, Baldwin's terms themselves (let alone what the audience is making of this) rest on shifting ground. He knows the price and he's still improvising. Performing. And, in order to carry the audience, he paints the picture in the stark terms of his own symbolic American discourse: it's a question of *white* people and *black* people and neither term, ultimately, is determined by skin color (although, of course, they're both guided by what history has made, and the present still makes, of skin color). Who in the audience understands this? Almost no one. But, as the uproar recorded in the auditorium indicates, what he said certainly provoked recognition.

I've played the speech for high school classrooms in the Bronx (actually in the high school Baldwin attended) in which there were almost no students from European-descended families at all and almost none from black families with origins in the American South. They felt left out! My task, then, was to explain why and how they're not left out and what their choices imply about where they're headed. How is it (and, indeed, it often is) that immigrants seek exactly the facets of the American dream that Baldwin aligns (or maligns) with whiteness and embrace the narrative of individual merit and personal, transcendent possibility all the while colluding with family and community in the United States and abroad? The pressures and delusions of whiteness Baldwin had in mind are, in fact, acute among non-European immigrants to the United States who have any intention of staying. Generations of conservatives (notably William F. Buckley when he debated Baldwin at Cambridge in 1965) have used this immigrant sleight of hand to assault the integrity of black people's "work ethic," and to wring hands about the mystical failure of black people to convert their condition into a state of mind like the rest of Americans. In the American theater, however, the white state of mind requires someone's condition remain available as a touchstone for what whiteness is not.

At least one American poet has picked up on Baldwin's call to collective, open-ended work on this theme. In his brilliant book, *Tocqueville*, Lybian-born Khaled Mattawa signifies on the longings for "whiteness" by people of whatever color, worldwide. Assessing the price of the twenty-first-century ticket, he wrote:

> You've got to admit that we're all white people now. Everybody that got killed in that war is White, all got killed for Whitie. Even the people in China are White people now. That's what a lot of these brown or yellow conservatives are really saying, and even they don't realize what they're getting at. They're saying race doesn't matter because they've become White.[41]

The twenty-five-page title poem of Mattawa's book comes at his point from many angles, but *all* the trajectories collide in the passage above. At UC Berkeley, Baldwin said, "when Americans talk about civilization, they mean how fast I can become white ... and I've drunk my share of dry martinis, but there is an irreducible difficulty [*sardonic laughter*] something doesn't work! [*More laughter.*]"

Now, consider the printed version of this section of Baldwin's speech published in the *Los Angeles Times* later that same week in April 1979:

> Our presence in this country terrifies every white man walking. This nation is not now, never has been and now never will be a

white country. There is not a white person in this country, including our President and all his friends, who can prove he's white.

The people who settled this country came from many places. It
was not so elsewhere in the world. In France, they were French; in
England they were English; in Greece they were Greek, in Russia
they were Russian. From this I want to point out a paradox: Blacks,
Indians, Chicanos, Asians and that beleaguered handful of white
people who understand their history are the only people who know
who they are.[42]

The printed version of the speech turns away from the moral white/black
vocabulary and implies that nonwhiteness in skin color and connection to
a living inheritance go together as a matter of course save a "beleaguered
handful" of exceptions. Mattawa begs to differ and Baldwin knew better.
But now the students in the Bronx find it much easier to see themselves
or their parents in Baldwin's statement. But, Mattawa's question—and
Baldwin's in the speech—that asks how many of them (and to what
degree) are choosing to be "white," by shedding the "condition" and
seeking an instrumental, American state of mind passes by completely.
The spoken version sounds jingoistic (the black people are the only
Americans who know the score) to someone passing by the classroom
door in the hall unacquainted with the structure of Baldwin's thought.
One has to guess that that's largely what Baldwin's audience at Berkeley
was applauding. He was fine with that at least in the public forum. The
printed version seems to leave one free to suppose (in ways alarmingly
similar to Reagan's quip that there was no word for *freedom* in Russian)
that there's no word for *safety* in Mandarin, Cantonese, Urdu, Ibo, Spanish, Quechua, or Farsi when spoken in the West.

The two versions of that point must be considered together in order to
understand the contradictory complexity of Baldwin's idea and to appre-
ciate the difficulty of rendering it in the public, everyday terms he chose.
All that *jazz*, indeed. Because, finally, the reason Baldwin's joke about dry
martinis not making him "civilized" in American terms is funny (at least
to him!) is that the "irreducible difficulty" isn't, in fact, his brown skin.
Instead, the difficulty is rooted in his living inheritance, in the black condition, and in the lyrical, peace-disturbing wisdom that comes from it.
The joke is that if he does become civilized then what will people measure their state of mind against? In *Just Above My Head*, he wrote "Our
history is each other";[43] in 1961 he told Studs Terkel, "If you're going to
learn [your name], you're going to have to learn mine."[44] He meant that
very deeply. He thought that the energy of people learning their own

names from each other was more important than privilege. That was the takeaway he intended in "The Hallelujah Chorus." We have to find a way to say our Amens to each other.

In effect, Baldwin argues that a state of mind can't learn anything from itself. Like living, like joy, learning takes place in relation to a *condition* one is struggling to clarify. That's the whole, lyrical, painful point in "The Uses of the Blues." In his 1976 essay "In Search of a Basis for Mutual Understanding," Baldwin criticized mainstream accounts of so-called American life, for instance, the "white furor" in South Boston over school busing. The distance between the terms of discussion and underlying situation thwarted any and all useful sense to be made:

> The details so authoritatively and painlessly amassed, as in political poles and public questionnaires, convey various reflexes (aka "facts") and have nothing whatever to do with the truth—the truth being contained in the point of view, and still more in the journey which creates the point of view. . . . But the truth is that the point of view dictated by their unlearned history has precipitated these people into nothing less than paranoia . . . if they had not forced themselves to forget the real reasons for their voyage, they might be better equipped to bear the promised land . . . on what basis can this panic-stricken multitude conceive of mutual understanding and racial harmony.[45]

In "The Uses of the Blues," Baldwin concluded that one might simply list the themes of the blues in the column marked "facts of life."[46] In "In Search of a Basis," he paused to note that no one is immune to eyes conditioned (blinded) by empire, to the invisible damage of privilege. Everyone has a state of mind; this is what human consciousness and culture do with experience. That's why artists disturb the peace. But, due to his sense of condition, Baldwin *doesn't* view this state of mind as an advantage. He recognizes the limitation and knows that, if one tries, one *can* recover one's sight from it: "Some of the things I've seen in other countries appalled me . . . one-eyed beggars, men amputated from the waist down. . . . But this says more about me than it says about the people I flattered myself as observing, and whom I failed to see. For the children of Sunset Boulevard are at least as devastated, and I have encountered more than one blind and stinking beggar in the executive suites and mansions of my own country."[47] In other words, one can't learn anyone's name by observation; real knowledge can't be "automatically and painlessly amassed." Details and facts acquired by these means, he thought, didn't bear upon anyone's experience. Equipped in this way, there's no way to tell who can afford what, who is a beggar, and who is a thief.

In short, he's saying that a "state of mind," shed of its condition, lacking its blues sense of itself (and therefore of its connection to others) can't make living sense of the world. As Baldwin had always insisted, therefore, the so-called advantages of whiteness are at least as destructive as the so-called disadvantages of poverty and blackness. They operate in different, although not unrelated, registers of experience. But, most of all, the destructive features of the various trajectories are *connected*. He elaborated this point in *Take This Hammer* better than anywhere else. It bears quotation in full:

A white liberal woman told me a few weeks ago, she had had the bad luck to be sitting in the same room with about twenty [black] students who were, you know, telling it like it is. Sterling Brown was there. She was one of the few white liberals in the room. And, what these kids were saying, in effect, was "white people don't know nothing about us to be able to help us, white people say one thing and do another" all of this [is] absolutely true. And, she was terribly terribly hurt, bitterly hurt, and she said "I'm sure I've done more for Negroes than they had ever done." And I got mad. And I said that's exactly what they were saying, they don't want you to do anything for Negroes, they want you to do it for you. And she said, "I'm not willing to damage my child." And, I said, "Well, then forget it." . . . After all, speaking for myself, you know, it's a kind of insult. Here I am, as they say, with no visible scars. I am not isolated, I've got a family and a history and I've got nieces and nephews. I can't protect them, you know, they're in tremendous danger. Every hour that they live just because they're black not because they're wicked. I mean this from the baby niece to the oldest nephew who is sixteen. Now, if this is where they are, you know, and I know every time I leave my nephew I don't know what will happen to him by the time I see him again I mean not only inside but physically. How do you expect me to take seriously someone who says "I'm willing to fight for you but I can't afford to let my children be damaged"? And, furthermore, how can I take seriously somebody who doesn't realize that their children are *being* damaged? By this. By the continuation of the system. . . . What I really mean at bottom is that if you can think of it in those terms then you don't see the gravity of the situation, you don't see that we are living in a segregated society and this does terrible things to my child and does terrible things to your child too. If you don't see that then I don't think you see anything. And most liberals don't see that.

The contemporary concept of privilege stands for exactly this invisible damage: the inanely single-minded, burrowed, state of mind imposed upon "white" children of whatever color—in order to *make* them "white"—to keep them free of the damage and danger of their condition. In that theater, black people serve as images of what to avoid. Then the culture makes *that* the bar and measures everyone else according to the *gap* (achievement gap, income gap, etc.) between their "condition" and the standard American "state of mind." If privilege and invisible damage aren't identical, the two are inseparable and their attributes switch places. Like the poetic eye in Sharon Olds's poem, "Race Riot, Tulsa, 1921," arguably, contemporary liberals are actually comfortable seeing and discussing "black damage," much of which, if not attributable directly to crimes naturalized by American culture, stands for the human constants of the blues, the facts of life. The liberal gaze, often mistakenly, sees this much while remaining blind to the invisible damage Baldwin points out. The fact that we're supposed to congratulate this "state of mind" as an advantage, call that damage a privilege, and aspire to it reveals much about the veiled assumptions of the contemporary culture. Calling such a state of mind privilege only intensifies the self-blindness of white people (in a particularly congratulatory way) and insidiously summons the aspirations of the so-called underprivileged out of their condition and into whatever version of a white state of mind they can afford. On credit. Something doesn't work, indeed.

By this dynamic, the *conditions* of people, everywhere, can only deteriorate as the pack, set in competition with each other, scuffles up the state-of-mind, privilege pyramid. Baldwin's work charted these invisible transactions going on beneath the chimerical terminology of change in America. The alternative is to remain in touch, or get back in touch, with the basic facts of life and health—if not salvation—gauged in one's relationship to others doing the same, or, as it happens, who knows, others doing something that seems *very* different. Or trying. As Baldwin noted of his mobility across the whole city during his early years in Paris, health must be the pursuit of relationships across the schisms of American life that quarantine our shared experience and prevent a sense of collective endeavor that would allow us to gauge—to *live*—our lives. By these actions we'd transform the two-dimensional portrait of power into a living tableau of shifting shades and multidimensional colors.

# Conclusion
## The Brilliance of Children, the Duty of Citizens

> Common knowledge say a US President
> can't save ya.
>
> —*Georgia Anne Muldrow, "Kneecap Jelly"*[1]

**A**s I complete this work, the question in the title, *Who Can Afford to Improvise?*, dangles above my head. This week in mid-August 2014, US audiences watched as tactical law enforcement mobilized in (many said occupied) the small, mostly black town of Ferguson, Missouri. Residents, protesters, and onlookers were stunned at the sight. Images that, for most of the twenty-first century, they had associated with military occupations far away in places like Mosul, Fallujah, and Baghdad (and, also, in the West Bank and Gaza), had appeared, as if out of nowhere, in the streets of the American Midwest. The killing by police in broad daylight of Michael Brown, an unarmed black teenager in Ferguson, had, once again, stirred up latent anger exposing the summertime rites of American poverty. The images played backward over the post-2001 era, the era of American Homeland Security, often known as the War on Terror. Largely initiated, constituted, and deployed by the Bush administrations (2000–2008) amid widespread disapproval around the world and periodic protests (such as those over the invasion of Iraq), this period of American history, since Barack Obama's election in 2008, has also borne the name the Obama era.

The coexistence between the image of President Obama—whose election fulfilled the predictions of Robert Kennedy and James Baldwin from the early 1960s (noted in Chapter 1)—and the War on Terror has been an uncomfortable riddle for people in the United States and in the world. There's absolutely no question as to the historic and symbolic importance of Obama's election. There was also never a question but that the symbol, like all symbols, would become part of the complex political machinery of the nation and the world. Political scientists, historians, and biographers will debate, deconstruct, and rebuild narratives of how this played out for generations. The following is one small glance at a convergence of events and forces that, to me, illustrated something new about the nature and staging of American political power, certainly American presidential power, in the early twenty-first century. It focuses on the functioning of President Obama's complex image in the theater of the American War on Terror in ways that draw directly upon angles of vision and lenses Baldwin provided in his work.

One key term in the riddle is the Nobel Peace Prize awarded President Obama in 2009, the year after he was elected. Many questioned the award, scanning the new president's brief record in national office (as US senator and as president) for "foreign policy" achievements worthy of the distinction. Rarely, at the time or since, did commentators seem to realize that, for the Swedes, for instance, Obama's election as the first black president of the United States was a signal "foreign" policy achievement in the world. His election indicated some kind of shift, maybe many, in racial attitudes among the populace of arguably the world's most powerful nation. In a distant echo of Nelson Mandela's election as president of South Africa in 1994, after (or, really, *while*) withholding full citizenship from its black population, the United States had elected a black president. Many criticisms of President Obama's foreign (and even some domestic) policies have turned upon the irony that the Nobel Peace Prize Laureate had sanctioned the use of force in some way or another. In this the commentaries usually lose track of the simultaneous, contrasting force of Obama's image that mitigates, every hour, feelings of alienation among many millions of black (as well as other) people across the class continuum in the United States. So powerful is that force that critiques of the president, even of the power of the US presidency, such as the one that follows, meet with editorial pressures not totally unlike those Baldwin dealt with during his career.[2] I don't wish to minimize the historic, peaceful force of President Obama's image here, not at all. I count myself and my family among those who benefit from it. It's a reality. At the same time, one has to make the effort to clarify operations in, and mobilizations of, forces that govern us.

On the morning of September 11, 2001, at the real dawn of the new age, I was teaching in Schenectady, New York, a small, brutally deindustrialized town near where the Mohawk River enters the Hudson. Later, the flight paths of the planes that crashed into the World Trade Center towers would be reconstructed to show that the flight from Boston had turned almost exactly overhead as it flew west, heading south at the Hudson and following the river to Manhattan. With the first, confused news reports on the radio that morning, I found a television set and, horrified and mesmerized, watched with my colleague Michelle and then with others as the second plane made its impact. This clarified the question as to whether the first crash had been an accident. As we watched, within hours, the towers disappeared into clouds of dust.

At some point that same day, an image from *Another Country* appeared in my memory. The novel begins with an epigraph by Henry James from the preface to the New York edition of his short novel from 1884, *Lady Barbarina*. As with the others, in his preface to *Lady Barbarina*, James reflected upon key questions and dilemmas of craft posed by the work. He recalled the problem of imagining "gages of identity" by which to measure "the diluvian presence" of American sensibilities. It no longer worked to approach them as "just the American vague variety of the dear old Anglo Saxon race."[3] The multitude in which "the general roll-call" of names "falls so strongly upon alien syllables and sounds" largely eluded his imagination which, he found, "doesn't rise to such people, who are obviously beyond my divination."[4] Baldwin's epigraph to *Another Country* recounts James's confusion before the alien spectacle of American sensibility: "They strike one, above all, as giving no account of themselves in any terms already consecrated by human use; to this inarticulate state they probably form, collectively, the most unprecedented of monuments; abysmal the mystery of what they think, what they feel, what they want, what they suppose themselves to be saying" (*ENS,* 363).

Amid his bafflement, however, James hazards that, at least for those "of position," American consciousness turned upon the attempt to stand beyond "any suspicion that convenience shall anywhere fail it: all its consciousness, on that general head, is that of itself representing and actively *being* the biggest convenience of the world."[5] Self-evident, he found, was "the guarantee of subjective ease involved with such an attitude." Assured that its gospel of convenience would be universally embraced by the world in a reciprocity that entitled it to "subjective ease," the American sensibility took itself and the world for granted via a flagrant series of absurd readings of history at home and abroad. So it was that Baldwin would aim his imagination at characters (Irish-Jewish, Polish, black) beyond the divination of James's concerned attention. Asked the title of the then-forthcoming novel by Studs Terkel in 1961, Baldwin said, "*Another Country*. It's about *this* country."[6]

At the outset of *Another Country*, the architecture of Manhattan confesses a brutally and commercially intensified Jamesian disregard for the people it uses as conveniences. Baldwin positions his protagonist, Rufus Scott—possibly his most densely interesting character—in mortal conflict with the complacent economic and cultural forces supporting the mid-twentieth-century American sensibility:

> A sign advertised the chewing gum which would help one to relax and keep smiling. A hotel's enormous neon name challenged the starless sky. So did the names of the movie stars and people currently appearing or scheduled to appear on Broadway, along with the mile-high names of the vehicles which would carry them into immortality. The great buildings, unlit, blunt like the phallus or sharp like the spear, guarded the city which never slept.
>
> Beneath them Rufus walked, one of the fallen—for the weight of this city was murderous—one of those who had been crushed on the day, which was every day, these towers fell. (*ENS*, 368)

Readers then supposed, and many now suppose (in ways rightly), that Rufus's danger hinged on his blackness. For Baldwin, Rufus was part of an "unprecedented multitude" which was not, in the end, bounded by American racial markers: "There were boys and girls drinking coffee at the drugstore counters who were held back from his condition by barriers as perishable as their dwindling cigarettes" (368). In an ominous signal, and in a violent reversal of the promise in the final scene of "Sonny's Blues," even the downtown jazz scene had been made into a "stunning corroboration" of American subjective ease. The music, "hurled at the crowd like a malediction in which not even those who hated most deeply any longer believed . . . reassured everyone that nothing terrible was happening" (368). In *Take This Hammer*, Baldwin returned to the image of convenience. Black people functioned in white people's imagination as they had for the mythic antebellum masters who "assumed that I was only there to give him his cigar and to cheer him up when he didn't feel too well." Summing up modern and postcolonial history, including the civil unrest in Birmingham during the previous week in May 1963, Baldwin concluded: "He suddenly discovered that that wasn't my role at all."

As the clouds of dust engulfed the World Trade Center towers, I had begun to remember a sentence that ended: "on the day, which was every day, these towers fell." In the lens of that image, the murderous contemporary events had spun on a global axis in my mind. The world had returned to proclaim its radical inconvenience. The domestic American attitude of convenience and "subjective ease" had encountered international terror. At a blow, Americans had been placed in an alternate subjective relation to the murderous weight of the city; the military and commercial shadow American power cast into the world had been spun into the American mirror. I remember e-mailing the quote to friends over the next few weeks.[7] I don't remember exactly what class I was teaching but I remember some Baldwin work was in it. Classes were cancelled that day but we met the next day, a Wednesday, and I brought in the passage above and another passage from *Just Above My Head*. I remember telling the class that we were all stunned and scared and that the dead needed to be mourned but, at the same time, we wouldn't in this classroom be party to, nor silent before, the spasm of nationalism and the theater of good versus evil that would most certainly be forthcoming. This attack had not come out of nowhere. We had authors on the syllabus, including James Baldwin, who had addressed these energies over the years. In the second passage, Hall Montana, the narrator of *Just Above My Head*, who very frequently in the novel speaks as if he is the author's ventriloquist puppet, discussed his memories of air travel and its relationship to global and domestic political ferocity:

> I was travelling before the days of electronic surveillance, before the hijackers and the terrorists arrived. For the arrival of these people, the people in the seats of power have only themselves to blame. Who, indeed, has hijacked more than England has, for example, or who is more skilled in the uses of terror than my own unhappy country? Yes, I know: nevertheless, children, what goes around comes around, what you send out comes back to you. A terrorist is called that only because he does not have the power of the State behind him—indeed, he has no State, which is why he is a terrorist. The State, at bottom, and when the chips are down, rules by means of a terror made legal—that is how Franco ruled so long, and is the undeniable truth concerning South Africa. No one called the late J. Edgar Hoover a terrorist, though that's precisely what he was: and if anyone wishes, now, in this context, to speak of "civilized" values or "democracy" or "morality," you will pardon this poor nigger if he puts his hand before his mouth, and snickers—if he laughs at you. I have endured your morality for a very long time, am still crawling up out of that dung heap; all that the slave can learn from his master is how to be a slave, and that is not morality.[8]

Baldwin knew very well that this wasn't the last, still less the only, word on the matter.[9] Even more, since at least 1967, when, writing from Istanbul, he addressed the complexities and contradictions in Lord Russell's

War Crimes Tribunal—which accused the United States of war crimes in Southeast Asia—, he'd been explicit that he "never had any interest in attacking America from abroad."[10] He maintained the effort to clarify the world from multiple points of view, emphasizing, increasingly, those of the stateless, the poor, and the powerless. In short, Baldwin's worldview reflected and refracted the perspectives of the least of these who were not, after all, to be expected to live lives of saintly abnegation and whose interests weren't to be always subordinated to the status quo that propped up the Jamesian "convenience" and "subjective ease" in the minds of Americans "of position."

During his career, Baldwin addressed the US presidency directly in multiple registers. With a brief exception after the election of Jimmy Carter in 1976, his public antagonism with American presidential power increased as the decades passed. I've noted Baldwin's parries with Robert F. Kennedy during his brother's term as US president, and during RFK's 1968 campaign, previously. One instance of Baldwin's public engagement with the Kennedy administration bears close attention. It clarifies the risky, wide brush with which Baldwin was willing to paint in this arena and the improvised acuity of such strokes. It also provides one instance of political censorship for which there is very clear evidence. This involves the final scene of *Take This Hammer*. The scene was shot in director Richard O. Moore's living room in May 1963. Viewers who watched the documentary on KQED in San Francisco on February 4, 1964, heard Baldwin say: "What is really crucial is whether or not the country, the people in the country, the citizenry, are able to recognize that there is no moral distance, no moral distance, which is to say no distance, between the facts of life in San Francisco and the facts of life in Birmingham. One has got to tell it like it is. And that's where it's at." He meant that the politics of race were national as well as regional or simply Southern issues. Racially inflected violence, overt and implicit, endangered citizens of all races across the nation. It was therefore, in Baldwin's mind and in the minds of many others, a federal issue. Between the final cut and the airing of the film, however, fifteen minutes of footage cut out by KQED directors who thought some statements—mostly by young black men affiliated with the Nation of Islam in San Francisco—incendiary. A few of them probably were incendiary—Baldwin's point being that the whole situation was thoroughly incendiary, *The Fire Next Time*—and remained in the film as aired. Baldwin was furious at the cuts. Even though Richard O. Moore had nothing to do with them, Baldwin still never spoke to him again.

In 2013, a director's cut of *Take This Hammer* was released with the edited footage restored wherein we find that even Baldwin's attempt "to tell it like it is" was cut and spliced before it aired. Baldwin actually said: "What is really crucial is whether or not the country, the people in the country, the citizenry, are able to recognize that there is no moral distance, no moral distance, which is to say no distance, between the facts of life in San Francisco and the facts of life in Birmingham. And there is no moral distance—which is to say no distance—between President Kennedy and Bull Connor because the same machine put them both in power. One has got to tell it like it is. And that's where it's at."[11] At the time, Baldwin's point was designed to put pressure on the Kennedy administration. There's no doubt about that. His point was also that it's difficult to tell exactly *where* it's at; the violence and danger of racial hatred and illegitimate power involve complex national and international networks. More than local weather, those forces create a volatile and unpredictable climate. The president, the president's brother, and many others viewed Baldwin's urgency as an exaggeration. Time would bear out just how dangerous (and to whom) those energies were. Interestingly, years later in the film *I Heard It Through the Grapevine*, Jerome Smith said that because Robert Kennedy, at the time of their meeting in 1963, had so little sense of the danger in other people's lives, he had no way of assessing the danger in his own life.

The pressure of the censors certainly didn't silence Baldwin's point of view. According to David Leeming, Baldwin once called Richard M. Nixon a "'motherfucker' from the pulpit of St. John the Divine."[12] For the record, when asked what he thought about it, the new dean of the cathedral was heard to remark, "It's about time someone did." Baldwin's political critique was nonstop, prohuman, antiviolent—as opposed to nonviolent—anticapitalist, deeply soulful, and he meant it and he lived it. He meant to salt the discourse with alternative images, observations, and analytical devices such that people would not be totally constrained by the political options sold to them in the consumer marketplace of American electoral arenas. He lived a lifestyle fluid—and difficult—enough to elude many of the choices compelling no-win decisions on the part of people in the nation and in the world. From that perch, he fired away letting people oppressed by or, at least, not accommodated in, the political and social mainstream know that they were not alone.

In "Notes on the House of Bondage," a November 1980 piece in the *Nation*, published just before Ronald Reagan's landslide defeat of Jimmy Carter, he wrote: "I certainly don't want [my tribe of nieces and nephews] to believe that Carter and Reagan—*or* [John B.] Anderson [the independent candidate]—are the best people this country can produce. That despair would force me onto the road taken by the late, Guyana-based Jim Jones" (*CE*, 799). Baldwin would certainly perceive the difference between President Obama and Ronald Reagan and, without a doubt, he would critique Obama's role and the role of the power wielded by the US presidency nonetheless. Maybe all the more. His political critique was far beyond distinctions between American political parties. Of the election preceding the one above, in "A Review of *Roots*," published in the *New York Times* in 1976, he wrote: "There is a carefully muffled pain and panic in the nation, which neither candidate, neither party, can coherently address, being, themselves, but vivid symptoms of it" (762). It seems appropriate to conclude the book by connecting Baldwin's musically analytical model from *The Fire Next Time* to the staging of American presidential power in international terms and in the image of President Barack Obama.

In *The Fire Next Time*, Baldwin wrote:

> It is the responsibility of free men to trust and to celebrate what is constant—birth, struggle, and death are constant, and so is love, though we may not think so—and to apprehend the nature of change. I speak of change not on the surface but in the depths—change in the sense of renewal. But renewal becomes impossible if one supposes things to be constant that are not—safety, for example, or money, or power. One clings then to chimeras, by which one can only be betrayed, and the entire hope—the entire possibility—of freedom disappears. (*CE*, 339)

I'll use this musically informed analytical model to examine the image of President Obama in one particularly revealing moment of performance concerning the use of American military power in the international theater of the War on Terror.

At the end of Chapter 1, I asked, "What changes, what constants and what chimeras made the United States the place that elects a black president?" And, "What does *black* president actually mean?" Consider a statement made—we're to assume—offhand and in jest by President Obama at the White House Correspondents Dinner on May 1, 2010. In his remarks, he noted the presence of the pop group Jonas Brothers. He went on to state the following, "Sasha and Malia are huge fans, but boys don't get any ideas. I have two words for you: Predator drones. You'll never see it coming." Like the young man in *Take This Hammer* who anticipated Baldwin's questions, I can see Jimmy Baldwin slipping on his shades. Everyone knows the president is a persona, highly crafted. It's interesting to see President Obama, here, consciously playing upon the protective father role. And, he's twisted the irony of his father/president persona precisely to enlist the deadly military force of the state to his shotgun-at-the-door-on-prom-night purposes as a father. He's working with changes and constants. A father's love of daughters? Constant! But, do we hear the smack of numb patriarchy, even an echo of the fathers of the white South's fear for their daughter's chastity? Change? A black man is commander and chief? Change! But, where and against whom are Predator drones actually mobilized when they're not metaphorically menacing teen idol pop groups? Even more, whose communities are endangered in these, often elective, attacks? Constant?

The threat and use of state violence against "insurgent" forces is nothing new. All American militant groups and many that weren't militant experienced levels of state terror as well as state apathy in the face of social terror in the twentieth century. Baldwin knew such state terror firsthand. He was conscious of state as well as vigilante threats against his privacy, his life, and his livelihood. Casual and tactical references to it litter his correspondence, affected his plans, and inflected his work in all kinds of ways. In Istanbul in 1969, for instance, he noted the proximity of his apartment to embassies not aligned with the United States in case he should need emergency political asylum. His family opened his mail, intercepted the death threats, and more than once attempted to dissuade him from returning to the United States for fear he would be killed. In his biography, James Weatherby quotes Baldwin from an interview with Italian press soon after the murder of Malcolm X: "He said his own mail had got 'so horrible' he had turned it over to the FBI. 'Maybe they were writing some of it.'"[13]

These were not unreasonable fears and precautions. They all knew their phones were tapped. Baldwin suspected that his mail was being opened. In 1968, he sent his brother David a (grimly) humorous greeting card. On one side, the card read "HI FROM PALM SPRINGS CALIFORNIA: I'd love to tell you what I've been doing here . . ." and featured a comic cartoon depiction of a naked conventioneer hiding his privates behind his briefcase. On the other side, the card concluded: "But you know how FUSSY they are at the POST OFFICE." In his own hand, Baldwin then assured his brother that they would discuss it all in person and told him to hold on. The FBI knew at least as much about Baldwin's progress on his script for the Malcolm X film as Columbia Studios executives did.

In a letter sent from Istanbul on September 10, 1969, Baldwin gave instructions that his brother not let anyone he hadn't explicitly authorized into his apartment. He followed the instructions with a thought that if the apartment was searched before David received the letter, they could then be sure who was reading the mail. In letters to David Leeming and others, at times, Baldwin included taunts and invective-streaming curses addressed to whatever agent he thought might read his mail. In "Re/Member This House," Baldwin recollects first meeting Robert Kennedy at the White House in April 1962 (although in "Re/Member This House" he mistakes the year for 1963). He recalls the sensation of feeling himself, mechanically and audibly, being slipped into an FBI file he sensed Kennedy kept in his brain. Baldwin's FBI file became active within hours of this third meeting with Kennedy in New York City on May 24, 1963.

Cases prosecuting American terrorists who as employees of or with the sanction of local governments menaced and murdered American citizens were brought to trial in the first decade of the twenty-first century in Florida, North Carolina, Mississippi, Alabama, Chicago, and elsewhere. Many other families were notified that their decades-old cases would never be solved and would be closed.[14] Stand-your-ground legislation such as that behind the George Zimmerman/Trayvon Martin case deputizes citizens in this posture. The blogosphere was full of commentary about the international politics of President Obama's Jonas Brothers joke before the first correct fork was lifted amid all the comic incorrectness at the Correspondents' Dinner. Frequent mistaken or collateral killings of Afghani, Pakistani, Somali, and Yemeni civilians and numerous intended murders of "suspects" by Predator drones immediately struck many as bizarre territory for a joke about a father protecting his daughters. It doesn't take much to mark the offense. But, the change/constant structure of Baldwin's work takes it further. The fact that vast numbers of bloggers stop at marking ironies with outrage opens and limits our discourse. The fact that the mainstream media often do less than that intensifies our need for clearer, deeper perspectives such as Baldwin's work offers. The firing of long-time White House correspondent Helen Thomas provides at least one clue as to why mainstream journalists operate the way they do.[15] If jokes are often funny because they flout convention, they're revealing for exactly the same reason. In *No Name in the Street*, Baldwin argued that one can learn a lot by listening to what people "think is funny, which is also what they think is real" (*CE,* 469). For instance, if I hold a mirror between us at arm's length, my one-year-old son sees my face at the end of my arm, but he doesn't laugh until he looks back at where my face actually is. Such is the brilliance of children. Such is also the *duty* of citizenship. How about a quick look back at where it's at?

Possibly, a small glimpse of what is change and what is constant in President Obama's America appears in this joke. And, more interestingly, the relationship appears between what is constant, what changes, and the dangerous chimeras of confusion between them. Less than two weeks after the Jonas Brothers joke, on May 13, Scott Shane's story entitled, "US Approval of Killing Cleric Causes Unease," in the *New York Times* began like this: "The Obama administration's decision to authorize the killing by the Central Intelligence Agency of a terrorism suspect who is an American citizen has set off a debate over the legal and political limits of drone missile strikes, a mainstay of the campaign against terrorism."[16] Moving the president's joke closer to home, by May 13 it was clear that the "suspects" targeted for killing by Predator drones could also be American citizens. In fact, Anwar al-Awlaki, the American-born cleric and "suspect" in question, and Samir Khan, an American-born editor of the English-language, militant online magazine *Inspire*, were intentionally killed in a CIA-led US drone strike while driving in Yemen on Friday, September 30, 2011.[17] Leading up to the 2012 election, *all* discussions of Nobel Peace Laureate, President Obama's foreign policy credentials began with his presiding over the murder of Osama bin Laden. In the so-called postracial age that bears his name, it became difficult for me during the 2012 election season to distinguish this credential from the old-fashioned, time-honored horror, the political spectacle in which the tough American man waves his trophy scalp.

Echoing as it does real-time state terror on Earth, President Obama's joke links the human constant of fatherly love with the capricious nature and terror of political power. Fathers and politicians are dangers in their own ways. That's constant; we can work with it. But, by this kind of gesture, ephemeral permanence, state power, borrows the universal permanence of a constant fact of life, fatherhood. And, the fact of life, fatherhood, adopts the (to me, a father, destructive) straight-backed, macho force of technologically abstracted military violence. Exactly as Baldwin's work diagrams, such chimerical traffic between changes and constants is dangerous to democracy *and* family life. And that's no joke.

Historically speaking, this is not "postracial" territory; and neither is it now. Cloaked in the constants of family, state terror becomes familiar, natural, to people while its ideological, unlawful and error-prone deployment is obscured. This impairs the mirror-and-back vision of citizens and makes the United States more dangerous to the world, and vice versa, than it has to be. And, dressed in the gleam and ferocity of an abstract killing force, the role of fatherhood becomes further dehumanized and abstracted from the lives of actual men and daughters attempting to live and communicate as persons. This obscures the privately panic-stricken texture of our errors as fathers. And, *that* makes our houses and neighborhoods more dangerous than they already are. In 1964, in "The Uses of the Blues," Baldwin charted the hidden transactions that prop up the structure of this American theater. He wrote: "People who don't know who they are privately, accept as we have accepted for nearly fifteen years, the fantastic disaster of American foreign policy, and the incoherence of the one is an exact reflection of the incoherence of the other. Now, the only way to change all this is to begin to ask ourselves very difficult questions" (*Cross*, 66). Here Baldwin connects the private panic in the American head and home to the forces of global terror played out on behalf of so-called American interests in the world. In case this is sounding rhetorical, consider—from progun bumper stickers to confederate insignia to the almost constant flow of promilitary discourse at sporting and civic events—the array of public, militaristic, basically antisocial signs and declarations that we pass through in our daily lives.

Ask, for instance, the driver of the SUV I came across in Georgia for his views on drone strikes, gun laws, neighborhood watch programs (see following photograph). All of this, at each level, is driven by private questions the language for which—to say nothing of any answers—is obscured by the whole pageant of guns, jokes, and (by whatever name) drones.

This paradigm is directly applicable, for example, in the relation between the neighborhood watch mentality with its reliance on progun legislation pervasive in much of the contemporary United States and the popular support, indeed demand, for preemptive strikes in the US War on Terror. In this sense, the War on Terror appears to be a "natural" (that is, veiled ideological) extension of the nexus of progun legislation and gated community and neighborhood watch mentality. So, we might ask who was piloting the *drone* named George Zimmerman in Florida when he shot an unarmed Trayvon Martin in "defense" of his neighborhood? How many of those drones are out there? How many black parents rehearse this with their children, especially their sons, and then dwell upon it before they go to sleep at night? And, as for the reality of "race" as a map to who "drones" whom, who is responsible for these armed *drones* when they malfunction like Adam Lanza in Connecticut or James Holmes in Colorado? Of course, as was Baldwin's point about the murders of Medgar Evers and Malcolm X and many others, in part,

Car in the parking lot at Publix grocery in Athens, Georgia. (Photo by author, 2012.)

these civic malfunctions are the result of a political climate, the product of cultural weather.

President Bush's War on Terror and homeland security policies—positioned constitutionally by John Yoo and Alberto Gonzales and kept, however ambivalently, basically intact by Eric Holder in the Obama administration—operate, in Baldwin's lens, precisely as a global neighborhood watch program.[18] The system of connections at work here is toxic to lives in ways few are conscious of and, maybe, in ways few want to know anything about. In this, then, as it was in 1964, Baldwin recommends that the place to start may not be located in Somalia or Afghanistan, not even in Washington, but with the lyrical resuscitation of a strangled blues self beginning with difficult questions in the hallway mirrors and across the dinner tables of American private life. And, as discussed in Chapter 10, the proportion of panic in the stricken vacuums produced by *these* reckonings—I would bet on Baldwinian logic—will decrease in direct proportion to the level of privileged bankruptcy afflicting the persons involved.

Nonetheless, we know some of what the first black president has in the bank. And, it's not because he's black and it's *not* not because he's black either. We know because he wrote it down, which is exactly the same reason so few of us know it. Which scarcity itself, it appears, is a crucial political (if not survival) tactic. I read Barack Obama's *Dreams from My Father* while flying to Kenya when the author was a newly elected US senator. I read parts of the book in shock and disbelief. The author of these paragraphs, the person possessed of this engaged and caring sense of human experience from the South Side of Chicago to Nairobi, is a US senator? Like Nikki Giovanni's opinion about the likelihood of a Ray Charles–inspired literary criticism in the 1970s, I hadn't thought it possible. Change. For one thing, we know for certain that Barack Obama understands what Baldwin wrote about gangrene and amputation. Consider the following two passages from *Dreams from My Father* where Obama riffed on Du Bois and described what he imagined about a Kenyan waiter in a restaurant frequented by Westerners:

> If he's ambitious he will do his best to learn the white man's language and use the white man's machines, trying to make ends meet the same way the computer repairman in Newark or the bus driver back in Chicago does, with alternating spurts of enthusiasm or frustration but mostly with resignation. And if you say to him that he's serving the interests of neocolonialism or some other such thing, he will reply that yes, he will serve if that is what is required. It is the lucky ones who serve; the unlucky ones drift into the murky tide of hustles and odd jobs; many will drown.[19]

That's textbook gangrene. And, amputation? Obama continued:

> Then again, maybe that's not all that the waiter is feeling. Maybe part of him still clings to the stories of Mau-Mau [essentially, revolutionary amputations of these complexities], the same part of him that remembers the hush of a village night or the sound of his mother grinding corn under a stone pallet. Something in him still says that the white man's ways are not his ways, that the objects he

may use every day are not of his making. He remembers a time, a way of imagining himself, that he leaves only at his peril. He can't escape the grip of his memories. And so he straddles two worlds, uncertain in each, always off balance, playing whichever game staves off the bottomless poverty, careful to let his anger vent itself only on those in the same condition.

A voice says to him yes, changes have come, the old ways lie broken, and you must find a way as fast as you can to feed your belly and stop the white man from laughing at you.

A voice says no, you will sooner burn the earth to the ground.[20]

The president of the United States wrote those paragraphs. Don't tell anyone. Widespread awareness of these paragraphs would be a political liability. The voting consumer public wants nothing to do with this. They want a clean winner and, if possible, it would be great to have losers who don't resemble them at all from the point of view of racists. And, in his first term in office, Barack Obama's Department of Justice successfully prosecuted long-time Chicago Police Commander John Burge (notorious for his administration of a decades-long campaign of harassment, torture, and false imprisonment).[21] But, don't tell anyone *that*! News such as that could give his "pro-American" opponents fuel; in American history, and from a perspective, albeit hideous, that Baldwin's line of sight forces us to acknowledge, such news could endanger the president's life. This is something so pervasively on people's minds that most refuse to talk (or even think) about it. At the same time, he jokes about the often mistaken and always extralegal use of Predator drones in killings across the globe which turns inevitable amputations—in this case militant urges for revolutionary freedom that echo Barack Obama's mention of the Mau-Mau above—into CIA-administered assassinations. Who is in dangerous rhetorical territory now?

This is beautiful, the president has those brilliant paragraphs from *Dreams from My Father*, and the sensibility they profile, in the bank. And, it's terrible. He must radically dissemble that profile to govern at all if not simply to survive. And, that's the nature of the view Baldwinian light gives up when we hold our eyes there long enough that they start to adjust. Who can afford such visions? Whose style can—"in a way must"—accommodate them? Constant? And, here we are. The truth is that there's no need for such critical perceptions to be secreted because the vast majority of Americans' lifestyles simply cannot accommodate what all this spells out. For reasons too numerable to list, they *cannot* afford to improvise. That's the trap, that's the twenty-first-century vacuumed panic, a widespread existential bankruptcy.

Comments like President Obama's joke—echoing as they do comments by Baldwin and Kennedy and many others—make me wonder again if this is the country that would elect a black president or not? And, to quote Miles's sardonic stylized-lyricizing, "So what?"[22] Do we aspire to clarify and further our shared (and distinct) condition or intensify our chimerical and bankrupt states of mind? Keep in mind, by Baldwin's angular improvisations in the language, a "state of mind" can't be shared, no matter to what extent whatever mob claims to hold it in common. A "state of mind" stifles the connection between the person and the people and back again; to the extent that can't happen, a person becomes unable to share anything. And, no one ever really changes their mind; or maybe we do nothing but change our minds? It doesn't really matter. The only way to really *develop* one's mind is to attach it to one's condition and set about changing that. And, no one does that alone.

Then, I wonder about it, again, vote by vote, person by person, and mirror by mirror. What's changed? What's constant? And, what would that mean? To whom? And in what way? James Baldwin's musical attention to this dynamic riding the dialectics of amputation and gangrene, refusing ephemeral change in search of a deeper development, offers a career of precise and useful guides to these massive and imprecise questions and to much that lurks within and behind them. These questions lurk in *who* we think we are (and aren't) in our intimate lives and when we look in our mirrors, and also in the way we're seen, as *what* we're seen (and not seen) to be, by our neighbors, our kids, our fellow citizens, and by people around the world.

His work also exposes some of why the answers and evidence have been so confusing and suggests some of how the confusion is still so dangerous. It also offers eyes to see—possibly, much more than we would like to see—and places us close enough to touch the living turbulence of political, social, and private life. It also prompts us to listen more closely to what's going on within, between, and around us. The living turbulence is, at times, painful and dangerous but, as Baldwin told Studs Terkel in 1961, the alternative is a joyless chaos. The contemporary choice Baldwin clarifies, written backward in the mirror, is clearly between "The Uses of the Blues" and the bankruptcy of privilege, between a risky, connected sense of salvation and a bunkered, paranoid route to suffocation. Over time the vocabularies will alter but the deep structure of change and constant, and the chimerical confusion of the two, will stay with us; it's one of the

constants, a fact of life. This book is a map of the grain in the voice behind that observation. Maybe in it, as well, there are images, rhythms, of
a range of styles useful in handling its truth.

There's no predesigned script. Jerome Smith had been a Freedom
Rider in the early 1960s when Baldwin sent for him to represent the
student movement in their meeting with Robert Kennedy on May 24,
1963. In that meeting, Lorraine Hansberry held Kennedy's attention and
pointed to Smith, saying "that man over there. That is the voice . . . of
22 million people" (*Cross*, 111). In *I Heard It Through the Grapevine* (1982),
Baldwin circled back and interviewed Smith who was immersed in work
with children in New Orleans. It was Smith who took Baldwin to see the
grave of his father's white brother, Robert Baldwin. As I listen to Smith
conclude his chat with Baldwin in the film, I wonder, had she lived, how
many people Lorraine Hansberry would have heard Jerome speaking for
in 1980? And how many now? Asked about the state of the movement
for human rights then, with something (maybe it's a self and its selfless
totality) open and gentle scored in his determined face and voice, and
with a slight lilt of the islands appearing in the timbre of his tone, Smith
said: "There's a feeling among some that says nothing is happening in
terms of struggle in the country. But that's a lie. That is a lie. No people,
no people nowhere, have ever really accept slavery. Some man, some one
man, some somebody, was in opposition." Slowing his speech and marking the rhythm with his upraised thumb, he concluded his thought: "So
in the quietness of the stillness of the night there is somebody that's in
motion."[23]

In a way increasingly like a lead sheet dashed off before a session, James
Baldwin's work provides chord changes and key signatures. Who's count-
ing off the tempo, the beat? And, indeed, at these prices, who can afford
to improvise? Baldwin's ready answer: those who can because "in a way
they must." The next question is obvious. And, it's ours. And, the answer
can't be written. Nor can it be sung. We give it back to the music, and to
each other—which is the music—in the lives we live. Following even as
it leads, the music takes it from there and gives it back to us. At that moment, which is always, it's time to listen closely, again.

# Acknowledgments

In addition to sources named in the text, this book encodes and enfolds conversations with many people over many years. In unavoidable ways, it charts realignments in relationships with some and the disappearances of others. In the writing and rewriting of this book and related work, as much as anything else, it often seemed I was encountering some of the many ways people (including me) had of appearing and disappearing. This travel with Jimmy Baldwin's voice, with his ever-shifting palette of tones and his always moving angles of sight, has been demanding and very, very rewarding. The following are brief thanks to some of those who appeared, and some who reappeared, and to some who disappeared in ways that directly informed what ended up in these pages.

Many thanks to the people who were present (and game) for discussions and conversations about Baldwin, music, and related subjects that turned out to be crucial to what this work contains: Stacey Cecile Barnum, Milan Pavlić, Suncana Pavlić, Adrienne Rich, Gloria Karefa-Smart, Binyavanga Wainaina, Yusef Komunyakaa, Greg Taylor, Diane McWhorter, Ekwueme Michael Thelwell, Craig Werner, Brent Edwards, Ntone Edjabe, Tim Tyson, Kim Fortuny, Gulen Gulen, Alonzo Levister, Lynn O. Scott, Ken Winfield, Randall Scott, Sascha Feinstein, Jono Rosenthal, Oluwatoni Campbell, Nigel Hatton, Michael Eric Dyson, Eddie Glaude, Mark Anthony Neal, Rich Blint, Helen Baldwin, Carole Weinstein, Michael Ondaatje, Alfredo Véa, the lovely staff at La Colombe d'Or (especially Pitou Roux), Magdalena Zaborowska, Dick Fontaine, Peniel Joseph, Frederick Douglass Opie, Emily Lordi, Malik Weaver, Sean

Jacobs, Elliot Ross, Florence Ladd, Maxine Gordon, Michelle Chilcoat, Andy Feffer, Nathalie Handal, Loye Miller, Hilton Als, David Leeming, Barry Jenkins, Doren Robbins, Ralph Black, Major Jackson, Terrance Hayes, Ralph Savarese, Doug Field, Brian Norman, Bill Schwarz, Karen Thorsen, Dwight McBride, Quentin Miller, Leah Mirakhor, L. Lamar Wilson, Suzanne Gardinier, Eric Darton, Gabrielle Fuentes, Shamala Gallagher, Ben Hudson, Valerie Babb, Barbara McKaskill, Susan Rosenbaum, Doug Anderson, Reginald McKnight, and Barbara Benzunas. Special thanks to Patrick J. Mattox for being there, for his energy of solidarity and rhythm at work, whether we met up at work or in the street, that guided much of the writing and rewriting of these pages. He knows. Last, thanks to David Dorsey, Roman Parrish, and Mr. William Jennings, who—while I was working on this book and teaching in Park Hall at the University of Georgia, and in an academic environment that, at times, seems to train people to act like they're alone even in crowded hallways— were (and are) always ready with a pound, a wave, even a quick nod, and often a good word, at work, any time of the day or night.

Also thanks to people and organizations for providing space, time, funding, and materials that were important to the work: The MacDowell Colony; the W. E. B. Du Bois Research Institute at the Hutchins Center, Harvard University (especially Henry Louis Gates Jr., Abby Wolf, and Krishna Lewis); the Harvard Film Archive (especially Robert Sennate and Liz Coffey); the Willson Center for the Humanities at the University of Georgia (especially Nicholas Allen, Dave Marr, and Winnie Smith); Manuscript, Archives and Rare Book Library, Robert W. Woodruff Library, Emory University (especially Kathleen Shoemaker); Doug Anderson and the Sterling Goodman Chair in English at the University of Georgia; and the Provost's Travel Grant at the University of Georgia.

Finally, special thanks to Eric Newman and the staff at Fordham University Press, most especially Richard Morrison, whose vision of what engaged scholarship can be was indispensible to this work and its shape; and to Michael Koch, Craig Werner, Emily Lordi, Daylanne English, and Yusef Komunyakaa, whose caring expertise and extreme generosity with their time and vision as readers of this manuscript improved the work in every dimension.

# Notes

### Introduction: "To the listeners, for those that have an ear for this"

The subtitle to this introduction comes from the first line in the song "To the Listeners" released in 1987 on the debut album, *Paid in Full*, of the hip-hop duo Eric B. & Rakim.

1. Gümüssuyu Caddesi is now called Inönö Caddessi. As of 2013, the Üçler building was the site of the Macedonian consulate. The historic Park Hotel was recently rebuilt and reopened in October 2013 as the Park Bosphorus Istanbul.

2. *James Baldwin: From Another Place*, directed by Sedat Pakay (Sedat Pakay and Hudson Film Works, 2000), DVD.

3. Baldwin, *Collected Essays*, 355. (Hereafter cited in text as *CE*.)

4. Baldwin's poem "For A.," published in *Jimmy's Blues and Other Poems*, offers a glimpse of the turmoil and pressure, and the deep caring, that Baldwin's love for Alain brought about for both of them, but especially the younger Alain. Hard lessons: "Love / love has no gifts to give / except the revelation that the soul can live." Baldwin stayed with Alain on Rue Passey, at the west edge of Paris, for a brief period in the summer of 1970 after leaving Istanbul and before moving to L'Hôtel Le Hameau (and finally to what would become his home across Route de la Colle from the hotel) in St. Paul de Vence.

5. Letters from James Baldwin to David Baldwin, the James Baldwin Estate. Unless otherwise noted, all references to Baldwin's correspondence with his brother David are from this collection.

6. Baldwin, *Cross of Redemption*, 57.

7. Baldwin, "The Uses of the Blues," 131.

8. Ibid.

9. Baldwin, *Early Novels and Stories*, 211. (Hereafter cited in text as *ENS*.)

10. *Collected Essays*, 306.

11. Zaborowska, *James Baldwin's Turkish Decade*, 211.

12. Baldwin, *A Dialogue*, 83.

13. Ibid., 84.

14. Ibid.

15. Baldwin, *Amen Corner*, 53–54.

16. Eckman, *Furious Passage*, 214.

17. In an undated letter to Mary Painter, which was sent from London and must have been written in late September 1961, Baldwin confided that he was focused on being more like Miles Davis in his attempt to deal with his mounting visibility. See "Mary Painter Letters," James Baldwin Early Manuscripts and Papers, Yale University.

18. Academic readers of this book will note a dearth of explicit references to critical readings of Baldwin's work. Nonetheless, I would like to thank and acknowledge the following critics, editors, and artists whose works informed the shape of this book and guided my listenings: Brimm, *James Baldwin and the Queer Imagination*; Edwards, *The Practice of Diaspora: Literature, Translation, and the Rise of Black Internationalism*; Field, *Historical Guide to James Baldwin*; Fortuny, *American Writers in Istanbul*; Glaude, *In a Shade of Blue*; Hubbard and Thomas, *Bearing Witness from Another Place*; Jones, *The Muse Is Music*; Komunyakaa, *Blue Notes*; Kun, *Audiotopia*; Lordi, *Black Resonance*; Mabanckou, *Letter to Jimmy*; Mackey, *Discrepant Engagement* and *Paracritical Hinge*; McBride, *James Baldwin Now*; Miller, *A Criminal Power*; Moten, *In the Break*; Nielsen, *Integral Music*; Ratliff, *Coltrane*; Rhodes-Pitts, *Harlem Is Nowhere*; Rich, *A Human Eye*; Scott, *James Baldwin's Later Fiction*; Thelwell, "A Prophet Is Not Without Honor"; Turner, *Awakening to Race*; Weheliye, *Phonographies*; Werner, *Playing the Changes* and *A Change Is Gonna Come*; and Zaborowska, *James Baldwin's Turkish Decade*. In addition, conversations with many of these writers and others (see acknowledgments) helped as well as this book took shape over the past few years.

19. Kun, *Audiotopia*, 92.

20. Hughes, *Collected Poems*, 387; emphasis added.

21. Baldwin, *Just Above My Head*, 500–501.

22. Kelley, *Thelonious Monk*, 202–203.

23. In an undated letter from the mid-1960s, sent from Istanbul to David Leeming in New York, Baldwin refers to the increasing demands of his work to come, to his need to be more immersed in it than ever, and to his increasing tendency to turn *inward* which, for him, does not mean turning away from other people such as Leeming himself. Turning inward and turning away from people, Baldwin stresses, are not, in fact, synonymous and, in his case, should not be confused with each other. See James Baldwin Early Manuscripts and Papers, Yale University.

24. Quoted in Kelley, *Thelonious Monk*, 172.

25. It's useful to imagine Hayden's repetition of the term "mean" in the line; one "mean" to signify the difficulty of the quest; another the intention, the will, and determination; and the third that freedom is about the average, the "mean," as much or more than it's about the elite. Baldwin addressed all of these resonances explicitly and implicitly during his career.

26. Ondaatje, *Cinnamon Peeler*, 183. As I will show, angularity in black music extends far beyond circles of friends and involves complexly personal and impersonal devices. Ondaatje notices that this is not an individual phenomenon and thus gives me a good start. Because he mentioned her more often in connection to his stay in Switzerland where he completed *Go Tell It on the Mountain*, Bessie Smith gets more credit than Fats Waller in the origins of Baldwin's musical, angular poetics. In Karen Thorsen's film *The Price of the Ticket*, Baldwin mentions that he found evidence he needed for the voices in the novel in records by Waller and Smith.

27. Ibid.

28. Ratliff, *Coltrane*, 83. Many thanks to Forrest Gander who recommended Ratliff's book on Coltrane and sound to me while we walked in Providence, Rhode Island, and talked about this work I was doing listening to Baldwin.

29. By musically angular, I mean an utterance that conveys a plurality of meanings that resonate in distinct ways with particular listeners (or readers) across an audience.

30. "UC Berkeley speech," *The James Baldwin Anthology*, directed by Claire Burch and Christopher Sorrenti (Regent Press, 2008), DVD.

31. Toni Morrison, "James Baldwin: His Voice Remembered; Life in His Language," *New York Times Book Review*, December 20, 1987, www.nytimes.com/books/98/03/29/specials/baldwin-morrison.html.

32. Barthes, "Listening," 255.

33. Standley and Pratt, *Conversations*, 150–151.

34. Thelwell, "Prophet," 98.

35. Ibid., 99.

36. Ibid.

37. Standley and Pratt, *Conversations*, 21.

38. Jane Howard, "Doom and Glory of Knowing Who You Are," *Life*, May 24, 1963, 86b.

39. In a letter dated November 21, 1962—four days after the appearance of Baldwin's "Letter from a Region in My Mind" (which, with a short introductory essay, would be published as *The Fire Next Time* in January 1963) in the *New Yorker*—Hannah Arendt wrote Baldwin, saying that his "article in the *New Yorker* is a political event of a very high order." She then went on to warn of the dangers of passion (love) in what should be rational, political discourse and action: "In politics, love is a stranger, and when it intrudes upon it nothing is being achieved except hypocrisy." For Arendt, the appeal of passion (love) in political terms only applied to oppressed people and its benefits "have never

survived the hour of liberation by even five minutes." Conscious of recent
European, fascist political disasters, Arendt concludes that "Hatred and love
belong together, and they are both destructive; you can afford them only in
the private and, as a people, only so long as you are not free" ("The Meaning of Love in Politics: A Letter by Hannah Arendt to James Baldwin," www
.hannaharendt.net/index.php/han/article/view/95/156).

40. Baldwin, "Go the Way Your Blood Beats: An Interview," by Richard
Goldstein, *Village Voice*, June 26, 1984, 13.

41. In the "Autobiographical Notes" at the beginning of *Notes of a Native
Son* (1955), Baldwin wrote: "I want to be an honest man and a good writer"
(*CE*, 9). He repeated the ambition to Studs Terkel in July 1961 (see Standley
and Pratt, *Conversations*, 23). In personal comments and correspondence from
the late 1960s and early 1970s (and thereafter), Baldwin explicitly describes his
ambition in terms that extend far beyond the edges of well-crafted pages. He
never gave up on literary craft, of course, but he absolutely and publically did
foreswear neatly crafted paragraphs and pages as the sole measure of literary
craft as he had (in the late 1950s) left behind personal success as the salient
measure of literary achievement. Even early in his career, Baldwin never made
a fetish of aesthetic fineness, in a letter to Mary Painter from 1955, he told his
good friend that he thought the yet-to-be-released *Giovanni's Room* was a good
novel, "(but not too good)." See James Baldwin Early Manuscripts and Papers,
Yale University.

42. *The James Baldwin Anthology*, directed by Burch and Sorrenti.

43. James Campbell, "Sorrow Wears and Uses Us," *New York Times*, September 12, 2010, and Elias Altman, "Watered Whiskey: James Baldwin's Uncollected Writings," *Nation*, May 2, 2011. Rehearsing the rise-and-fall narrative
of Baldwin's (pre-1963) timeless aesthetics ruined by his (post-1963) historical,
cultural, and political engagements, Campbell and Altman both dismiss or dis-
count the merit and relevance of Baldwin's most angular, lyrical, and directly
political writings.

44. Darryl Pinckney, "Jimmy Baldwin: Stirring the Waters," *New York Review
of Books*, November 25, 2010. Linking Baldwin directly to Emerson and to
"the authority of the individual" in ways that distort the deeply interactive and
complexly collective elements of Baldwin's lyrical work and cultural-political
thought, Pinckney's review inflects Baldwin in ways that the mainstream
literary culture can accommodate. Even in "Looking for James Baldwin"—his
caring deeply thoughtful introduction to *The Cross of Redemption: Uncollected
Writings*—Randall Kenan, apparently seeking to reassure mainstream readers, mitigates the contemporary intensity of what Baldwin saw as the artist's
"lover's war" (*CE*, 672) with society: "I'm sure [Baldwin] would believe the
possibilities for his country were looking up since [1961]" (xxiii). In short,
reception of Baldwin's work suffers from: (1) the need to protect and promote
the transcendent (more than historically contingent) and aesthetic (more than
political) features of the American literary tradition; (2) the need to depict that

aesthetic tradition as the province of individual genius (as opposed to collective and dialogic processes); and (3) the need to create a tale of American success and progress that helps frame salable images (and books) in the contemporary marketplace.

45. See Baldwin and Stein, *Native Sons*, 93–103 for an example of one instance of such pressure. In a letter dated December 7, 1956, Baldwin's good friend and editor Sol Stein advised that Baldwin would be better off once he had "made some real peace with yourself, your old man, and the white world" (93). In midst of Baldwin's vehement response to—and dissent from—his good friend's point of view, he notes: "If I were trying to escape my environment, I wouldn't be covering the earth to do it. The best way to escape one's environment is to surrender to it. I, personally, am trying to understand mine, in which endeavor I may possibly be retarded—but I don't think I'm romantic enough, any longer, to imagine that anything is ever escaped" (97).

46. Ratliff, *Coltrane*, 63.

47. *I Heard It Through the Grapevine*, directed by Dick Fontaine and Pat Hartley (London: Central TV, 1982), DVD.

48. Jane Howard, "Doom and Glory of Knowing Who You Are," *Life*, May 24, 1963, 88.

49. Rich, *A Human Eye*, 96.

50. Baldwin, *Just Above My Head*, 584.


## 1. "Not the country we're sitting in now": Amputation/Gangrene Past and Present

1. The letters portray Baldwin as an individual with a sensitive, reflective, and above all international literary and political sensibility. In the five-page piece, Baldwin posts letters to Mills from France, Switzerland, Israel, and Turkey, and discusses impending engagements in Dakar, Brazzaville, Monterey, Mallorca, Ghana, Nigeria, and Kenya.

2. Dispatches from *Time* magazine correspondents: second series, 1956–1968 (MS Am 2090.1), Houghton Library, Harvard University. (Hereafter cited as *Time* dispatches.)

3. Ibid.

4. On his first trip to the South in October 1957, Baldwin had stayed in the A. G. Gaston Motel in Birmingham, Alabama. He wrote his friend Mary Painter that the dishwasher at the motel was taking him to meet a man who'd been castrated in a racially motivated attack during the previous month. Six years later, when asked if he'd go back to Birmingham, this was the image that came to mind. The man was named Edward "Judge" Aaron whose case became widely reported. His attackers were convicted but pardoned by George Wallace when he took office in 1962. See "Mary Painter Letters," James Baldwin Early Manuscripts and Papers, Yale University.

5. *Take This Hammer*, directed by Richard O. Moore (WNET, 1963). In a

televised interview with Kenneth B. Clark on May 24, 1963, Baldwin, referring to the filming of *Take This Hammer*, said: "A boy last week, he was sixteen, in San Francisco, told me on television—thank God we got him to talk.... He said, 'I got no country, I got no flag.'" That's the best date I've been able to come up with for the filming. See Standley and Pratt, *Conversations*, 42.

6. Of the many photos in the *Life* magazine story—taken with kids on the streets of New Orleans, in homes, and at a party in New York with Geraldine Page and Rip Torn—one shows a "Negro girl" in New York thrusting her finger in Baldwin's face and saying, "You're not my spokesman, James Baldwin!" Baldwin looks surprised by the confrontation but ready to engage.

7. See the major Baldwin biographies: Eckman, *Furious Passage of James Baldwin*; Weatherby, *James Baldwin*; Campbell, *Talking at the Gates*; and Leeming, *James Baldwin*.

8. *Time* dispatches.

9. Baldwin, "Lorraine Hansberry," 270.

10. Ibid.

11. Ibid., 269.

12. Leeming, *James Baldwin*, 224.

13. Baldwin gave a talk on June 2, 1961, at a forum hosted by the Liberation Committee for Africa on nationalism and colonialism and US foreign policy. The contents have been published as "From Nationalism, Colonialism, and the United States: One Minute to Twelve—A Forum," in Baldwin, *Cross of Redemption*, 10–18.

14. *Take This Hammer*, directed by Moore. All excerpts in this book refer to the 2013 director's cut of Moore's documentary available online at https://diva.sfsu.edu/collections/sfbatv/bundles/216518.

15. Hughes, *Collected Poems*, 390.

16. Leeming, *James Baldwin*, 221.

17. *Black San Francisco*, directed by Caroline Bins (2013), http://www.carolinebinsmedia.com/experimental-work/#/short-docs/. Bins's short documentary contains interviews with some of the participants from *Take This Hammer*: Famios Bell, Tyrone Primus, and James Lockett.

18. See, for example, James Campbell's dismissive review of *The Cross of Redemption*, "Sorrow Wears and Uses Us," *New York Times*, September 12, 2010. Campbell essentially writes off the relevance of much of the material behind the present reading of Baldwin's importance.

## 2. Blues Constants, Jazz Changes: Toward a Writing Immune to Bullshit

1. Baldwin, "Uses of the Blues," 131.

2. Ibid.

3. Jones, *Black Music*, 180.

4. Baldwin, "Uses of the Blues," 131.

5. "UC Berkeley speech," *The James Baldwin Anthology*, directed by Claire Burch and Christopher Sorrenti (Regent Press, 2008), DVD.

6. Here I'm drawing upon a distinction made by Paul Gilroy, in his essay, "It's a Family Affair." Gilroy wrote: "If we are to think of ourselves as a diaspora people, how do we then understand the notion of space? . . . One thing we might do is take a cue from Manuel Castells, who describes the shift from an understanding of space based on notions of place and fixity to an understanding of space based on flows. Or, what another exiled Englishman, Iain Chambers, introduces in his very suggestive distinction between roots and routes" (303). So, considering identity as a mobile process of becoming by tracing the routes of one's and one's forebearers' experiences presents an alternative to the search for the essential place of origins, roots.

7. Charles Mingus, "An Open Letter to Miles Davis." *Charles Mingus*, http://mingusmingusmingus.com/mingus/an-open-letter-to-miles-davis.

8. Baldwin, "Uses of the Blues," 241.

9. Jones, *Black Music*, 180.

10. Komunyakaa, *Pleasure Dome*, 31.

11. "James Baldwin Talks with Studs Terkel," by Studs Terkel, September 29, 1962, https://archive.org/details/popuparchive-1854433; my transcription.

12. Jones, *Black Music*, 181.

13. Baldwin, "Letters from a Journey," 52, http://harpers.org/archive/1963/05/letters-from-a-journey-2/.

14. Ibid.

15. "James Baldwin Talks with Studs Terkel"; my transcription.

16. As for revision of terms, as his letters and almost all of his public statements show, Baldwin used the term *jazz* itself most often as a synonym for "bullshit," sardonically spitting out, "all that *jazz*" and "later for that *jazz*." His deep respect for and connections with many jazz musicians—from his lover, Arnold, in the mid-1950s who was the model for Sonny in "Sonny's Blues," to Billie Holiday, Alonzo Levister, and Miles Davis—as well as his brilliant and near-constant use of the deep structure of the blues-jazz continuum, "the changing same," makes it obvious that Baldwin knew the term meant far more than what it evoked in the popular mind.

17. Jones, *Black Music*, 180.

### 3. "Making words *do* something": Retracing James Baldwin's Career

1. Jane Howard, "Doom and Glory of Knowing Who You Are," *Life*, May 24, 1963, 88.

2. Ibid., 86b.

3. Baldwin, "Mass Culture," 373.

4. Ibid., 374.

5. Ibid., 376.

6. Baldwin, "Modern Rover Boys," 12.

7. Ibid.

8. Baldwin, *Cross of Redemption*, 240. (Hereafter cited in text as *Cross*.)

9. Baldwin, "On an Author," 3.

10. Baldwin, "Me and My House," 61.

11. These faculties would remain irresolvable in Baldwin's mind. He thought resolving them led to romance and sentimentality, to a stable and unified self. That in no way implied, however, that the impasse was static; in fact he thought the opposite. In a 1972 interview, John Hall asked Baldwin about this passage, if he still held "the same position," and "if so, how do you reconcile the opposing outlooks?" ( Hall and Baldwin, "*Transition* Interview," 24). Baldwin replied: "I don't think you do. I think it's a great mistake to be sentimental about human beings, and to be sentimental about oneself. One doesn't know what one can do until one does it. . . . You accept life as it is before you can change it. In order to change myself, I have to admit that I am not six feet tall, I'm not blue-eyed. I've got to accept [my] limitations before I can discover my possibilities" (ibid.).

12. Baldwin, "Me and My House," 64.

13. Ibid.

14. Stone dispatches from *Time* magazine correspondents: second series, 1956–1968 (MS Am 2090.1), Houghton Library, Harvard University.

15. Ibid.

16. "Sonny's Blues" was published in *Partisan Review* in summer 1957. "A Letter from a Region in My Mind" appeared in *The New Yorker* on November 17, 1962. The 86-page essay was reprinted in January 1963 as "Down at the Cross," comprising most of Baldwin's most famous single book, *The Fire Next Time*.

17. Baldwin, "A Word from a Writer," 20.

18. See introduction, note 23.

19. My (more accurate) transcription of the recorded interview with Baldwin by Terkel—"James Baldwin Talks with Studs Terkel on WFMT," July 15, 1961, www.popuparchive.com/collections/938/items/6901—which differs from the published transcript edited by Standley and Pratt. See also, Standley and Pratt, *Conversations*, 20.

20. Editor's introduction to Baldwin, "Me and My House," 54.

21. Baldwin, "Me and My House," 61.

22. My transcription of the recorded interview with Baldwin by Terkel. See also, Standley and Pratt, *Conversations*, 23.

23. Ibid., 21.

24. Alonzo Levister in an e-mail to the author, June 8, 2013.

25. Baldwin, "At a Crucial Time," 83.

26. James Baldwin, "Artist's Struggle," 9.

27. Miller dispatch, May 9–10, 1963, *Time* magazine correspondents: second series, 1956–1968 (MS Am 2090.1), Houghton Library, Harvard University.

28. Ibid.

29. Ibid.

30. Baldwin, *Tell Me How Long*, 12.

31. Baldwin, "Uses of the Blues," 241.

32. Ibid., 244.

33. Baldwin, *Just Above My Head*, 222.

34. Baldwin, "Letter to Americans," 115.

35. Baldwin, "Dear Sister," 15.

36. Ibid.

37. Ibid.

38. In *Talking at the Gates*, James Campbell lists the following entry from Baldwin's FBI file: "('advised . . . James Baldwin arrived in Istanbul, Turkey, from Athens, Greece, via Air France on July 13, 1969')" (232).

39. Baldwin understood the long odds involved with the project. His agent Robby Lantz pushed the deal forward and Baldwin seems to have gone along with the project out of a mix of his cultural and political ambitions during the era and loyalty to Malcolm X. Malcolm's widow received part of the advance paid by Columbia Studios; directing funds to Malcolm's family, especially his children, was also part of Baldwin's motivation. Elia Kazan had met with Baldwin and Alex Haley (and photographer Frank Dandridge) on Long Island in 1967 to discuss a stage version of Haley's book written by Baldwin and directed by Kazan. Kazan warned Baldwin about dealing directly with Hollywood before a successful stage production (as Kazan had done, for instance, with *A Streetcar Named Desire* in 1951). On November 29, 1967, Kazan wrote to Baldwin: "With love. I think you will be happiest, finally, in the long run, if you don't get involved with agents, studios and movie people on this yet. In my opinion, there is no way any big movie company, no matter what they tell you, can put on the screen what you and your conscience—not to mention the pressures of the times and Negro America—must needs [*sic*] put on the screen. What's the use of fooling yourself?" (Kazan, *Selected Letters*, 549).

Kazan's advice that Baldwin take his time, write a great play, and lead with a successful stage production was obviously impossibly out of sync with the intensity of Baldwin's personal and political engagements with the culture of the times. It might have been impossible as well, but, in hindsight, Kazan's approach makes practical, tactical sense: "Then—if you do a successful play, watch them come for it, the movie people. They'll kill themselves to get it, and fork up much more money, too" (549–550). By the late 1960s, Kazan had known Baldwin for a decade since Baldwin worked with him at the Actor's Studio in the spring of 1958. On February 3, 1967, Kazan wrote to Alex Haley with advice about how to bring the play about, saying that the first thing was to have the strongest possible script. When it came to producing, Kazan knew that Baldwin, like many authors, could be a "slippery fish," and he thought that, "again and again," they'd have to "turn Jimmy around and point him to the table with the typewriter on it" (541).

40. Hall and Baldwin, "*Transition* Interview," 23. This interview is included

in Standley and Pratt, *Conversations*, 98–107. Standley and Pratt list the year of the interview as 1970 and the source as *Transatlantic Review* (Autumn/Winter 1970–71): 37–38. I am quoting from the published transcript in *Transition*. See also Standley and Pratt, *Conversations*, 103.

41. Baldwin, "In Search of a Basis," 235.

42. Baldwin, *Beale Street*, 191.

43. Ibid.

44. Baldwin, *Devil Finds Work*, 537.

45. "James Baldwin," by Jo Durden-Smith, *Ink*, July 31, 1971, 9.

46. Baldwin, *Beale Street*, 189.

47. On September 22, 1969, after leaving Hollywood and while living in Istanbul, Baldwin sent his brother a copy of a letter, and a copy of a check, he'd sent to Susan Sontag in support of the Conspiracy. He told Sontag that he had gone to Turkey to finish a book and regain his sanity. He asked to be considered part of the movement and to be put to any use possible given his present location. This letter is not available to the public.

48. Baldwin, *Beale Street*, 169–170.

49. Mead and Baldwin, *Rap on Race*, 217.

50. Baldwin and Giovanni, *A Dialogue*, 34.

51. Ibid., 18.

52. Ibid., 33.

53. Ibid., 35.

54. Mead and Baldwin, *Rap on Race*, 187.

55. Ibid., 183.

56. Hall and Baldwin, "*Transition* Interview," 24.

57. Ibid.

58. Ibid., 23.

59. Ibid.

60. Weatherby, *James Baldwin*, 24.

61. Standley and Pratt, *Conversations*, 155.

62. Ibid., 155.

63. Baldwin, "In Search of a Basis," 232–233.

64. Ibid., 233.

65. Here Baldwin uses "Rhodesia" as an image of colonial power and anti-colonial struggle in general.

66. Standley and Pratt, *Conversations*, 19.

67. Baldwin and Giovanni, *A Dialogue*, 36.

68. "The Hallelujah Chorus," Dick Fontaine Collection, Harvard Film Archive, Harvard University, 1973; my transcription.

69. Hall and Baldwin, "*Transition* Interview," 24.

70. Baldwin, *Just Above My Head*, 109.

71. Ibid., 109–110.

72. Baldwin, "In Search of a Basis," 236.

73. Ibid., 237.

74. Ibid.

75. Baldwin, *Just Above My Head*, 110.

76. Ibid., 110.

77. Mead and Baldwin, *Rap on Race*, 90.

78. Ibid., 94.

79. *The James Baldwin Anthology*, directed by Burch and Sorrenti.

80. Baldwin, *Just Above My Head*, 214.

81. Ibid., 215.

82. Ibid., 216.

83. "The Black Situation Now: An Interview with James Baldwin," *Washington Post*, July 21, 1974, C1.

84. Ibid.

85. "James Baldwin: The Fire Still Burns," by Hollie I. West, *Washington Post*, April 8, 1979, F1.

86. Ibid.

87. Ibid.

88. Standley and Pratt, *Conversations*, 160.

89. Ibid., 158.

90. Ibid., 150.

91. *I Heard It Through the Grapevine*, directed by Dick Fontaine and Pat Hatley (Living Archives, 1982), DVD.

92. Baldwin, *Blues for Mister Charlie*, 77.

93. Fontaine, box 9, file 10, roll 1, 1, Dick Fontaine Collection, Harvard Film Archive, Harvard University.

94. Baldwin and Giovanni, *A Dialogue*, 62.

95. Baldwin, *Just Above My Head*, 333.

96. Ibid., 334.

97. Ibid., 335.

98. Baldwin, "Atlanta," 141.

99. See Massey and Denton, *American Apartheid* and Wilson, *The Truly Disadvantaged*.

100. A very brief excerpt of this conversation was published as "Revolutionary Hope: A Conversation between James Baldwin and Audre Lorde" in *Essence* magazine, December 1984. The published excerpt of the conversation emphasizes the difficulty the two writers had communicating fully about the reality of intraracial violence between black men and black women. How, as Baldwin put it, "in what is in effect occupied territory," can one remember that a person's actions are quite often "his *responsibility* but . . . not his *fault*."

At over seventy pages, the full transcript of the conversation ranges much more widely over the contemporary, embattled sense of black resistance, struggle, and survival at the time. Thankfully, the Audre Lorde Estate allowed me to quote from Lorde's statements not published in *Essence*. It would have been great if the James Baldwin Estate had permitted accompanying quotes. Sadly, they didn't. I hope at some point the full transcript of that historic conversation can be available to the public. Unless otherwise noted, all quotations of Lorde's statements from their conversation here are from the full manuscript: "Revolutionary Hope: Teaching the Young," conversation at Hampshire College, Audre Lorde Estate, 1983. All of the quotations of Baldwin's comments are either paraphrased or come directly from the excerpts in *Essence*.

101. Baldwin and Lorde, "Revolutionary Hope," 130.

102. Ibid.

103. Ibid., 133.

104. Ibid.

105. The phrase comes up in correspondence as early as the mid-1950s. Baldwin also concludes his April 1979 speech at UC Berkeley with that phrase.

106. Standley and Pratt, *Conversations*, 181.

107. Fontaine, box 9, file 4, 3, Dick Fontaine Collection, Harvard Film Archive, Harvard University.

108. Baldwin, "Atlanta," 310.

109. Ibid., 314.

110. *The James Baldwin Anthology, directed by Burch and Sorrenti.*

111. Baldwin, "Go the Way Your Blood Beats: An Interview," by Richard Goldstein, *Village Voice*, June 26, 1984, 14.

112. Ibid., 13.

113. Ibid.

114. Ibid., 14.

115. Ibid., 16.

116. Ibid.

117. "James Baldwin's National Press Club Speech," *YouTube*, December, 22, 2014, www.youtube.com/watch?v=qDNkT4xH3YE. All subsequent quotes from this event refer to this source.

118. Baldwin, "Re/Member This House: A Memoir by James Baldwin," the James Baldwin Estate.

119. Baldwin, "Architectural Digest," 122–123.


## 4. Billie Holiday: Radical Lyricist

1. On January 20, 1960, Baldwin wrote a letter to Mary Painter, recounting, among other things, his impressions after having interviewed Piaf. His description glows and swells with his immense regard for her spiritual power as a singer and as a person. Mary Painter Letters in James Baldwin Early Manuscripts and Papers, James Weldon Johnson Collection in the Yale Collection of American Literature, Beinecke Rare Book and Manuscript Library.

2. In a letter to his brother from 1971, Baldwin suggested that they contact Abbey Lincoln to play Margaret in a possible production *The Amen Corner*. His reasoning stressed the power of her voice and what he thought of as her obvious (if untested) skill as an actress.

3. Standley and Pratt, *Conversations,* 155.

4. AAB form is a traditional form in which verses state a line (A), repeat that line (A), and then complete the thought with a third line (B) that rhymes with the first two.

5. *The Complete Billie Holiday on Verve 1945–1959*, Verve, 1993, CD, liner notes.

6. Maher and Dorr, *Miles on Miles*, 14.

7. *The Complete Billie Holiday on Verve, 1945–1959*, liner notes.

8. *Billie Holiday: The Complete Decca Recordings*, MCA, 1991, CD, liner notes.

9. I would like to provide a brief explanation for my characterization of Billie Holiday as a great "radical lyricist." Our vision of her radical importance to the kinds of explorations, strengths, and resistances fundamental to Baldwin's work, among others, is clouded by many mythologies and obstructed by many historical forces. Consider the following. In "When We Dead Awaken: Writing as Re-Vision" (1971), Adrienne Rich closes the essay with a dream she had the previous summer: "I was asked to read my poetry at a mass women's meeting but when I began to read, what came out were the lyrics of a blues song. I share this dream with you because it seemed to me to say something about the problems and the future of the woman writer, and probably of women in general. The awakening of consciousness is not like the crossing of a frontier—one step and you are in another country. Much of women's poetry has been of the nature of the blues song: a cry of pain, of victimization, or a lyric of seduction" (*On Lies, Secrets, and Silence*, 48). Her perspective here, in part, echoes so-called radical writings by black nationalists of that era—such as Mulana Karenga and Eldridge Cleaver—that dismissed the blues along with all other supposed signs of "victimhood."

Going back to the essay in 1978 in preparation for its inclusion in her book, *On Lies, Secrets, and Silence*, Rich added the following footnote: "When I dreamed that dream, was I wholly ignorant of the tradition of Bessie Smith and other women's blues lyrics which transcended victimization to sing resistance and independence?" (48). As ever, Rich's statement is complex; in keeping with her idea of awakening as process, her understanding of the complexity and importance of black music to resonant political consciousness continued to develop throughout her life. Her study of Marx and further poetic explorations deepened her view in ways that distilled her idea of "resistance" and convinced her to critique the notion of "transcendence" itself (Ralph Ellison's view of "the blues" as transcendence from *Shadow and Act* [1964] likely played a role in Rich's first stage of awakening to these issues).

By the year 2001, in a foreword to my first book of poems, *Paraph of Bone and Other Kinds of Blue*, she would describe "the blues and jazz" as "our most profound American art" and credit its role in exploring "a mesh of experience extraneous to literary theories" (xi). Such a "mesh of experience" beyond the scope of (at least) literary theory and ideology, accessible via lyric exploration of experience, is clearly part of what Rich, by the latest stages of her career, understood as "radical, meaning root-tangled in the grit of human arrangements and relationships: *how we are with each other*" (Rich, *A Human Eye*, 96).

It's worth noting that, beginning in the late 1940s and throughout her life, Adrienne Rich was a reader and re-reader of Baldwin's work. The appearance of "another country" as part of her description of "awakening" is likely subconscious, even accidental, but it's accurate enough, in fact. Recently, Angela Davis, Daphne Brooks, and Emily Lordi have added important views to the deep and complex, decades-long grappling with these issues by black women writers (and, certainly, many who aren't black women). But, as is the case with Baldwin, traveling with Billie Holiday is still, and will always be, an encounter with "a mesh of experience extraneous" to all attempts at prose paraphrase. All great lyrics are—which is the whole, lyrical point.

### 5. Dinah Washington's Blues and the Trans-Digressive Ocean

1. Standley and Pratt, *Conversations*, 23.

2. Ibid., 4. Baldwin's accounts of his time in Switzerland emphasize the Bessie Smith records he had with him. In Karen Thorsen's film, Baldwin mentions having had records by Fats Waller with him as he finished *Go Tell It on the Mountain* as well. See *James Baldwin: The Price of the Ticket*, directed by Karen Thorsen (California Newsreel, 1989).

3. In a vexing and revealing letter to Mary Painter from 1955, Baldwin explained to his friend that Lucien thought Baldwin was kicking him out of the relationship but that, for him, two men in love could never be "married" without one of them ceasing to be a man and therefore canceling out the whole point of the love between the lovers anyway. In *James Baldwin and the Queer Imagination*, Matt Brimm explores Baldwin's complex, "unqueer," disruptions of categories of "transcendent queer thought" throughout his career. James Baldwin Early Manuscripts and Papers, James Weldon Johnson Collection in the Yale Collection of American Literature, Beinecke Rare Book and Manuscript Library.

4. Baldwin, "Uses of the Blues," 131.

5. Ibid., 131.

6. Joyce, *Portrait of the Artist*, 176.

7. Ezra Pound, "A Few Don'ts by an Imagiste" (1913), reprinted on *Poetry Foundation*, www.poetryfoundation.org/poetrymagazine/article/335.

8. Baldwin, "Uses of the Blues," 241.

9. Ibid., 241.

10. Ibid., 131.

11. Ellison, *Collected Essays*, 129.

12. Joyce, *Portrait of the Artist*, 176.

13. Dispatches from *Time* Magazine Correspondents: Second Series, 1956–1968 (MS Am 2090.1), Houghton Library, Harvard University.

14. James Baldwin Letters to David Moses, Manuscript, Archives and Rare Book Library, Robert W. Woodruff Library, Emory University.

15. Elia Kazan, *The Selected Letters of Elia Kazan, 541.*

16. Baldwin, "Architectural Digest," 123.

17. Ahmann, *New Negro*, 113.

18. Ibid.

19. Lawrence, *Studies in Classic American Literature*, 9.

20. Standley and Pratt, *Conversations*, 19.

21. Baldwin, "Uses of the Blues," 272.

## 6. "But Amen is the price": James Baldwin and Ray Charles in "The Hallelujah Chorus"

1. "Cicely Tyson, Ray Charles in Concert," *New York Amsterdam News,* June 23, 1973, D 11.

2. George Goodman, "For James Baldwin, A Rap on Baldwin," *New York Times,* June 26, 1972, 38.

3. In an undated letter from mid-September 1961, Baldwin wrote to Mary Painter in advance of leaving for his trip to Israel. Discussing his struggles in dealing with his new fame, he told his friend that he was trying to deal with it like Miles Davis had, allowing that when he'd first met Miles he was surprised to find that Miles was even more shy and afraid than he was. See "Mary Painter Letters," James Baldwin Early Manuscripts and Papers, Yale University.

4. *Village Voice* advertisement, Bob Stumpel, *The Ray Charles Video Museum*, http://raycharlesvideomuseum.blogspot.com/2010/05/life-and-times-of-ray-charles-live.html.

5. "Baldwin Honors Ray Charles at the Newport Jazz Fest," *Jet*, July 19, 1973, 60.

6. On July 24, 1973, Baldwin answered a letter from David Moses who was shaken by his sense of the performance and the reviews. Writing as his friend, director, and as a veteran of the public maelstrom, he told Moses to avoid listening to the chaos of responses. Baldwin concluded writing, simply, "Sweetheart, you were beautiful."

7. Balliett, *Collected Works*, 397.

8. Tom Buckley, "Baldwin Enunciates Ray Charles' Soul," *New York Times,* June 30, 1971, 28.

9. Beckett, *Molloy*, in *Selected Works*, 2:56.

10. Lawrence, *Studies*, 9.

11. The important thing here is the crucial role of emotional and, at whatever level, erotic discoveries to Baldwin's personal, aesthetic, and political work, and thought. The connection between the two men appears in Baldwin's letters as well as in poems in *Jimmy's Blues and Other Poems*.

Baldwin found the poem titled "Ballad (for Yoran)" in a notebook years after the immediate connection between the men had passed. After a thought to destroy the poem, he decided to save it. The lines "you / and / you" and the line "Oh, Brother, say: / I couldn't hear nobody pray" (*Jimmy's Blues,* 93) echo very precisely moments in the script for "The Hallelujah Chorus" where Baldwin asks Ray Charles to explain "the wedding: between you and you" and, at the conclusion, where Baldwin refers back to "The valley—where you couldn't hear nobody pray." In that context, we can hear the echoes between "Oh, brother, say" from the poem and "Brother Ray" from the performance. In addition, the poem titled "Munich, Winter 1973 (for Y.S.)," from *Jimmy's Blues and Other Poems*, was originally titled, simply, "For Yoran." The poem depicts a person waiting for the arrival of a beloved, "I know / I will see you tonight" (28). The poem likens the desirous pair to "the birds above our heads" who are "making choices / are using what they have. / They are aware / that, on long journeys, / each bears the other, / whirring, / stirring / love occurring / in the middle of the terrifying air" (29).

Precise echoes between Baldwin's descriptions of what he learned from his connection to Cazac, even the phrase "above our heads," appear in the deep, complex emotional, ethical and erotic energies at work in Baldwin's next (and last) novel, *Just Above My Head*. Among the crucial and challenging features of this novel are the deeply complex, at times dangerous, connections between brotherly, friendly and erotic energy and between sexual/emotional and social/ political dimensions of experience. Baldwin saw these dimensions of experience as reciprocal and, finally, as inextricable. In *Just Above My Head*, he writes, "Love forces, at last, this humility: you cannot love if you cannot *be* loved, you cannot see if you cannot be seen" (84). In Baldwin's mind, somehow, his connection with Cazac had caused him to confront and understand the depth of this necessity in a new way.

12. Buckley, "Baldwin Enunciates," 28.

13. Ed Reavis, "Viewpoint: James Baldwin," *Stars and Stripes*, February 27, 1973, www.stripes.com/news/viewpoint-james-baldwin-1.17013.

14. Ibid.

15. My transcription of the recorded interview with Baldwin by Terkel, "James Baldwin Talks with Studs Terkel on WFMT," July 15, 1961, www .popuparchive.com/collections/938/items/6901. This interview can also be found in Standley and Pratt, *Conversations*, 3–23. Note that throughout this book, I am citing two versions of Terkel's interview with Baldwin: the published version in Standley and Pratt and my own transcription. The published version in Standley and Pratt, however, contains some transcription errors. Therefore, I have provided my own transcriptions where errors in the published version of the interview impede understanding of what Baldwin was trying to say or where Baldwin's vocal emphasis of a term makes a difference in my listening in a way the published version doesn't mark. In this instance, the published transcription of the present statement is inaccurate and misleading. Standley and Pratt quote: "Well, I may be able to tell you who I am, but I am also discovering who I am not" (23).

16. Ibid.

17. Goodman, "For James Baldwin, A Rap on Baldwin," 38.

18. Baldwin, *Just Above My Head*, 500.

19. Ibid., 501.

20. Cowie, *Stayin' Alive*, 155.

21. "New York Crime Rates 1960–2013," www.disastercenter.com/crime/nycrime.htm.

22. Sanders and Cohen, *Zebra Murders*, 235. According to Sanders and Cohen, between 1972 and 1974 there were scores—up to eighty-one in some reports—of so-called motiveless murders of white people across the state of California. The investigating officer (and eventual chief of police) in San Francisco, Prentice Earl Sanders, discounts links between these murders and the verified fourteen or so "zebra killings" of white people in San Francisco he investigated in 1973 and 1974.

23. For about a week in mid-April 1974, for instance, black neighborhoods in San Francisco were under formal occupation by uniformed and undercover police who stopped, frisked, and assigned an ID card, a "zebra card," to all black men in the street after dark. Needless to say, extreme measures such as these enraged black communities. Less extreme but similar practices would be common in American cities throughout the twentieth and into the twenty-first century. See Sanders and Cohen, *Zebra Murders*, 201–217. I take up a few of the implications of these contemporary practices in the Conclusion.

24. Reavis, "Viewpoint: James Baldwin."

25. *The Hallelujah Chorus*, Fontaine, box 8, file 6, Dick Fontaine Collection, Harvard Film Archive, Harvard University.

26. Baldwin and Giovanni, *Dialogue*, 84.

27. Ibid.

28. *The Great Ray Charles*, Rhino, 2004, CD, liner notes.

29. Transcripts from interviews not contained in the final cut of *I Heard It Through the Grapevine*. Dick Fontaine Collection, box 8, file 6, Harvard Film Archive, Harvard University.

30. "The Inheritance," n.d., (ca. 1971), Dick Fontaine Collection, Harvard Film Archive, Harvard University.

31. John S. Wilson, "Ray Charles Times," *New York Times*, July 3, 1973, 10.

32. Balliett, *Collected Works*, 397.

33. *The Hallelujah Chorus*, Dick Fontaine Collection.

34. Baldwin, "Sonny's Blues," 340.

35. Ibid.

36. *The Great Ray Charles*, Rhino, 2004, CD, liner notes.

37. *The Hallelujah Chorus*, Dick Fontaine Collection.

38. Baldwin, *A Dialogue*, 84.

39. "Baldwin Honors Ray Charles at the Newport Jazz Fest," *Jet*, July 19, 1973, 60.

40. Balliett, *Collected Works*, 397.

41. "Ray Charles honored at Jazz Festival," *Chicago Defender*, July 5, 1973, 15.

42. Wilson, "Ray Charles Times," 10.

43. Richard Williams, "Tribute to Ray—A Virtual Disaster," *Melody Maker*, July 7, 1973, 20.

44. Ibid.

45. Ernie Santosuosso, "Ray Charles Holds forth at Carnegie," *Boston Evening Globe,* July 2, 1973, 28.

46. Baldwin, "Many Thousands Gone," in *Collected Essays*, 19.

47. *Baldwin's Nigger*, directed by Horace Ové (1969), YouTube, www .youtube.com/watch?v=ryuAW_gnjYQ.

48. Williams, "Tribute to Ray," 20.

49. Balliett, *Collected Works*, 397.

50. Ibid.

51. Wein, *Myself Among Others,* 388.

52. Bob Stumpel, *The Ray Charles Video Museum,* http://raycharlesvideo museum.blogspot.com/2010/05/life-and-times-of-ray-charles-live.html.

53. Leeming, *James Baldwin*, 319.

54. Wein, *Myself Among Others*, 388.

## 7. On Camden Row: Amy Winehouse's Lyric Lines in a Living Inheritance

1. Maura Johnston characterized the advent of the Internet "point-and-gawk cycle" and Winehouse's unfortunate place in the limelight of online "gossip sites that were ascendant (and definitely outdrawing music-centered sites)" in 2006 when Winehouse's *Back to Black* album was released. See Johnston, "Amy Winehouse, R.I.P.," *Village Voice (blog)*, July 23, 2011, http://blogs .villagevoice.com/music/2011/07/amy_winehouse_obituary.php.

2. Jess Harvel, "Afterward: Amy Winehouse," *Pitchfork*, July 24, 2011, http:// pitchfork.com/features/afterword/8011-appreciation-amy-winehouse/.

3. Bill Wyman, "Amy Winehouse: Why Her Music Will Last," *Slate .com*, July 26, 2011, www.slate.com/articles/arts/music_box/2011/07/amy _winehouse.html.

4. Laura Barton, "Amy Winehouse Sang of a Deeply Feminine Suffering," *Guardian*, July 26, 2011, www.theguardian.com/music/2011/jul/26/amy -winehouse-lyrics.

5. Ibid.

6. Ibid.

7. Randall Roberts, "Amy Winehouse: An Appreciation," *Los Angeles Times (music blog)*, July 24, 2011, http://latimesblogs.latimes.com/music_blog/2011/ 07/amy-winehouse-an-appreciation.html.

8. Nitsuh Abebe, "Amy Winehouse's Intelligent Soul," *Vulture*, July 26, 2011, www.vulture.com/2011/07/amy_winehouse_1.html.

9. Ibid.

10. Ibid.

11. Ibid.

12. Julianne Escobedo Shepherd, "Lady Sings the Blues: Remembering Amy

Winehouse," *MTV Hive*, July 25, 2011, www.mtvhive.com/2011/07/25/lady
-sings-the-blues-remembering-amy-winehouse/.

13. Daphne Brooks, "Amy Winehouse and the (Black) Art of Appropriation," *Nation,* September 29, 2008, www.thenation.com/article/amy-wine
house-and-black-art-appropriation.

14. Brown, *Collected Poems*, 63.

15. Rich, *Diving into the Wreck*, 57.

16. Ibid., 57.

17. Adrienne Rich, in an e-mail to me, wrote about these notes and her
discovery of this connection after reading my essay "'Something Patterned,
Wild and Free': Robert Hayden's Angles of Descent and the Democratic Unconscious."

18. Rich, *Diving into the Wreck*, 58.

19. Ibid., 58.

20. Lidija Haas, "Spirit of the Beehive," London Review of Books
(blog), July 26, 2011, www.lrb.co.uk/blog/2011/07/26/lidija-haas/spirit
-of-the-beehive/.

21. Standley and Pratt, *Conversations*, 155.

22. Brooks, "Amy Winehouse and the (Black) Art of Appropriation."

23. Winehouse's studio version of "A Song for You," also recorded famously
by Donny Hathaway, is the final track on the posthumously released album,
*Amy Winehouse: Lioness Hidden Treasures*. At the end of the record which closes
the album, she says: "You know what, Donny Hathaway, you what? I see
Donny Hathaway as like, my Carleen Anderson. Like on Marvin Gaye, like,
great but, Donny Hathaway, like . . . he couldn't contain himself he had something killing him you know."

24. See Suzanne Goldenberg, "US election 2008:'I want to cut his nuts
out'—Jackson Gaffe Turns Focus on Obama's Move to the Right," *Guardian*, July 10, 2008, www.theguardian.com/world/2008/jul/11/barackobama
.uselections2008; and "Spain Basketball Team Pictured in Controversial Pose,"
*Guardian*, August 10, 2008.

25. Brooks, "Amy Winehouse and the (Black) Art of Appropriation."

26. Hall and Baldwin, "*Transition* Interview," 23.

27. Even then Winehouse's lyric force, a few years after her death, clearly
has made a space for a whole generation of voices even younger than hers to
come into being. Clear borrowings from Winehouse's tonal palette appear in
the consciously diasporic stylings of the Cuban and French duo, Ibeyi. These
confluences in songs such as "Come to the River" and "Mama Says" sound
clearly in the work (and, one guesses, in the lives) of the most interesting and
powerful inheritors, or "devotees," of Winehouse's phonemic domain to date.

28. Standley and Pratt, *Conversations*, 22.

29. Joyce, *Portrait of the Artist*, 176.

30. Rich, *Diving into the Wreck*, 58.

31. Smokey Robinson, "18: Marvin Gaye," in "100 Greatest Artists,"
*Rolling Stone*, www.rollingstone.com/music/lists/100-greatest-artists-of-all-time-19691231/marvin-gaye-20110420.

32. Clarke, *Billie Holiday*, 110.

33. Quoted in ibid., 191.

34. Ibid.

35. Barthes, "Listening," 255.

36. Clarke, *Billie Holiday*, 191.

37. Standley and Pratt, *Conversations*, 20.

38. Baldwin, *Just Above My Head*, 500.

39. Baldwin understood very well how changing the sound changes the text as well. He had a similar reaction to at least one version of the "Star Spangled Banner." On May 25, 2014, jazz critic and historian Dan Morgenstern, in an e-mail message to the author, wrote that he had met Baldwin "at San Remo in Village" in 1947 and that he and Baldwin were "never close but crossed paths." Describing one crossing, he continued: "I was about [the] only person he knew when attending Newport Jazz Festival, I think '59, his sister was covering for *Ebony*, so we listened to Louis Armstrong together—great late night, closed by Louis with National Anthem (his way of warding off more demands for encores), after which Jimmy said, 'You know, that's the first time I've liked that song!'"

40. *Billie Holiday: The Complete Decca Recordings*, MCA, 1991, CD, liner notes.

41. In the district court of the Eastern District of Pennsylvania, Judge J. Cullen Ganey sentenced Holiday to one year and one day at the Federal Reformatory for Women in Alderson, Virginia. She served nine and a half months and was released on March 16, 1948. Banned from performing in New York City clubs serving alcohol, less than two weeks after her release, Holiday's concert on March 27 set a Carnegie Hall box office record requiring three hundred seats to be arranged on stage. On April 17, she performed at Carnegie Hall again breaking her own box office record. See Ramshaw, "He's my man!" See also, "1948 Billie Holiday Makes Her Carnegie Hall Debut as a Headliner," www.carnegiehall.org/History/Timeline/Timeline.aspx?id=4294968798.

42. Juliet, *Conversations with Samuel Beckett,* 27.

43. Ibid., 33.

44. *Doubt*, directed by John Patrick Stanley (Miramax Films, 2008), DVD.

45. Rich, "The Blue Ghazals," in *Collected Early Poems*, 370.

46. Rich, *Diving into the Wreck*, 57

47. See Zoboroska, *James Baldwin's Turkish Decade*, 161.

48. Baldwin, *Beale Street*, 151.

49. Ibid., 152.

50. Ibid.

51. Ibid.

### 8. Speechless in San Francisco. "A somewhat better place to lie about": An Inter-View

1. *Medicine for Melancholy*, directed by Barry Jenkins (Strike Anywhere Films, 2009), DVD.

2. When *Take This Hammer* originally aired, editors spliced Baldwin's statement in order to omit his positioning of Kennedy and Bull Conner in a way that connected federal power and Southern racism. The splice cut out: "And there's no moral distance, which is to say no distance, between President Kennedy and Bull Connor because the same machine put them both in power." This enraged Baldwin who never spoke to the director of the film again. In 2013, a director's cut of *Take This Hammer* was made available with nearly fifteen minutes of restored footage. In this passage, I'm quoting the director's cut version available online at https://diva.sfsu.edu/collections/sfbatv/bundles/216518. For more on Baldwin and censorship, see my "Welcome to the Errordome: Are Editors Still Afraid of James Baldwin?" *Worldvoices.pen.org*, April 9, 2014, http://worldvoices.pen.org/nonfiction/"welcome-errordome"-are-editors-still-afraid-james-baldwin.

3. Standley and Pratt, *Conversations*, 21.

4. Barry Jenkins in an e-mail to the author.

5. See my discussion of "inheritance," "birthright," and the cultural and political obstruction (what Baldwin called "the rock of ages") between the two at the beginning of Chapter 7.

6. After noticing one of the working women in Jean-Luc Godard's *Two or Three Things I Know about Her* reading a translation of Ray Bradbury's book, *Medicine for Melancholy*, I thought about the role of the city as language and the language of the city in Barry Jenkins's eponymous film. Jenkins confirmed that he'd titled his film after remarking that phrase while viewing Godard's film in San Francisco. It strikes me that much of what Jenkins does with the music of the soundtrack can be considered a musical translation of the semiotic and linguistic treatise Godard laces into his film about the role of the city in the language of its inhabitants and vice versa.

7. Roy Ayers was a close friend of David Baldwin, a fixture at Mikell's, a bar and music venue at 97th and Columbus Avenue in Manhattan where David worked as a bartender. Ayers later rented David Baldwin's apartment. Mikell's has since been razed. A Whole Foods grocery store now occupies the corner.

8. Baldwin, *Just Above My Head*, 375.

9. Ibid.

10. Standley and Pratt, *Conversations*, 3.

11. Rich, *Collected Early Poems*, 366.

### 9. "In a way they must . . .": *Turf Feinz* and Black Style in an Age of Sights for the Speechless

1. See Cristi Hegranes, "What's Really Wrong with the Lower Fillmore," *San Francisco Weekly News*, September 21, 2005, http://www.sfweekly.com/2005-09-21/news/what-s-really-wrong-with-the-lower-fillmore/.

2. Baldwin, *Just Above My Head*, 375.

3. "James Baldwin talks with Studs Terkel," September 29, 1962, https://archive.org/details/popuparchive-1854433.

4. Yoram Savion, "Turf Feinz," YouTube, October 27, 2009, www.youtube.com/watch?v=JQRRnAhmB58. The original title of the video was "RIP Rich D." In an e-mail to the author, Savion mentioned it was later renamed "Dancing in the Rain" by popular and mainstream media attention.

5. Savion, in an e-mail message to the author, noted: "Other dancers were also present that morning in the YU center, part of the Turf Feinz crew, but didn't want to dance because of the cold weather and rain. The dancers that accepted to follow Dreal in his performance were more closely related to him (Gary being a distant cousin, and Man and BJ are brothers, all close friends of Dreal)."

6. Baldwin, *Price of the Ticket*, 651.

7. Ibid., 648.

8. Baldwin, *Price of the Ticket*, 651.

9. Rachel Swan, "Turf Feinz Go Viral," *East Bay Express*, August 11, 2010, www.eastbayexpress.com/ebx/the-turf-feinz-goviral/Content?oid=1987041.

10. In an e-mail message to the author, Savion corrected the details, "the video was made in early October 2009 and released online October 27, 2009." He added that the original title, "RIP Rich D," referred to Dreal's brother's death; he also added: "We had already produced a RIP dance video for another Turf Feinz member, Chonkie, who lost a childhood friend to gun violence in Oakland http://youtu.be/uqH9s5mwTEY. We also did it in December 2009 for a victim of police violence, close friend to the dancers, http://youtu.be/g-t01opsPos. And, again in 2010 for Oscar Grant, http://youtu.be/atyTZ8prhCg."

### 10. "Shades cannot be fixed": On Privilege, Blindness, and Second Sight

1. Leeming, *James Baldwin*, 47.

2. Ibid., 48.

3. James, *Literary Criticism*, 1214.

4. Standley and Pratt, *Conversations*, 6.

5. Ibid., 235.

6. Delaney's own use of color in paintings was deeply involved with his sense of rhythm, generally, and African American music particularly. He was a

lifelong lover of jazz, among many other musical forms. Delaney was personally acquainted with W. C. Handy and many other black musicians of the 1930s, '40s and early '50s while he lived in New York City. In *Amazing Grace: A Life of Beauford Delaney*, David Leeming includes a journal entry written soon after Delaney met Teddy Wilson in the mid-1930s. Signaling the relation between music and color in his way of imagining the world and his work, and responding to a boogie-woogie-style rendition of Handy's "St. Louis Blues," Delaney wrote: "For the first time I have really felt the enormity of the jazz idiom. Of course . . . it most certainly takes light suffused with pink and smokey atmosphere" (61).

7. Baldwin, *Just Above My Head*, 461.

8. Ibid., 487.

9. Ibid., 500.

10. Ibid., 502.

11. Ibid.

12. Ibid.

13. Ibid., 503.

14. Ibid.

15. "James Baldwin Writing and Talking: An Interview," by Mel Watkins, *New York Times Book Review,* September 23, 1979, 36.

16. Ibid.

17. "UC Berkeley speech," *The James Baldwin Anthology*, directed by Claire Burch and Christopher Sorrenti (Regent Press, 2008), DVD. Unless otherwise noted, all references to this speech are transcribed from this DVD.

18. "Go the Way Your Blood Beats: An Interview," by Richard Goldstein, *Village Voice*, June 26, 1984, 14.

19. Standley and Pratt, *Conversations*, 19.

20. Ibid., 19.

21. "James Baldwin talks with Studs Terkel on WFMT," July 15, 1961, www.popuparchive.com/collections/938/items/6901; my transcription.

22. Addonizio, *Ordinary Genius*, 165.

23. Rich, *On Lies, Secrets, and Silence*, 300.

24. Rich, *An Atlas of the Difficult World*, 19.

25. Ibid.

26. Beckett, *Waiting for Godot*, in *Selected Works*, 350.

27. Olds, *Dead and Living*, 7.

28. Ibid.

29. Hayden, *Collected Poems*, 15.

30. Ibid.

31. Ibid., 16.

32. Ibid., 7.

33. Baldwin, "How Can We," 52.

34. Ibid.

35. Ibid.

36. Baldwin, "On Being White," 92.

37. Rich, "5:30 A.M.," in *Collected Early Poems*, 304. Rich changed the pronouns that refer to the fox in this poem to "her" at some point. There are published versions that refer to "his" and some that refer to "her."

38. Baldwin, "In Search of a Basis," 235.

39. An early appearance of this perspective on whiteness appears in a letter to his brother David concerning his choice, unpopular with radicals, of Elia Kazan as the director for the Malcolm X film project that Baldwin would work on for years. He told David that he was the only person Malcolm and Betty Shabazz would trust with the duty to write the script so they would trust him to choose the director. And, he added, in the end, no one could *prove* that Kazan was white, there being, when it really came down to it, no such thing as a white person. See Letters from James Baldwin to David Baldwin, the James Baldwin Estate.

40. Donny Hathaway, *Everything Is Everything* (Atco, 1970), CD.

41. Mattawa, *Tocqueville,* 43.

42. Baldwin, "On Language, Race, and the Black Writer," 1.

43. Baldwin, *Just Above My Head,* 501.

44. "James Baldwin talks with Studs Terkel on WFMT," July 15, 1961, www.popuparchive.com/collections/938/items/6901; my transcription.

45. Baldwin, "In Search of a Basis," 236.

46. Baldwin, "Uses of the Blues," 131.

47. Baldwin, "In Search of a Basis," 236.

## Conclusion: The Brilliance of Children, the Duty of Citizens

1. Georgia Anne Muldrow, *Seeds* (Entertainment One Music, 2012), CD.

2. See Pavlić, "Welcome to the Errordome: Are Editors Still Afraid of James Baldwin?" *Worldvoices.pen.org*, April 9, 2014, http://worldvoices.pen.org/nonfiction/"welcome-errordome"-are-editors-still-afraid-james-baldwin.

3. James, *Literary Criticism*, 1217.

4. Ibid., 1218.

5. Ibid., 1217.

6. "James Baldwin Talks with Studs Terkel" by Studs Terkel, September 29, 1962, https://archive.org/details/popuparchive-1854433; my transcription.

7. My memory is that I was e-mailing friends that passage very quickly. I know I had the quote (along with the one that follows from *Just Above My Head*) in class with me the following day, which was a Wednesday. Adrienne Rich—in "Six Meditations in Place of a Lecture," a chapter added to the 2003 reissue of *What Is Found There*—quoted the Baldwin quote as I had e-mailed it to her. Rich notes: "A poet friend, Ed Pavlić, sent me, in late September 2001, a passage from James Baldwin's 1961 [*sic*] novel, *Another Country*" (262).

8. Baldwin, *Just Above My Head*, 342.

9. John Edgar Wideman—in "Whose War: The Color of Terror," *Harper's* (March 2002), http://harpers.org/archive/2002/03/whose-war/—echoes much of Baldwin's sense in this passage from *Just Above My Head.*

10. Baldwin, "The War Crimes Tribunal," 242.

11. These kinds of elisions are insidious and important. Even the great staff at the San Francisco Bay Area Television Archive where the preparation and restoration of the director's cut of *Take This Hammer* was performed, and where it can be viewed, quoted the censored version of Baldwin's comment about telling it like it is until I notified them of the error on October 12, 2014. On the website, they also quote the one KQED board member about the cuts made to the aired version of the film as well as about the film in its entirety: "I believe we would all agree that it is not the function of KQED to produce inflammatory, distorted, sacrilegious, extremist programming under the name of educational television. I believe this program is all of these." We should be thankful to Richard O. Moore and his crew for the work in 1963. And, we should thank Alex Cherian, Alex Rosen, and others at the Film Archive for restoring the film and for making it available at https://diva.sfsu.edu/collections/sfbatv/bundles/216518.

12. Leeming, *James Baldwin*, 322.

13. Weatherby, *James Baldwin*, 264.

14. See Dan Barry, Campbell Robertson, and Robbie Brown, "When Cold Cases Stay Cold," *New York Times*, March 16, 2013, www.nytimes.com/2013/03/17/us/souths-cold-cases-reopened-but-still-unresolved.html.

15. Sheryl Gay Stolberg, "Helen Thomas Retires in Wake of Anti-Israeli Remarks," *Caucus* (Times blog), June 7, 2010, http://thecaucus.blogs.nytimes.com/2010/06/07/white-house-blasts-reporters-remarks/.

16. Scott Shane, "US Approval of Killing Cleric Causes Unease," *New York Times,* May 13, 2010, www.nytimes.com/2010/05/14/world/14awlaki.html.

17. Mark Massetti, Eric Schmitt, and Robert F. Worth, "Two-Year Man Hunt Led to Killing of Awlaki in Yemen," *New York Times*, September 30, 2011, www.nytimes.com/2011/10/01/world/middleeast/anwar-al-awlaki-is-killed-in-yemen.html.

18. On August 1, 2014, President Obama minimized but admitted that some practices on the part of US Military and Government personnel were "contrary to our values." The president said, "we tortured some folks." Robert Frampton and Steven Holland, "Obama says that after 9/11, 'we tortured some folks,'" Reuters, August 1, 2014, www.reuters.com/article/2014/08/01/us-usa-cia-obama-idUSKBN0G14YY20140801.

19. Obama, *Dreams*, 314.

20. Ibid., 314.

21. Matthew Walberg and William Lee, "Burge Found Guilty," *Chicago Tribune*, June 28, 2010, http://articles.chicagotribune.com/2010-06-28/news/ct-met-burge-trial-0629-20100628_1_burge-chicago-police-cmdr-special-cook-county-prosecutors.

22. I can hear Miles's comment about racial identity politics in his 1962 *Playboy* interview, "A Candid Conversation with the World's Premier Iconoclast," *Playboy*, September 1962, 57–66. Asked about black players who were angry that he hired white musicians such as Bill Evans and Lee Konitz, Miles said: "If a cat could play like Lee, I would hire him, I didn't give a damn if he was green and had red breath" (62). In a letter to Bob Mills from February 1962 published in *Harper's* in May 1963, Baldwin wrote: "There is a very grim secret hidden in the fact that so many of the people one hoped to rescue could not be rescued because the prison of color had become their hiding place" ("Letters from a Journey," in *Cross*, 198).

23. *I Heard It Through the Grapevine*, directed by Dick Fontaine and Pat Hartley (New York: Living Archives, 1982), DVD, www.dickfontaine.com/ 1980page.html. Note: My transcription of Jerome Smith's comments are accurate based upon what I hear. His unique rhythms and cadences in speech are, for me, one key to the lyrical power of his point of view and the truth it bears. Out of respect for the power of that point of view and the message it carries, as well as for Mr. Smith's hard-won eloquence, I haven't placed [*sic*] within these quotes.

# Bibliography

Addonizio, Kim. *Ordinary Genius: A True and Beautiful Course in Writing Poetry.* New York: Norton, 2009.

Ahmann, Mathew H., ed. *The New Negro.* Notre Dame, IN: Fides Publishers, 1961.

Arendt, Hannah. "The Meaning of Love in Politics: A Letter by Hannah Arendt to James Baldwin." November 21, 1962. www.hannaharendt.net/index.php/han/article/view/95/156.

Baldwin, James. *The Amen Corner.* New York: Samuel French, 1968.

———. *Another Country.* 1962. Reprinted New York: Random House, 1993.

———. "At a Crucial Time a Negro Talks Tough: 'There's a bill due that has to be paid.'" *Life*, May 24, 1963.

———. "The Artist's Struggle for Integrity." *Liberation* 8 (March 1963): 9–11.

———. *Blues for Mister Charlie.* 1964. Reprinted New York: Dial Press, 1995.

———. *Collected Essays.* Edited by Toni Morrison. New York: Library of America, 1998.

———. *The Cross of Redemption: Uncollected Writings.* Edited by Randal Kenan. New York: Pantheon, 2010.

———. "Dear Sister." *Manchester Guardian Weekly*, December 17, 1970.

———. *Early Novels and Stories.* Edited by Toni Morrison. New York: Library of America, 1998.

———. *The Evidence of Things Not Seen.* New York: Henry Holt, 1985.

———. "How Can We Get the Black People to Cool It?" *Esquire*, July 1968.

———. *If Beale Street Could Talk.* 1974. Reprinted New York: Vintage, 2002.

———. "In Search of a Basis for Mutual Understanding and Racial Harmony." In *The Nature of a Humane Society*, edited by H. Ober Hess, 231–240. Philadelphia: Fortress, 1979.

————. *Jimmy's Blues and Other Poems*. Boston, MA: Beacon Press, 2014.

————. *Just Above My Head*. 1979. Reprinted New York: Delta, 2000.

————. "A Letter from a Region in My Mind." *New Yorker*, November 17, 1962: 59–145.

————. "A Letter to Americans." *Freedomways* 8 (Spring 1968): 112–116.

————. "Letters from a Journey." *Harper's*, May 1963. http://harpers.org/archive/1963/05/letters-from-a-journey-2/.

————. *Little Man, Little Man: A Story of Childhood*. New York: Dial Press, 1976.

————. "Lorraine Hansberry at the Summit." *Freedomways* 19 (1979): 269–272.

————. "Mass Culture and the Creative Artist: Some Personal Notes." *Deadalus* 89 (1960): 373–376.

————. "Me and My House." *Harper's*, November 1955.

————. "Modern Rover Boys." *New Leader*, August 14, 1948.

————. "On an Author." *New York Herald Tribune Book Review*, May 31, 1953.

————. "On Being White and Other Lies." *Essence* 14, no. 12 (April 1984): 90–92.

————. "On Language, Race, and the Black Writer." *Los Angeles Times*, April 29, 1979.

————. *The Price of the Ticket*. New York: St. Martin's, 1985.

————. "Sonny's Blues," *Partisan Review* (Summer 1957): 327–358.

————. *Tell Me How Long the Train's Been Gone*. New York: Dial Press, 1968.

————. "The Uses of the Blues." *Playboy*, January 1964.

————. "The War Crimes Tribunal." *Freedomways* 7 (Summer 1967): 242–244.

————. "A Word from a Writer Directly to a Reader." In *Fiction of the Fifties*, edited by Herbert Gold, 18–19. New York: Doubleday, 1959.

Baldwin, James, and Audre Lorde. "Revolutionary Hope: A Conversation between James Baldwin and Audre Lorde." *Essence* 15, no. 8 (December 1984): 72–74, 129–30, 133.

Baldwin, James, and Nikki Giovanni. *A Dialogue*. New York: Lippincott, 1973.

Baldwin, James, and Sol Stein. *Native Sons*. New York: Random House, 2004.

Baldwin, James and Studs Terkel. "James Baldwin Talks with Studs Terkel." July 15, 1961. www.popuparchive.com/collections/938/items/6901.

————. "James Baldwin Talks with Studs Terkel." September 29, 1962. https://archive.org/details/popuparchive-1854433.

Balliett, Whitney. *Collected Works: A Journal of Jazz 1954–2001*. New York: St. Martin's, 2002.

Barthes, Roland. "Listening." In *The Responsibility of Forms*, translated by Richard Howard, 245–260. Berkley: University of California Press, 1985.

Beckett, Samuel. *The Selected Works of Samuel Beckett*. Vols. 2 and 3, edited by Paul Auster. New York: Grove, 2010.

Brimm, Matt. *James Baldwin and the Queer Imagination*. Ann Arbor: University of Michigan Press, 2014.

Cézanne, Paul. *The Letters of Paul Cézanne*. Edited by Alex Danchev. Los Angeles: J. Paul Getty Museum, 2013.

Campbell, James. *Talking at the Gates: A Life of James Baldwin*. Berkeley: University of California Press, 1991.

Clarke, Donald. *Billie Holiday: Wishing on the Moon*. Cambridge, MA: De Capo Press, 2000.

Cliff, Michelle. *If I Could Write This in Fire*. Minneapolis: University of Minnesota Press, 2008.

Cowie, Malcolm. *Stayin' Alive: The 1970s and the Last Days of the Working Class*. New York: New Press, 2010.

Du Bois, W. E. B. 1903. *The Souls of Black Folk*. New York: Vintage, 1990.

Eckman, Fern. *The Furious Passage of James Baldwin*. New York: Lippincott, 1966.

Edwards, Brent Hayes. *The Practice of Diaspora: Literature, Translation, and the Rise of Black Internationalism*. Cambridge, MA: Harvard University Press, 2003.

Ellison, Ralph. *The Collected Essays of Ralph Ellison*. New York: Modern Library, 1995.

Field, Douglas, ed. *A Historical Guide to James Baldwin*. New York: Oxford University Press, 2009.

Gilroy, Paul. "It's a Family Affair." In *Black Popular Culture*, edited by Gina Dent, 303–316. Seattle: Bay Press, 1992.

Glaude, Eddie. *In a Shade of Blue: Pragmatism and the Politics of Black America*. Chicago: University of Chicago Press, 2007.

Hall, John and James Baldwin. "James Baldwin: A *Transition* Interview." *Transition* 41 (1972): 20–24.

Hayden, Robert. *Collected Poems*. New York: W.W. Norton, 1985.

Herbert, John. *Fortune and Men's Eyes*. New York: Grove Press, 1967.

Hewitt, Christopher. *Political Violence and Terrorism in Modern America*. Westport, CT: Praeger Security International, 2005.

Holiday, Billie, with William Dufty. *Lady Sings the Blues*. 1956. Reprinted New York: Harlem Moon Classics, 2006.

Hubbard, Barbara, and Barbara Earl Thomas, eds. *Bearing Witness from Another Place: James Baldwin in Turkey*. Seattle: University of Washington Press, 2012.

Hughes, Langston. *The Collected Poems of Langston Hughes*. Edited by Arnold Rampersad. New York: Vintage, 1995.

Jackson, George. *Soledad Brother: The Prison Letters of George Jackson*. 1970. Reprinted Chicago: Chicago Review Press, 1997.

James, Henry. *Literary Criticism: French Writers, Other European Writers, The Prefaces to the New York Edition*. Edited by Leon Edel. New York: Library of America, 1984.

Jones, LeRoi (Amiri Baraka). *Black Music*. New York: William Morrow and Co., 1968.

Jones, Meta DuEwa. *The Muse Is Music: Jazz Poetry from the Harlem Renaissance to Spoken Word*. Champaign: University of Illinois, 2011.

Joyce, James. *A Portrait of the Artist as a Young Man*. 1916. Reprinted New York: Penguin, 1992.

Juliet, Charles. *Conversations with Samuel Beckett and Bram Van Velde*, Champaign, IL: Dalkey Archive Press, 2009.

Kazan, Elia. *The Selected Letters of Elia Kazan*. Edited by Albert J. Devlin with Marlene J. Delvin. New York: Knopf, 2014.

Kelley, Robin D. G. *Thelonious Monk: The Life and Times of an American Original*. New York: Free Press, 2009.

Komunyakaa, Yusef. *Blue Notes: Essays, Interviews, and Commentaries*. Edited by Radiclani Clytus. Ann Arbor: University of Michigan Press, 2000.

———. *Pleasure Dome: New and Collected Poems*. Middletown, CT: Wesleyan University Press, 2001.

Kun, Josh. *Audiotopia: Music, Race, and America*. Berkeley: University of California Press, 2005.

Lawrence, D. H. *Studies in Classic American Literature*. 1923. Reprinted New York: Penguin, 1977.

Leeming, David. *Amazing Grace: A Life of Beauford Delaney*. New York: Oxford University Press, 1998.

———. *James Baldwin: A Biography*. New York: Knopf, 1994.

Lordi, Emily. *Black Resonance: Iconic Women Singers and African American Literature*. New Brunswick, NJ: Rutgers University Press, 2013.

Mabankou, Alain. *Letter to Jimmy*. Translated by Sara Meli Ansari. Berkeley, CA: Soft Skull, 2014.

Mackey, Nathaniel. *Discrepant Engagement: Dissonance, Cross-Culturality, and Experimental Writing*. Tuscaloosa: University of Alabama Press, 1993.

———. *Paracritical Hinge: Essays, Talks, Notes, Interviews*. Madison: University of Wisconsin Press, 2005.

Maher, Paul, Jr., and Michael K. Dorr. *Miles on Miles: Interviews and Encounters with Miles Davis*. Chicago: Chicago Review Press, 2008.

Malcolm X with Alex Haley. *The Autobiography of Malcolm X: As Told to Alex Haley*. New York: Ballantine, 1987.

Massey, Douglas, and Nancy Denton. *American Apartheid: Segregation and the Making of the Underclass*. Cambridge, MA: Harvard University Press, 1998.

Mattawa, Khaled. *Tocqueville*. Kalamazoo, MI: New Issues, 2010.

McBride, Dwight, ed. *James Baldwin Now*. New York: New York University Press, 1999.

Mead, Margaret, and James Baldwin. *A Rap on Race*. New York: Lippincott, 1971.

Miller, Quentin. *A Criminal Power: James Baldwin and the Law*. Columbus: Ohio State University Press, 2012.

Moten, Fred. *In the Break: The Aesthetics of the Black Radical Tradition.* Minneapolis: University of Minnesota Press, 2003.

Nielson, Aldon Lynn. *Integral Music: Languages of African American Innovation.* Tuscaloosa: University of Alabama Press, 2004.

Obama, Barack. 1995. *Dreams from My Father.* New York: Crown, 2007.

Olds, Sharon. *The Dead and the Living.* New York: Knopf, 1984.

Ondaatje, Michael. *The Cinnamon Peeler.* New York: Vintage, 1997.

Oppen, George. *Of Being Numerous.* New York: New Directions, 1968.

———. *Selected Prose, Daybooks, and Papers.* Berkeley: University of California Press, 2007.

Pavlić, Ed. *Paraph of Bone and Other Kinds of Blue.* Port Townsend, WA: Copper Canyon Press, 2001.

Pound, Ezra. "A Few Don'ts by an Imagiste." 1913. Reprinted *Poetry Foundation .org.* www.poetryfoundation.org/poetrymagazine/article/335.

Ramshaw, Sara. "'He's my man!': Lyrics of Innocence and Betrayal in The People v. Billie Holiday." *Canadian Journal of Women and the Law* 16, no. 1 (2004): 86–105.

Ratliff, Ben. *Coltrane: The Story of a Sound.* New York: Picador, 2007.

Rhodes-Pitts, Sharifa. *Harlem Is Nowhere: A Journey to the Mecca of Black America.* New York: Little Brown and Company, 2011.

Rich, Adrienne. *An Atlas of the Difficult World: Poems 1988–1991.* New York: W.W. Norton, 1991.

———. *Collected Early Poems 1950–1970.* New York: W.W. Norton, 1993.

———. *Diving into the Wreck.* New York: W.W. Norton, 1973.

———. *A Human Eye: Essays on Art in Society, 1997–2008.* New York: W.W. Norton, 2009.

———. *On Lies, Secrets, and Silence: Selected Prose.* New York: W.W. Norton, 1979.

———. *What Is Found There: Notebooks on Poetry and Politics.* New York: W.W. Norton, 2003.

Sanders, Prentice, and Ben Cohen. *The Zebra Murders: A Season of Killing, Racial Madness, and Civil Rights.* New York: Arcade, 2011.

Scott, Lynn O. *James Baldwin's Later Fiction: Witness to the Journey.* Lansing: Michigan State University Press, 2002.

Standley, Fred L., and Louis Pratt, eds. *Conversations with James Baldwin.* Jackson: University of Mississippi Press, 1989.

Thelwell, Ekwueme Michael. "A Prophet Is Not Without Honor." *Transition* 58 (1992): 90–113.

Turner, Jack. *Awakening to Race: Individualism and Social Consciousness.* Chicago: University of Chicago Press, 2012.

Wein, George. *Myself Among Others: A Life in Music.* New York: Da Capo, 2004.

Weatherby, William J. *James Baldwin: Artist on Fire.* New York: Donald Fine, 1989.

Weheliye, Alexander. *Phonographies: Grooves in Sonic Afro-Modernity*. Durham, NC: Duke University Press, 2005.

Werner, Craig. *A Change Is Gonna Come: Music, Race and the Soul of America*. New York: Plume, 1999.

———. *Playing the Changes: From Afro-Modernism to the Jazz Impulse*. Champaign: University of Illinois Press, 1994.

Wilson, William Julius. *The Truly Disadvantaged: The Inner City, the Underclass and Public Policy*. Chicago: University of Chicago Press, 1987.

Zaborowska, Magdalena. *James Baldwin's Turkish Decade: Erotics of Exile*. Durham: Duke University Press, 2009.

# Index